JCMS Annual Review of the European Union in 2013

Edited by

Nathaniel Copsey
and
Tim Haughton

General Editors: Michelle Cini and Amy Verdun

This edition first published 2014
© 2014 John Wiley & Sons Ltd except for editorial material and organization

Registered Office
John Wiley & Sons Ltd, The Atrium, Southern Gate, Chichester, West Sussex, PO19 8SQ, UK

Editorial Offices
350 Main Street, Malden, MA 02148--5020, USA
9600 Garsington Road, Oxford, OX4 2DQ, UK
The Atrium, Southern Gate, Chichester, West Sussex, PO19 8SQ, UK

For details of our global editorial offices, for customer services, and for information about how to apply for permission to reuse the copyright material in this book please see our website at www.wiley.com/wiley-blackwell.

Library of Congress Cataloging-in-Publication Data

ISBN 978-111883550-0
ISSN 0021-9886 (print) 1468-5965 (online)

A catalogue record for this book is available from the British Library.

Set in 11/12.5 pt Times by Toppan Best-set Premedia Limited
Printed in Singapore

1   2014

CONTENTS

JCMS 2014 Volume 52 Annual Review pp. 1–4   DOI: 10.1111/jcms.12181

Editorial: Opening Pandora's Box? The EU in 2013

NATHANIEL COPSEY[1] and TIM HAUGHTON[2]
[1] Aston University. [2] University of Birmingham

The year 2013 could be characterized as notable both for what materialized and what did not. In terms of the latter, for the first time since 2007 Europe's economic woes did not dominate the continent's affairs. True, the eurozone crisis and the fall-out from the Great Recession remained very much in evidence. Economic growth disappointed, government borrowing remained excessive and unemployment remained high across much of the European Union, especially in the troubled southern periphery where it edged towards 30 per cent in Spain and Greece. There was also another high-profile eurozone bail-out, this time of Cyprus, whose banking system needed to be rescued in March. But news of the eurozone crisis was not all unremittingly bad. Indeed, Ireland exited its bail-out arrangements and returned to the bond markets in December, showing there was light at the end of the tunnel for the programme countries.

Somewhat unusually, the really important action in 2013 took place at some distance from Brussels, Strasbourg, Frankfurt, Paris or Berlin towards the western and eastern periphery of the European continent. The consequences of 2013's two top stories could be far-reaching not only for Europe's security, but also for the strength of its economy and, perhaps, for the ultimate destination of a beleaguered European integration project.

At the very beginning and close to the end of the year 2013, two very different European political leaders, Britain's David Cameron and Russia's Vladimir Putin, unleashed potent forces over which they had no ultimate control. In January, Cameron announced his intention to hold a referendum by 2017 on the UK's continued membership of the EU should his party be re-elected in 2015. In November, Vladimir Putin launched a full-bodied assault on the eastwards expansion of the European integration project, torpedoing the EU's flagship Eastern Partnership summit at the last minute by using a potent combination of credible threats and tantalizing sweeteners to convince Armenia and Ukraine to pull back from signing historic association agreements with the EU. The ultimate consequences of these two acts may prove crucial for the future deepening and widening of the European integration project. And the long-term consequences of these two decisions may prove to be rather different to what Cameron and Putin intended. For this reason, we dub these two top stories 'opening Pandora's box'.

Beyond these two headline-grabbing stories from the periphery, closer to the heart of the Union, the year 2013 was a time of transitions. With European Parliament elections looming in May 2014, a new European Commission to emerge soon afterwards and a whole raft of top jobs up for grabs in the following year, 2013 – particularly in the final months – had the feel of a lame duck year for outgoing and often long-serving EU leaders, with much activity and speculation focused on who would fill the shoes of the current incumbents. One of Europe's most active politicians during 2013 was the President of the European Parliament, Martin Schulz, who used his position to pursue his barely concealed ambitions for another job – that of Commission President. As Desmond Dinan's contribution to this *Annual Review* shows, Schulz's dogged attempts to ensure the EP and its President's voice was heard and given significant weight *vis-à-vis* the Council and the Commission not only ruffled feathers, but also may come back to haunt him if his personal ambitions are realized. More significantly, the efforts of Schulz and Klaus Welle, the EP's politically astute Secretary-General, in advancing the institution's interests and standing with particular reference to the Lisbon Treaty, highlighted the underlying power and weight of the dry legal language of treaties and agreements. Indeed, it was the wording of the proposed association agreement and the implications for Russia that provoked Vladimir Putin into pressurizing Ukrainian President Yanukovych not to sign up to the deal offered by the EU in Vilnius. This decision set in train mass demonstrations in Kyiv that spread across the centre and west of the country, leading to the ignominious fall of Yanukovych's government and the forced departure of the ex-President for political asylum in Russia. Extraordinarily, it also set in motion forces that led to Russia's astonishing and largely bloodless annexation of Crimea just a few months later.

***

This is our sixth issue of the *JCMS AR* as editors and we have continued our policy of commissioning special contributions from academics and from practitioners outside the academic world. We are delighted that almost all of our regular contributors have continued for another year. After three years explaining clearly the legal complexities of new financial mechanisms and other developments, Fabian Amtenbrink stepped down from the team. We are very grateful to him for his contributions to the *Annual Review*. Unfortunately, the scholar recruited to write on legal developments this year was inexplicably unable to meet the deadline. However, we will ensure there is a contribution covering both 2013 and 2014 in next year's publication.

In contrast to previous lectures under our tenure as editors that have focused largely on internal challenges facing the EU, examining central themes of European integration such as solidarity, sustainability and democracy (Schmidt, 2009; Nicolaïdis, 2010; Tsoukalis, 2011; Jones, 2012; Falkner, 2013), Anand Menon's lecture focused on 'Europe as a Global Power' with the accent placed on what he terms the 'choice between collective empowerment and autonomous decline'. This year's *Annual Review* Lecture was delivered at Jawaharlal Nehru University (JNU) in Delhi, and we are grateful to Professor Gulshan Sachdeva and his colleagues for hosting us there and for the fruitful discussions that took place. We would also like to extend our thanks to Ambassador Bhatia and his team at the Indian Council of World Affairs (ICWA) at Sapru House for organizing a workshop on the EU's place in the world after the eurozone crisis.

India was an appropriate location for discussion on Europe as a global actor. As Daniel Hamilton argues in his contribution to the *Annual Review*, for more than two centuries,

> either Europeans or Americans, or both together, have been accustomed to setting global rules. Yet as new powers rise, older powers rise again, and the West faces challenges at home, the prospect now looms that Europeans and Americans could become standard-takers rather than standard-makers.

Hamilton's contribution assesses US–EU efforts to forge a more operational and strategic partnership. Although he charts significant progress in a number of areas, including steps to create a transatlantic trade and investment partnership, he reminds politicians on both sides of the Atlantic that time is not neutral: 'In a globalizing world of more diffuse power and a multitude of rising countries, the window is closing on the ability of the transatlantic partners individually to set standards and assert influence'.

The theme of the 'transformative power' of the EU forms the focus of Heather Grabbe's reflections a decade on from the big bang enlargement of 2004. Drawing on her experiences from inside and outside EU institutions, she identifies six lessons to be learned from the process of enlargement. She reminds us that two events in 2013 'showed the opportunities, risks and challenges of EU enlargement': Croatian accession, and the turmoil in Ukraine. She concludes by arguing that the EU faces a major strategic choice:

> [P]reserve the current Union by continuing to prioritize internal consensus over external effectiveness; or respond to the new external challenge by exerting its transformative power across the European continent to strengthen its neighbours and counter Russian influence?

Despite the salience of external themes in 2013, Europe's economic woes remained central to political debate. The year marked another anniversary: a decade since the publication of the landmark report by a high-level group of independent experts commissioned by the then Commission President Romano Prodi. The report was designed to offer a strategy for delivering faster growth together with stability and cohesion on the eve of the big bang enlargement of 2004. We commissioned the chair of the report, André Sapir, to reflect on the state of the European economy today. After charting developments over the past decade, he argues strongly that the growth strategy is 'not only still relevant today but that the crisis has made it even more urgently needed than it was ten years ago'.

Following the last two issues of the *Annual Review* in which William Paterson (2011) examined Germany as a 'reluctant hegemon' and Christian Lequesne (2013) explored the consequences of a new Socialist President in the Elysée, in the light of David Cameron's referendum pledge it seemed appropriate for this year's *Annual Review* to contain a contribution examining the UK and the EU. We highlight some of the continuities and changes of Britain's stance towards European integration and EU membership by drawing on the notion of 'issue capture', which we argue is the reason why Britain is now threatening exit from the EU.

We would like to thank all the contributors to this issue of the *JCMS AR* for their efforts and efficiency in producing such excellent copy within the usual tight time constraints. Moreover, we would like to express our gratitude to a couple of the unsung heroes who worked on many issues of the *Annual Review*, but moved on to other challenges during the course of the year. As the Chinese proverb goes, many hands make light work. Our workload has been lightened in recent years by the efficiency of our production manager at Wiley, Rowena Micah Sula, and the eagle-eyes of the proofs collator, Anne Rickard, who retired in 2013. Melissa Henson has taken over as production manager and we thank her for all her work on this *Annual Review*. Finally, we would also like to thank the editors of the *JCMS*, Michelle Cini and Amy Verdun, for their continuing support over the past year and indeed during their entire tenure as editors of the journal. We look forward to working with their successors.

References

Falkner, G. (2013) 'The JCMS Annual Review Lecture: Is the European Union Losing Its Credibility?' *JCMS*, Vol. 51, No. s1, pp. 13–30.

Jones, E. (2012) 'The JCMS Annual Review Lecture: European Crisis, European Solidarity'. *JCMS*, Vol. 50, No. s2, pp. 53–67.

Lequesne, C. (2013) 'A New Socialist President in the Elysée: Continuity and Change in French EU Politics'. *JCMS*, Vol. 51, No. s1, pp. 42–54.

Nicolaïdis, K. (2010) 'The JCMS Annual Review Lecture: Sustainable Integration – Towards EU 2.0?' *JCMS*, Vol. 48, No. s1, pp. 21–54.

Paterson, W. (2011) 'The Reluctant Hegemon? Germany Moves Centre Stage in the European Union'. *JCMS*, Vol. 49, No. s1, pp. 57–75.

Schmidt, V. (2009) 'Re-Envisioning the European Union: Identity, Democracy, Economy'. *JCMS*, Vol. 47, No. s1, pp. 17–42.

Tsoukalis, L. (2011) 'The JCMS Annual Review Lecture: The Shattering of Illusions – And What Next?' *JCMS*, Vol. 49, No. s1, pp. 19–44.

JCMS 2014 Volume 52 Annual Review pp. 5–24   DOI: 10.1111/jcms.12172

The JCMS Annual Review Lecture
Divided and Declining? Europe in a Changing World*

ANAND MENON
Kings College London

> Europe consists only of small countries – some of which know it and some of which don't yet. (Paul-Henri Spaak, as quoted in Renard and Biscop, 2012)

International politics is changing and the implications for Europe are potentially highly significant. Western pre-eminence in world affairs, so long taken for granted (at least within that same west) is being challenged by the rise of emerging powers. Closer to home, unrest in the neighbourhood, ranging from brutal civil war in Syria, to invasion and annexation in Ukraine, to the reversal of democratic gains made during the Arab Spring combine to make the near abroad a source of countless threats to European prosperity and stability.[1] Added to this, the continued impact of the economic crisis has rendered Europeans both more inward-looking and less able to address the myriad external challenges confronting them.

Faced with such turbulent times, it is appropriate indeed that the editors have chosen this as the moment for the first *JCMS AR* annual lecture on Europe's external role during their tenure. Clearly, issues such as solidarity (Jones, 2012), compliance with EU rules (Falkner, 2013), and, above all, economic crisis (Tsoukalis, 2011) remain fundamental to the Union's future. But the world beyond Europe's borders constitutes an equally important challenge for Europeans and for the EU itself.

Perceptions of Europe's world role have fluctuated as that world has itself changed. The triumphalism of the post-Cold War world and supposed end of history (Fukuyama, 1989) quickly gave way to disillusionment as Europeans watched the Balkans burn. As the new millennium dawned, the mood shifted again. The crisis in Iraq spawned withering critiques of Europe's international ineffectiveness (Kagan, 2003), which were quickly countered by claims that traditional power-based analyses of international politics were themselves misleading and that the EU's unique international influence stemmed from a new kind of non-material, 'normative' power (Manners, 2002). It was not long before observers were once again happily proclaiming that the EU was about to become a – if not the – major player in world affairs (Leonard, 2005; McCormick, 2007; Reid, 2004).

A similar debate has characterized assessments of the potential impact of the economic crisis. Initially, the tone was sombre as scholars for the first time began ruminating on the conditions under which European integration itself might unravel (Webber, 2013).

* The author gratefully acknowledges the support of ESRC Grant RES-062-23-2717 for funding the research on which this contribution was based. He would also like to express his grateful thanks to the audience at the lecture at Jawaharlal Nehru University in New Dehli, Loukas Tsoukalis and the editors of the *JCMS Annual Review*, Nathaniel Copsey and Tim Haughton, for invaluable comments on earlier drafts. All remaining errors of fact and interpretation are the author's own.

[1] See also Whitman and Juncos's contribution to this volume.

Sobering accounts of the impact of the swingeing defence spending cuts necessitated by austerity were accompanied by claims that the EU came second in a list of the world's biggest losers in international affairs in 2013 (Mead, 2014). Subsequently, others have been moved to argue that it is adversity itself that prompts Europeans to act. Confronted with economic contraction and a perception of declining international clout, the current crisis might lead to dramatic progress in the area of external policy by provoking 'more positive spillover dynamics' (Youngs, 2014, p. 31).

Contemporary arguments along these lines frequently draw succour from the example of economic integration. In response to the economic crisis, European leaders have taken a series of decisions that would have been unthinkable before it erupted, leading some to identify a renaissance in the functionalist strategy that drove European integration forward for many decades (Tsoukalis, 2011). Foreign policy specialists have expressed the hope that the example of greater integration of economic policies may itself alert Member States to the benefits of greater unity in foreign policy (Youngs, 2014, p. 4).

What follows takes issue with such optimistic analyses. Building on an assessment of the increasing volatility of international relations both globally and in Europe's own backyard, it goes on to consider European responses. It argues that these have been inadequate when it comes to addressing the impact of rising powers in Asia, unrest in the neighbourhood, and the need to supplement softer forms of power with military force. A common feature across all three areas has been the absence of effective collective European action. Indeed, and in contrast to claims regarding the importance of functionalist logic, it demonstrates that, while myriad functional pressures militate in favour of more concerted European action, they have not generated much in the way of an effective collective response. There is little evidence of the EU providing a framework within which Member States can aggregate their foreign and security policy capabilities and multiply their external influence. Rather, Europe's foreign policy actions remain, for the most part, divided, delayed, incoherent and consequently relatively ineffective.

The contribution is divided into four sections. The first considers the contemporary challenges confronting European policy-makers. It spells out not only the changes that have occurred in Europe's international environment, and their potential implications, but also the internal pressures stemming from the economic crisis which have constrained European reactions to them. The second section considers European actions in three areas that have been high on the agenda over recent years: Europe's response to the emergence of Asian rising powers, its policies towards its own neighbourhood and its ability to deploy military force in response to perceived threats to its security. The third contrasts these findings with the kinds of functionalist claims outlined above, while a final section concludes.

I. The Challenges

A Changing World

Europeans live in a world that is changing rapidly, where power is, by some measures, diffusing away from the west (Mahbubani, 2008; Zakaria, 2008), where the institutions and rules governing international politics are increasingly questioned, where democracy is being challenged in many places, and even democratic regimes display little proclivity to act as Europe's allies, where the European neighbourhood is becoming ever more unstable, and where the threat of armed conflict looms large in many regions. In the words of Catherine Ashton, High Representative for Foreign and Security Policy, they confront, 'increased volatility, complexity and uncertainty' (High Representative of the Union for Foreign Affairs and Security Policy, 2013).

Foremost among global trends has been the gradual emergence of 'rising powers' such as China, India, Russia and Brazil (dubbed the 'BRICs' since a 2001 Goldman Sachs report coined the term). The American National Intelligence Council predicted that the three largest national economies in purchasing power parity (PPP) terms by 2025 would be the US, China and India, adding that in 'terms of size, speed and directional flow, the global shift in relative wealth and power – roughly from West to East – is without precedent in modern history' (National Intelligence Council, 2008). Subsequent developments seem to have borne out such predictions – not least given the outbreak of the financial and subsequent economic crisis. The combined gross domestic product (GDP) of the BRICs has risen by more than US$6 trillion since 2000 – as compared to US$4.5 trillion for the US (Moyo, 2011, p. 182). In 2013, China became the world's largest trader in goods.

A series of caveats is in order at his point. Population size alone does not necessarily equate to global influence. Moreover, the west continues to enjoy several advantages over rising powers in terms of income per head, innovation and a massive preponderance as a destination for, and source of, foreign direct investment (Matthijs, 2012). Studies point to both the dependence of the Chinese economy on the west (Gilboy, 2004) and the unsustainable roots of the rise of non-western economies in a commodity bubble that cannot endure (Sharma, 2013). The rise of the rest, even in economic terms, then, is far from assured. More broadly, if it is methodologically suspect to base economic predictions on linear extrapolations of current economic trends, it is all the more so to base political predictions on such logic (Judt, 2006, pp. 25–6).

Nonetheless, while longer-term trends are impossible to predict with any degree of certainty, the rise of emerging powers has certainly added spice (so to speak) to debates concerning the place of the west in the international system. Its political implications are already discernible. Beijing's designation of an air defence zone in the South China Sea,[2] along with growing discord with Japan over ownership of the Senkaku Islands,[3] mark a willingness to translate economic self-confidence into foreign policy actions. Asian middle powers are also becoming increasingly active in international diplomacy (Gowan, 2012).

Political assertiveness has been accompanied by a steady shift in military power. The Asia-Pacific region is the only one to have seen military spending grow steadily since 2008; China has more than quadrupled its military spending since 2000; by 2015 it will be outspending the UK, France and Germany combined, and by some measures it could match US defence outlays by the 2020s. Asia is already outspending Europe on defence for the first time in modern history. Outside Asia, Saudi Arabian defence spending has overtaken that of Britain, while Russia's has increased 30 per cent since 2008.[4] Of course, rising powers have significant catching up to do before defence spending translates into usable capabilities. British armed forces will continue to enjoy a qualitative edge over

---

[2] The creation of such a zone is not, in itself, unusual – both Japan and the US have them. The Chinese zone, however, overlaps with Japan's.
[3] Known as the Diaoyu Islands in Chinese.
[4] *Reuters*, 12 February 2013; *The Economist*, 24 March 2012.

Asian military forces until at least well into the 2020s (Chalmers, 2011). Nonetheless, the direction of travel seems clear.

Scholars (for the most part based in the US) have vigorously debated the nature and implications of the changes taking place in international politics. For liberal theorists, the emerging world can be socialized into the liberal international order led by the US, (Ikenberry, 2008, p. 37) and, consequently, the 'road to the East runs through the West' (Ikenberry, 2008, p. 25). Others have taken issue with this (for the west) optimistic reading of the emergent international system. For some, we have entered an age of divergence (Kagan, 2008) with potential for growing antagonism between the world's democracies and autocracies. Others see the challenge in terms of the need to deal with an increasingly democratic world, yet one in which rising democracies have interests of their own and challenge the west in a 'clash of democratizations' (Harrison and McLaughlin Mitchell, 2014).

Liberal thinkers overlook too easily that, to 'non-liberals, the international liberal order is not progress. It is oppression' (Kagan, 2008, p. 6). Equally, and as was made abundantly clear by the audience at *JCMS AR* lecture in New Delhi, even liberal rising powers bridle at the domination of the current system by the west. The contemporary liberal international system was designed not merely by, but for, the west (Bull, 1985, pp. 217–18). Consequently, it is hardly surprising that emerging powers argue for revisions to the existing order (Mahbubani, 2008, p. 235) and are increasingly prone to challenge western positions. India – a temporary member of the Security Council in 2011 – took many aback with its criticism of the NATO intervention in Libya and reluctance to sanction interference in the Syrian conflict. Both India and Brazil abstained in the UN General Assembly vote on Crimea, while they, along with China and South Africa, opposed any restriction on Vladimir Putin's participation in the G20 meeting in Australia in November.

Certainly, the growth of Asia has presented Europe with numerous opportunities. Recent years have witnessed an enormous increase in EU trade with China; ASEAN, for its part, has become the EU's third largest trading partner (Stokes and Whitman, 2013, p. 1098). Asia now accounts for 28 per cent of European trade, as opposed to the 25 per cent constituted by the US. EU maritime trade with Asia accounts for more than a quarter of transcontinental container shipping traffic – making it the most important trade route on earth (Casarini, 2012, p. 47).

Equally, however, the close economic relationships being fostered with Asian states mean that Europeans are, whether they like it or not, invested in the stability and security of that continent. Instability in Asia will have unpredictable implications for Europe, if only via the disruption of trade routes, instability in financial markets and the damage caused to key political and economic partners in the region. Australia, South Korea and Japan, among others, would certainly look askance if Europe were simply to look away in the event of turmoil in their region.

No one can be sure whether the emergence of rising powers will lead to a sustained challenge to the rules and institutions governing the liberal international order. Equally, it is impossible to predict the degree to which China's new found assertiveness will lead to greater tensions or even conflict within Asia – by miscalculation or design. What is clear, however, is that shifts in global economic and political power will have profound implications and must be factored into calculations underpinning any European foreign policy worthy of the name.

Volatility and uncertainty are also features of international politics far closer to home. The initial optimism provoked by the Arab Spring quickly gave way to concerns about emergent regimes and the significant potential for instability to Europe's immediate south. In Egypt, a failed experiment in Muslim Brotherhood rule gave way to military control hardly distinguishable from the *ancien régime*. Military intervention in Libya has helped produce an anarchic land governed by warlords. Meanwhile, Syria has descended into brutal civil war. The triangle of Iraq, Libya and Syria is now a breeding ground for terrorism; Libya in particular is awash with both militias and weapons and increasingly used by affiliates of Al-Qaeda in the Islamic Maghreb as a base of operations and a conduit for arms (Boukhars, 2014, p. 28). Meanwhile, Iran remains a source of insecurity and sponsor of violence across the region. To the east, meanwhile, Russia annexed by force the territory of a state that, until recently, had genuine aspirations to EU membership.

With uncertainly and potential insecurity in plentiful supply, Europeans face the prospect of confronting these various challenges without the unquestioning support of their traditional American protector. The US no longer has the ability, resources or desire to play the role of global policeman to the extent it has in the past. Scarred by its experiences in Iraq and Afghanistan, 'nation-building at home' has become a priority at a time of economic retrenchment. Public opinion mirrors these elite-level trends. A *New York Times*/CBS poll reported in June 2013 that almost six out of ten Americans thought the US should not play a leading role in trying to resolve international conflicts (as compared to 48 per cent in April 2003).[5]

This reduced appetite for foreign adventures has coincided with a rethinking of US foreign policy priorities. In 2010, the Obama administration initiated its so-called 'pivot' to Asia, predicated on a belief that American well-being will in future be inextricably linked to security in Asia, and that 'the maintenance of peace, stability, the free flow of commerce, and of US influence in this dynamic region will depend in part on an underlying balance of military capability and presence' (US Department of Defense, 2012, p. 2). As if to underline the point, Washington sent two B52 bombers into the Chinese air defence identification zone soon after its creation.

Certainly, one should not exaggerate the scale of the shift in US foreign policy represented by the 'rebalancing'. American officials could hardly have been clearer when it comes to stressing their continued commitment to their European allies. Hillary Clinton made almost 40 trips to Europe as Secretary of State, while Obama's current foreign policy team of John Kerry and Chuck Hagel are both traditional Atlanticists. However, the priority accorded to Asia will have significant implications for Europe. For one thing, there is the possibility that the US might seek to assist rising powers in rebalancing the institutions of global governance by redistributing power from Europe to Asia (Leonard, 2012). Perhaps more significantly, shifting American priorities and decreasing US taste and resources for interventionism imply that Europeans will need, at a minimum, to take greater responsibility for the stability of their own neighbourhood.

Internal Pressures

Confronted with an ever more unstable and unpredictable world, Europe finds itself hobbled in its response by challenges from within. Foremost among these, of course, is the

[5] *The New York Times*, 6 June 2013.

continuing impact of the economic crisis. As the banking crisis transformed itself into a crisis of the real economy and, subsequently, sovereign debt crisis, European and North American economies experienced negative growth rates and steeply rising unemployment.[6] For those Member States that had pinned their economic futures on the single European currency, the stakes could hardly have been higher. In November 2010, European Council President Herman van Rompuy announced that 'we are in a survival crisis', adding that the end of the euro would mean the end of the European Union.[7]

The details of the crisis – its origins, impact and longer-term implications – have been widely commented upon. Less often discussed, however, are its implications for Europe's international role.[8] Implications, however, there are aplenty, and particularly for a continent whose recent ability to influence international politics has been largely based on economics. For the EU in particular, it hardly needs saying that an institution frequently referred to as an economic giant but a political pygmy would be gravely affected should even its economic strength be called into question.

A number of scholarly accounts of the EU's role in world politics emphasize the centrality to this role of Europe's economic strength. It has led to the coining of phrases such as the 'world's regulatory superpower' (Reid, 2004, p. 235), or 'market power Europe' (Damro, 2012). The European Commission itself has argued that the single market 'gives the EU the potential to shape global norms and to ensure that fair rules are applied to worldwide trade and investment', adding that the 'single market of the future' should be 'the launch pad of an ambitious global agenda' (Commission, 2007, p. 7). Studies of external perceptions of the EU confirm that its power is seen to lie more in the economic than the political realm (Larsen, 2002).

Europe's relative economic strength has been directly affected by the crisis, which has accelerated a pre-existing trend of relative western decline (Ferguson, 2011, p. 308). The US, Canada and EU together accounted for 50 per cent of world GDP in 2000, 47.3 per cent in 2005 and 41.8 per cent in 2010 – and is predicted by the International Monetary Fund to fall to 37.6 per cent in 2015 (Matthijs, 2012, p. 41). While, as Tsoukalis (2011, p. 25) points out, western observers have been keen to label the crisis as 'global' – their Asian counterparts refer to the 'western financial crisis' (Mahbubani, 2011) – its major impact has been felt in the west. As Europe struggled with negative growth rates, the Chinese economy barely slowed in 2009, while India maintained growth of around 5 per cent.

Early indications are that the crisis has damaged Europe's share of global trade and investment, its weight in global currency matters and its ability to act as a leader in global financial regulation (Youngs, 2014, chapter 3). Even in areas where its economic power had traditionally provided the Union with a degree of international leverage – such as in international environmental negotiations – recent years have witnessed a decline in its clout (Lehmann, 2010). Moreover, economic weakness has left the continent vulnerable to what some have dubbed a 'scramble for Europe' as Beijing buys up assets in Europe's cash-strapped south (Godement and Parello-Plesner, 2011).

More indirectly, the crisis has impacted on Europe's international standing (Whitman and Juncos, 2012, pp. 148–9). Prior to the collapse of the banks and subsequent crisis in

---

[6] For perhaps the clearest analysis of the crisis, its causes and implications, see Tsoukalis (2011).
[7] *euobserver*, 16 November 2010.
[8] Recent exceptions are Hodson (2011) and Youngs (2014).

the eurozone – and doubtless somewhat exaggeratedly even then – Europe's cheerleaders made ambitious claims regarding the continent's ability to act as a model for other regions. Yet even at that time, emerging countries were displaying frustration with what they perceived as the hectoring tone adopted by the west in general (Kagan, 2008). Economic collapse reinforced such attitudes, as Europe lost its allure (Youngs, 2014, p. 4), and the idea that EU experience could serve as a template for others came to seem somewhat fanciful (Hollis, 2012, p. 81). Even when it comes to showcasing the benefits of multilateralism, the ugly tone that has characterized interactions *within* the Union during past five years has undermined Europe's credibility.

Finally, austerity has, and will continue to, put a strain on direct investment in the apparatus of foreign and security policy (Youngs, 2014, pp. 34–6). The EU's own putative foreign service – the European External Action Service (EEAS) – is already badly resourced, with administrative funding in 2012 roughly equivalent to that of the foreign ministries of Spain and the Netherlands – and a staff that puts it eighth in a list of Member State ministries of foreign affairs in terms of personnel (Balfour and Kristi, 2013, p. 38). Perhaps most obviously, severe cuts in military spending have affected the ability of national militaries to undertake effective deployments (Larrabee *et al.*, 2012; Valasek, 2011) – on which more below.

II. European Responses

Rising China, Changing World

At the rhetorical level at least, Europeans have recognized that fundamental shifts in the nature of international politics are underway. In economic terms, as the Commission (2007) put it, '21st century Europe is indivisible from the world economy'. High Representative Catherine Ashton, for her part, acknowledged that economic indivisibility has political implications:

> I intend to invest a lot in strengthening partnerships across the world: China, India, South Africa, Brazil, Mexico, and Indonesia. For too long we have seen these countries mainly through an economic prism. But it is clear that they are major political and security players too with increasing political clout. Our mental map has to adjust – and fast. (Ashton, 2010)

As yet, however, there are few signs of practical steps reflecting such adjustment. Even economically, direct European economic engagement with China remains surprisingly limited – the Union invests less in China than in Norway, while Chinese investments in the EU are even smaller (Youngs, 2014, p. 78). Certainly, trade represents an important element of contemporary foreign relations. And the EU remains a powerful player in such relations, given the size of its single market. However, serious problems are apparent in the current European approach to Asia, which seems grounded in a one-dimensional vision of Asia's rise being purely about economic opportunities (Parello-Plesner, 2012). A visit by British Prime Minister David Cameron to Beijing at the end of 2013 was striking not merely in terms of his 'embarrassingly enthusiastic self-abasement', but because the political leader of a western state that prides itself on its continued membership of the UN Security Council had nothing to say to the leadership in Beijing on geopolitics, including the Chinese decision to implement its expansive air identification zone (Stephens, 2013).

Even in the economic realm, moreover, there is a striking lack of a common European approach. Rather, political leaders have attempted to extract as many national benefits as possible from their relationships in Asia. Germany has proven more willing than most to prioritize its own narrow economic interests (Youngs, 2014, p. 61). One prominent commentator was moved to imagine that 'China's leaders sit around in that compound next to the Forbidden City, chortling into their tea about the undignified antics of the Europeans who [. . .] appear like mendicants before the imperial throne, begging for business to lift their faltering economies' (Garton Ash, 2010).

A proclivity to focus on economic issues is nothing new. Talk of trade often appears as a kind of displacement activity for Europeans anxious not to embroil themselves in more problematic matters of geopolitics (Menon, 2013b, p. 9). It is also, however, profoundly short sighted. The liberal international system and the institutions that underpin it are not self-sustaining. It will require active participation by both Europe and the US to preserve them (Erickson and Strange, 2012, p. 38). To take but one prosaic example, trade depends crucially on the maintenance of trade routes. Open sea-lanes represent a particular priority, as 90 per cent of European trade is moved by sea.

In this sense, the American pivot to Asia represents more of an opportunity for Europeans than their reactions to it (focused on the risk of abandonment), have implied. Europe and the US have significant shared interests in the Asia Pacific (Erickson and Strange, 2012; Pawlak and Ekmektsioglou, 2012). Indeed, for many Americans, engagement with China would be more effective if carried out in partnership with Europe (Erickson and Strange, 2012, p. 38). Far from marking a turn away from Europe, the rebalancing represented an invitation to Europeans. As former Secretary of Defence Leon Panetta put it in a speech at Kings College London in January 2013: 'Europe should not fear our rebalance to Asia; Europe should join it'.

Yet Europeans have continued to leave matters related to Asian stability to the US. For all the fine words – and one can hardly set foot in a conference on any aspect of Europe's external dealings without hearing repeated references to the changes taking place in world politics – Europeans are yet to engage effectively with the political challenges that these changes have spawned. At the very least, those in charge of planning European foreign policies must adopt a precautionary approach. Should liberal hopes of a peaceful and seamless incorporation of rising powers into the liberal international system be fulfilled, so much the better in terms of Europe's ability to continue to benefit from that order. If, on the other hand – and as seems more likely to this author – these states prove less than eager to accept the western order as it stands, and begin to assert themselves in less co-operative ways, it is as well for Europeans to understand that their interests would be in play and thus that they should not simply abstain from any role in defence of a system on which their continued prosperity depends.

I am not suggesting the dispatch of a European fleet to the South China Sea (which, as intimated below, would not be possible anyway). Yet it is time Europeans acknowledged – in deeds as well as in words – their interest in the maintenance of security and stability beyond their immediate neighbourhood. For one thing, genuine recognition of the grievances of many rising powers should engender immediate discussion about how to address the problem of chronic European over-representation in many international fora. More broadly, European governments should not shy away from involving themselves in discussions about threats to Asian stability and security. Clearly it is only the US that has the wherewithal to provide meaningful security guarantees in the region, but a European commitment to regional security could be clearly stated, and reinforced by a willingness to 'back-fill' for the US as Washington commits more resources to the Asia Pacific. In particular, this would imply Europeans taking greater responsibility for the security of their own neighbourhood.

Neighbourhood

Whatever the broader challenges confronting them, the international credibility of Europe hinges critically on its ability to shape events in its own near abroad.[9] Yet frantic attempts to revamp European approaches to the neighbourhood notwithstanding, the region has become increasingly unstable and unpredictable. To the south, European leaders were largely unprepared for the Arab Spring, and their reactions to it left much to be desired. 'Money, mobility and market access', while doubtless promising significant longer-term benefits, was a wholly inappropriate and flat-footed response to the seismic changes sweeping the region. European reactions focused on technical aspects of co-operation, rather than initiating franker and more strategic relationships with key political players in the region intended to shape developments to suit European interests.

If EU reactions to developments to the south have been disappointing, this pales into insignificance when compared to events in the east. The Union had intended to sign or initial trade and association agreements with Ukraine, Moldova, Armenia and Georgia at a special summit in Vilnius in November 2013. This crowning achievement of the revamped Eastern Partnership imploded spectacularly following the refusal of both Ukraine and Armenia, under intense pressure from Moscow, to sign the deals on offer. This episode, and the subsequent crisis over Russian intervention in Crimea and eastern Ukraine, underlined several rather unsettling truths about the Union. Its neighbourhood policy – like the majority of its foreign policy armoury – is a project-based undertaking, intended for lengthy engagement and consisting largely of technocratic tools, programmatic objectives and benchmarks (Stokes and Whitman, 2013, p. 1095). Consequently, and as was the case with reactions to the Arab Spring, it lacks effective means to react in a timely and effective manner to crisis. The EU offer to Ukraine was for a long-term deep and comprehensive free trade agreement (DCFTA). DCFTAs require partners to approximate the bulk of the EU trade *acquis*, which involves the adoption of numerous EU rules. In return, the EU pledges access to its markets. This implies considerable short-term costs in the expectation of longer-term gains (predictions of potential gains for the Ukrainian economy range from 5–12 per cent).

Such trade-offs might make sense in a relatively benign environment where no obvious competition to EU influence exists. In the case of Ukraine, however, European leaders evinced considerable naivety. Specifically, they failed to anticipate Russian unease at the prospect of Kyiv signing an agreement that was incompatible with membership of Moscow's own pet project, the Eurasian customs union. More broadly, the EU has been slow to elucidate a way of dealing with the increasing number of potentially rival powers – including Russia, Turkey, Iran and the Gulf States – in its own backyard (Grevi, 2014, p. 17). To take but one example, Saudi Arabia, Kuwait and the United Arab Emirates

[9] See Whitman and Juncos in this volume.

offered the military government that deposed the Muslim Brotherhood in Egypt aid totaling some €9 billion, thereby reducing any influence that the EU could bring to bear via its own aid package.

Ukraine, for its part, was confronted with a genuinely difficult choice: 33 per cent of its total external trade (imports and exports) in 2012 were with the EU, and 29 per cent with the Eurasian customs union; 25 per cent of Ukrainian exports go to the EU and 30 per cent to the customs union. By signing the agreement with the EU, Ukraine faced the prospect of losing access to crucial Russian markets, with only longer-term economic gains to be had from association with the EU. Russia, in contrast, proved willing to exert direct and immediate pressure on Kyiv. It imposed customs 'checks' on Ukrainian exports, while threatening hikes in already high energy prices and an embargo on the import of some Ukrainian goods. President Putin also offered immediate and significant cash incentives were the Ukrainians to refuse to sign the EU agreement. In response, the EU could offer very little in the way of immediate palliatives. A chronic inability to deal with Russian competition in the neighbourhood has been a feature of EU policies over recent years, being all too evident even at the time of the invasion of Georgia in 2008 (Forsberg, 2013).

Moreover, the Union's toolbox for dealing with its eastern neighbourhood has been depleted since the 1990s. Following the end of the Cold War, enlargement was the key tool used to deal with the former Soviet states, which partly reflected the inability of Member States to think up any workable foreign policy alternative (Jones, 2006). The EU still enjoys some transformational power in the western Balkans, where states have a reasonable expectation of ultimate EU membership.[10] However, the unwillingness of Member States to countenance further enlargement to the east represents a significant erosion of the EU's ability to shape developments there. Association, comprising – in the words of former Commission President Romano Prodi – 'everything but institutions', simply does not provide the same incentives for neighbouring states to accept short-term adjustment costs.

Absent the carrot of membership, and given the EU's inability to provide effective short-term support in response to unrest in North Africa, both the 2008 union for the Mediterranean and the 2009 Eastern Partnership are in serious trouble. The less the EU is able to shape developments in its near abroad, the more challenges to European prosperity and security these regions will pose.

Hard Powerlessness and Normative Delusions

If the power of attraction and long-term economic agreements no longer wield the influence they once did in Europe's neighbourhood, so, too, are European states increasingly unable and unwilling to deploy 'harder' forms of international influence. Europe is not as 'soft' a power as exaggerated accounts of the continent's decline might have us believe (Giegerich and Wallace, 2004). Troops have recently been deployed in Afghanistan, Kosovo, Mali, Libya, Bosnia and off the Horn of Africa. Since the inception of its common security and defence policy (CSDP) in 1999, the EU has carried out six military

[10] See Grabbe in this volume.

missions – all of which have accomplished their stated objectives (Engberg, 2014; Menon, 2009).[11]

However, the limits of European military interventions are perhaps more striking still. CSDP missions to date have been 'small, lacking in ambition and strategically irrelevant' (Korski and Gowan, 2009, p. 11). The EU's first autonomous military intervention – Operation Artemis in the Democratic Republic of Congo – was 'limited, brief, risk-averse and ultimately ineffective' (Haine and Giegerich, 2006). Moreover, a significant proportion of the EU's military interventions have either followed, or accompanied, action on the ground by other institutions (NATO troops preceded those of the EU in both Macedonia and Bosnia, while the EU operated alongside UN forces in Congo).

The crucial explanation for the limits of European military ambitions is an absence of requisite capabilities. Shrinking defence budgets as a consequence of austerity policies have compounded the capability problems confronting European militaries (Valasek, 2011). Individual European states are finding it increasingly difficult to maintain sufficient capabilities for their stated levels of military ambitions. One defence specialist, who subsequently became the director of the EU's own Institute for Security Studies, pointed to the danger of the emergence of 'Bonsai armies', with functional gaps undermining the capacity of Member States to launch even joint missions (Missiroli, 2013, p. 12). This applies even to the EU's most militarily powerful states: the UK and France. Former US Defence Secretary Robert Gates has hinted that cuts to defence spending in the UK have engendered a situation in which London can no longer bring full-spectrum capabilities to the table in its military partnership with the US.[12]

Capability problems have been highlighted in recent operations. In Libya, shortages of operationally capable fighter aircraft, munitions, refueling tankers and intelligence surveillance and reconnaissance (ISR) soon became evident (Chivvis, 2014, pp. 34–7, 110–2). For all the political rhetoric about Washington 'leading from behind', the contribution of the US was vital, whether in the form of the hundreds of American staff transferred to analyze intelligence information, or the re-introduction of Predator drones (Chivvis, 2014, pp. 4, 21, 90, 113). French Defence Minister Jean-Yves Le Drian described as 'incomprehensible' France's lack of such drones.

There is no lack of analyses pointing to the need for European states to collaborate in order to address such shortfalls. Catherine Ashton herself has regularly pointed to the dangers of fragmentation, duplication and inefficiency stemming from the lack of effective collaboration between Member States (Ashton, 2013). A recent attempt to quantify the 'costs of non-Europe' in the defence sector arrived (albeit via a somewhat questionable methodological route) at an estimate for the money wasted as a result of the lack of an integrated European defence of up to €120 billion annually (Briani, 2013).

For all this, however, and for all the rhetoric about the need to 'pool and share' military capabilities, the focus of national defence policies remains resolutely national. Indeed, even when implementing cuts necessitated by austerity, Member States have largely failed to consult or even inform their partners as to their plans. The consequent constraints created by shrinking national capabilities and a lack of compensatory collaboration at the European level have resulted in what I have elsewhere termed a 'European defence

---

[11] See «http://eunavfor.eu/key-facts-and-figures».
[12] *The Guardian*, 16 January 2014.

deficit', or the gap between the military resources needed and those available (Menon, 2013a).

The perhaps unpalatable fact is that Europeans have become reliant on the US for their security. It is a reliance that has been implicit since the start of the twentieth century and explicit since the start of the Cold War, but one which has, if anything, increased in recent years. According to an analysis by the NATO Secretary General, the share of the NATO defence burden falling on the US has increased from 63 per cent in 2001 to 72 per cent today.

Safe under the American security umbrella, Europeans have enjoyed the luxury of aspiring to play a world role without the backing of military force (Krastev, 2012). Indeed, anxious to develop a narrative to legitimize this stance, some have formulated the notion that inaction itself represents a new, more effective, form of power. As the doyen of studies of 'normative power' has put it, the 'most important factor shaping the international role of the EU is not what it does or what it says but what it is' (Manners, 2002, p. 252). Policy-makers are always quick to pick up on academic insights that suit their purposes. Consequently, it was not long before European Commission President Barroso, was declaring that: 'We are one of the most important, if not the most important, normative powers in the world' (Peterson, 2008, p. 69).

For all the fine words, however, evidence suggests that 'normative power' cannot form a credible basis for Europe's global ambitions. For one thing, it is not perceived as such. Lorenzo Fioramonti and Sonia Lucarelli conclude their study of perceptions of the Union in eight key countries with the observation that 'the EU does not seem to be widely regarded as a "normative power". [It] tends to be regarded as a (neo-)liberal power, not too dissimilar from the USA' (Fioramonti and Lucarelli, 2008). Perhaps unsurprisingly, in some former European colonies, the EU is seen not as a normative but, rather, a neocolonial actor (Larsen, 2002). The Union was memorably described by one discussant at the *JCMS AR* lecture in India as a 'regulatory imperialist'.

Moreover, numerous aspects of the EU's dealings with the outside world belie its claims to 'normative' status. While setting great store by its claims to be the leading international provider of development aid, the cost to the global south of the Union's common agricultural policy amounts to several times the value of all the European aid monies disbursed (Grant *et al.*, 2004). For all its claims to be a friend of the democratic movements that appeared during the Arab Spring, the Union had propped up many of the regimes they overthrew (Cavatorta, 2001, p. 184). Even when foreign policy tools are deliberately intended to promote 'European values', the outcome is not always as intended. An audit by the European Court of Auditors, for instance, discovered that €1 billion provided to Egypt over a seven-year period had done little to improve democracy or human rights in the country.[13]

More insidiously, claims to normative status enable Member States intent on the pursuit of their own narrow interests to deploy the EU as a useful shield. As one caustic observer has put it:

> [T]he EU's more militarily active members are deliberately casting the ESDP in the role of the 'nice cop': as the shop front where they advertise themselves as friendly and 'safe' interveners, with bloodied hands discreetly held behind backs. (Bailes, 2008, pp. 120–1)

[13] *Financial Times*, 17 June 2013.

Numerous concerns have been expressed, for instance, over French instrumentalization of the EU for collective interventions in Africa designed to serve the interests of Paris. Similarly, in relations with rising powers, the EU can serve as a 'normative distraction'. Member States, as we have seen, have tried to maintain good relations with Chinese leaders, avoiding discussion of sensitive issues such as Tibet or human rights, in order to ensure access to lucrative contracts. Meanwhile, the EU is deployed to apply a small amount of critical pressure (Casarini, 2012, p. 60).

Finally, and crucially, normative power depends on more traditional forms of power. It was, after all, the triumph of western economic and military power that imbued Europeans with confidence that 'modern civilization was synonymous with European ways and standards, which it was their duty and their interest to spread in order to make the world a better and safer place' (Watson, 1985, p. 27). The spread of western values, in other words, was due not to their universal appeal, but to the material dominance of the west (Kupchan, 2012b, p. 6). Turning to the present, the fact that Europeans are able to experiment with novel forms of international influence is itself a function of the fact that they are safe to do so under the protection of the US. Even then, normative power will be most effective in a world where its objects are at least 'proto-Kantian' (Marquand, 2011, p. 155) – something which, to take one obvious example, Vladimir Putin is not.

Increasingly, it is hard to avoid the impression that European claims to 'normative power' serve as a handy alibi legitimizing free riding on American power and reflecting a European incapacity – and in some Member States, distaste – for the deployment of hard power. As former French President Nicolas Sarkozy put it, evocations of 'soft power' can act as 'a screen for surrendering responsibility', frequently accompanied by 'a blindness to threats' (Sarkozy, 2008). Indeed, a 'normative' European approach to world politics itself raises normative problems, in that a 'state of dependence on others [. . .] ought not to be compatible with the dignity of nations with the wealth, skills and historical position of those of Western Europe' (Bull, 1982, p. 156).

Europe confronts a series of potential threats to its security and its prosperity both in the neighbourhood and further afield. And while the US is already shifting its focus eastwards, American patience is starting to wear thin with European states that, in the words of a recent Secretary of Defence, 'are apparently unwilling to devote the necessary resources [. . .] to be serious and capable partners in their own defense' (Gates, 2011). None of this is to argue that Europeans should simply attach themselves unquestioningly to a global security agenda defined in Washington. As Iraq underlined all too clearly, the Americans are as capable of making bad strategic calls as anyone. However, a greater European contribution to the preservation of shared interests makes sense. In addition, a Europe that acts as a more responsible partner could credibly claim a greater role in the joint definition of these interests, which would include arguing for the importance of continued American engagement in Europe itself.

III. The Limits of Functional Logic

Jean Monnet, one of the founding fathers of European integration, once remarked that 'crises are opportunities' (Duchêne, 1994, p. 23). As we have seen, more recent observers have also argued that the economic crisis might finally provoke European states into acting collectively – and hence more effectively – in world politics. Such predictions have not, however, been borne out. This is not because of a lack of functional pressures. Indeed, European states are increasingly unable individually to achieve their desired ends.

Perhaps the most critical factors explaining this failure to collaborate are the reluctance of Member States to give real authority over foreign and security policy to EU institutions and, related, their differing attitudes towards the challenges they confront. The quest for elusive consensus profoundly shapes Europe's dealings with the outside world in an era when even the largest among them struggles individually to wield influence in international politics. Recent experience suggests that, when the EU is given a degree of autonomy to act in the name of Member States, it can perform the task creditably. In April 2013, Catherine Ashton successfully negotiated an agreement between Serbia and Kosovo. She has also been highly effective in chairing the six power talks with Iran, while she was the only foreign representative allowed to visit former Egyptian President Morsi in prison.

Problematically, however, the EU is allowed to represent European interests only in very limited circumstances. Member States are jealous guardians of their foreign policy prerogatives and tend only to allow the EU such autonomy over issues that are geographically remote or non-salient, where efficiency considerations can be allowed to take precedence over the balance of competence between national and EU levels (Balfour and Kristi, 2013, p. 36). Moreover, the kinds of second-order concerns that are pursued through the EU will always be side-lined if they clash with core national interests (Hyde-Price, 2006, p. 222). Thus, national political leaders are quick to try to hog the limelight when it suits them. Member States hastened to be the first to respond to the Tunisian and Egyptian revolutions, leading to a 'cacophony of voices' (Balfour and Kristi, 2013, p. 26), impeding and delaying the emergence of the collective European response that would have been far more effective given the scale of the challenges at hand.

The inherent duality of the EU's role is evident in the contradictory mandates of the European External Action Service. The EEAS is tasked, on the one hand, with co-ordinating policy and providing leadership and policy entrepreneurship. On the other, it is expected to respect the sensibilities of national governments and not 'step on the toes of national diplomacies, or interfere with national priorities and interests' (Balfour and Kristi, 2013, p. 13). Thus, while some Member States have been quick to criticize Catherine Ashton for failing to be more assertive and provide leadership for EU foreign policy, many of those same states would be only too willing to complain should she take an initiative that did not meet their approval. Little wonder, then, that she has tended to carry out consultations with national capitals before acting, spawning delayed reactions and inadequate responses.

Scholars have, for many years, argued that the stubborn persistence of different national interests based on history and geography prevent the emergence of consensus among Member States on key foreign policy issues (Gordon, 1997–1998; Hoffmann, 1995). One result of the economic crisis has been to inflame tensions between Member States, with commentators rushing to speak of a renationalization of EU politics (Kupchan, 2012a).

The degree to which intra-European divisions and even competition impedes effective foreign and security policy was made all too clear during the 2013–14 crisis in Ukraine. In the run up to the 2013 Vilnius summit, Sweden, Lithuania, Poland and

Slovakia actively promoted closer links with Ukraine, while other Member States, including Spain, Italy and the UK, anxious to restore relations with Russia, were far more cautious. Meanwhile, reports emerged in 2014 that a German defence contractor had been training the Russian special forces used in Ukraine for some years.[14] Following Russian intervention in Crimea, the situation did not improve. Senior British officials referred to the principle of 'equal pain' as underlying the UK approach to the Russian annexation.[15] Rather, however, than implying that Russia should be made to suffer proportionately to the scale of its infraction, the principle implies that if EU sanctions on Russia were to damage UK interests, these would only be acceptable if they inflicted comparable harm on the UK's main EU partners. Estonian President Toomas Ilves had reason to complain, at the Brussels Forum in March 2014, about the EU 'sitting and watching' while Russia annexed Crimea, and giving Moscow 'a minor slap on the wrist' subsequently – a reaction which Russia 'laughed at'.[16]

In the area of defence policy, EU military deployments can take place only in those instances where all Member States can agree that the potential gains are high and the costs (in terms of both blood and treasure) low (Toje, 2008, p. 206). Hardly surprising, then, that missions have tended to be small scale and of limited duration. On those occasions when potentially difficult operations reach the agenda – as in December 2008 when the UN Secretary General requested an EU intervention in the Democratic Republic of Congo (Menon, 2009, pp. 231–2) – the Union has simply failed to respond.

It is not only in the realm of foreign and security policy that such divisions have undermined collective action. In May 2013, as the EU was preparing to impose duties on Chinese solar panels in a massive anti-dumping case, a group of Member States led by Germany blocked the move. Beijing had made it clear that it would retaliate in the event that duties were imposed, and had opened its own trade investigation into European wine, while threatening further action against German car manufacturers. Indeed, China has gone so far as to institutionalize relations with a subset of EU Member States, announcing in August 2012 a new initiative comprising of a special credit line for central and eastern Europe, along with a new investment fund and the creation of 5,000 scholarships for students from those same states. Subsequently, Beijing has announced its intention to create a secretariat for the initiative.

Rather than permitting the EU to act as a multiplier of influence or a power aggregator, thereby allowing them to do together what is beyond them individually, Member States have limited its autonomy and ability to initiate foreign policy actions. National control has exaggerated the importance of intra-state disagreements on substantive issues. Consequently, European reactions to the challenges of a rapidly changing world remain inadequate.

Conclusions

Buffeted by changes in the world around it, constrained by the direct and indirect effects of the economic crisis, Europe has struggled to react effectively as its neighbourhood has

---

[14] *Daily Beast*, 22 April 2014.
[15] Interviews with the author, March 2014.
[16] *euobserver*, 22 March 2014.

descended into violence, Russia deploys force to secure its territorial ambitions and an increasingly assertive China flexes its muscles in Asia and further afield.

It is obviously important not to overstate the case. Changes in world politics provide opportunities as well as posing challenges. European states, untroubled by the kinds of (real or perceived) threats to their territorial integrity that confront many of their competitors, enjoying the fruits of the world's largest market and the international influence it confers and benefitting from an international order they played a decisive role in structuring to suit their own interests, hardly lack the tools of global influence. It is thus far too early to claim, as some have (Moyo, 2011), that the west as a whole is about to squander all it has achieved in the way of economic, military and political supremacy. Nonetheless, Europeans have failed to punch their collective weight on the world stage, and it is difficult to argue with the warning issued by the US National Intelligence Council that Europe risks becoming a 'hobbled giant, distracted by internal bickering and competing national agendas' (National Intelligence Council, 2008, p. 32).

The foregoing discussion has suggested a number of ways in which Europeans could increase the effectiveness of their international dealings. All of these – from more explicit engagement with the geostrategic implications of Asia's rise, to more decisive action in the European neighbourhood, to greater military self-sufficiency – require effective collaborative action between Member States increasingly incapable of achieving these objectives alone. To date, however, such collaboration has been distinctly limited in scope, contributing to the ineffectiveness of European external policies. The EU itself cannot be held responsible for the relative lack of progress achieved. Clearly, its institutions are not optimally configured for foreign policy. A rich and detailed literature testifies to the problems of co-ordination, of lack of leadership and of competing institutions that bedevil its quest for effectiveness in this sphere. However, the fundamental problems lie not in the precise constellation of institutions in Brussels, but rather in the continued divergences between the interests of Member State anxious to retain their foreign policy prerogatives.

Partly, this is because Member States do not seem to have properly thought through the implications of the shift of economic and political power eastward (Marquand, 2011, p. 23). Indeed, one of the side effects of long-term dependence on American power has been that Europeans have increasingly outsourced strategic activity as a whole to Washington (Stokes and Whitman, 2013, p. 1096). Partly, too, it is because national governments are all too willing to seek short-term national advantage, even if they are aware that, over the longer term, European influence will need to be wielded collectively rather than individually in a world dominated by continent-sized states.

Given the shifts occurring in world politics and the direct and indirect threats that they imply, simply opting out of world politics is not a viable alternative (Laqueur, 2011, p. 275). Crudely put, the choice confronting Member States is one between collective empowerment and autonomous decline. To date, they have largely plumped for the latter, emphasizing the pursuit of narrow national interests over effective multilateral action. In the near abroad, the Ukrainian crisis of 2013–14 provided a clear illustration of this. Further afield, European governments compete to win favour and contracts from Beijing, avoiding discussion of controversial geopolitical issues in their quest to secure comparative advantage over each other. Meanwhile, their ability to deal with security crisis diminishes as national capabilities are not supplemented by the kinds of multilateral collaboration increasingly required. Should shifts in world politics continue along their present trajectory, the stark trade-offs implied by such choices, as well as the significant costs they imply, look set to become increasingly clear.

References

Ashton, C. (2010) 'Remarks by EU HR Ashton at the Munich Security Conference'. Available at: «http://www.eu-un.europa.eu/articles/en/article_9472_en.htm».

Ashton, C. (2013) 'Opening Address by High Representative Catherine Ashton at the symposium on the Common Security and Defence Policy'. Available at: «http://www.consilium.europa.eu/uedocs/cms_data/docs/pressdata/en/esdp/137066.pdf».

Bailes, A.J.K. (2008) 'The EU and a "Better World": What Role for the European Security and Defence Policy?' *International Affairs*, Vol. 84, No. 1, pp. 115–30.

Balfour, R. and Kristi, R. (2013) *Equipping the European Union for the 21st Century: National Diplomacies, the European External Action Service and the Making of EU Foreign Policy* (Brussels: European Policy Centre).

Boukhars, A. (2014) 'North Africa: Back to the Future'. In Grevi, G. and Keohane, D. (eds) *Challenges for European Foreign Policy in 2014: The EU's Extended Neighbourhood* (Madrid: FRIDE).

Briani, V. (2013) *The Costs of Non-Europe in the Defence Field* (Moncalieri/Rome: Centre for Studies on Federalism/Istitutor Affari Internazionale).

Bull, H. (1982) 'Civilian Power Europe: A Contradiction in Terms?' *JCMS*, Vol. 12, No. 2, pp. 149–64.

Bull, H. (1985) 'The Revolt against the West'. In Bull, H. and Watson, A. (eds) *The Expansion of International Society* (Oxford: Oxford University Press).

Casarini, N. (2012) 'The EU's Approach to China: Implications for Transatlantic Relations'. In Pawlak, P. (ed.) *Look East, Act East: Transatlantic Agendas in the Asia Pacific* (Paris: EU Institute for Security Studies).

Cavatorta, F. (2001) 'Geopolitical Challenges to the Success of Democracy in North Africa: Algeria, Tunisia and Morocco'. *Democratization*, Vol. 8, No. 4, pp. 175–94.

Chalmers, M. (2011) *Looking into the Black Hole: Is the UK Defence Budget Crisis Really Over?* (London: Royal United Services Institute).

Chivvis, C.S. (2014) *Toppling Qaddafi: Libya and the Limits of Liberal Intervention* (New York: Cambridge University Press).

Commission of the European Communities (2007) *A Single Market for Citizens* (Brussels: Commission of the European Communities).

Damro, C. (2012) 'Market Power Europe'. *Journal of European Public Policy*, Vol. 19, No. 5, pp. 682–99.

Duchêne, F. (1994) *Jean Monnet: The First Statesman of Interdependence* (New York: Norton).

Engberg, K. (2014) *The EU and Military Operations: A Comparative Analysis* (Abingdon: Routledge).

Erickson, A.S. and Strange, A.M. (2012) 'Transatlantic Security Cooperation in the Asia Pacific'. In Pawlak, P. (ed.) *Look East, Act East: Transatlantic Agendas in the Asia Pacific* (Paris: EU Institute for Security Studies).

Falkner, G. (2013) 'The JCMS Annual Review Lecture: Is the European Union Losing its Credibility?' *JCMS*, Vol. 51, No. S1, pp. 13–30.

Ferguson, N. (2011) *Civlization: The West and the Rest* (London: Penguin Books).

Fioramonti, L. and Lucarelli, S. (2008) 'How Do the Others See Us? European Political Identity and the External Image of the EU'. In Cerutti, F. and Lucarelli, S. (eds) *The Search for a European Identity: Values, Policies and Legitimacy of the EU* (London: Routledge).

Forsberg, T. (2013) 'The Power of the European Union: What Explains the EU's (Lack of) Influence on Russia?' *Politique européenne*, No. 39, pp. 22–42.

Fukuyama, F. (1989) 'The End of History?' *The National Interest*, Vol. 16, pp. 3–18.

Garton Ash, T. (2010) 'The View from Beiling Tells You Why We Need a European Foreign Policy'. *The Guardian*, 10 November.

Gates, R.M. (2011) 'The Security and Defence Agenda (Future of NATO)'. Speech, Brussels. Available at: «http://www.defense.gov/speeches/speech.aspx?speechid=1581».

Giegerich, B. and Wallace, W. (2004) 'Not Such a Soft Power: The External Deployment'. *Survival*, Vol. 46, No. 2, pp. 163–82.

Gilboy, G.J. (2004) 'The Myth Behind China's Miracle'. *Foreign Affairs*, Vol. 83, No. 4, pp. 33–48.

Godement, F. and Parello-Plesner, J. (2011) 'The Scramble'. ECFR Policy Brief (London: European Council on Foreign Relations).

Gordon, P.H. (1997–1998) 'Europe's Uncommon Foreign Policy'. *International Security*, Vol. 22, No. 3, pp. 74–100.

Gowan, R. (2012) 'The US, Europe and Asia's Rising Multilateralists'. In Pawlak, P. (ed.) *Look East, Act East: Transatlantic Agendas in the Asia Pacific* (Paris: EU Institute for Security Studies).

Grant, W., Coleman, W. and Josling, T. (2004) *Agriculture in the New Global Economy* (Cheltenham: Edward Elgar).

Grevi, G. (2014) 'Re-defining the EU's Neighbourhood'. In Grevi, G. and Keohane, D. (eds) *Challenges for European Foreign Policy in 2014: The EU's Extended Neighbourhood* (Madrid: FRIDE).

Haine, J.-Y. and Giegerich, B. (2006) 'In Congo, a Cosmetic EU Operation'. *International Herald Tribune*, 12 June.

Harrison, E. and McLaughlin Mitchell, S. (2014) *The Triumph of Democracy and the Eclipse of the West* (New York: Palgrave Macmillan).

High Representative of the Union for Foreign Affairs and Security Policy (2013) Preparing the December 2013 European Council on Security and Defence: Final Report by the High Representative/Head of the EDA on The Common Security and Defence Policy. Brussels, 15 October. Available at: «http://eeas.europa.eu/statements/docs/2013/131015_02_en.pdf».

Hodson, D. (2011) *Governing the Euro Area in Good Times and Bad* (Oxford: Oxford University Press).

Hoffmann, S. (1995) 'Obstinate or Obsolete? France, European Integration and the Fate of the Nation-State'. In Hoffmann, S. (ed.) *The European Sisyphus: Essays on Europe, 1964–1994* (Boulder, CO: Westview Press).

Hollis, R. (2012) 'No Friend of Democratization: Europe's Role in the Genesis of the "Arab Spring" '. *International Affairs*, Vol. 88, No. 1, pp. 81–94.

Hyde-Price, A. (2006) ' "Normative" Power Europe: A Realist Critique'. *Journal of European Public Policy*, Vol. 13, No. 2, pp. 217–34.

Ikenberry, G.J. (2008) 'The Rise of China and the Future of the West'. *Foreign Affairs*, Vol. 87, No. 1, pp. 23–37.

Jones, E. (2006) 'Mis-selling Europe'. *The World Today*, Vol. 62, No. 1, pp. 17–19.

Jones, E. (2012) 'The JCMS Annual Review Lecture: European Crisis, European Solidarity'. *JCMS*, Vol. 50, No. S2, pp. 53–67.

Judt, T. (2006) *The Future of Decadent Europe* (Washington, DC: Brookings Institution).

Kagan, R. (2003) *Paradise and Power: America and Europe in the New World Order* (London: Atlantic Books).

Kagan, R. (2008) 'The End of the End of History'. *The New Republic*, 23 April.

Korski, D. and Gowan, R. (2009) Can the EU Rebuild Failing States? A Review of Europe's Civilian Capacities (London: European Council on Foreign Relations).

Krastev, I. (2012) 'Authoritarian Capitalism versus Democracy'. *Policy Review*, Vol. 172, pp. 47–57.

Kupchan, C.A. (2012a) 'Centrifugal Europe'. *Survival*, Vol. 54, No. 1, pp. 111–18.

Kupchan, C.A. (2012b) *No One's World: The West, the Rising Rest and the Coming Global Turn* (Oxford: Oxford University Press).

Laqueur, W. (2011) *After the Fall: The End of the European Dream and the Decline of a Continent* (New York: St Martin's Press).

Larrabee, F.S., Johnson, S.E., Wilson, P.A., Baxter, C., Lai, D. and Trenkov-Wermuth, C. (2012) *NATO and the Challenges of Austerity* (Santa Monica, CA: RAND).

Larsen, H. (2002) 'The EU: A Global Military Actor?' *Cooperation and Conflict*, Vol. 37, No. 3, pp. 283–302.

Lehmann, J.-P. (2010) 'Fallout from Copenhagen: Has the EU Lost Its Global Relevance?' *Yale Global Online*. Available at: «http://yaleglobal.yale.edu/content/fallout-copenhagen-has-eu-lost-its-global-relevance».

Leonard, M. (2005) *Why Europe Will Run the 21st Century* (London: Fourth Estate).

Leonard, M. (2012) *The Central Challenge to the Western Liberal Order* (London: ECFR).

Mahbubani, K. (2008) *The New Asian Hemisphere: The Irresistable Shift of Global Power to the East* (New York: Public Affairs).

Mahbubani, K. (2011) 'Asia has had Enough of Excusing the West'. *Financial Times*, 25 January.

Manners, I. (2002) 'Normative Power Europe: A Contradiction in Terms?' *JCMS*, Vol. 40, No. 2, pp. 235–58.

Marquand, D. (2011) *The End of the West: The Once and Future Europe* (Princeton, NJ: Princeton University Press).

Matthijs, M. (2012) 'Crying Wolf Again? The Decline of Western Economic Influence after the Great Recession'. *The International Spectator*, Vol. 47, No. 3, pp. 37–52.

McCormick, M. (2007) *The European Superpower* (London: Palgrave Macmillan).

Mead, W.R. (2014) '2013: The World's Biggest Losers'. *The American Interest*, 5 January.

Menon, A. (2009) 'Empowering Paradise? ESDP at Ten'. *International Affairs*, Vol. 85, No. 2, pp. 227–46.

Menon, A. (2013a) 'The Other Euro Crisis: Why Europe Desperately Needs Military Collaboration'. *Foreign Affairs*, 10 December. Available at: «http://www.foreignaffairs.com/articles/140380/anand-menon/the-other-euro-crisis».

Menon, A. (2013b) 'Time for Tough Love in Transatlantic Relations'. *The International Spectator*, Vol. 48, No. 3, pp. 7–14.

Missiroli, A. (2013) *Enabling the Future: European Military Capabilities, 2013–2025: Challenges and Avenues* (Paris: EU Institute for Security Studies).

Moyo, D. (2011) *How the West was Lost: Fifty Years of Economic Folly – and the Stark Choices Ahead* (London: Allen Lane).

National Intelligence Council (2008) *Global Trends, 2025: A Transformed World* (Washington, DC: National Intelligence Council).

Parello-Plesner, J. (2012) 'Europe's Mini-pivot to Asia'. *China-US Focus*.

Pawlak, P. and Ekmektsioglou, E. (2012) 'Introduction'. In Pawlak, P. (ed.) *Look East, Act East: Transatlantic Agendas in the Asia Pacific* (Paris: EU Institute for Security Studies).

Peterson, J. (2008) 'José Manuel Barroso: Political Scientist, ECPR Member'. *European Political Science*, Vol. 7, pp. 64–77.

Reid, T.R. (2004) *The United States of Europe* (London: Penguin).

Renard, T. and Biscop, S. (2012) 'Introduction'. In Renard, T. and Biscop, S. (eds) *The European Union and Emerging Powers in the 21st Century: How Europe Can Shape a New Global Order* (Farnham: Ashgate).

Sarkozy, N. (2008) Speech by M. Nicolas Sarkozy, President of the Republic, at the Seventeenth Ambassadors' Conference, Paris.

Sharma, R. (2013) *Breakout Nations* (New York: Norton).

Stephens, P. (2013) 'A Painful Lesson in How Not to Deal with China'. *Financial Times*, 6 December.

Stokes, D. and Whitman, R.G. (2013) 'Transatlantic Triage? European and UK "Grand Strategy" after the US Rebalance to Asia'. *International Affairs*, Vol. 89, No. 5, pp. 1087–107.

Toje, A. (2008) 'The European Union as a Small Power, or Conceptualizing Europe's Strategic Actorness'. *European Integration*, Vol. 30, No. 2, pp. 199–215.

Tsoukalis, L. (2011) 'The JCMS Annual Review Lecture: The Shattering of Illustions – and What Next?' *JCMS*, Vol. 49, No. s1, pp. 19–44.

US Department of Defense (2012) *Sustaining US Global Leadership: Priorities for 21st Century Defense* (Washington, DC: Department of Defense).

Valasek, T. (2011) *Surviving Austerity: The Case for a New Approach to EU Military Collaboration* (London: Centre for European Reform).

Watson, A. (1985) 'European International Soceity and Its Expansion'. In Bull, H. and Watson, A. (eds) *The Expansion of International Society* (Oxford: Oxford University Press).

Webber, D. (2013) 'How Likely is It that the European Union Will Disintegrate? A Critical Analysis of Competing Theoretical Perspectives'. *European Journal of International Relations*. doi:10.1177/1354066112461286.

Whitman, R.G. and Juncos, A.E. (2012) 'The Arab Spring, the Eurozone Crisis and the Neighbourhood: A Region in Flux'. *JCMS*, Vol. 50, No. s2, pp. 147–61.

Youngs, R. (2014) *The Uncertain Legacy of Crisis: European Foreign Policy Faces the Future* (Washington, DC: Carnegie Endowment for International Peace).

Zakaria, F. (2008) *The Post-American World* (New York: Norton).

JCMS 2014 Volume 52 Annual Review pp. 25–39   DOI: 10.1111/jcms.12175

Transatlantic Challenges: Ukraine, TTIP and the Struggle to be Strategic

DANIEL S. HAMILTON
Center for Transatlantic Relations, Johns Hopkins University SAIS

Introduction

In terms of values and interests, economic interactions and human bonds, the United States and the European Union are closer to one another than either is to any other major international actor. The US-EU relationship is among the most complex and multilayered economic, diplomatic, societal and security relationship that either partner has, especially if it is seen to encompass the relationships Washington maintains with the EU's 28 Member States, its '*European institutions*', and with NATO allies and other European partners. North Atlantic networks of interdependence have become so dense that they transcend *foreign* relations and reach deeply into each other's societies. The US$5 trillion transatlantic economy employs up to 15 million people on both sides of the Atlantic (Hamilton and Quinlan, 2014).

Nonetheless, the US and Europe have often found it difficult to harness the full potential of their partnership. Of course, spectacular successes have been achieved, including the peaceful end of the Cold War and unification of Germany; extending the space of democratic stability in Europe where war simply does not happen; and expanding prosperity and rules-based norms for hundreds of millions of people across the Atlantic and billions of people around the world. But relations are also beset by competitive impulses, underlying questions of trust, and mutual doubts about relative commitment and capacity. NATO is busier than ever, yet only encompasses the political-military aspects of transatlantic partnership. And while the US-EU relationship is close, it is not strategic in the sense that partners would share assessments about issues vital to both on a continuous and interactive basis; be able to deal with the daily grind of immediate policy demands while identifying longer-term challenges to their security, prosperity and values; and be able to prioritize those challenges and harness the full range of resources at their disposal to advance common or complementary responses (Hamilton, 2010).

The US-EU relationship has still not overcome its image as a technocratic exercise with an overabundance of process disproportionate to actual output, a repository of issues dealt with in rather ad hoc fashion by a range of disparate agencies, with little sense of urgency or overall direction. The relationship is still dominated by an economic and commercial agenda even though it has expanded far beyond that original core set of issues. The EU remains best understood as a carefully negotiated and continuously evolving framework by which its Member States can live together and advance common interests, rather than as a unitary actor with the operational capacity to shape international events in real time. The operational effectiveness of the US-EU relationship is thus heavily contingent on the evolving nature of the EU itself. Obstacles to effective transatlantic co-ordination often have less to do with American reluctance to engage or support the EU as a strategic partner than with the limits of European capability, consensus and political will. Of course, both US and EU officials are often tempted to bypass formalized US-EU structures and advance their interests bilaterally.[1] As a result, the partnership punches below its weight. Priorities are often mismatched, as the US looks for efficiency and concrete outcomes, European institutions seek legitimacy and symbolic American validation of the ongoing process of European integration, and EU Member States alternate between efforts to band together to resist American influence and a competitive scramble to secure US favour for their own particular national interests.

In recent decades, the US and Europe have found they can live with these challenges since they still hold great sway over most key issues of global consequence. Yet these hurdles to transatlantic effectiveness are now looming larger in a world of rising markets and diffuse power. The billions of workers around the world who have joined the global economy are providing Americans and Europeans with fresh sources of competition at a time when the West's political, financial and economic credibility has been damaged considerably by the financial crisis and the Great Recession, as well as by the spectacle of America's domestic political dysfunction and Europe's incessant navel-gazing. As Chinese Deputy Premier Wang Qishan reportedly noted when the financial crisis broke, 'the teachers now have some problems' (Asghar, 2008).

For more than two centuries, either Europeans or Americans, or both together, have been accustomed to setting global rules. Yet as new powers rise, older powers rise again, and the West faces challenges at home, the prospect now looms that Europeans and Americans could become standard-takers rather than standard-makers. In addition, the fashionable notion that Western liberal democracy is on the march, which accompanied the opening of the Iron Curtain, has been challenged by the rise of alternative models of state capitalism; reluctance by emerging powers that are also democracies, such as Brazil and India, to associate themselves fully with the West; and the turmoil that has followed the initial promise of the Arab Awakening.[2] As a result, the window is closing on the ability of the US and Europe alone to set the rules and reap the benefits of an open global economy supported by *Pax Americana*, unless they can more effectively harness partnership to purpose. During the coming decade both transatlantic partners will be challenged to make their own pivot away from a legacy relationship structured to tackle twentieth-century challenges to a more effective partnership that is more global, more equal and better positioned for a very new world rising.

This contribution assesses US-EU efforts to forge a more operational, useful and strategic partnership in three broad areas of engagement. The first is the common goal of advancing a Europe that is whole, free and secure. For the first two decades of the post-Cold War era, western powers joined with emerging leaders in Wider Europe – the vast area beyond the EU and NATO – to drive change towards a more stable, democratic and prosperous continent. Attention flagged, however, and now the transatlantic partners are scrambling to adjust to Moscow's annexation of Crimea, its active efforts to destabilize Ukraine more broadly and its assertion of a Russian sphere of influence over its neighbourhood.

---

[1] See Anand Menon's contribution to this volume.
[2] See, for example, Ikenberry (2011).

The second area focuses on US and European efforts to build competitive economies. Traditionally, Americans and Europeans have been as much competitors as partners in this area. Today, however, the US and the EU are driving a new agenda through negotiations on an ambitious transatlantic trade and investment partnership (TTIP) that is intended not only to open markets and align standards across the Atlantic, but to use the power of such a large Euro-Atlantic market and high transatlantic standards to open other markets and form the core of global standards.

The third area relates to the ability and desire of transatlantic partners to extend their co-operation beyond the North Atlantic to address together a range of other regional and global challenges. Traditionally, both sides of the Atlantic have been largely ambivalent about such co-operation. Today each partner has been pushing for more effective co-ordination, but with uneven results.

I. The Setting: A Shifting Transatlantic Agenda

Before turning to these issues, however, it is important to set the context. The Obama administration has approached transatlantic partnership far more pragmatically, and with less of a Eurocentric focus, than many Europeans had originally expected (Hamilton and Foster, 2009). Barack Obama assumed the Presidency believing that Europe had stopped being the central challenge to American foreign policy, as it had been in the twentieth century, and he and his team came to judge the value of transatlantic partnership largely in relation to Europe's willingness and ability to assume greater leadership in addressing its own challenges, as well as tackling together with the US a host of problems far beyond European shores. This unnerved many in Europe who had grown accustomed to having Americans instinctively turn first to Europe on most major issues. It was particularly challenging for central European elites, many of whom had been feted by both the Clinton and Bush administrations as they moved from dictatorship to democracy and joined NATO, the EU and other Euro-Atlantic institutions.

Europeans west and east were then further unnerved by administration announcements of a *pivot* to the Asia-Pacific region. While the Obama administration portrayed the turn – which it has subsequently labeled a 'rebalance'[3] – as a shift of US security focus from the Middle East, not from Europe, the simultaneous downsizing of US forces in Europe was interpreted widely in Europe as further evidence of an American shift away from the region. Many European elites feared that Washington would pay less heed to their concerns even as it demanded more from them in terms of assistance with challenges far from their region, at a time when many European countries were struggling with economic recovery.

Most Europeans cheered when Barack Obama won the Presidency, but their support was tied to a perception that he would deliver on issues important to Europe. Yet on challenges ranging from climate change to Guantanamo, the US has not necessarily obliged. Most recently, disclosures of extensive spying operations by the US National Security Agency against European allies and other governments have put a major strain on relations with key European countries, particularly Germany, and forced serious debate

---

[3] To track the administration's changing descriptions, see Clinton (2011); US Department of Defense (2012); Campbell and Andrews (2014); Binnendijk (2014).

about the proper relationship between liberty and security in democratic societies and about the nature and effectiveness of the US-European link in a rapidly changing world. Although President Obama has defended the intelligence community's activities, he also embraced some, but not all, recommendations provided to him by a review group to rein in the most egregious abuses. He has ended the Bush administration's rhetoric about a 'war on terror', begun to alter US policy on use of drones, and sought to shift America's domestic framework towards greater transparency and rules legitimized by democratic consent and oversight. An unlikely assemblage of conservative Republicans and liberal Democrats in the US Congress is pushing legislation pointing in the same direction. Others, however, believe that European reactions are incredibly naive. They contend that the US is being singled out for activities conducted by many countries. They argue vociferously that terrorism and other threats to the US warrant such extensive surveillance methods. They also point out that Germany and other European allies co-operate regularly with US intelligence services, and that such co-operation has helped to foil various terrorist plots, including against European targets.

Current debates underscore once again that the question of how democratic societies can best relate individual freedom and fundamental values such as privacy to expectations of individual and national security has long been contentious across the Atlantic. Despite such differences, however, the US and the EU have reached agreement in past years on 'safe harbour' provisions for data privacy; passenger name recognition arrangements providing for safe air travel; and access to financial transactions that could be related to terrorist financing. This time, however, mutual trust and confidence has been eroded to such an extent that some in Europe are calling for the EU to suspend various agreements with the US and to halt bilateral negotiations on the TTIP. European leaders have resisted such demands since they know that Europe has a great stake in a successful TTIP agreement. Nonetheless, given that the TTIP is likely to be a 'mixed agreement' requiring support from the European Parliament as well as all 28 EU Member State parliaments, it is unlikely to succeed unless transatlantic arrangements on data protection also win the support of European legislators.

The relationship has also been buffeted by daunting economic challenges on each side of the Atlantic. The 2008 financial crisis, ensuing Great Recession and related eurozone crisis have all cast a long shadow over transatlantic relations and generated tensions between Washington and Berlin in particular. Obama and other American officials have publicly challenged Berlin's policies of austerity and tight monetary policies while actively supporting calls by France, Italy and Spain for pro-growth strategies. Meanwhile, many European officials generally believed that the US was largely responsible for the financial crisis and failed to grasp the nature of the eurozone's problems and the rationale behind the EU's response. They urged Washington to put its own house in order before lecturing others.

These tensions have eased somewhat, now that the eurozone crisis has been contained, at least for now, and as both sides of the Atlantic are returning to somewhat higher growth rates. Yet the bickering underscored that solid economic growth is fundamental to a vibrant transatlantic partnership. Without US fiscal solvency, economic growth and job creation, Washington is unlikely to be the type of consistent, outward-looking partner that Europeans need and want. The US has the same stake in Europe's success. Europe's protracted sovereign debt crisis drained US confidence in Europe and its institutions and threatened to derail American support for major transatlantic policy initiatives. Economic turmoil at home also undermines the influence of the US and Europe elsewhere, since in a world in which competing models are emerging the normative appeal and continued relevance of the American and European models for others depends heavily on how well they are seen to be working for their own people.

II. Ukraine and the Changing Strategic Landscape in Europe

When the Iron Curtain parted, the George H.W. Bush administration worked brilliantly with European partners to ensure peaceful change. The administrations of both Bill Clinton and George W. Bush then worked energetically with European partners to stabilize and integrate as much as possible the spaces of Europe that were not part of European or Euro-Atlantic institutions. The Clinton administration led efforts to enlarge NATO to Poland, the Czech Republic and Hungary and set the stage for later integration of the Baltic States, even as it supported EU enlargement and, after initial hesitations and immense human tragedy, worked with European allies to quench the fires ravaging the Balkans and set that region on a path to European integration. The George W. Bush administration and European allies continued the process of NATO enlargement to more countries in the region as the EU also continued to enlarge. The transatlantic partners also consulted on ways to advance democratic stability in the wake of the 2003–4 'colour revolutions' in Ukraine and Georgia. The administration exceeded the bounds of Western consensus, however, by pushing for rapid NATO expansion to the two countries, over determined Russian opposition and despite reservations by some allies who were unconvinced that the two countries were prepared for NATO membership or that membership at that time would enhance security in Europe. Ultimately, the strategy of the second Bush administration foundered; it had no fallback plan to stabilize the region through means other than institutional expansion of the NATO alliance, and the energetic phase of eastern enlargement ended.

The Obama administration and most EU Member States have been much more cautious and circumspect in their approach to Wider Europe, reflecting widespread reluctance within the EU to continue the process of enlargement, given challenges of absorbing new members at a time of economic and financial crisis. In addition, Ukraine under Victor Yanukovych withdrew its interest in NATO membership. Overall, the post-communist countries of the region were seen to be weaker and poorer than earlier membership aspirants, still to embrace sustained democratic reforms, and were less well known to western legislators and to broader publics. While the transatlantic partners continued to engage the countries of the region, such efforts lost coherence and were accorded far less priority by Western capitals.

Renewed turmoil in Ukraine and Russia's annexation of Crimea have jolted transatlantic leaders and publics awake to the reality that the European continent is still not fully whole, free and at peace. They are also digesting the fact that Russia under Putin is now prepared to challenge western influence and undermine wherever possible efforts at democratic transformation in the region. Russia's aggression against Ukraine presents a significant challenge to Europe's security, its stability and to transatlantic credibility. Russian President Vladimir Putin has sought to weaken neighbouring states and assert Russian hegemony over the region by utilizing cyber warfare, corruption and criminal networks, political provocateurs, separatist groups, unresolved borders, energy embargoes and military force, among other means. Russia's incursion into Crimea was an unprovoked violation of the territorial sovereignty of one of Europe's largest nations and a direct assault on the vision of a Europe whole, free and at peace. It was a direct violation of Russian commitments to the Council of Europe; pledges made in the 1994 Budapest Agreement to respect and protect Ukraine's territorial integrity; and to Putin's own commitment on behalf of Russia, in the 2002 NATO-Russia Rome Declaration, to 'observe in good faith our obligations under international law, including the UN Charter, provisions and principles contained in the Helsinki Final Act and the OSCE Charter for European Security', and to affirm the basic principles set forth in the 1997 NATO-Russia Founding Act, to 'creat[e] in Europe a common space of security and stability, without dividing lines or spheres of influence', and to show 'respect for [the] sovereignty, independence and territorial integrity of all states and their inherent right to choose the means to ensure their own security'.[4] Putin's assertion he has the unilateral right to redraw borders on the grounds that he is protecting ethnic Russians re-introduces into Europe a dangerous principle that has provoked European conflict resulting in millions of deaths (Brzezinski, 2014).

Above all, the turmoil surrounding Ukraine underscores that Europe's turbulent spaces to the east and south of the EU and NATO are still beset with historical animosities and multiple crises, including a number of festering conflicts that in some way affect all the countries of the region. Despite reassuring notions that Europe had settled into a comfortable state of peace following two world wars and the Cold War, it is becoming clear that the continent is still caught up in the geopolitics of the post-Soviet succession – and when you are in the middle of an earthquake, the best prediction you can make is that things will keep shaking.

The evolving situation in Ukraine is emblematic of these changes. Russia's war with Georgia is also still fresh in our memories. And tensions over Transniestria, Nagorno-Karabakh, Abkhazia and South Ossetia, which some euphemistically label '*frozen conflicts*', represent additional festering wounds that absorb energy and drain resources from countries that are already weak and poor. They inhibit the process of state-building as well as the development of democratic societies. They generate corruption and organized crime. They foster the proliferation of arms and a climate of intimidation. They are a major source of instability within these countries and the broader region. Overall, Wider Europe is significantly less democratic, less settled and more prone to violent conflict than it was five years ago.

Successes in this region – more effective democratic governance grounded in the rule of law, progress against corruption and trafficking, peaceful resolution of conflicts, secure energy production and transit, more confident and prosperous market economies – could resonate significantly across the post-Soviet space and into the broader Middle East, and enhance the region's potential as a strategic bridge. Failure to deal with the region's problems risks destabilizing competition and confrontation among both regional and external actors; separatist conflicts; greater transnational challenges; and dysfunctional energy markets, the negative consequences of which could spill over into Europe, Eurasia

---

[4] 'NATO-Russia Relations: A New Quality', Declaration by Heads of State and Government of NATO Member States and the Russian Federation, Rome, 28 May 2002; Founding Act on Mutual Relations, Cooperation and Security between NATO and the Russian Federation signed in Paris, 27 May 1997.

and the Middle East. The ability of countries in the region to deal with these issues, and the willingness and ability of Europe and the US to work together with those countries to address these issues, could determine not only where Europe ends, but what it represents (Asmus, 2006; Hamilton, 2010; King, 2008; Stent, 2007).

Russia's annexation of Crimea has prompted a remarkable alignment of tactical responses by North American and European responses, ranging from economic support and an International Monetary Fund package for Ukraine, financial and other sanctions against Russia, reinforcement of Baltic, Polish and Romanian airspace and territory, and efforts to deepen US and EU ties with the new Ukrainian government. But these tactics are clearly insufficient. Throughout the spring of 2014, tens of thousands of Russian troops were mobilized in high readiness on Ukraine's border and the Kremlin had shown no signs of backing down. Such tactical responses are also unlikely to be sustainable unless they are tied to a long-term western strategy towards Wider Europe, which itself is framed by a recognition that geopolitics has returned to (it never left) the European continent. NATO has acted to reassure nervous allies, but it is not prepared to engage militarily to protect Ukraine. Ukrainians have been left to doubt the credibility of commitments made by the US and the United Kingdom in the 1994 Budapest Agreement to assure Ukraine's territorial integrity, and to the value of such instruments as the Partnership for Peace and the NATO-Ukraine Commission. The Alliance has yet to develop a coherent strategy of projecting stability and resilience forward, beyond the bounds of NATO territory itself, to partner countries in Wider Europe.

US-EU efforts have been similarly challenged. The EU's Eastern Partnership and european neighbourhood policies were developed as technocratic exercises largely devoid of political purpose and drive; their credibility is also now in doubt. The EU-Ukraine deep and comprehensive free trade agreement is ambitious, but in the wake of the crisis the EU stepped back from its original willingness to proceed with the full agreement, and by March 2014 was only prepared to sign the political provisions of the agreement while delaying implementation of the pact's economic provisions. The US has offered US$1 billion in loan guarantees and technical assistance with financial, energy and political reforms. This is an important signal of support, but remains far below what Ukraine needs for success. US-EU co-ordination of such assistance has been patchy – and the transatlantic partners have yet to harness their assorted efforts to a more strategic effort to project stability and opportunities for integration to this region.

Ukraine has grabbed the headlines, but the erosion of the transatlantic vision of a Europe whole, free and at peace extends to unfinished business in the Balkans. Croatia has joined the EU and NATO, but others are struggling. Serbia and Kosovo have made some progress in resolving their differences, but some EU Member States do not recognize Kosovo's independence, damaging its ability to move forward and obstructing wider progress in the region. Greece continues to block progress with Macedonia due to issues surrounding its name. Bosnia is mired in a swamp of corruption amid squabbles among ethnically based politicians; most reform efforts have gone nowhere.[5] Continued US and European engagement remains essential if the Balkans are to continue along the path towards Europe's mainstream.

---

[5] See Whitman and Juncos's contribution to this volume.

III. Advancing an Economic Partnership that Delivers

While the US and Europe are playing catch-up in Wider Europe, they have seized the initiative in another area. If successful, the TTIP promises to be a major political, strategic and economic driver of the transatlantic relationship over the course of this decade and beyond. Yet challenges have emerged here as well. The TTIP is about more than trade. At its core, it is about generating regulatory coherence and breaking down barriers to transatlantic commerce in ways that can generate growth and jobs without piling on debt. It is also about creating a more strategic, dynamic and holistic US-EU relationship that is better positioned with regard to third countries to open markets and strengthen the ground rules of the international order. There is also a reassurance element to the TTIP. Many view NATO as wobbly, and many Europeans are worried that the American rebalance to Asia will translate into less attention and commitment to Europe. Creation of what would essentially be a Euro-American market of over 800 million people from Hawaii to the Baltic and Black seas, together with a commitment to work together to advance core western norms and standards, would offer reassurance that Europe is in fact America's 'partner of choice'. In this regard, TTIP has the potential to serve as a new binding element for the transatlantic partnership. It is not an 'economic NATO' – a term that can easily be misinterpreted – but it can be a second transatlantic anchor, rooted in deep and growing transatlantic economic integration. TTIP can be both a symbolic and practical assertion of western renewal, vigour and commitment, not only to each other but to high rules-based standards and core principles of international order. It is an initiative that can be assertive without being aggressive, and that challenges fashionable notions about a 'weakened west'.

All in all, the transatlantic economy remains the world's preeminent economic force. Rising powers are resetting the global economy, but they have not done so yet. Such a transformation is neither complete nor pre-ordained. And a different world economy is not necessarily a worse one for Americans and Europeans – if they use the coming decade to leverage global growth, human talent and innovation while tackling related challenges of deficits and debt, building on their own considerable strengths and exploiting the full potential of their own economic ties.

Despite the rise of other powers, the US and Europe remain the fulcrum of the world economy, each other's most important and profitable market and main source of onshored jobs. The transatlantic economy accounts for three-quarters of global financial markets and over half of world trade. It accounts for 50 per cent of world gross domestic product (GDP) in terms of value and 41 per cent in terms of purchasing power. No other commercial artery is as integrated. The EU exports twice as many goods to the US as to China, and the US exports three times as many goods to Europe as to China (Hamilton and Quinlan, 2014). Average transatlantic tariffs are relatively low, at about 3–4 per cent on average, but since the volume of US-EU trade is so huge, eliminating even relatively low tariffs could boost trade significantly. The European think tank ECIPE estimates that a transatlantic zero-tariff agreement would be worth five times more than the US-Korea free trade deal ratified in 2011 (Erixon and Bauer, 2010).

Even greater gains could be had if TTIP opens the transatlantic services economy. Most American and European jobs are in the services economy, which accounts for over 70 per cent of US and EU GDP. The US and EU are each other's most important commercial partners and major growth markets when it comes to services trade and investment. The services economies of the US and Europe have never been as intertwined as they are today in financial services, telecommunications, utilities, insurance, advertising, computer services and other related activities. Deep transatlantic connections in services industries, provided by mutual investment flows, are not only important in their own right; they are also the foundation for the global competitiveness of American and European services companies. A good share of American services exports to the world are generated by European companies based in the US, just as a good share of EU services exports to the world are generated by American companies based in Europe. Protected services sectors on both sides of the Atlantic account for about 20 per cent of combined US-EU GDP – more than the protected agricultural and manufacturing sectors combined. Major services sectors such as electricity, transport, distribution and business services suffer from particularly high levels of protection. A targeted opening of services could present vast opportunities to firms and huge gains to consumers in both the EU and the US. Removing barriers in these sectors would be equivalent to 50 years' worth of GATT and WTO liberalization of trade in goods (Hamilton, 2010). An initial transatlantic initiative can be a building block for more global arrangements. Such negotiations are likely to trigger plurilateral negotiations to include other partners. Beyond these areas however, the greatest impact of the TTIP is likely to lie in efforts to generate greater regulatory coherence across the Atlantic. Estimates indicate that 80 per cent of the overall potential wealth gains resulting from TTIP will come from cutting costs imposed by bureaucracy and regulation, as well as from liberalizing trade in services and public procurement (Francois, 2013).

Given the relatively open US-EU trading relationship and the importance of mutual investment, the most important hurdles to greater transatlantic commerce are 'behind the border' regulatory differences rather than 'at the border' trade barriers. The US and the EU boast two of the most sophisticated regulatory systems in the world. American and European regulators uphold high health, welfare and environmental standards. Yet given the deep integration of the transatlantic economy, the economic friction generated by differences in regulatory approaches or procedures – many of which are relatively minor – can mean big costs for companies and consumers. For instance, although EU chemical exports to America face a modest 1.2 per cent tariff rate, non-tariff barriers to chemicals result in a tariff equivalent of 19.1 per cent (Stelzer, 2013).

This does not mean that the regulatory pillar of TTIP is simply another element to be subjected to the inevitable trade-offs involved in traditional trade agreements; there will be no deal, for instance, in which the EU would sacrifice its position banning hormone beef in exchange for US agreement to open its public procurement market. Yet negotiators have not explained well how the regulatory dimension will in fact work, giving rise to concerns, particularly among a range of stakeholder groups in Europe, that TTIP is nothing less than a new mechanism by which the 'American system' will eviscerate European standards and simply steamroll the European way of life.

In the face of such high levels of concern, EU officials have been adamant that laws intended to protect human life and health, animal health and welfare, or environment and consumer interests will not be part of the negotiations. This includes genetically modified organisms. The intent, rather, is to improve US-EU exchange of information on testing procedures, sharing of scientific data and reducing costs of compliance without sacrificing safety assessment and risk procedures, such as those carried out by the European Food

Safety Authority. Examples of such co-operation include a US-EU agreement on the equivalency of organic foods; progress along similar lines for communications equipment, common standards for electric vehicles; and mutual agreement to recognize as substantially equivalent each other's safety tests for aircraft. Where harmonization or mutual recognition of existing regulations and standards cannot be achieved, then the TTIP seeks to create a 'living agreement' that would include other forward-looking mechanisms to head off conflicts, including early consultations, impact assessments and regulatory reviews (De Gucht, 2013).

A related public outcry, particularly in Europe, has appeared over TTIP negotiations towards a transatlantic approach to investor-state dispute settlement. This provision, first introduced by Germany in the 1950s out of a perceived need to ensure clear legal guidelines with countries with relatively underdeveloped legal systems, particularly with regard to potential issues such as expropriation or nationalization, is now part of over 3,000 economic agreements worldwide, including between nine different EU Member States with the US and between the EU and Canada as part of their nearly-completed economic agreement known as CETA (comprehensive economic and trade agreement) (Federation of German Industry, 2014). Even though European countries make greater use of investor-state provisions than all other countries in the world combined, considerable concern has emerged among stakeholder groups in Europe that such a provision with the US would dilute governments' 'right to regulate' by giving corporations a preferential ability to sue public authorities.

In the case of both the regulatory elements of TTIP and investor-state dispute settlement, the original intent of US and EU negotiators was not simply to focus on the renewal and further opening of the transatlantic market, but to use more efficient, high-standard regulatory alignment and modernized investor-state provisions to strengthen the ground rules of the international economic order itself by repositioning the transatlantic partnership with regard to third countries. Domestic single-issue critics of particular TTIP efforts have by and large failed to take account of this 'second' purpose: to open transatlantic markets in ways that can also be used to open global markets and lift international standards. This 'second purpose' – and perhaps the one that finally galvanized political will among EU and US leaders to launch the TTIP negotiations – was prompted by a common sense that in a more diffuse, globalizing world the window is closing on the ability of the US and Europe to set standards informing the ground rules of the international system. The multilateral system administered by the World Trade Organization is under challenge, especially by emerging growth markets that have benefited substantially from the system. A number of rapidly emerging countries do not share the core principles or basic structures that underpin open rules-based commerce, and are now showing no real interest in new market opening initiatives. As a result, the global economy is drifting dangerously towards the use of national discriminatory trade, regulatory and investment practices.

In this regard, the US and the EU are now committed to invest in new forms of transatlantic collaboration that strengthen multilateral rules and lift international standards. Given the size and scope of the transatlantic economy, standards negotiated by the US and EU are still likely to become the benchmark for global models, reducing the chances that others will impose more stringent, protectionist requirements for either products or services. Mutual recognition of essentially equivalent norms and regulatory coherence across the transatlantic space, in areas ranging from consumer safety and intellectual property to investment policy and labour mobility, not only promise to lift lives, but form the core of broader international norms and standards. Both sides hope that by aligning their domestic standards, they will be able to set the benchmark for developing global rules in ways that avoid lowest-common denominator outcomes when dealing with rising powers that may not necessarily share the same such standards with regard to health and safety or consumer, worker and environmental protection.

Greater trade and investment opportunities and alignment on high standards and norms are important not only in terms of how the transatlantic partners relate to each other, but how they together might best relate to rising powers, especially emerging growth markets, whose leaders are still debating their role in the international system. Whether those powers choose to challenge the current international economic order and its rules or promote themselves within it depends significantly on how the transatlantic partners engage not only with them, but also with each other. The stronger those transatlantic bonds, the better the chances that rising partners will emerge as responsible stakeholders in the international trading system; the looser or weaker those bonds, the greater the likelihood that rising powers will challenge this order.

TTIP has also become important in the context of changing energy realities. Over the past few years America's oil and gas boom has rendered the US over 80 per cent self-sufficient in energy production and use. It will soon become an exporter of natural gas and surpass both Russia and Saudi Arabia to become the world's largest producer of oil and liquid natural gas. A successful TTIP would enable the US to export gas to Europe since American law prohibits such exports (or requires onerous licensing procedures) except to countries with which the US has a free trade agreement. American gas exports to Europe could alleviate European dependence on unpredictable suppliers; just the prospect has forced Russia to break the link between oil and gas prices and to negotiate better terms with a number of European customers. Critics are sceptical that substantial US energy flows could happen anytime soon, given the need to build appropriate new infrastructure that could take years to complete. Yet investors likely to fund such a project are deciding today on such multi-year projects, and thus a strong political signal of intent can in fact influence such investment decisions.

Unfortunately, Americans and Europeans often talk past each other when it comes to energy issues. At times it seems to be a 'clash of religions': Americans tend to believe that European preoccupation with their image as the 'champion' of climate issues has blinded them to key dependencies and the need for a clear and common energy policy. Europeans tend to believe that American preoccupation with the notion of energy independence has blinded them to the dangers posed by a changing climate and caused them to pull back from vigorous efforts to develop breakthrough energy solutions. Neither view is entirely true, but these differing perceptions have contributed to a dialogue of the deaf that often finds the US and the EU in opposing camps globally. Of course, different stakeholders on each side of the Atlantic may have competing or even conflicting interests among themselves; the issues cannot be boiled down to a simple Europe versus America debate. However, the depth of the transatlantic strategic relationship, the nature of global energy trends, and the further integration of the US and EU economies warrant a new approach to energy issues.

Getting a TTIP deal will be tough. Remaining transatlantic tariff barriers, especially in agriculture, often reflect the most politically difficult cases. Some of the most intense transatlantic disagreements have arisen over differences in regulatory policy. Issues such as food safety or environmental standards have strong public constituencies and are often extremely sensitive in the domestic political arena. Responsibility for regulation is split in the EU between Brussels and the Member States, and in the US between the federal and state governments. Investment barriers, especially in terms of infrastructure and transport sector ownership, will be very difficult to change. The potential payoff of such an initiative is high, however, and will translate into jobs and economic opportunity not only for Americans and Europeans, but for billions around the world.

IV. The Transatlantic Agenda beyond Europe

In the first area under examination transatlantic leadership used to drive change; now the transatlantic partners are being forced to react to changes set elsewhere. In the second area, the transatlantic actors have set aside tactical differences to advance an ambitious and potentially transformative economic partnership, yet are struggling to deal with challenges raised by domestic stakeholders. In the third area to be explored, the US and Europe continue to struggle to use their partnership to tackle common challenges in other regions of the world.

During the Cold War, 'transatlantic' relations primarily meant stabilizing the European continent. Today, however, Europeans and Americans are each challenged by such issues as climate change, radicalism and ungoverned spaces, the rise of China, Iran's nuclear ambitions and a host of issues far from European shores. The question is whether they can use their relationship to address these issues more effectively together, or whether differences will inhibit the development of a more global transatlantic partnership. The record thus far is quite mixed. It indicates considerable ambivalence on the part of each partner, underscores continued disparities in American and European priorities and capacities, and in some cases demonstrates the limits of western influence even when the US and its European partners work closely together. Of course, this is a vast field. The US and European countries work daily to co-ordinate their efforts in a wide range of areas beyond the scope of this essay, but efforts with regard to the broader Middle East and to Asia loom particularly large.

President Obama is using his second term to consolidate his administration's 'rebalance' toward the Asia-Pacific region. Although there is considerable European apprehension and misunderstanding about this perceived shift in US focus, until now policy statements about the 'rebalance' have not been accompanied by a substantial boost in resources for the Pacific, and to the extent the US is seeking to build a new regional architecture of co-operation in the Pacific, it regularly uses transatlantic co-operation as a template and reference. In addition, the military element of the shift has been from two theatres of war in Iraq and Afghanistan. It is not intended as a 'pivot' from the Atlantic to the Pacific, and turmoil in Europe's eastern neighbourhood is likely to ensure continued US focus on Europe as well. Nonetheless, there are serious reasons behind renewed American attention to Asia-Pacific dynamics, which contain the seeds for severe political confrontation and possible great power conflict. Defence budgets are increasing everywhere in Asia; in 2012, total defence spending in Asia exceeded total defence spending in Europe. Moreover, there are inadequate institutions and insufficient agreement on basic norms of behaviour in Asia compared to those that have developed in Europe.

These developments, together with Europe's own vested interests in Asian stability and growth, offer an opportunity for Washington to embrace a pivot 'with Europe', not 'from Europe'. This does not mean that Washington would seek to push Europe to play a role in Asia commensurate with America's, or to slavishly follow US direction, but rather to signal that Europe would draw on its comparative advantages to pursue common interests and co-ordinate policies towards Asia with the US wherever possible (Binnendijk, 2014). Both partners will have to develop new habits of working together if they are to make a common pivot more operational. Moreover, the basic drivers behind US and European approaches to the region differ. Europe's Asia policy is largely driven by the drive for markets and investment, although some see a bigger role for European soft power, particularly attention to the rule of law. American economic interests in Asia are also substantial, but they are tempered by the real obligations it has as an underwriter of regional security and stability.

Attention to Asia notwithstanding, Middle East troubles are not going away. In fact, despite all the rhetoric about an American pivot to Asia, US Secretary of State John Kerry has spent most of his tenure trying to contain Middle Eastern instabilities and insecurities. The ongoing human tragedy in Syria is the most immediate of these challenges. The US and most European countries have been reluctant to become involved militarily in Syria. Yet western hesitation has created a political vacuum that jihadist forces associated with al-Qaeda have exploited to their advantage. The Syrian crisis has already destabilized Iraq and threatens to do the same to Lebanon, Jordan and even Turkey. How the US and Europe approach the crisis will have considerable implications for their relations with other key actors in the region. And tensions with Russia over Moscow's intentions towards Ukraine and its neighbourhood are certain to affect the ability of the US and Europe to work with Russia to ameliorate the situation in Syria, as well as to move forward with Iran.

The transatlantic partners have aligned their dual-track approach of pressure and engagement with Iran and secured an interim agreement with Tehran that provides for a six-month suspension of Iranian nuclear activity in exchange for some sanctions relief and negotiations for a final and comprehensive agreement. Yet the next phase of negotiations is far more difficult, and prospects for a final arrangement remain highly uncertain.

The US and European partners provide the majority of funding for the stabilization of Afghanistan and have co-ordinated their messages on the need for peaceful and inclusive change, even though it is unclear whether Afghan forces can assume primary responsibility for their own security as the western presence diminishes. The urgent agenda now is to develop a credible political strategy to complement the military drawdown.

Americans and Europeans have broadly agreed in their analysis of what needs to be done to support Arab countries in transition, and US and European aid officials have actively co-ordinated their efforts. Yet donor co-ordination is notoriously difficult on the ground, and the Deauville format of assistance co-ordination, which was launched by the G8 in 2011, has not delivered. Moreover, while both the US and the EU were concerned with the coup that deposed the Morsi government in Egypt and want Egypt to do more to restore democracy, they have been unwilling to cut off aid or pressure the military regime.

In short, until now American and European efforts to extend their partnership beyond their traditional focus on Europe has had mixed results. In many areas there is relative convergence of views on overall goals, but this often contrasts with differences over tactics.

Conclusions

Twenty-five years after the opening of the Iron Curtain, the transatlantic partnership has evolved from its primary focus on stabilizing the European continent to a three-pronged agenda: strengthening the community of prosperous democratic European societies while extending that stability to as much of Europe as possible; seizing opportunities inherent in deep integration of the transatlantic economy, both to create jobs and spark growth in a more open Euro-Atlantic market and to use the potential of such a market to strengthen the international system and lift standards worldwide; and to address together a range of regional and global issues beyond the traditional confines of the North Atlantic space. In each area significant progress has been made, and yet it can fairly be said that the US and the EU have yet to forge a truly effective strategic partnership in any of these three areas. Moreover, time is not neutral. In a globalizing world of more diffuse power and a multitude of rising countries, the window is closing on the ability of the transatlantic partners individually to set standards and assert influence.

Through TTIP the transatlantic partners are charting new ground in their efforts to reposition their economies for a new world rising. Yet they are losing ground with regard to concerns raised by domestic stakeholders. Their most promising legacy – very real progress toward a Europe whole, free and at peace – is being challenged by Russia and by continued turmoil in Wider Europe. And efforts to extend their partnership to other regions and to global challenges remain hampered by asymmetrical institutional frameworks, strategic-action capacity and inadequate tools at their disposal.

In short, this three-fold transatlantic pivot to a new and more relevant relationship is not proving to be easy. It is unclear whether Europeans have the desire, and Americans the patience, for the nuanced and painstaking work required for it to work. If they do, the first 'Pacific President' and his EU partners may well be remembered for having re-founded the Atlantic Partnership. If they do not, then issues of failing trust and confidence, in the context of mutual retrenchment and attention to domestic challenges, so visible today, will continue to eat away at the relationship like termites in the woodwork.

References

Asghar, I. (2008) 'Flipside of US Politics'. *The Nation*, 30 October.
Asmus, R. (ed.) (2006) *Next Steps in Forging a Euroatlantic Strategy for the Wider Black Sea* (Washington, DC: German Marshall Fund of the United States).
Binnendijk, H. (ed.) (2014) *A Transatlantic Pivot to Asia: Towards New Trilateral Partnerships* (Washington, DC: Center for Transatlantic Relations).
Brzezinski, I.J. (2014) 'Transatlantic Security Challenges: Central and Eastern Europe'. Testimony before the US Senate Committee on Foreign Relations, 10 April.
Campbell, K. and Andrews, B. (2014) *Explaining the US 'Pivot' to Asia* (London: Chatham House).
Clinton, H.R. (2011) 'America's Pacific Century'. *Foreign Policy*, 11 October.
De Gucht, K. (2013) 'Transatlantic Trade and Investment Partnership (TTIP): Solving the Regulatory Puzzle'. Speech by EU Trade Commissioner Karel De Gucht, 10 October.
Erixon, F. and Bauer, M. (2010) 'A Transatlantic Zero Agreement: Estimating the Gains from Transatlantic Free Trade in Goods'. ECIPE Occasional Paper 4/2010 (Brussels: European Centre for International Political Economy).

Federation of German Industry (2014) *Background: Facts and Figures – International Investment Agreements and Investor-State Dispute Settlement* (Berlin: Federation of German Industry).

Francois, J. (2013) *Reducing Transatlantic Barriers to Trade and Investment: An Economic Assessment* (London: Centre for Economic Policy Research).

Hamilton, D. (ed.) (2010) *Shoulder to Shoulder: Forging a Strategic US-EU Partnership* (Washington, DC: Center for Transatlantic Relations).

Hamilton, D. and Foster, N. (2009) 'The Obama Administration and Europe'. In Vasconcelos, A. de and Zaborowski, M. (eds) *The Obama Moment: European and American Perspectives* (Paris: EU ISS).

Hamilton, D. and Quinlan, J. (2014) *The Transatlantic Economy 2014: Annual Survey of Jobs, Trade and Investment between the United States and Europe* (Washington, DC: Center for Transatlantic Relations).

Ikenberry, G.J. (2011) *Liberal Leviathan: The Origins, Crisis and Transformation of the American World Order* (Princeton, NJ: Princeton University Press).

King, C. (2008) 'The Wider Black Sea Region in the Twenty-First Century'. In Hamilton, D. and Mangott, G. (eds) *The Wider Black Sea Region in the 21st Century: Strategic, Economic and Energy Perspectives* (Washington, DC: Center for Transatlantic Relations).

Stelzer, I. (2013) 'USTR Hopes TTIP + TPP = Faster Growth'. *Weekly Standard*, 13 July.

Stent, A. (2007) 'The Lands In-Between: The New Eastern Europe in the Twenty-First Century'. In Hamilton, D. and Mangott, G. (eds) *The New Eastern Europe: Ukraine, Belarus and Moldova* (Washington, DC: Center for Transatlantic Relations).

US Department of Defense (2012) *Sustaining US Global Leadership: Priorities for 21st Century Defense* (Washington, DC: US Department of Defense).

JCMS 2014 Volume 52 Annual Review pp. 40–56 DOI: 10.1111/jcms.12174

Six Lessons of Enlargement Ten Years On: The EU's Transformative Power in Retrospect and Prospect

HEATHER GRABBE
Open Society European Policy Institute

Introduction

Two events in 2013 showed the opportunities, risks and challenges of EU enlargement: Croatia joined the Union, having been at war only two decades previously, while the prospect of more former Soviet countries getting closer to the EU (although well short of membership) frightened Russia enough to deploy soft and hard power to prevent Armenia and Ukraine from signing association agreements.

It was the end of the EU's monopoly on transformative power. For a quarter-century, the EU's gravitational pull had been largely unrivalled. It was a remarkable period in European history. After the fall of communism, nearly every country in central and eastern Europe had turned towards the west, seeking to join the EU and NATO. Sooner or later, even the most tenacious regimes were felled by popular movements inspired by calls for 'reform' and a 'European future'. Some took longer than others to oust their communist parties, but there was no serious rival for regional integration and international standing. Only Belarus remained in the Soviet mould, tied to Russian markets by its autocratic leader. After the Balkan wars finally ended with a series of peace deals around the turn of the century, the former Yugoslav republics and Albania also sought EU membership. Moldovan and Ukrainian leaders enquired about a membership perspective, but were discouraged by the EU from applying.

The EU's appeal came from its combination of stability, prosperity, security and personal freedoms. Open markets and open societies were extremely attractive to people who had lived under state socialism. The previous political and economic systems were thoroughly discredited, and the EU provided a successful alternative model combined with a framework of support for the reforms to get there, crowned with the possibility of joining a powerful and rich regional club.

For two decades, it seemed that Francis Fukuyama was right in proclaiming 'the end of history' in Europe at least. Central and Eastern Europe embraced western liberal democracy as the 'final form of human government' (Fukuyama, 1992). The EU offered a fast-track to this form of government by providing models for new policies and institutions, as well as deep political engagement, trade, investment and financial aid. The US was also an important source of inspiration and support for post-communist transition, and it offered access to NATO membership. But the EU had by far the deepest impact on domestic policies, institutions and expectations of the societies emerging from communism after 1989, working through social norms and the construction of identity as well as material incentives.

However, the EU's agenda for the region was never a full plan for democracy and development. It was focused on the core requirements for EU membership, a much narrower set of goals focused on ensuring countries can participate in a common market, a shared budget and policies (Grabbe, 2006). The limits of EU influence on political culture are now becoming evident. Bulgaria, Hungary and Romania have experienced rollback of various EU-inspired changes, while populist xenophobic politics has emerged also in Slovakia and elsewhere.

This contribution reviews six major lessons drawn by EU policy-makers about the first decade of eastward enlargement. Some of these lessons are corroborated by academic research, particularly on how the new members fared in the EU, from their compliance with EU law (which was better than expected) to their practice of democracy (in some cases worse than expected). The Commission and Member States responded to these lessons by altering how the accession conditionality was applied to the Balkans and Turkey by, for example, prioritizing institution-building, the rule of law and anti-corruption measures much earlier in the process.

There are also lessons about the domestic constraints on EU external policies. Politics within the EU have affected enlargement policy much more, changing it from an elite-led and largely consensus-based project before 2004 to a much more contested one. Populist politics began to surge in both the EU and enlargement countries as the crisis hit, bringing controversy to issues such as migration from poorer to richer parts of the EU. Political uncertainty has affected the consistency and credibility of the accession process for would-be joiners of the future. As a result, the prospects for transformative power in the Balkans are much dimmer than they were for post-communist Europe.

The Outlook for Enlargement Ten Years On

Just months before Russia struck back in the east, the Union celebrated the accession of its 28th member. Beethoven's 'Ode to Joy' was sung in public squares when Croatia joined the European Union on 1 July 2013. It was a rare moment of celebration for an EU riven by strife, in a brief pause between the internal crisis over the euro and the external crisis of Russia moving into Ukraine.

The 2013 enlargement was an historic moment in many senses: Croatia was the second ex-Yugoslav country to join and the first that had been deeply embroiled in the terrible wars of the 1990s. That gave hope to the rest of the region that they really could make it into the EU. However, Croatia's accession treaty may prove to be the last to be signed this decade, and the last to be passed without a referendum in one or more of the existing Member States. Croatia may also be the last joiner not to face permanent derogations of one kind or another – particularly on free movement of workers after accession. The EU already stated in its 2005 negotiating framework for Turkey that there might be permanent derogations on labour mobility, and now some Member States are considering ways of introducing indefinite limits on free movement after other countries join, beyond the temporary transition periods of the past. That opens the possibility of a status permanently less than full membership for future joiners.

The outlook for the EU to use its transformative power in the Balkans and Turkey is very different from what happened in central Europe. The accession process is moving much more slowly and the feedback loop between accession prospects, domestic reforms and economic improvements is not functioning positively. The state of play at the end of 2013 was three countries in negotiations for EU membership (Montenegro, Serbia and Turkey); one with candidate status but no date for starting negotiations (Macedonia); one with a Commission recommendation for candidate status that has not yet been agreed by the Council (Albania); and two that have yet to apply (Kosovo and Bosnia-Herzegovina).[1] These fine gradations in the stages in the accession process are one of the many new elements introduced since the 'big bang' enlargement of 2004, which brought ten new members into the EU.

This contribution draws on academic research about enlargement and its effects, and on the personal experience of the author, who was senior adviser to the Commissioner for Enlargement in the European Commission from 2004 to 2009, and thereafter worked on the Balkans, Turkey and the new Member States of the EU for the Open Society Foundations in Brussels. The observations presented draw on direct involvement in policy-making, as well many conversations with the main actors in the EU institutions, Member States and enlargement countries. This experience showed EU officials to be very responsive to the needs and problems faced by the enlargement countries, and also the concerns of Member States. They took lesson-learning very seriously. However, Commission officials could not control the politics of enlargement in the Member States, which changed considerably after 2004 because of growing domestic debates about the effects of enlargement, especially migration across the EU.

Lessons Learned about the EU's Transformative Power since 2004

In Brussels and national capitals, there is widespread consensus about the lessons learned since 2004. This contribution sets out the six lessons most widely cited among officials and politicians in the EU – including policy-makers from the newer Member States – and matches them with academic research findings where possible.

1. EU Influence Dwindles on Politically Hot Topics Once the Accession Date is Guaranteed – but Compliance on Laws and Policies is Surprisingly Long-Lasting

Threats from the EU start to lose their power once the country gets into the Union because the strongest conditionality is attached to membership itself. The lesson drawn by EU policy-makers is that more vigilance is needed in ensuring that candidates deliver on their commitments before negotiating chapters are closed rather than on the basis of promises, as happened before 2004. But in less politically controversial areas, new members have complied better with EU law than the old ones.

Two of the most often cited examples of new members reneging on their commitments were provided by Romania and Croatia. Shortly after Romania joined the EU in 2007, the government sacked Justice Minister Monica Macovei, who had been in charge of the enormous reform effort to clean up the judiciary so that the country could join the EU on time rather than being delayed by a year to 2008. Her efforts had been vital to improving the rule of law and expanding the capacity of Romanian courts to apply EU law properly.

---

[1] See Whitman and Juncos's contribution to this volume.

The reform plan was not complete, but the government chose to get rid of a crusading minister who was bitterly opposed by the interests who benefited from corruption in the judiciary – including some of those in power.

Enlargement Commissioner Olli Rehn was concerned about this problem, and tried to prevent the EU from fixing an accession date for Bulgaria and Romania accessions at the December 2004 European Council; however, France in particular insisted on a date in order to ensure that nominally Francophone countries would join soon after the central Europeans. The resulting compromise on the EU side was the possibility of a one-year delay from 2007 to 2008 if the remaining conditions were not met. But once the 2007 date approached, both Commission officials and EU members worried that a delay might not lead to a significant improvement in meeting the conditions, but it could cause a political backlash that created unhappy future members. The Commission sought to maintain some pressure by imposing a 'co-operation and verification mechanism' of post-accession monitoring on Bulgaria and Romania. The naming and shaming effect of annual reports still had some restraining effect – but much less so once new members had a seat at the table and could argue against sanctions both within the Commission and the Council. This lesson was learned to the extent that Croatia's negotiations slowed down markedly in their final phase because the Commission and several Member States were unconvinced that the judiciary was clean enough and that rule of law would function adequately after accession. Croatia had to jump through many more hurdles than Bulgaria and Romania had done, on corruption and judicial reform as well as on delivering indicted war criminals to the Hague Tribunal.

Nevertheless, political actors resisted on an issue of high political salience once the date of accession was fixed and sure. In 2013, EU officials were shocked when the Croatian parliament voted just days before accession to change its laws to prevent the arrest of Yugoslav-era secret police chief Josip Perković, who was wanted in Germany for the murder of a Croatian dissident on its territory. During the accession negotiations, the EU had insisted that Croatia lift its prohibition on the extradition of Croatian citizens, so that the country could apply the European arrest warrant for automatic extradition between Member States. The parliament tried to change the law to prevent extradition for crimes committed prior to 2002 when the European arrest warrant came into force – including the 1983 murder in which Perković is implicated. This move caused outrage in Berlin as well as Brussels, and eventually Perković was extradited in 2014.

What is remarkable about EU influence is not so much that countries sought to renege on hotly contested commitments, but rather that they continued to comply in many other fields. EU social pressure only works sometimes at the political level, as the cases of Croatia and Romania show, but it has continued to influence state administrations after accession. Ministries got used to following EU norms, and continued to apply EU law. There were widespread concerns before 2004 that new members might not be able to apply EU law properly. The third Copenhagen condition on 'ability to take on the obligations of membership' was the focus of attention in most of the negotiations. Extensive research on post-accession compliance shows that implementation of EU law among the central European members who joined in 2004 has been strong in the first decade after accession (Sedelmeier, 2012). This is all the more remarkable given that non-compliance has grown elsewhere in the EU during the euro crisis (Falkner, 2013).

Why has the compliance of the 2004 joiners been so durable? This cannot have happened only because of the threat of material sanctions such as infringement proceedings, which apply to all members, but must also be because of the transfer of norms through social learning and persuasion during the accession process. There are both rational choice and constructivist reasons for this outcome. The threat of material sanctions is limited in practice. The Commission is cautious about using infringement proceedings to go after Member States for fear of damaging its own credibility. If a Member State defies the Commission or ignores a ruling by the Court of Justice of the EU, it undermines the community of law that underpins European integration. Commission officials are very aware of the fragility of the system and do not seek confrontation with Member States. Usually they try to warn Member States and find solutions before taking them to court. There was no need to do this in the case of central Europeans, whose records are better than those of the older Member States over the past decade, especially on compliance with the *acquis communautaire*. Most have also continued to comply with the political conditionality, although that has now started to change with Hungary. If the new members had adopted EU laws and norms instrumentally only to achieve the objective of membership, then they would have stopped complying when the incentive structure changed. Beneath formal compliance, there were problems in implementation in some areas of high political salience, such as minority rights (Sasse, 2009), but there are now plenty of instances where the EU and other international organizations went beyond conditionality to influence countries at a very deep level within the state and society, as well as in post-communist politics (see the contributions to Epstein and Sedelmeier, 2009).

There is much academic literature on how and why normative pressures had long-lasting effects. One finding is that conditionality was applied in a social context (see Epstein, 2008; Kelley, 2004). The accession process was not just about EU officials talking to a small group of bureaucrats, but the formation of a vast network of ties to the economy and society that gave elites a greater stake in integration (Levitsky and Way, 2010). The 'return to Europe' was a national project in which officials and politicians ended up sharing much of the EU's reform agenda rather than resisting it. Rather than the EU overcoming resistant domestic actors, the two worked together. As Jacoby (2006) argues, external actors lengthened the time horizons of post-communist politicians, expanded the circle of interested reformers and deterred opponents of reform.

This shared agenda is central to explaining the success of the 2004 enlargement. The EU was going with the tide of history in central Europe. It could help domestically driven reforms to go faster and further by empowering reformers and giving them technical and financial assistance. The incentive of joining the EU overwhelmed other domestic interests because there was such a strong sense among political elites and the public that Europe was their destiny in terms of identity, as well as their preferred destination in terms of prosperity, stability and security. This factor explains much of the difference between what happened in central Europe and the EU's lack of traction in Turkey and Iceland, where membership was not a widely shared goal in society.

Where the accession process runs against the political tide in a country, it cannot gain momentum to overcome domestic obstacles consistently enough to achieve systemic transformation. The EU's combination of membership conditionality, material incentives and social pressure depends on widespread orientation towards future membership. Where the accession date seems very far away, rent-seeking elites, weak bureaucracies and nationalist leaders can stop EU-motivated reforms even if the public wants to join. And when the EU pushes issues of high domestic salience in more contested political arenas, it has less impact, as shown in Croatia, Serbia and Turkey (Schimmelfennig, 2009).

On Bulgaria and Romania, the phrase most often heard in Brussels and national capitals is: 'They came in too early, before they were ready.' This view is not matched by international comparisons of the performance of Bulgaria and Romania on broad democracy and governance indicators with the 2004 joiners (see Levitz and Pop-Eleches, 2010), but it is a very widespread perception in the rest of the EU.

Would more time have brought deeper transformation in these countries? There are many reasons why conditions were different in Bulgaria and Romania. The main lesson the Commission drew was that the weak capacity of the state – especially in enforcing the rule of law – limited the transformative effect. Following the 2007 enlargement and Croatia's troubled final phase of negotiations, the EU pushed reform of the judiciary and improvements in the rule of law up the list of priorities. DG Enlargement changed the sequencing of the negotiations and priorities in technical and financial assistance to focus on reforms of the judiciary and law enforcement from the beginning, instead of leaving the relevant chapters (23 and 24) until after the more straightforward parts of the negotiations.

2. Democratic Transition is Not a One Way Street and It Does Not Guarantee Good Governance

Lesson 1 is about the deep effects of the accession process on the state at many levels, from ministries to local government. The top political level can turn against the EU even while its functionaries continue to comply with EU law. The EU is strong in guiding and supporting reformers, but weak when nation-based populism dominates domestic politics. Even in countries where the incentive of accession can overcome domestic resistance to the EU agenda, EU influence can be weak because it has no answers to fundamental questions of national identity or how to unseat rent-seeking elites. In other words, its influence on democracy and governance is much more limited than on laws and policies. As a result, Italy and Greece still showed severe problems decades after joining the EU. The path for post-communist countries was assumed to be more linear. And the Member States have never wanted to give the EU powers to sanction undemocratic practices or corruption at the national level – only in the misuse of EU funds. This is mainly because the EU never set out to be a holistic development agency, and its Member States have avoided giving the EU's institutions powers to criticize their democracy or governance.

The mandate for enlargement policy set by the Copenhagen conditions is both broad and narrow. The first condition is political: 'stability of institutions guaranteeing democracy, the rule of law, human rights and respect for and protection of minorities'. Where there is no *acquis* or clear link between the political conditions and the 'obligations of membership', and particularly where the Commission lacks expertise and hence self-confidence in setting standards, the EU cannot easily widen the scope of its conditionality. The Commission had a major influence on the shape and mandate of regulatory institutions that affected the *acquis*, especially the Single Market, but not on the checks and balances between political institutions.

When it comes to the most sensitive and difficult issues in democratic transition, such as the status and treatment of minorities, human rights, corruption and organized crime, the EU is often agnostic about what policies countries should adopt. Although potential members have to meet the political conditions, the EU has no democratic *acquis* on which to draw to provide guidance to the candidates – and tends to outsource the issue to the Council of Europe. The Member States are themselves diverse in their policies on issues like provision of bilingual education for the children of ethnic minorities, or on tackling corruption in the public sector. Although the members form part of a community of nations and share norms on what is and is not acceptable behaviour on the part of the state, the EU has no codified guidance on how to solve the trickiest dilemmas of democracy. Moreover, most EU processes are designed to turn insoluble political questions into manageable technical issues. This is the heart of the 'Monnet method' of European integration: focus on practical economic integration and knit interests together so that people will stop paying so much attention to nationalist claims. The downside of this approach is that if the unsolved political question re-emerges, it can disrupt all the careful technical work.

The most unexpected rollback happened in Hungary, where state institutions proved to be much more vulnerable to capture than the EU side expected. During the accession process, Hungary was long regarded by the EU – and its own officials – as 'the best pupil in the class' who got its homework done fastest and was better prepared than any other candidate by the mid-1990s (Grabbe and Hughes, 1998). The Commission praised Hungary's institutions, laws and policies every year in its annual progress reports prior to membership – and these were achieved under a government led by Viktor Orbán during 1998–2002. But after accession, these institutions proved to be easily captured by a single party led by the same person.

Hungarian civil society reacted initially with protests, but they did not succeed in reducing the dominance of the ruling Fidesz party over the judiciary and media. It seems that Hungarians were not so attached to their new institutions to fight hard for their independence in the absence of effective opposition parties. The limits of socialization were shown when checks and balances in the constitutional order were easily overcome by a determined and popular premier (see Haughton, 2014). Commission President Barroso and Justice Commissioner Reding complained, while others used what small levers they had available: Economic and Monetary Affairs Commissioner Olli Rehn cut financial assistance because the central bank's independence had been compromised, while Digital Affairs Commissioner Neelie Kroes tried to use her legal toehold of preventing discrimination against foreign media companies.

The Commission's powers to sanction anti-democratic or even unconstitutional measures in a Member State are tiny. Its power to name and shame through public criticism only works when democracy is functioning well enough that the domestic opposition can use Commission criticism as ammunition against the government. This did not happen in the Hungarian case, although it was more effective in Romania in 2012. Hungary made some small changes in response to EU pressure, and the fuss died down, enabling the Orbán government to gain a new super-majority in the 2014 elections.

Why did the EU not use its measures to try to bring rogue members into line? The answer lies in a combination of partisan politics and weak normative consensus, which thwarted the EU's ability to use the sanctioning mechanism of Article 7 of the Treaty on European Union (see Sedelmeier, 2014). The Commission's criticism was undermined by a lack of support from other EU institutions. In the European Parliament, the European People's Party used its relative majority to block an attempt by other parties to censure Fidesz. Rather than holding its member to account, the EPP used its power to protect a member of its party family. In the Council, the leaders of other Member States were not inclined to give the EU level new sanctions on democracy at the national level – lest they might themselves fall foul of them someday. Furthermore, officials had tended to assume that progress on democracy and governance went together. However, Alina Mungiu-Pippidi (2014) points out that democracy does not by itself ensure good governance – that is, the set of formal and informal institutions that determine how public goods are allocated in a country. She criticizes the EU for relying on building legal constraints to fight corruption rather than reducing the opportunities for graft such as increasing transparency and reducing red tape. Her research indicates that accession makes the problem worst in the least developed countries because EU structural funds increase resources for corruption (Mungiu-Pippidi, 2014).

One of the great disappointments for citizens in central Europe is that EU membership has not protected them from power-concentrating politicians and rent-seeking elites. Hungarians and Bulgarians may vote for politicians who defy the EU, but polls show that they still support EU membership – because they are hoping for some external constraints on national politics. Will it get them now? The EU has never been effective at countering state capture. However, the silver lining of the euro crisis might be that the EU starts to develop a more elaborate governance agenda. The crisis revealed very deep problems of governance in Greece, an old Member State, which had enormous effects on the whole eurozone. Germany became liable for Greece's problems with governance through eurozone debt. The creditor countries are keen to avoid such spill-overs in the future, and the EU has now set up much more robust systems of discipline on fiscal policy.

The combination of enlargement and the euro crisis are now pushing the EU to develop new mechanisms and competences in the areas of rule of law and democratic practice as well – still hesitantly and with resistance from some members. The impetus for new EU powers on democracy comes not just from problems with democratic pluralism and governance in recent joiners, but also founding Member States (media pluralism in Italy) and the poor governance revealed by the euro crisis (Greece). The public has also been making its voice heard, with large-scale protests in Bulgaria over corruption and in Greece, Spain and Italy over austerity measures.

The Commission has recently been working on plans for a European Public Prosecutor and monitoring of the rule of law in Member States, and it could go further by using the Copenhagen conditions to assess existing Member States (see the proposal by Müller, 2013). But the problem is that the Member States ultimately decide who has power over them, and every one of the governments has to agree, including those likely to be caught out by such new powers. The turkeys would have to vote unanimously for Christmas.

3. Transformation of the Economy and the State Depends on a Self-Sustaining Dynamic between Domestic Reforms, the Accession Process and Economic Prospects

Because of the lessons it drew from the 2004 and 2007 enlargements, the Commission has developed a much more explicit state-building agenda for the Balkans. The requirements of membership have become ever more demanding as the *acquis* has grown and the euro crisis has focused much more attention on governance. In the Balkans, the starting conditions are also much more difficult because states are weak and administrative capacity low. Serbia inherited the state institutions of Yugoslavia, but the other countries had to build them from scratch after their independence. The region has still not recovered from the legacy of the post-Yugoslav wars, with unresolved status issues long preventing regional co-operation and economic integration. The prerequisites are not in place for reformers in most of the Balkan countries to take advantage of the accession process to cause systemic transformation. In central Europe, the most important proved to be: a well-functioning state administration; inflows of foreign direct investment (FDI) to get a virtuous circle working between reforms and economic growth; and a cross-party consensus on the importance of joining the EU and the need for reforms to succeed in doing it.

In order to respond to the incentives that the EU has to offer, countries need to have fairly strong states. The EU negotiates with a small executive team, which it expects to co-ordinate the process of preparing for membership. This team needs strong political backing so that it can override the priorities of other ministries, and it needs to be highly competent in the approximation of laws – often overriding parliamentary objections, too. And the judiciary needs to be able to enforce EU-inspired laws, or they simply foster a culture of non-compliance. Weak states – as in several Balkan countries – cannot take full advantage of the twinning projects, financial and technical assistance that the EU can offer.

The state-building agenda that is now part of the accession process is much needed in the Balkans. The question is whether domestic administrative capacity and governance can improve fast enough to allow the countries to move forward in the accession process and motivate further improvements. This political momentum is vital to overcoming domestic interests that oppose the EU reform agenda. It is also essential for allowing the countries to use their access to EU markets to improve the economic outlook and opportunities for the population, and thereby maintain public support for the whole process. FDI was a vital part of this dynamic in central Europe, acting as the grease that kept the wheels turning towards the EU by offering capital, skills and expertise, employment and hope. Countries that undertook economic reform and gained FDI as a consequence maintained a virtuous circle where their efforts were rewarded by approbation from the EU, which encouraged more foreign investors, and enabled them to undertake the next phase of reforms (Bevan *et al.*, 2001). But the Balkans have had the bad luck of wars delaying their economic transitions until the supply of global capital was drying up in the early 2000s. As a result, problems of de-industrialization have gotten worse and access to EU markets is not bringing profits, jobs and growth as it did in central Europe.

A basic cross-party consensus is also essential in order to ensure consistency of policy on the EU across governments. Otherwise the efforts of one government are wasted, and the country gets no benefits from the painful reforms already undertaken – causing further disillusionment among voters. If the EU becomes a political football in domestic politics, hotly contested between different groups, then the virtuous circle between reforms and progress towards accession disappears.

4. Transformative Power Depends on Consistency and Credibility

In his famous comparison of Europeans from Venus and Americans from Mars, Robert Kagan criticized the EU for not having a 'hammer' of hard power and consequently avoiding foreign policy problems that look like nails (Kagan, 2003). He did not consider how the EU's most effective foreign policy works, however. Enlargement has an effect more like a screwdriver: it does not force change by hitting hard and suddenly; rather, it slowly but surely works deeply into the wood through consistent pressure. Once the screw is deeply embedded, it holds better than a nail. This kind of force depends on consistent pressure. If the EU keeps changing direction during the accession process, the conditionality doesn't hold – just like the screw. In the case of Romania, conditionality was either overlooked or downgraded on at least three occasions (Phinnemore, 2010), exacerbating the problems with weak commitment to EU-imposed reforms. In the early years of its accession negotiations, Croatia's champions among the Member States gave the Sanader government the impression that diplomatic lobbying would let the country off the reforms demanded by the Commission. Only after the problems following the 2007 accessions became evident did the Member States allow the Commission to get much tougher on Croatia.

If the EU is to have a transformative effect in the rest of the Balkans, it has to be much more consistent in its demands and credible in the promise of membership (see Grabbe *et al.*, 2010). This is difficult because the EU has wanted to use its most powerful tool on several different problems at the same time. In addition to domestic reforms, the EU wanted the countries to transfer suspected war criminals to the International Criminal Tribunal for the former Yugoslavia, and settle the status of Kosovo. Perhaps that was the right choice of priorities, but it had a cost: multiple goals dissipated the leverage of EU conditionality during the critical postwar years to start reform of the state and economy.

The challenge is all the greater in the Balkans because the EU's anti-corruption and rule of law agenda runs against the interests of political elites who have captured parts of the state in some countries. The accession process cannot work through empowering reformers as it did in central Europe. The EU's dilemma is worst in the countries that are moving most slowly; it wants to use conditionality, but not to the point where the worst-performing countries in the region – notably Bosnia-Herzegovina – fall out of the accession process altogether (see Vachudova, 2014).

In the case of Turkey, lack of consistency about the accession promise has undermined the credibility of the whole process. Several Member States have blocked chapters and questioned whether the ultimate goal was really membership. In Turkey, the identity incentive to join the EU was strong for several decades, but repeated questioning of the EU's commitment to accession undermined trust in the process and Turkey's ruling party turned against it. When it came to power in 2002, the AKP embraced the EU's agenda as a means of overcoming suspicion among the liberal and secularist elites of its intentions (Barysch *et al.*, 2005). However, Prime Minister Erdogan found the constraints of EU conditionality irksome to his style of government and increasingly contrary to his domestic political and economic agendas. Unlike central Europeans who were seeking to change discredited political and economic systems radically after the fall of communism, Turks were much more comfortable with the *status quo* in their country. When the accession process began to threaten Turkish domestic interests, especially those of the ruling party, it was impossible to sustain support for the negotiations – and both sides found it convenient to go as slowly as possible.

No wonder Turkey's transformation had moved in another direction by 2013. The protestors at Gezi Park waved EU flags, but public support for the EU had already nose-dived. Now Turkey is facing huge challenges to democratic pluralism and individual freedoms – but the EU's power to influence its choices is very weak.

5. Never Allow In a Country with an Unresolved Conflict over Its Status

Ask any non-Cypriot policy-maker – whether in the EU institutions, national diplomats or politician – about Cyprus, and they will tell you that the EU made an enormous mistake in allowing a divided island to join. The unresolved conflict has caused myriad problems for the rest of the EU as the Republic of Cyprus used its membership to pursue the interests and concerns of the Greek Cypriot community. Members that were already reluctant to see Turkey enter found it convenient that Cyprus set up new obstacles in Turkey's accession negotiations and blocked progress on many chapters. The stakes got higher for all Member States when Cyprus hindered EU-NATO co-operation to the extent that it disrupted communication on EU military and civilian missions. The problem escalated from an irritant to other members to a major concern when Cyprus had to apply for a bail-out from other euro members in March 2013. The lack of a settlement had encouraged the Cypriot economy to rely on providing financial and legal services for other countries. The size of Russian assets held on the island (widely estimated at some 450 per cent of Cypriot gross domestic product) became more widely known, and other EU members began asking what influence – through Cyprus – this dependence was giving Moscow in the EU.

Cyprus is unique among EU members in its single-issue focus. It is the only Member State facing an existential security threat, with a population that has lived with an occupying power on part of its territory for several decades. This results in behaviour that other countries' officials find frustrating because Cyprus is not playing in multiple dimensions of European integration, but rather focusing on pursuing its own interests and not following the EU norm of at least pretending to accommodate wider European interests. 'This siege mentality is exasperating,' mutter the representatives of other Member States. As a result, they showed very little sympathy to Cyprus in 2013 when its economy nearly collapsed.

Have they learned the lesson about unresolved conflicts? EU and national policy-makers complain often about the Cyprus problem, but they have not found a way to ensure it never happens again. Bilateral disputes remain time-bombs that could disrupt accession talks at any point, and the EU has found no way of reliably defusing them. The Member States have never mustered the political will to commit themselves to not using the accession process to resolve grievances and disagreements – even just to commit to taking issues to international arbitration and not hindering the accession process (as proposed in Grabbe *et al.*, 2010). The EU has proved to have almost no leverage over its Member States when they enter into a bilateral dispute with a would-be member. Quite the opposite: the Member State has every opportunity to use many levers inside the EU's decision-making system to its advantage. Croatia was forced to come to an agreement with Slovenia over its sea border, just as Slovenia had been pressured into a settlement with Italy over postwar restitution before it could join. The rest of the EU could do little to prevent a future Croatian government from blocking the progress of its neighbours if a local politician started a campaign over one of the many unresolved issues left over from the dissolution of Yugoslavia.

   The most high-profile bilateral dispute in the region is over the name of the 'former Yugoslav Republic of Macedonia', as Greece has insisted the UN and EU call this country since its independence in 1991. Twenty-three years later, the name issue seems as far from resolution as ever. It could still block Macedonia's accession to the EU, as happened with NATO accession in 2008. As a result, the EU's transformative power has had little impact in Macedonia. The name issue has encouraged the growth of a nationalist movement that has distracted the country from the reforms that would be necessary to prepare for EU membership. Since it gained candidate status in 2005, the country's preparedness has moved backwards and the EU's influence has waned, to the extent that the Commission has privately threatened to recommend withdrawal of candidate status. When a prime minister can claim to be fending off a threat to national identity, he can maintain his popularity despite rising unemployment, falling living standards, lack of pluralism and poor governance. He can always blame Greece for lack of progress towards EU and NATO membership, fending off legitimate criticism in the Commission's annual progress reports by claiming it is Greek propaganda.

   The EU has made significant progress is resolving the other major status issue in the Balkans. The High Representative for Foreign and Security Policy, Catherine Ashton, achieved a deal between Belgrade and Pristina in 2013 to remove many obstacles to Kosovo's participation in the accession process. However, the EU has a dilemma: should all the former Yugoslav republics come in together? That would resolve the bilateral disputes problem and reduce the number of potential referendums in existing Member States on Balkan accessions. It would also avoid the risk of Serbia government blocking Kosovo's accession. But the whole region would have to wait a long time before Kosovo caught up, and a package accession would run against the principle of each country progressing on its own merits in meeting the accession conditionality. The lesson is well understood, but the answer to avoid the problem in future is not in sight. The EU's political system is good at finding consensus but not at creating compromises. When major national interests are at stake, the EU is designed to find the lowest common denominator – not to force Member States into deals.

6. Enlargement cannot be Treated as an Elite-Led Foreign Policy

Until the 2004 and 2007 accessions, enlargement had been a largely elite project, known to foreign policy wonks and officials but barely figuring in public debates in many EU countries. There was more controversy in countries that were close to the potential new members, where business stood to benefit but the public was less sure, such as Austria and parts of Germany, and among elites who wanted to keep their influence in the club, such as in France. But in many countries, the media debate about central Europe was small – although the prospects for Turkey have always been more controversial. This changed when the 'Polish plumber' arrived. After 2004, he became a folk villain, even though millions of Europeans relied on his services regularly at home. Most of the EU-15 countries used the transition periods for two, five or seven years on migration of workers, but the accession treaties allowed central Europeans to set up their own businesses throughout the EU, and many started working in construction and household maintenance trades in self-employment.

© 2014 The Author(s) JCMS: Journal of Common Market Studies © 2014 John Wiley & Sons Ltd

Only Ireland, Sweden and the UK opened their labour markets fully in 2004, and many more central Europeans moved to work in these countries than would have done if Germany and other closer neighbours had opened theirs as well. There are no reliable statistics because the UK does not register who leaves the country, but the figures most widely quoted in the debate in Britain are that a government-commissioned academic study estimated that some 13,000 would arrive but around one million Poles came (many have since left). Moreover, many of them moved to rural areas in the UK and Ireland that had experienced little immigration since the Second World War, creating a much bigger social effect than if the central Europeans had moved to the multicultural cities like other migrants.

In 2013, the migration debate turned nasty when it connected with another major public fear: pressure on social welfare systems. Populism surged in European politics just at the time when the transition periods on free movement of labour from the new members were expiring after 2010 – at the height of the euro crisis. With high unemployment in many eurozone countries, fear of labour migration was already growing, even though the economics of a single currency area require labour mobility to correct imbalances in the absence of a central redistributive budget. Meanwhile, the euro crisis had created an atmosphere of fear about the impact of budget cuts on national social security systems, even in the Northern European countries that were suffering much less from austerity. When the seven-year transition periods for Bulgarians and Romanians were about to expire at the end of 2013, the backlash really started. For the first time, tabloid newspapers could put three vilified groups – 'migrants, benefits fraudsters and Eurocrats' – in the same headline. The result was political wildfire. Scare stories about millions of Bulgarians and Romanians moving to richer countries in northern Europe spread rapidly, creating hysteria especially in the British press.

The Austrian, British, Dutch and German interior ministers wrote to the European Council President in 2013 to complain about poorer Europeans moving to their countries to claim welfare benefits. They could not produce evidence of significant numbers of people doing this when challenged by the Commission – and there was no wave of immigrants once they were free to move. But the panic had already had a huge impact, especially in the UK, where parliamentarians started to ask about how new obstacles to free movement could be made permanent for any future joiners. The front-runner in accession negotiations is currently Montenegro, with a tiny population of 621,000 and a joining date probably beyond 2020, but already the British Parliament is asking whether it can stop Montenegrins from moving to work in the UK permanently. More collateral damage to enlargement from austerity politics in the eurozone and worries about the sustainability of welfare systems is likely in future.

The migration panic has made enlargement much more visible to the public and in the media. It will further increase the re-nationalization of enlargement policy by the Member States. Since 2004, they have sought a more active role, initially because of the security and postwar issues for the Balkans, as well as the controversy surrounding Turkey's accession process. Enlargement has moved from the hands of the Commission and foreign ministries into those of national politicians and domestic ministries, especially those responsible for internal security. Perhaps the Ukraine crisis will make it again a geopolitical issue, but at the moment interior ministries are playing the most assertive and active role, especially on final decisions about moving countries from one stage to the next in the accession process. Border controls, corruption and organized crime are the central domestic issues, in addition to the focus on migration.

Other political institutions are also increasing their role. The German Constitutional Court in Karlsruhe gave a more prominent role to the Bundestag in making European policy, and this has increased its role also in enlargement decisions. The reviews of EU competences by the Dutch parliament and UK government are also covering enlargement. Commercial interests, especially from energy industries and banks, are still lobbying governments about enlargement, largely in favour, but sometimes to use the accession process to put pressure on the countries.

The European Parliament has brought a new actor into enlargement, too: party politics on a European scale. The European party families had offered observer or associate membership to parties in the enlargement countries, initially with the aim of socializing them into EU democratic practices. However, in some cases the effect has worked in the opposite direction. For example, MEPs from the European People's Party (EPP) on several occasions blocked the European Parliament from criticizing undemocratic practices in Macedonia because the ruling party in Skopje had signed up as an EPP associate. Instead of holding its associate member to the highest standards of democracy, the EPP protected one of its own from EU criticism.

The much larger role of domestic and party politics in the accession process will make it less predictable and more prone to special-interest lobbying within the EU – reducing the consistency and credibility that are vital for the transformative effect to happen in the Balkans and Turkey.

Conclusions: Transformative Power Redux?

Some of the lessons of the past decade have improved the accession process – particularly the first, second and third presented above – but others are beyond the reach of diligent officials. Policy-makers are very aware of lessons four, five and six, but they cannot change the EU's nature as a consensus-based political institution where every member has a veto over future members. Sometimes the EU is portrayed as a colonizer, teacher or parent to wannabe members. In practice, it is a conflicted, uncertain and reluctant power in its own region.

Some of the lessons reviewed here were predictable in 2004 (see Grabbe, 2004). Perhaps the most surprising to academic researchers is that compliance with the *acquis* has been so strong and enduring in the 2004 joiners. Large parts of the state administrations have continued to comply with EU law, but the Union's impact on political culture was much more superficial. The assumption in 2004 was that the EU-25 would divide over Atlanticism and US interventionism, but Russia was always the most divisive issue – not between east and west but across the Union. It is too early to draw a lesson about Russia's role, but it sets a new political challenge and research agenda. Since 2013, Russia's overt rivalry for influence has cast the EU's role in a different light – and not a flattering one. Russia proved that history did not end in 1989 by pushing back the reach of the most influential western liberal model in eastern Europe. Russia has many routes of influence in the enlargement countries and neighbourhood, as well as in the EU itself. How will the EU respond to the rival pressures on its periphery? Will it pull in its horns, or might Russian pressure forge a new political will in the EU to make enlargement and neighbourhood policies more effective?

One immediate result is the return of the geopolitical and security rationale for enlargement. For the first time in 25 years, EU members can see a hard security threat not far from the external border of the Union. Interest is rising in projects that create a ring of stable, well-governed countries around them, with the initial focus on beefing up the neighbourhood policy. But the relevance of enlargement as a security project – which had been almost forgotten in the EU since NATO's expansion eastwards – has suddenly returned. The Balkans and Turkey raise internal security concerns such as organized crime, trafficking and migration that Member States are seeking to protect themselves against through tougher border controls. Russian influence in southeastern Europe is a different order of problem for the EU.

A possibly apocryphal story told by long-time Commission officials is that Jacques Delors used the fall of the Soviet Union in 1991 to persuade the EU's members to overcome their reluctance to offer trade access to Hungary, Poland and the other central European countries which were then struggling to re-orient their markets. He argued successfully that geopolitics was more important than protecting domestic industries – and he carried the day. Could Russian competition make EU members more generous again today? Or might Russia try to prevent some of the Balkan countries from joining the EU, using its leverage on energy and infrastructure? This is a new prospect for the EU to contend with. Russia's resurgence will cause a few Member States (Sweden, the Baltic States, perhaps the UK) to urge faster progress towards accession to counter Russian influence in the region. But other EU members will want to pull back, either to avoid antagonizing Moscow or because their own populations are turning inwards and against foreign ventures of any kind.

Will Russian pressure in the east drive Member States together or apart? In the EU, division is the biggest obstacle to enlargement because every country has a veto at each step along the path – and Russia is the foreign policy issue that divides them most. Distraction of political attention tends to slow the process down. The Commission's DG Enlargement is experienced at keeping the wheels turning on accession negotiations even when Member States are not paying much notice, but four of the Balkan countries are not in negotiations yet and it is becoming ever more difficult to get them over the threshold of candidate status and into formal talks.

The EU faces a major strategic choice now: preserve the current Union by continuing to prioritize internal consensus over external effectiveness, or respond to the new external challenge by exerting its transformative power across the European continent to strengthen its neighbours and counter Russian influence? The first choice would mean another generation of stagnation in the Balkans and the loss of the EU's remaining influence on Turkey's choices. The abandonment of enlargement would not necessarily lead to a deepening of European integration, which happens largely independently of enlargement. Rather, it would mean a retreat from deep engagement with neighbours and the avoidance of interdependence. The question that EU policy-makers should ask themselves is whether this is a sustainable strategy: can they ultimately avoid spill-over from poor governance and desperate poverty on their periphery? Or should they rather use the best tool the EU has to improve the outlook for people who live in those countries – and hence the EU's own security? The second choice is still available to the EU; it still has many routes of influence through the accession process and neighbourhood policies that can bring domestic transformation over time. Yet transformative power redux would require vision, patience, consistency and credibility – all of which are in short supply in post-crisis European politics. It might be that the EU is pulling out of the euro crisis just in time to start paying attention to its periphery again. Or maybe the EU was distracted for so long that Russia will end the European dream on its borders.

References

Barysch, K., Grabbe, H. and Everts, S. (2005) *Why Europe should embrace Turkey* (London: Centre for European Reform).

Bevan, A., Estrin, S. and Grabbe, H. (2001) 'The Impact of EU Accession Prospects on FDI Inflows to Central and Eastern Europe'. ESRC 'One Europe or Several?' Programme Policy Paper 06/01 (Brighton: Sussex European Institute).

Epstein, R.A. (2008) *In Pursuit of Liberalism: International Institutions in Postcommunist Europe* (Baltimore, MD: Johns Hopkins University Press).

Epstein, R.A. and Sedelmeier, U. (eds) (2009) *International Influence beyond Conditionality: Postcommunist Europe after EU Enlargement* (Abingdon: Routledge).

Falkner, G. (2013) 'Is the European Union Losing Its Credibility?' *JCMS*, Vol. 51, No. s1, pp. 13–30.

Fukuyama, F. (1992) *The End of History and the Last Man* (New York: Free Press).

Grabbe, H. (2004) *The Constellations of Europe: How Enlargement Will Transform the EU* (London: Centre for European Reform).

Grabbe, H. (2006) *The EU's Transformative Power: Europeanization through Conditionality in Central and Eastern Europe* (Basingstoke: Palgrave Macmillan).

Grabbe, H. and Hughes, K. (1998) *Enlarging the EU Eastwards* (London: Cassell/Royal Institute of International Affairs).

Grabbe, H., Knaus, G. and Korski, D. (2010) 'Beyond Wait-and-See: The Way Forward for EU Balkans Policy'. Policy Brief (London: European Council on Foreign Relations).

Haughton, T. (2014) 'Money, Margins and the Motors of Politics: The EU and the Development of Party Politics in Central and Eastern Europe'. *JCMS*, Vol. 52, No. 1, pp. 71–87.

Jacoby, W. (2006) 'Inspiration, Coalition and Substitution: External Influences on Postcommunist Transformations'. *World Politics*, Vol. 58, No. 4, pp. 623–51.

Kagan, R. (2003) *Paradise and Power: America and Europe in the New World Order* (London: Atlantic Books).

Kelley, J. (2004) *Ethnic Politics in Europe: The Power of Norms and Incentives* (Princeton, NJ: Princeton University Press).

Levitz, P. and Pop-Eleches, G. (2010) 'Monitoring, Money and Migrants: Countering Post-Accession Backsliding in Bulgaria and Romania'. *Europe-Asia Studies*, Vol. 62, No. 3, pp. 461–79.

Levitsky, S. and Way, L.A. (2010) *Competitive Authoritarianism: Hybrid Regimes after the Cold War* (Cambridge: Cambridge University Press).

Müller, J.-W. (2013) 'Safeguarding Democracy Inside the EU: Brussels and the Future of Liberal Order'. Transatlantic Academy Paper 3. Available at: «http://www.transatlantic academy.org/».

Mungiu-Pippidi, A. (2014) 'The Transformative Power of Europe Revisited'. *Journal of Democracy*, Vol. 25, No. 1, pp. 20–32.

Phinnemore, D. (2010) 'And We'd Like to Thank [. . .] Romania's Integration into the European Union, 1989–2007'. *Journal of European Integration*, Vol. 32, No. 3, pp. 291–308.

Sasse, G. (2009) 'The Politics of EU Conditionality: The Norm of Minority Protection during and beyond Accession'. In Epstein, R.A. and Sedelmeier, U. (eds).

Schimmelfennig, F. (2009) 'EU Political Accession Conditionality after the 2004 Enlargement: Consistency and Effectiveness'. In Epstein, R.A. and Sedelmeier, U. (eds).

Sedelmeier, U. (2012) 'Is Europeanisation through Conditionality Sustainable? Lock-In of Institutional Change after EU Accession'. *West European Politics*, Vol. 35, No. 1, pp. 20–38.

Sedelmeier, U. (2014) 'Anchoring Democracy from Above? The European Union and Democratic Backsliding in Hungary and Romania after Accession'. *JCMS*, Vol. 52, No 1, pp. 105–21.

Vachudova, M.A. (2014) 'EU Leverage and National Interests in the Balkans: The Puzzles of Enlargement Ten Years On'. *JCMS*, Vol. 52, No. 1, pp. 1–17.

JCMS 2014 Volume 52 Annual Review pp. 57–73   DOI: 10.1111/jcms.12176

Still the Right Agenda for Europe? The Sapir Report Ten Years On*

ANDRÉ SAPIR
Université Libre de Bruxelles and Bruegel

Introduction

In 2002, the President of the European Commission, Romano Prodi, invited me to chair a high-level group of independent experts to review the entire system of European Union economic policies and to propose a strategy for delivering faster growth together with stability and cohesion in a Union that would soon, after its eastern enlargement, count more than 25 Member States. The group was invited to seek inspiration from a report by Tommaso Padoa-Schioppa and others, whom Commission President Delors had invited in 1986 to reflect on the economic consequences of the single market programme and of the southern enlargement. The report (Padoa-Schioppa *et al.*, 1987) was extremely influential. It laid down the intellectual foundation for the construction of a coherent economic edifice resting on three pillars: the single market, to improve economic efficiency; an effective monetary arrangement, to ensure monetary stability; and an expanded Community budget, to foster cohesion. Our task was therefore challenging. The members of the group were all eminent scholars: Philippe Aghion, Giuseppe Bertola, Martin Hellwig, Jean Pisani-Ferry, Dariusz Rosati, José Viñals and Helen Wallace. The group worked closely with the Commission's group of policy advisors (GOPA), to which I and the three rapporteurs – Marco Buti, Mario Nava and Peter Smith – belonged, and whose director, Ricardo (Ricky) Levi, also participated actively in our deliberations.

What came to be known as the 'Sapir Report' was completed and published as a Commission document in July 2003, and published the following year by Oxford University Press (Sapir *et al.*, 2003; 2004). The purpose of this contribution is to examine whether the Sapir Report is still relevant ten years after its publication. The analysis is divided into three parts. The first section recalls the main findings and recommendations of the report. The second section examines what has been the political and policy impact of the report. Finally, the third section looks at the development of the European economy during the past ten years. I find that an EU growth strategy is not only still relevant today, but that the crisis has made it even more urgently needed than it was ten years ago. In designing a new growth strategy, which should blend both demand and supply measures, European leaders can probably seek inspiration from our report on how to better use European instruments to foster growth.

* I am grateful to the editors, Nathaniel Copsey and Tim Haughton, for helpful and constructive comments.

I. The 2003 Report

The report identified a growing gap between the EU's institutional and economic achieve-ments. On the one hand, EU integration had made huge progress with the establishment of the single market in 1993, the introduction of the single currency in 1999 and the preparation for the eastern enlargement, which eventually occurred in 2004 and 2007 when a total of 12 new Member States joined the EU. On the other hand, economic performance had been mixed. While macroeconomic stability had significantly improved and a high degree of cohesion, both between and within Member States, had continued, growth was unsatisfactory. The report regarded this under-performance as striking because it contrasted not only with expectations, but with past EU performance and a record of accomplishment in the US. In the EU-15, there had been a steady decline of the average growth rate decade after decade and per capita gross domestic product (GDP) had stagnated at about 70 per cent of the American level since the early 1980s. The disparity between the EU and the US was particularly remarkable in the 1990s. During the second half of the decade, the US was responsible for over 60 per cent of the cumulative expansion in world GDP, while the EU, with only a slightly smaller economy, contributed less than 10 per cent.

The report ascribed Europe's disappointing growth performance during the 1990s to its inability to adapt an antiquated economic and social model to two major changes: the information technology revolution and globalization, which called for new organizational forms of production with less vertically integrated firms, greater mobility within and across firms, greater flexibility of labour markets, greater reliance on market finance and higher investment in both research and development and higher education. In other words, this required massive change in economic institutions and organizations that had not yet occurred on a large scale in Europe when the study was completed.

The report considered it urgent that the EU economic system be reconfigured so as to deliver higher growth. Failure to do this, it argued, would gravely endanger the sustain-ability of the European model with its emphasis on cohesion. It identified accelerating trends in population ageing, technological change and globalization – all of which greatly increase the demand for social protection – as a potential cause of worry for the EU and its citizens, while at the same time recognizing that technological change and globalization also hold the potential for higher EU growth. It viewed the forthcoming EU enlargement in the same light. By increasing income and factor endowment disparity among EU countries, enlargement held the prospect of both higher demand for social protection in old Member States and higher growth in the EU as a whole.

The key to meet these challenges was to deliver on the commitments of the Lisbon Agenda, the strategic economic goal of the EU for the decade ending in 2010 to become a competitive and dynamic knowledge-based economy with sustainable economic growth, more and better jobs and greater social cohesion. In order to achieve this goal the report proposed a six-point agenda focusing on reforms where it considered that EU policies had the biggest potential to improve EU growth. Point 1 of the agenda was to make the single market more dynamic as such a market was considered the keystone to Europe's eco-nomic growth. While acknowledging that much progress had been achieved in goods markets, it was viewed that integration in services and in network industries remained very limited. Moreover, a truly dynamic single market needed not only more integration, but also better regulation to facilitate entry by new players and the development of risk capital. Hindrances to intra- and extra-EU labour mobility were also viewed as problematic. In addition, the report proposed action to promote major infrastructure for connecting the about-to-be-enlarged EU territory.

Point 2 was to boost investment in knowledge. The integration of goods, services and capital markets was considered as only a first step. Innovation was viewed as a key driver of growth, calling not only for a dynamic market environment but also major investments in knowledge. The report argued that increased EU funding for innovation and research could make a significant contribution, and that such funding should be managed by an independent European Agency for Science and Research modelled after the US National Science Foundation (NSF).

Point 3 was to improve the macroeconomic policy framework of economic and monetary union (EMU). The report argued the monetary and fiscal policy framework of EMU should be made more symmetric over the phases of the cycle. There was a call for the implementation of the stability and growth pact to focus more on long-term sustainability by taking into account both explicit and implicit public liabilities in the assessment of national budgetary positions. The policy framework for EMU was also judged to be in need of reform to improve policy co-ordination among eurozone countries, especially in the budgetary area. In particular, the report proposed that the budgetary calendar be divided into a 'European semester', in which common orientations would be agreed at the EU level, and a 'national semester', in which such orientations would be reflected into national budgetary processes. The report considered that such development would help ensure that the national fiscal policies add up to a consistent fiscal stance for the eurozone as a whole. In terms of budgetary surveillance, the report proposed an enhanced role for the Commission accompanied by the creation of independent national fiscal councils, both relying on budgetary statistics provided by independent national statistical institutes.

Point 4 was to redesign EU policies for convergence and restructuring. The report proposed that EU convergence policy should focus on countries rather than regions, and that only low-income countries be eligible for EU convergence funding. Such money should be used first to improve the administrative capacity of low-income countries. Allocation of EU money to these countries for other eligible purposes (investment in human and physical capital) should be conditional on verified progress towards reasonable administrative capacity. The report also proposed the creation of an EU restructuring fund, complementing national policies, for workers laid off as a result of technological change or (intra- or extra-EU) trade. The EU money should help displaced workers to re-enter the labour market via retraining, geographic relocation or assistance to create new firms.

Point 5 was to improve EU governance methods. The report argued that the EU should have more power to oversee the correct application of single market rules. Independent EU bodies should be created in certain specific areas, while more authority could be devolved to decentralized, but co-ordinated, systems of authorities which would operate within the same legal norms. The report also proposed a number of institutional reforms aimed at strengthening strategic capabilities, including: reducing the size of the European Commission to 15 members; extending the scope for qualified majority voting in the economic field; increasing the scope and removing the threshold of nine members for enhanced co-operation among subsets of EU countries, while at the same reinforcing the procedures to ensure transparency and guarantee that the rights of non-participating Member States are preserved.

Point 6 was to restructure the EU budget. The report famously declared that the EU budget was an 'historical relic', its expenditures, revenues and procedures all being inconsistent with the 'present and future state of EU integration' (p. 162). It argued that for the next multiannual financial framework (2007–13) the EU should redirect its expenditure to the goals of creating a dynamic knowledge-based economy and of helping new Member States to catch up with the rest of the EU as rapidly as possible. In other words, the EU budget should become a budget for Europe. The report recognized that the EU budget was, and would remain, very small (roughly 1 per cent of EU GDP devoted to domestic economic policies) and therefore that it could only act as a 'facilitator' to improve the composition of national budgets. The report proposed a 'radical restructuring of the EU budget' (p. 166) into three funds: a 'growth fund' (45 per cent of the EU budget for domestic economic policies) for research and development, innovation, education and training, and infrastructure; a 'convergence fund' (35 per cent of EU economic budget) to help low-income countries catch up; and a 'restructuring fund' (20 per cent of the EU economic budget) to support economic restructuring, including for agriculture. This new structure would have cut the share of the common agricultural policy (CAP) in the EU budget for domestic economic policies from 50 to 15 per cent. The authors of the report were well aware that the notion of an economically more rational 'budget for Europe' was incompatible with the approach of 'net balances' or '*juste retour*' that typically dominated EU budget negotiations between Member States. Hence two further proposals: reducing the weight of national contributions to the EU budget in favour of revenue sources with a clear EU dimension; and qualified majority voting rather than unanimity for the multiannual budgetary framework.

II. Impact of the 2003 Sapir Report

Although the report has been widely cited in the academic literature (1,065 citations in Google Scholar, of which 413 since 2009),[1] its main impact was political and on policy. The political impact was greatest in the weeks and months after the report was published; the policy impact, like the academic impact, was naturally slower but is still evident ten years later.

Political Impact

The report had a significant political impact. I ascribe this to five factors. First, it presented a comprehensive and thorough analysis of the EU's economic situation and the challenges it faced, which very few disputed, and it made a limited, though equally comprehensive and thorough, set of recommendations with whose logic it was hard to disagree. European leaders had set two strategic economic goals for the decade ending in 2010, which we took for granted, and we were spelling out what should be done at the EU level to achieve them. It was as simple as that.

The second factor was the quality of the team that produced the report, who between themselves had an exceptional scientific and policy track record that made them credible to both the academic and policy worlds. The entire team, rather than only the chairman and the

[1] The 1,065 citations divide into 413 citations for the original 2003 version of the report and 652 for the Oxford University Press 2004 version. Google Scholar search, 12 May 2014.

rapporteurs as is often the case for such reports, actually wrote the entire report, which greatly helped it become a good and respected blend of academic and policy contributions. The members of the group came from relatively diverse backgrounds not only in geographical terms as is generally the case with EU reports, but also in ideological terms: they had different views about the merits of government intervention and of deeper European integration to foster growth. This posed a challenge to the chairman of the group to avoid producing a bland report with which all members could easily agree. The alternative, producing an ambitious report with bold recommendations, might, and did to some extent, require a laborious process to reach a consensus based on a shared analysis of Europe's problems.

The third factor was the qualities of the person who had appointed our high-level group and who was the first and prime addressee. One of the qualities of Romano Prodi was obviously that he was President of the European Commission and that as such he had some degree of latitude in trying to implement the recommendations of the report if he happened to share them. Another quality of President Prodi was that, like us, he was an economist and one who straddled the worlds of academia and policy. This had several important consequences. First, he really gave us his full support, but yet allowed us to work in complete independence. While this was perhaps obvious as far as the members of the group (none of whom was employed or even paid by the Commission) were concerned, it was less so for the chairman. I was indeed at the time not only a university professor (though on partial leave) but also economic advisor to Romano Prodi himself and a member of his group of policy advisors (and therefore employed and paid by the Commission) to which the rapporteurs also belonged and whose director, President Prodi's confidant, closely interacted with the group. Yet President Prodi never put any direct or indirect pressure on me or on others to write or not write certain specific things. This does not mean that he did not impact on the orientation of the report. As a group, we met President Prodi just twice. The first time was in summer 2002 when the group was launched. During the meeting, he shared with us his concern that the EU economic system lacked sufficient coherence. This concern guided the work of the group and became a major theme of the report. The second meeting took place in July 2003 when we formally handed him the report which I had given to him informally a few days earlier. He had read it and said he appreciated our analysis and recommendations, but did not necessary share them all.

The fourth factor was the timing of the report. At our first meeting with him, President Prodi had asked us to conclude our work by early spring 2003 so it could potentially feed into the work of the Convention on the Future of Europe, chaired by Valery Giscard d'Estaing, which was due to end in summer 2003. Unfortunately, our work proved more complicated than anticipated and the bold consensus that I was aiming at was not easy to reach. As a result we were unable to meet the original deadline and only handed him the report in July 2003, a few days before the end of the Convention. We had missed an opportunity to reform the EU economic system. But the timing of our second meeting with President Prodi opened, by accident, a different opportunity. That coming Sunday, President Prodi was gathering his fellow Commissioners for a first informal discussion on the 2007–13 EU budget framework. This prompted a heated discussion between the President and his advisors about the desirability to invite me to make a presentation of our report at this discussion. I waited nervously for several days for the decision, not wanting to influence it, yet hoping it would be positive. The green light finally came on

Saturday, with the result that Commissioners only received the report one day before the presentation. My presentation did not focus on the EU budget. Instead I presented our analysis of the EU economic challenges and our entire six-point agenda, closing with one slide showing our proposal to restructure the EU budget by insisting that it should be judged in the context of the other five proposals. When my presentation ended there was a clamour in the Commission's meeting room, some Commissioners violently protesting against our radical budget proposal, while others applauded our boldness and efforts to present a coherent strategy to seriously tackle the EU's key objectives for the beginning of the new millennium.

Last but not least was the press coverage that the report received immediately after the presentation to the Commission. The first article, published in the Spanish daily *El Pais*, came out just two days after the presentation and was provocatively titled 'Prodi Presents a Plan to Dismantle the CAP and the EU Regional Funds' (Yarnoz, 2003a). The next day the same newspaper published an even more provocative article about the high-level group entitled 'A Group of Advisers under the Command of the President of the European Commission' (Yarnoz, 2003b). In view of the mounting controversy, and not only in the Spanish media, the Commission decided that a press conference should be held the following day to present and explain the report to the media. I stood (alone) in front of a packed audience in the Commission's press room and repeated the presentation I had made a few days earlier in the Commission's meeting room. I then answered many questions. This led to dozens of newspapers articles as well as radio and television interviews in the European media, which contributed to political debates on the report not just in Brussels but also in most European capitals. Quickly the media started to refer to our report as the 'Sapir Report' (see, for instance, Chatignoux, 2003) – an expression we had never used within our group, but which had been popularized by some EU Commissioners soon after their Sunday meeting and which we then used as subtitle of the 2004 book version.[2]

Policy Impact

The report was widely discussed not only in the media and in political circles, but also in policy circles. It is probably fair to say that it was intellectually influential. Whether or not it actually shaped European policies is far more difficult to assess, if only because the process of European policy-making is so complex. Rather than attempting to gauge whether the report actually impacted on European policies, I will instead describe policy changes that have been implemented since the report's publication and that are in line with our recommendations. The description follows our six-point agenda.

The idea of making the single market more dynamic was not new. Mario Monti had already put it forward when he was EU Commissioner for Customs, Taxation and the Internal Market in the 1990s (see, for instance, Monti, 1997). What was perhaps new, however, was the idea that making the single market more dynamic essentially meant designing rules to promote the entry of new players rather than to protect incumbents. This idea is now well established in EU policy circles, especially among competition officials, though its implementation still faces formidable opponents.

---

[2] In the team, especially those of us working in the Commission's group of policy advisers, we always referred to our report during its preparation as the 'TPS2 report' – that is, the second Tommaso Padoa-Schioppa report.

The idea of boosting investment in the knowledge-based economy was not new either, but our report probably gave it a strong boost in policy circles. We had insisted that Europe needed not only to allocate more money to research and development and innovation, but that it needed to spend its money better by creating an independent body modelled after the American NSF, which should focus on financing bottom-up academic research. This body – the European Research Council (ERC) – was created in 2007. And while it would be incorrect to state that the ERC is simply the product of our report, it is widely acknowledged that it was among the reports that 'were, without doubt, highly influential in persuading the EC of the need for its involvement in the creation of the ERC' (Simons and Featherstone, 2005).

Our report contained several specific recommendations to improve the EMU's macroeconomic policy framework that were eventually implemented. First, the reform of the stability and growth pact, proposed by the Prodi Commission in 2004 and adopted during the first Barroso Commission in 2005, contained several ideas we had defended, such as introducing a higher degree of country differentiation in evaluating national stability programmes and in formulating recommendations in case of an excessive deficit, and redefining the 'exceptional conditions' rule when an excess over the 3 per cent of GDP deficit threshold is allowed as simply a negative annual GDP growth rate rather than the earlier more demanding –2 per cent growth rate. A second recommendation that was implemented is the European Semester, which was established in 2010 as a part of a wider reform of the EU economic governance introduced in the wake of the eurozone sovereign debt crisis.[3] However, while the European Semester procedure should help the avoidance of excessive deficits and excessive macroeconomic imbalances, it falls short of the report's hope that it would also help ensure that the national fiscal policies add up to a consistent fiscal stance for the eurozone as a whole. A third recommendation that was also implemented in the wake of the crisis is the requirement that all signatories of the fiscal compact (that is, all EU countries except the United Kingdom and the Czech Republic) set up national fiscal councils.[4]

Our recommendation to redesign EU policies for convergence and restructuring had a mixed reception. The proposal that EU convergence policy focuses on countries rather than regions and that only low-income countries be eligible for EU convergence funding was flatly rejected by a wide coalition of interests. Sadly our proposal that EU funding should be used as a priority to improve the administrative capacity of low-income countries and that funding for other projects should be made conditional on verified progress towards reasonable administrative capacity was also ignored. On the other hand, our proposal for an EU restructuring fund for laid-off workers was implemented in 2006 with the European globalization adjustment fund established 'to provide support for workers made redundant as a result of major structural changes in world trade patterns due to globalisation' and funded by the EU budget.[5]

The Report's recommendation to improve EU governance methods, even those that would not have necessitated changes in the EU treaty, was basically ignored.

---

[3] See Hodson's contribution to this volume.
[4] The fiscal compact (a part of the Treaty on Stability, Co-ordination and Governance in the Economic and Monetary Union) entered into force in January 2013.
[5] Regulation (EC) 1927/2006.

Finally, our recommendation to restructure the EU budget was the source of much political drama, but had relatively minor effect on actual policy. This was not surprising given that our proposal would have basically eliminated agricultural support (and transferred it from the EU to the national level) and radically revamped EU support for low-income regions and countries (although not its share in the EU budget), which together account for roughly 80 per cent of EU budgetary expenditure. Within the Commission opposition came not only from the Commissioners and their services in charge of agricultural and regional policies, but also from many Commissioners coming from countries that are 'net beneficiaries' of the EU budget. The dividing line was the same outside the Commission. The powerful agricultural and regional lobbies were fiercely opposed to our proposal as were net beneficiary countries, whereas net contributors (in particular the Netherlands, Sweden and the UK) as well as many employers' and employees' federations were resolutely in favour of our growth agenda and budgetary proposals. Together with the unanimity rule in the Council for the EU budget, the strong opposition by farm and regional interests led the Prodi Commission to propose only relatively modest budgetary changes for the programming period 2007–13. This led one observer to state that: 'One of only two new elements in the Commission proposal was an increase in spending on "policies for growth and competitiveness" [. . .] a token gesture to the Sapir report' (Peet, 2005).

After nearly two years of negotiations, and by then under the first Barroso Commission, the new seven-year EU budget was due to be adopted by EU leaders at their June 2005 summit, on the eve of the UK Presidency of the EU, but the deal was blocked by British Prime Minister Tony Blair, with the support of the Dutch and Swedish leaders. Barely a week after rejecting the budget compromise, Tony Blair made a speech at the European Parliament outlining his ambitions for the UK Presidency, including the need for EU budgetary reform. He passionately argued for a modern 'policy agenda for Europe' and the budget to go with it, stating that:

> The Sapir report shows the way. Published by the European Commission in 2003, it sets out in clear detail what a modern European budget would look like. Let us put it into practice. But a modern budget for Europe is not one that ten years from now is still spending 40 per cent of its money on the common agricultural policy. (Blair, 2005)

This mention of our report did a lot to revive interest in our recommendations, but in the end they had little effect and the UK accepted in December 2005 a budget compromise very similar to the one it had rejected six months earlier. This led another observer to remark that the 'sensible' ideas of the Sapir Report

> have been seized on by Mr Blair, but he has signally failed to make any progress in achieving them. One reason is that he ignored the other half of Prof Sapir's recommendations: that without an equally radical change in contributions to finance the budget from a dedicated tax, rather than 90 per cent from national contributions as it is today, no reform would be politically possible. (Peel, 2005)

The outcome of the December 2005 deal for the 2007–13 budgetary allocation of EU expenditure on growth, cohesion and agriculture as a share of total expenditures on domestic economic policies is shown in Table 1. The table also shows the new allocation

Table 1: The EU Budget for Growth, Cohesion and Agriculture (as a Percentage of Total Expenditure for Domestic Economic Policies)

Budget item	2007–2013		2014–2020	
	Agreed budget	Sapir Report proposal	Agreed budget	Sapir Report proposal
Growth	11	45	15	53
Cohesion	41	40	40	41
Agriculture	48	15	45	6
Total	100	100	100	100

Source: Author's own calculations.

for the budget 2014–20 agreed in December 2013. These allocations are compared to the allocation we had proposed for 2007–13, which included phasing outs for certain regions in rich countries and for certain agricultural expenditures, and for 2014–20, when the phasing out was supposed to have ended. As can be seen there is no disagreement between the report and the actual EU decisions regarding the share of cohesion policy (which includes in the table expenditures for low-income countries or regions as well as the expenditures for displaced workers). On the other hand, there is a huge discrepancy as far as growth and agricultural expenditures are concerned. For the 2007–13 budget, we would have allocated 45 per cent of the relevant expenditures to growth and only 15 per cent to agriculture; the actual budget was almost the exact reverse: 11 and 48 per cent, respectively. The 2014–20 budget greatly increased the share for growth-related expenditure compared to the earlier budget (from 11 to 15 per cent), but it still falls very short of our proposal, essentially because agriculture retains such as large share of the EU budget, while we would have practically eliminated it by transferring agricultural expenditures back to national budgets.

To conclude, my sense is that although our report was widely read in policy and political circles, including often at the top, and was generally considered to be an important contribution to addressing Europe's main economic challenges, its influence was limited to a few specific policy measures. It failed to change the main thrust of the European policy agenda and to convince policy-makers that they needed to do more than pay lip service to the necessity of a European growth strategy. In particular it failed to radically restructure the EU budget and send a clear signal that Europe was willing and able to adapt its policy agenda to the realities of the twenty-first century. But this was perhaps not surprising. It would be easy to ascribe this failure to the limited influence of Tony Blair or even the UK in EU affairs, but the fact of the matter is that it reflects a deeper problem that the report had clearly identified: EU governance. As far as the EU budget is concerned, the decision-making process – with unanimity of the Member States and revenues almost entirely financed by national contributions – introduced a strong *status quo* bias against radical changes that is still present today.

Only paying lip service to the necessity of an EU growth strategy is what eventually led the Lisbon strategy to be declared unsuccessful in 2010. Although it was succeeded by a new ten-year EU growth strategy, Europe 2020, that contains some useful improvements, there is a real danger that it will not be much more successful than its predecessor. If so, Europe will have wasted two decades in talking about growth rather than implementing the necessary measures.

Table 2: Growth of Gross Domestic Product, Employment, Labour Productivity and Gross Domestic Product Per Capita (% Per Annum)

	GDP			Employment			Labour productivity			GDP per capita		
	EU-27	EU-15	US	EU-27	EU-15	US	EU-27	EU-15	US	EU-27	EU-15	US
1992–2000	n.a.	2.2	3.9	n.a.	0.3	1.6	n.a.	1.9	2.2	n.a.	1.9	2.6
1999–2008	2.3	2.2	2.6	1.1	1.2	1.0	1.2	1.0	1.6	2.0	1.7	1.6
2009–2013	–0.2	–0.3	1.2	–0.5	–0.5	–0.2	0.3	0.2	1.3	–0.5	–0.7	0.4

Source: Author's own calculations based on AMECO.

III. Ten Years On: Old and New Challenges to the European Economy

In the early 2000s the EU was starting to feel the need to adjust its economy to a series of tectonic trends: globalization, technological change and ageing. Unfortunately, the policy response was feeble. Ten years later Europe is still confronting these massive changes, but the economic and financial crisis has compounded them by accelerating the previous trends and decreasing the room for manoeuvre of governments to tackle them.

Growth Performance during 2000–13, before and after the Financial Crisis

The 2003 report found that Europe's performance had been unsatisfactory since the early 1980s, with a steady decline of both GDP and productivity growth and per capita GDP stagnating at about 70 per cent of the American level. What happened after the early 2000s and the publication of the report? Table 2 shows the growth of GDP, employment, labour productivity and GDP per capita in the EU and the US during the 1990s and during the period 1999–2013, which is divided into two sub-periods: 1999–2008, from the start of the euro to the start of the crisis; and 2009–13. During the first sub-period, the gap in GDP growth between the EU and the US narrowed significantly compared to the 1990s and even per capita GDP grew faster in the EU than in the US. This raised the hope that the European growth problem had finally been surmounted thanks to the introduction of the euro and the eastern enlargement. Yet not all was well in comparison with the US.[6] Labour productivity growth in the EU-15 continued to decline and was now well below US productivity growth. But this alarming trend was overshadowed by the good news elsewhere. Employment in the EU was now growing faster than in any of the previous three decades and even faster than in the US, where, on the contrary, employment growth was slower than in any of the previous three decades.

What explains the sharp increase in EU employment growth during the period 1999–2008?[7] The euro was often viewed has having played the leading role since the vast majority of the new EU jobs were in fact created in the eurozone. For instance, in its assessment of the first ten years of EMU, the European Commission (2008, p. 3) concluded that the 'launch of the euro represented a sea change in the macroeconomic environment of its participating Member States', which

---

[6] I use the US as comparator as we did in the report.

[7] The pre-crisis US employment 'sag' of the 2000s has been widely recognized but little understood by economists. One attempt to provide an explanation is the paper by Acemoglu *et al.* (2013), which ascribes the poor employment performance mainly to import competition from China.

culminated in the creation of a record 16 million jobs during the first decade of EMU in the euro area. Employment has risen by almost 15 per cent since the launch of the single currency while unemployment has fallen to about 7 per cent of the labour force, the lowest rate in more than fifteen years. Importantly, job growth outpaced that of other mature economies, including the United States. (Commission, 2008, p. 6)

A closer look at the evidence suggests that two countries – Italy and Spain – were responsible for more than half the jobs created in the eurozone between 1999 and 2008, and well over 40 per cent of those created in the EU-15 or even EU-27. The role of Spain is only partly surprising as a relatively large country, which experienced a huge boom in the labour-intensive construction sector. Yet the fact that one in three jobs created during this period in the eurozone was essentially due to the Spanish housing boom is quite astounding. The finding about Italy is more puzzling since it had the lowest GDP growth in the eurozone (and even in EU-27 and the wider Organization for Economic Co-operation and Development area) during 1999–2008, but yet managed to create one in five new jobs in the eurozone.[8] The flip side of the unprecedented employment growth in Italy and Spain, was a stagnant (in Italy) or even negative (in Spain) labour productivity growth. Second, and even more importantly, the situation proved unsustainable when the financial crisis hit. All this was reversed after the start of the crisis. Between 2008 and 2013, 70 per cent of the jobs created in Spain since 1999 were destroyed. And although the situation was less severe in Italy, it was far worse in two other southern eurozone countries – Greece and Portugal – which lost during the next five years, 150 and 240 per cent, respectively, of the jobs they had created between 1999 and 2008.

More generally, the sub-period 2009–13 saw once again the EU underperform the US economy with average GDP growth negative in the EU, but above 1 per cent in the US, resulting in a growth differential between the two sides of the Atlantic not far below the record level reached in the 1990s. At the same time, GDP per capita contracted by 0.5 per cent in the EU-27 (and 0.7 per cent in the EU-15), while it grew by 0.4 per cent in the US, thereby reversing the process of convergence in per capita GDP witnessed during the period sub-period.

Table 3 provides detailed information about GDP per capita (this time measured at purchasing power parities) for all EU-27 countries (plus Croatia which joined in EU in July 2013) in 2001, 2008 and 2012. It shows that the EU-27 converged towards the US until 2008, but remained at the same relative level thereafter. However, this aggregate picture hides two very different situations in the EU-15 and in the 12 countries that joined the EU in 2004 and 2007.

In the new Member States there was very rapid catching-up between 2001 and 2008, which continued between 2008 and 2012, though generally at a more moderate pace. This confirms that the EU is still a successful 'convergence machine', capable of bringing in low-income countries and providing them with an environment conducive to rapid catching-up (see Gill and Raiser, 2012). In the EU-15, the situation was more mixed. Two sets of countries can be distinguished: those that converged on the US before 2008, and those that did not. The first sub-group includes 11 countries: some which rapidly

---

[8] With a far bigger economy and a higher GDP growth than Italy, Germany only succeeded in creating half as many jobs as Italy during this period.

Table 3: Gross Domestic Product Per Capita at Current Market Prices and Purchasing Power
Parity, 2001, 2008 and 2012 (US = 100)

	2001	2008	2012		2001	2008	2012
Austria	78	83	86	Ireland	82	87	85
Belgium	77	77	79	Italy	73	69	66
Bulgaria	19	29	31	Latvia	24	39	42
Croatia	31	42	41	Lithuania	26	42	47
Cyprus	56	66	61	Luxembourg	144	175	173
Czech Republic	45	54	53	Malta	51	54	57
Denmark	79	83	83	Netherlands	83	89	84
Estonia	29	46	47	Poland	30	37	44
EU-15	71	74	71	Portugal	50	52	50
EU-27	62	66	66	Romania	17	31	33
Finland	71	79	76	Slovakia	33	48	50
France	72	71	72	Slovenia	49	60	55
Germany	72	77	81	Spain	60	69	63
Greece	54	62	49	Sweden	76	82	83
Hungary	36	42	44	UK	75	75	70

Source: Eurostat.

converged before 2008, but lost ground thereafter, with Greece in the extreme case of
being further away from the US in 2012 than it was in 2001; others which moderately
converged first but either lost a bit of ground or stagnated *vis-à-vis* the US after 2008; and
Austria and Germany, which converged both before and after 2008. The second sub-group
includes the four countries that did not converge before 2008: two (Belgium and France)
that basically held the same position *vis-à-vis* the US throughout the period between 2001
and 2012; the UK, which stagnated before 2008 and lost ground afterwards, hence ending
up in 2012 at a lower relative level than in 2001; and Italy, the only EU-27 country that
suffered a deterioration of its relative position both before and after the crisis, dropping
from high-income to medium-income status. In 2012, per capita GDP in the EU-15 was,
on average, around 70 per cent of the US level – the same as in 2001 and during the 20
years before.

The period 2001–12 was therefore one of great upheavals in the fortunes of EU
countries: the 12 countries that joined the EU during the 2000s all did very well
between 2001 and 2012, even the two (Cyprus and Slovenia) that lost ground between
2008 and 2012.[9] Among the EU-15 countries those belonging to the eurozone had a
very different performance: some (like Austria and Germany) did rather well, others did
very poorly (Greece and Italy) or the rest either progressed a bit (like Ireland and
Spain) or stagnated (like France and Portugal). The situation was the same outside the
eurozone, with Sweden doing rather well, the UK doing very poorly and Denmark
progressing a bit.[10]

[9] Other countries, like Estonia, Latvia and Lithuania, suffered major setbacks in 2009–10, but more than recovered
afterwards.
[10] For accounts of the development of individual European economies in recent times, see Hodson's and Connolly and
Hartwell's contributions to this volume.

Implications of the Crisis

The EU's growth performance improved after our report was released, suggesting that perhaps the introduction of the euro and the eastern enlargement had solved Europe's growth problem. Unfortunately the gains were short-lived. The crisis has revealed three issues. First, with the advent of the crisis, the EU's growth performance became doubly disappointing. Not only has the growth differential with the US nearly gone back to the situation in the 1990s, but, even worse, the EU's average annual growth during 2009–13 was negative. The result has been record unemployment rates, reaching in 2013 nearly 11 per cent in the EU-27 and 12 per cent in the EU-15 and the eurozone.

Why such disappointing performance since 2009? There is no single explanation but both supply and demand factors have probably been at play, though their relative weight likely varies across countries, although there is no doubt an important eurozone dimension to the problem. Three main factors seem to have played a role. The first is financial. The combination of excessive (private and public) debt, high bank intermediation and low bank capitalization has been a problem in many countries. In addition the lack of a European 'banking union', with common supervision, resolution and deposit insurance mechanisms, has greatly hampered the cleaning up of the European banking system in the wake of the financial crisis. By contrast, in the US, federal institutions – including the Federal Deposit Insurance Corporation (FDIC), the Federal Reserve (Fed) and the US Treasury – were able to deal decisively with banking problems already in 2009. Sadly the Maastricht Treaty did not set up a European banking union as part of the EMU, and our report did not suggest that one be created. Both fell into the trap of ignoring the dangers of financial stability and the lack of readiness of the European system to deal with a financial crisis should one occur.[11] This mistake started to be remedied in June 2012, at the height of the eurozone sovereign debt crisis, when EU governments decided to improve the governance of the eurozone by creating a European banking union. If all goes well, the eurozone will overcome its financial crisis by late 2014, after the European Central Bank (ECB) concludes what amounts to an entry examination for the 130 banks that it will directly supervise under the single supervisory mechanism (SSM), which along with the single resolution mechanism (SRM), constitutes an important part of the European banking union.[12] The second factor is structural. Many EU countries, and especially, but not only, those in the eurozone periphery have poorly functioning product and labour markets that are certainly not compatible with membership of the eurozone, where the absence of the exchange rate instrument requires market flexibility to adjust to economic shocks, or with the reality of globalization. The third factor is macroeconomic policy. National fiscal policies in many EU countries have been too restrictive, especially in the eurozone, where the risk of self-fulfilling sovereign debt crises was not well understood before the financial crisis and was only (and partially) remedied in September 2012 with the announcement of the ECB's outright monetary transactions (OMT).[13] At the same time, the ECB's monetary policy has not been sufficiently expansionary, especially compared with the Fed's, resulting both in low inflation (with outright deflation in some

---

[11] On the lack of readiness of the European system to deal with financial crises, see Pisani-Ferry and Sapir (2010); Sapir (2011).

[12] On banking union, see Pisani-Ferry *et al.* (2012) and Howarth and Quaglia's contribution to this volume.

[13] On the issue of self-fulfilling sovereign debt crises in the eurozone, see De Grauwe (2011).

eurozone countries) and a high euro-dollar exchange rate. This inadequate policy mix has weighted down on eurozone aggregate demand and resulted in a relatively large and persistent output gap.

The second issue revealed by the crisis is the heterogeneity in the growth and unemployment performance of EU Member States, which has become more important than ever before in the EU's history. In the euro periphery, the improvement of the growth performance, when it occurred, proved elusory. After the boom that followed the introduction of the euro came the bust, which generated sovereign debt crises in Greece, Ireland, Italy, Portugal and Spain (the so-called 'GIIPS' countries) and later in Cyprus. In all these countries, the unemployment rate in December 2013 was at least 12 per cent, and more than 25 per cent in Greece and Spain.

By contrast, in the central and eastern countries that joined the EU in 2004 and 2007, there has been a powerful catching-up process that, on the whole, has resisted fairly well to the financial crisis, despite the fact that these countries were the first ones in the EU to be hit by the crisis since they had relied most on capital inflows. In December 2013, only two of these countries had unemployment rates of more than 12 per cent and six had rates below 10 per cent. The eastern enlargement contributed to the revival of the German economy – the 'sick man of Europe' at the start of the euro mainly because of the country's reunification in 1991. Germany's revival was not only the result of supply-side structural reforms, like the Harz reforms and the reorganization of its manufacturing sector by outsourcing some activities to its eastern neighbours. It was also helped by the boost of demand coming from peripheral eurozone countries that had attracted massive capital inflows after the start of the euro. When the financial crisis happened, these countries were hit by a sudden stop in capital inflows and their longstanding structural weaknesses, which such inflows had helped conceal for a while, became suddenly exposed (see, for instance, Merler and Pisani-Ferry, 2012). The other factor responsible for the sovereign debt crisis in these countries was an EMU policy framework originally lacking appropriate instruments for crisis management and resolution, especially in the banking sector (see, for instance, Darvas et al., 2011). By contrast, Germany, which by the time the financial crisis started had undertaken deep structural and fiscal reforms, was well placed to act as the anchor of the eurozone and to benefit from exceptionally low government bond yields. In December 2013, its unemployment rate was barely above 5 per cent. Consequently, the old economic divide between a successful Germany and its neighbours (now comprising not just countries in western Europe, but also those in central and eastern Europe), on the one hand, and the less successful countries of southern Europe, on the other, has re-emerged, with France having one foot on both sides of the divide. Concomitantly, the economic dominant role of Germany has substantially increased. At the beginning of the 2000s, its level of per capita GDP lagged behind the next three largest EU economies. In 2012, it was higher than in France (by 12 per cent), the UK (by 16 per cent) and Italy (by 22 per cent), leaving no doubt about which country is Europe's powerhouse.

In terms of the third issue, Europe's many immediate economic, political and social problems have unfortunately distracted its leaders from focusing on Europe's longer-term challenges. These are still the same as before the crisis – globalization, technological change, energy and climate, ageing – but two things have changed. On the one hand, the crisis has accelerated some trends – in particular the distance between us and the emerging

Table 4: Gross Domestic Product at Purchasing Power Parity and Gross Public Debts: Advanced Economies versus Emerging and Developing Economies, 1991, 2000 and 2013

	GDP at PPP (as percentage of world total)			Gross public debt (as percentage of GDP)		
	1991	2000	2013	1991	2000	2013
World	100.0	100.0	100.0	n.a.	63.0	71.9
Advanced economies	68.9	63.0	49.6	59.5	71.4	107.7
EU-28	27.9	24.8	18.7	n.a.	62.1	89.5
Eurozone	21.6	18.1	13.1	54.1	69.3	95.7
Emerging and developing economies	31.1	37.0	50.4	n.a.	48.7	36.7

Source: IMF (2014).

countries, especially China, has decreased. On the other hand, our capacity to address the challenges seems to have decreased partly as a result of the accumulation of public debts due to the crisis. Here again the contrast between the EU and the emerging countries is striking. Table 4 illustrates clearly both the acceleration of the catching-up by emerging countries and our public debt situation compared to theirs.

Whither a New Growth Agenda?

The previous discussion suggests that the time has come for European leaders to switch from a mode of crisis response to one of strategic action and to propose a new growth agenda. The growth agenda proposed by the Sapir Report mainly emphasized supply measures because at the time Europe's main problem was indeed structural. Yet it also argued that the monetary and fiscal policy framework of EMU should be made more symmetric over the phases of the cycle. Today's growth agenda ought to provide a convincing response to Europe's immediate and longer-term challenges, which entails both closing the output gap and increasing potential output. The strategy needs therefore to be two-handed: demand measures to close the output gap, and supply measures to increase potential output.

On the supply side, the priority must to implement the EU growth strategy, Europe 2020, the successor of the Lisbon strategy, with an emphasis on three areas. The first is the completion of the single market and the implementation of complementary structural reforms by the Member States to foster competition in product markets. Second, national labour market and social policies (including formal education, training and life-long learning) need to be modernized in the direction of greater flexibility and security for workers, along the lines of the successful Nordic model (Sapir, 2006). The EU could help the facilitation of national reforms with a proper use of the EU budget. Third, the EU budget can also help to increase Europe's research effort and to build a genuine European research area (ERA). Significant progress in these three areas would help Europe becoming a knowledge-based innovation society and economy able to confidently respond to the challenges of the twenty-first century.

On the demand side, the overall policy mix of the eurozone needs to be more conducive to reducing the existing output gap. The key here is greater symmetry in the conduct of macroeconomic policy. Restrictive fiscal policy in crisis countries must be accompanied by looser policy in countries that enjoy fiscal space; it would also be useful if the EU budget could play a role in fiscal stabilization. As far as monetary policy is concerned, the ECB must make clear that it is committed to a symmetric attitude towards both inflation and deflation risks. It must also clearly communicate to the public that its objective of an inflation rate of below but close to 2 per cent in the medium term applies to the eurozone on average rather than each and every eurozone country, and therefore that achieving both disinflation in the GIIPS countries and the 2 per cent objective implies an inflation rate of probably close to 3 per cent in core eurozone countries. Symmetry in the conduct of fiscal and monetary policies would result in an adjustment within the eurozone that would contrast with the current asymmetric adjustment supported mainly by the crisis countries.

One area that would probably deserve close attention is energy. Apart from reducing Europe's carbon emission and its dependency on foreign supply, an ambitious EU energy policy could be an important component of a new EU growth agenda given the importance of energy for all EU countries and the size of the investment needed in the coming years. Such policy would involve the creation of a single energy market (which would imply both regulatory measures and investment in infrastructure to be financed partly by the EU budget and the European Investment Bank) and research and development in new energy technologies (which could also be partly financed by the EU budget and the EIB).

Conclusions

Europe is going through a testing period. In addition to having to respond to a number of long-term challenges that were already underway a decade ago when our report was published, it has to deal with the consequences of a severe crisis which has left behind high levels of debt and unemployment in many Member States. Tackling these issues requires a European growth strategy. Had Europe implemented the Lisbon strategy launched in 2000 and the related proposals made by our report, it would probably not have avoided the financial crisis but at least it would have been in much better shape to rebound more strongly and quickly. Today, Europe must put forward a new growth strategy that not only incorporates the supply-side ideas of the Lisbon strategy and its successor Europe 2020, but also recognizes that insufficient demand is currently a constraint on growth in many of its Member States. Reading (or re-reading!) our report with a fresh eye might help convince European leaders of the need for such strategy and give them inspiration on how to better use European instruments to foster growth. As I wrote ten years ago: 'Growth must become Europe's number one economic priority – not only in the declarations of its leaders but first and foremost in their actions' (Sapir *et al.*, 2004, p. i).

References

Acemoglu, D., Autor, D., Dorn, D., Hanson, G.H. and Price, B. (2013) 'Import Competition and the Great US Employment Sag of the 2000s', mimeo.

Blair, T. (2005) Speech to the European Parliament, 23 June. Available at: «http://www .europarl.europa.eu/sides/getDoc.do?pubRef=-//EP//TEXT+CRE+20050623+ITEM-004 +DOC+XML+V0//EN».

Chatignoux, C. (2003) 'Europe: le rapport Sapir jette un pavé dans la marre'. *Les Echos*, 18 September.

Darvas, Z., Pisani-Ferry, J. and Sapir, A. (2011) 'A Comprehensive Approach to the Euro-Area Debt Crisis'. Policy Brief 2011/02 (Brussels: Bruegel).

De Grauwe, P. (2011) 'The Governance of a Fragile Eurozone'. CEPS Working Document (Brussels: Centre for European Policy Studies).

European Commission (2008) 'EMU@10: Successes and Challenges after Ten Years of Economic and Monetary Union'. *European Economy*, No. 2, pp. 1–328.

Gill, I.S. and Raiser, M. (2012) *Golden Growth: Restoring the Lustre of the European Economic Model* (Washington, DC: World Bank).

International Monetary Fund (IMF) (2014) *World Economic Outlook, April 2014* (Washington, DC: IMF).

Merler, S. and Pisani-Ferry, J. (2012) 'Sudden Stops in the Euro Area'. Policy Contribution 2012/06 (Brussels: Bruegel).

Monti, M. (1997) 'Making the Single Market Work: The Next Steps'. Opening speech at the 'Priorities for the Single Market' Conference, Brussels, 7 March.

Padoa-Schioppa, T., Emerson, M., King, M., Milleron, J.C., Paelinck, J.H.P., Papademos, L.D., Pastor, A. and Scharpf, F.W. (1987) *Efficiency, Stability and Equity: A Strategy for the Evolution of the Economic System of the European Community* (Oxford: Oxford University Press).

Peel, Q. (2005) 'Europe's Leaders Must Shake Off Their Gloom'. *Financial Times*, 15 December.

Peet, J. (2005) 'The EU Budget: A Way Forward'. Policy Brief (London: Centre for Economic Reform).

Pisani-Ferry, J. and Sapir, A. (2010) 'Banking Crisis Management in the EU: An Early Assessment'. *Economic Policy*, Vol. 62, pp. 343–73.

Pisani-Ferry, J., Sapir, A., Véron, N. and Wolff, G. (2012) 'What Kind of European Banking Union?' Policy Contribution 2012/12 (Brussels: Bruegel).

Sapir, A. (2006) 'Globalization and the Reform of European Social Models'. *JCMS*, Vol. 44, No. 2, pp. 369–90.

Sapir, A. (2011) 'Europe after the Crisis: Less or More Role for Nation States in Money and Finance?' *Oxford Review of Economic Policy*, Vol. 27, No. 4, pp. 608–19.

Sapir, A., Aghion, P., Bertola, G., Hellwig, M., Pisani-Ferry, J., Rosati, D., Viñals, J. and Wallace, H. (2003) *An Agenda for a Growing Europe: Making the EU Economic System Deliver – Report of an Independent High-Level Study Group Established on the Initiative of the President of the European Commission* (Brussels: European Commission).

Sapir, A., Aghion, P., Bertola, G., Hellwig, M., Pisani-Ferry, J., Rosati, D., Viñals, J., Wallace, H. with Buti, M., Nava, M. and Smith, P.M. (2004) *An Agenda for a Growing Europe: The Sapir Report* (Oxford: Oxford University Press).

Simons, K. and Featherstone, C. (2005) 'The European Research Council on the Brink'. *Cell*, Vol. 123, pp. 747–50.

Yarnoz, C. (2003a) 'Prodi presenta un plan para desmantelar la PAC y los fondos regionales en la UE'. *El Pais*, 15 July.

Yarnoz, C. (2003b) 'Un grupo de asesores, a las órdenes del presidente de la Comisión Europea'. *El Pais*, 16 July.

JCMS 2014 Volume 52 Annual Review pp. 74–89

DOI: 10.1111/jcms.12177

Farewell Britannia? 'Issue Capture' and the Politics of David Cameron's 2013 EU Referendum Pledge*

NATHANIEL COPSEY[1] and TIM HAUGHTON[2]
[1] Aston University. [2] University of Birmingham

Introduction

On 23 January 2013, the terms of Britain's long-running debate on the nature of its relationship with the European Union underwent a dramatic transformation. For the first time in nearly 40 years, a British Prime Minister announced his intention to hold a plebiscite on membership of the EU with the promise to include the possibility of a British exit as a response on the ballot paper. David Cameron's speech had been trailed for several months in order both to soften up the audience and to wait for an appropriate juncture at which to make such a momentous announcement. Nonetheless, its impact was dramatic in setting out a scenario under which the UK could leave the EU in perhaps little more than five years after the date on which the speech was given. Cameron's language was conciliatory – in places even rather Europhile in the grand Tory statesman tradition, name-checking Sir Winston Churchill and the 'twin marauders of war and tyranny' that the EU had banished. Cameron also spoke of Britain's role as a 'haven for those fleeing tyranny and persecution' and the 'hundreds of thousands of British servicemen who have given their lives for Europe's freedom' (Cameron, 2013). He was also adamant that his speech was a 'positive vision for the future of the European Union. A future in which Britain wants, and should want, to play a committed and active part.' He set out a number of familiar principles on which a reformed EU should be built: flexibility, competitiveness, democratic accountability, the return of powers to the Member States and fairness (Cameron, 2013). Such calls for EU reform along the lines set out by Cameron could have been made by any British Prime Minister, or leader of the opposition, of the past quarter of a century.

It was not, however, the statesman-like part of the speech that provided the dramatic transformation. Rather it was the second part of his discourse, the segment containing a more narrowly political, even party-political element that captured the headlines. Cameron's speech also included a commitment that 'the next Conservative Manifesto in 2015 will ask for a mandate from the British people for a Conservative Government to negotiate a new settlement with our European partners in the next Parliament'. In other words, he would be seeking a re-negotiation of the terms of British membership. Cameron promised that 'we will give the British people a referendum with a very simple in or out choice': to stay in the EU on these new terms; or come out altogether. These final words marked the most radical change in Conservative policy towards the EU since the referendum of 1975

* The authors are grateful to Simon Bulmer, Paul Copeland, Kai Oppermann and Willie Paterson for their insightful comments on earlier drafts. Thanks are also due to Pamela Atanga and Mark Webber for bringing a number of articles to our attention and participants at the 'Way Out and Exit? Britain and the EU' seminar at the University of Birmingham on 12 March 2014.

when 67 per cent voted to remain inside the European Community. Even if Cameron's junior coalition partners, the Liberal Democrats, did not sign up to this agenda, his announcement changed the terms of the British debate on the EU decisively.

Given that all three major political parties in the UK, including Cameron's Conservatives, are officially in favour of EU membership, the questions of why a re-negotiation was deemed necessary and why a referendum on its outcome should be held are highly pertinent. Indeed, at the heart of the call lies a fundamental paradox. Britain is threatening exit at a point where the EU is wider, more liberal and much more Anglophone (if not always more Anglophile) than at almost any point since the UK joined the EEC in 1973. Forty years of determined, even bloody-minded negotiations have won the British what amount to the most privileged terms of membership of any Member State in the EU. Britain gets a substantial rebate on its contribution to the EU budget and is under no commitment to join the euro. With its impressive array of 'opt-ins' and 'opt-outs', the British are seemingly able to have their cake *and* eat it. Given such favourable terms, why ask for more?

In the wake of this seminal policy change, this contribution attempts to analyse and explain the announcement of a possible referendum in Cameron's speech. The first section provides an analysis of the background to the speech, charting the course of Britain's relationship with the EU over the longer-term, looking at the way in which British relations with the EU have become subject to what we term 'issue capture'. It also looks at public opinion in the UK on the EU with a view to understanding the extent to which Cameron's policy shift was likely to resonate with the electorate. Having established that public opinion is far more nuanced than is sometimes assumed, the second section of the article focuses on domestic politics. It explains why the referendum pledge was made with a focus on the politics of party management within the Conservative Party, in the context of a rise in support for anti-European political parties. Subsequently, it maps how elite attitudes towards the EU have been shaped over the long term with a view to understanding why – given that the UK is far from being the only Eurosceptic Member State – an in-or-out referendum pledge was made in the UK and not elsewhere. It concludes with a look at what new research avenues in the study of European integration have been opened up by the announcement.

I. The Context to Cameron's Speech: The Politics of 'Issue Capture'

As a result of the announcement of a possible 'in-or-out' referendum, the coming few years will be an extraordinarily turbulent period in the UK's relationship with the EU. Two elements[1] were driving this process of radical change. In addition to the Conservative referendum pledge, as Cameron himself was keen to stress in his speech, at the EU level a number of institutional, policy and political shifts were taking place in the nature of the economic and political union that have been prompted by the eurozone crisis. Indeed, formalization of the eurozone could have far-reaching efforts on Britain's capacity for influence within the Union (and that of other permanent non-members of the eurozone).

The UK has had a difficult relationship with the European integration project since Robert Schuman's declaration proposed the first common European institutions in 1950.

[1] A third element is the September 2014 Scottish independence referendum, which is excluded here for reasons of space.

As Geddes (2013, p. 1) observed, the 'debate about Britain and the European Union is about the past, present and future of British politics, about Britain's place in the world and about national self-understandings'. Trenchant as this particular observation is, it is also equally applicable to all 28 Member States, in addition to candidate countries, potential candidate countries and other European states that have not yet joined the EU. Why should the UK be different?

No other Member State has had quite so difficult a relationship with the EU as the UK. Some other Member States negotiated opt-outs, but no other Member State has negotiated quite so many as the British. Apart from Ireland, there is no other longstanding Member State that does not participate in the Schengen area of free movement – and this in part is a reflection of Britain's choice to remain outside, since Ireland's only land border is with the UK. No other Member State has ever held a referendum on leaving the EU, having joined it.[2] The British have been difficult, or at least separate from the rest of the herd, about European integration for a very long time; their reticence has been apparent since the first negotiations on a coal and steel community in the very early 1950s and has never quite gone away. After failing to join the European Economic Community in the 1950s, the UK changed its mind and tried, unsuccessfully, to join in 1963 and 1967. After joining in 1973, the UK held its first in-or-out referendum on the terms of an allegedly renegotiated and improved membership settlement in 1975 (George, 1990; Crowson, 2010). In the 1980s, dogged negotiation on the part of Mrs Thatcher won the UK its cherished rebate on its contribution to the Community budget. In the 1990s, the Major government secured the UK a permanent opt-in/out from the single currency, and the Blair administration saw no reason to change its policy on the euro.

Britain's relationship with the EU has been described as 'semi-detached' and between 1973 and 2010 – despite the protestations of Jacques Delors that the British were 'allergic' to Europe – it might also have been characterized as 'stable yet sceptical' since membership of the EU was regarded as a fixed feature of the British and European political landscapes. Since the general election of 2010 and the formation of a Conservative–Liberal Democrat coalition, that situation has changed quite radically. As a precursor of what was to come, in July 2012, the British Foreign and Commonwealth Office (FCO) announced its intention to launch what it dubbed in the EU-speak that is a mix of West European languages a 'balance of competences' review – in standard English, it might more lucidly be termed a 'balance of powers' review. The purpose of the review was to look across the entirety of those areas of government policy where the EU acts in addition to, or instead of, the British state (understood to include devolved and local government) to determine whether matters might be better arranged in another way. More precisely, the review was to consider if it would make more sense in each policy area for the UK government to act instead of the EU, whether there was need for more European integration, or whether things were working just fine as they were. One popular interpretation of the balance of competences review was that the government was drawing up a 'shopping list' of powers to be 'repatriated' from the EU. Another, Liberal Democrat, view was that the exercise was designed to scotch plans for a re-negotiation by showing that the present delineation of powers was working to the UK's best advantage.

---

[2] Although it is worth noting that Greenland did vote in 1982 to leave following the entry into force of Home Rule from Denmark after 1979, thereby becoming an overseas territory of the EU.

Six months later, in January 2013, during an exceptionally long-trailed speech, which was put back on at least two occasions, David Cameron announced that he would be seeking a re-negotiation (details not specified) of the current terms of the UK's membership of the EU. Following a re-negotiation, and not later than 2017 (the reasons for this date were also not specified), a future Conservative government would put the results of the renegotiation to a referendum, which would include the option of staying in or leaving the EU. Two points were of exceptional importance here. First, and most clearly, in the event of a Conservative victory in the general election of 2015, Cameron had committed the UK to a referendum that could lead to an exit. By doing so, he made himself hostage to the outcome of both an unknown international renegotiation and an unknown domestic referendum result. Second, in political terms, Cameron's announcement made clear that the terms of the debate on Britain's membership of the EU were to be set by what remained in party political terms a Eurosceptic minority. Why did a British Prime Minister in command of a safe majority in the House of Commons undermine his own position so drastically in order to appease a minority? The next section addresses this question, yet before moving any further, it is necessary to evidence some of the claim we make that Eurosceptics are a minority in the UK.

Beginning with public opinion, long-term data are available from Eurobarometer on British attitudes to the EU that chart positive or negative sentiments towards membership since 1973 (Eurobarometer, 1973–2014). Over the very long term (that is, 1973–2009), those who thought British membership of the EU to be a bad thing ranged from 12 to 48 per cent; those who thought it a good thing ranged from 25 to 58 per cent; those who were neutral ranged from 18 to 37 per cent; and the 'don't knows' amounted to between 6 and 24 per cent. A first observation is that while attitudes were neither overwhelmingly Europhile nor overwhelmingly Eurosceptic, they were very volatile, indicating that public opinion was not settled one way or another. It is also worth stressing that the salience of Europe as an issue has also varied over time. Europe is usually not that uppermost in the minds of voters, but occasionally – such as on the question of whether Britain should join the euro in the early days of the Blair administration – it was much more salient. A second observation is that the peak of Eurosceptic sentiment (48 per cent in the late 1970s) was ten percentage points lower than the peak of Europhile sentiment (at 58 per cent in the early 1990s). A third observation is that the nadir of support for the EU in the UK was 25 per cent, whereas the low point of Eurosceptic support was just 12 per cent. This would seem to indicate that diehard supporters of the EU in all circumstances are twice as numerous as diehard Eurosceptics. These observations are counterintuitive. A fourth and final observation is that if the 'don't knows' and neutrals are added together they amount to between 24 and 61 per cent of voters. In simple terms, therefore, the great majority of British voters change their view of Europe over time, waxing and waning in their support for the EU, but the Europhiles seem to outnumber the Eurosceptics.

It is instructive to compare these results with those conducted by the Pew Centre, several years into the EU's worst crisis in its entire history. Pew polling in May 2013 found that those with a 'favourable' view of the EU had fallen across the then EU-27, but that the British were by no means the most sceptical in their attitude towards the EU. Some 43 per cent of the British had a favourable view of the EU, in comparison to just 41 per cent of the French. The figures for Spain, Germany and Italy were higher, with 46 per cent of Spaniards, 58 per cent of Germans and 60 per cent of Italians favourable to the EU.

What seems more striking is the lack of exceptionalism in the British figures, which were almost identical to an EU-wide 45 per cent expressing a favourable view of the EU. Turning, however, to the question of whether to stay in the EU or leave it, some 46 per cent of Britons were inclined to stay in and an identical 46 per cent wanted to leave. This question was not asked of other Member States since they had not announced a referendum. In public opinion terms, therefore, the data suggest that British public opinion is sceptical towards the EU but not more sceptical than in other Member States. They also suggest that in the UK support for EU membership is higher during periods of economic expansion, i.e. during the Barber, Lawson and Brown booms, than during economic downturns where a dip in support for the EU was observed in the early-1980s recession and since 2008. An exception is the Lamont recession of the early 1990s, which of course included Britain's ignominious exit from the Exchange Rate Mechanism (ERM) when Cameron was working as a special adviser for the then Chancellor of the Exchequer Norman Lamont.

Moving away from the mass of public opinion towards political decision-makers a first direct observation is that all three major British political parties – the Conservative, Labour and Liberal Democrat parties – were all in favour of EU membership. Of the three, the Liberal Democrats were traditionally the most pro-European. While the Labour Party did not have a reputation or profile as an especially pro-European party – and indeed was only converted to pro-Europeanism during the long years of opposition between 1979 and 1997 – it went along with most EU developments from enlargement to the Lisbon Treaty and has not advocated withdrawal from the EU since its disastrous election manifesto of 1983.

The Conservative Party was far more complicated, having moved from its position as the 'party of Europe' that took the UK into the then EEC in 1973 towards Euroscepticism from the 1990s onwards was more obviously split on European policy than Labour or the Liberal Democrats. Conservative policy on Europe since the 1990s has been heavily influenced by the intertwined themes of the ERM debacle of 1992 and Margaret Thatcher's legacy. Sterling's unplanned exit from the ERM and the devaluation that went with it shattered the Conservatives' long-established reputation for economic competence. The link to Margaret Thatcher lies in the fact that she had opposed the plans of two of her Chancellors – Nigel Lawson and John Major (as well as the majority of her Cabinet) – to join the ERM. Between her departure from office in 1990 and the pound crashing out of the ERM in 1992, Margaret Thatcher's increasingly strident Euroscepticism had made her seem out of touch with voters, the mainstream Conservative Party and perhaps even something of an embarrassment. In the wake of the ERM crisis, to many on the Conservative right it seemed that she had been spot-on in her judgement. In the 20 years that followed the ERM crisis, the right-wing came increasingly to dominate the Conservative Party and no new ideologues emerged to challenge, or even rethink the Thatcher legacy. The attitude of the increasingly Eurosceptic parliamentary party was best illustrated by the letter, signed by 95 Conservative MPs (out of a total of 303), to David Cameron demanding a bill to give the Westminster Parliament a veto on European legislation. All signatories to the letter must have known that this was incompatible with remaining in the EU under the terms of the British 1972 European Communities Act. The aim of carrying out such a doomed-to-failure grandstanding exercise was therefore simply to highlight a *status quo* that they viewed as intolerable. It is not unreasonable to suggest therefore that perhaps around a third of the Conservative parliamentary party would like to leave the EU.

Given the absence of United Kingdom Independence Party (UKIP) MPs in the Westminster Parliament, it is safe to conclude therefore that something in the region of 100 MPs out of a total of 646 would like to leave the EU. Here again, that seems to be a small minority, albeit crucially one larger than the government's working majority. Finally, turning to the legislature in which the most avowed Eurosceptic, perhaps Europhobic, politicians sit, the European Parliament, only 13 UKIP MEPs (amounting to 18 per cent of British MEPs) were returned in the 2009 election (several of whom left the party between 2009 and the 2014 European Parliament election).

In sum, this review of British public opinion and British parliamentarians reveals that while Eurosceptic views are reasonably common, they remain very much a minority faith among MPs and MEPs and subject to a very high degree of volatility in terms of public attitudes over time. Moreover, the evidence suggests that diehard Europhiles outnumber diehard Eurosceptics. Herein lies our research puzzle. If Eurosceptic views are minority views, why do they apparently set the terms of the UK national debate about the EU? This contribution argues that what has taken place in terms of the British debate on Europe amounts to what we term 'issue capture'. This concept draws some inspiration from Petrocik's (1996) classic work on 'issue ownership' – the basic idea of which is that voters associate certain issues with certain parties. Issue capture moves beyond this and refers to the way in which a given political debate can be 'occupied' and 'dominated' by a minority group with deeply-held strong views on a given political issue. British debate on Europe is certainly not 'owned' by a particular party or even set of parties, but the terms of the debate are determined by the vocal, Eurosceptic minority in the UK. What matters is that from the point that issue capture occurs, the terms of the political debate become set by the vocal minority until such time as the issue in question can be 'recaptured' by the political mainstream.

The next section moves onto the *domestic* politics of Cameron's speech viewed through the prism of issue capture, with a special focus on both UKIP and the Conservative Party, before looking at the very pertinent question of the interplay between UK domestic politics and relations with the rest of the EU. We conclude the article by raising some important and pressing questions worthy of further research.

II. The Domestic Politics of Cameron's Speech

The problem with vocal minorities is that they are vocal. Put simply, for many diehard Eurosceptics the issue of Britain and the EU assumes a salience beyond its objective significance. If such vocal minorities are appeased or accommodated or simply not challenged, they can move from the periphery to dominate the debate, eventually achieving a position of complete 'issue capture', where alternative views are almost automatically discarded. This is what we argue has happened in the UK. The consequence is that it has been almost impossible for political leaders to make an unreserved defence of the EU and Britain's role in it. Although Labour leader Ed Miliband[3] and Liberal Democrat leader Nick Clegg (2013) gave speeches warning that Britain was sleepwalking out of Europe and of the 'economic suicide' of exit, respectively, these fell on deaf ears. Clegg's strong advocacy of continued membership during the televised debates with UKIP leader

---

[3] *BBC News*, 19 November 2012.

Nigel Farage in spring 2014 confirmed this rule as Clegg struggled to move the debate away from Eurosceptic ground. Moreover, despite the array of pressure groups such as the European Movement and the oddly-named 'British Influence', there has been no real concerted effort to make the case for Britain in Europe – indeed, the only campaigning group to hold this particular name went out of business in 2005.

These failures, however, stretch back long before Cameron took up residence in Downing Street. Few British Prime Ministers, and not one recent Prime Minister, have set out strongly pro-European stalls and been listened to with approval – the last such was probably Mrs Thatcher in launching the single market in the mid-1980s. Tony Blair made high-profile speeches in Birmingham, Oxford and Strasbourg full of pro-European rhetoric, but these seemed aimed at domestic Europhiles and the foreign audience. His purpose was not to change hearts and minds at home. Not only Blair, but other pro-Europeans failed to transform the view of successive British governments that the EC/EU was in essence a foreign policy issue which did not need domestic consensus behind it (Allen, 2005). This was a serious strategic error that in great part explains the UK's current predicament. If successive governments continue to stress to voters that the EU is harmful to their interests, eventually the public will start to believe them.

In contrast to the muted voices and silence on the Europhile side, UKIP and the Eurosceptic tendency in the Conservative Party have become more vocal. Within the Conservative Party their domination is so complete that it is hard to imagine a pro-European candidate winning a selection to stand as a parliamentary candidate on the Tory ticket.[4] The explanation for the shift in the terms of debate owes much to deep-seated continuities in Britain's relations with Europe and shifts in both the Conservative Party and the EU. The areas of particular focus include party politics, media cues, identity politics and the performance of the UK economy relative to the EU average. These issues are worth dealing with in turn.

Two continuities are worth immediate mention: cues and party divisions. In terms of the former, the British electorate tends to take its cues from the media and politicians on European integration. The EU is perceived as boring and distant in the minds of most voters who rely not on 'police-patrol oversight' to obtain information on the EU, but rather 'fire-alarm oversight' by third parties – that is, the media and opposition parties (Oppermann, 2008, p. 158). The shift in the media portrayal of European integration has been stark. In the words of Oliver Daddow (2012), the UK print media have moved from 'permissive consensus' to 'destructive dissent'. Although the impact of newspapers can be over-emphasized in the era of social media and when most news is consumed from television and radio which remain relatively impartial, it is nonetheless striking that the daily diet of Brussels bashing served up by the *Daily Mail* (the British newspaper with the second-highest circulation at 1.9 million)[5] and others is a far cry from the 1975 referendum when only the Communist *Morning Star* backed the 'no' campaign. The fire alarms began going off almost every day thanks to the rise of UKIP, in more recent times prompted by the linkage between the EU and immigration. In terms of party divisions, it is worth remembering that the two main parties have from time to time been subject to

[4] Some pro-Europeans such as Neil Carmichael (Stroud) were elected in 2010, but it is noticeable he had been the Conservative candidate in the constituency for both the 2001 and 2005 elections.
[5] ABC newspaper circulation figures reported in *The Guardian*, 8 February 2013, available at: «http://www.theguardian.com/media/table/2013/feb/08/abcs-national-newspapers».

internal spats about European integration, albeit to different degrees, since the 1950s (see, for example, Crowson, 2007; George, 1990).

There is, however, a more fundamental building block of Eurosceptic opinion in the UK: identity. In contrast to Germans who have tended to see 'Europe' as an integral part of national identity and the French who see European integration as a chance to further national identity (Schmidt, 2006), Britons – or perhaps more accurately the English – tend to see *Europe* as a threat to national identity. They have difficulty reconciling themselves to the idea of being both British and European.[6] In common discourse 'Europe' refers to something different and distinct. 'Europe' is 'the Continent' over the Channel – a place to which Britons go rather than belong.[7] This distinction is reinforced by the meanings attached to the historical narratives of Shakespeare's 'Sceptred Isle', the Empire, victory in many wars, Whiggish self-perceptions of historical progress, keeping a 'balance of power' between European states, and so on. It is also an epiphenomenon of the principle of British parliamentary sovereignty, and is strongly reinforced by the nature of the British polity (Schmidt, 2010). The English electorate – unlike the Scots, Welsh or the Irish of Ulster let alone the Germans, Italians or Spaniards – live in a highly centralized state and find multiple locations of power beyond Westminster hard to comprehend and undesirable (and have tended to vote against devolution of powers to regional assemblies or elected city mayors).[8] Local government in England (regional government does not exist) is merely charged with the implementation of nationally designed policy and is overwhelmingly reliant on central government for revenues over which it has almost no discretion in spending. In this regard, it surely is not mere coincidence that Euroscepticism is more of a minority creed in Wales, Scotland and Northern Ireland, which all enjoy devolved government, even if attitudes are not so far removed from those of the English as the Scottish National Party has suggested (Curtice, 2014).

Moving beyond questions of culture or the institutional structure of the polity, central to Britain's relationship with the process of European integration is economics. It was symbolic that Cameron's speech was delivered at the financial news agency Bloomberg and Miliband's riposte in March 2014 was given at the London Business School. At the core of the United Kingdom's waxing and waning enthusiasm for the EU has not been love, passion or duty, but an economic calculation based on 'cost–benefit analysis' (Matthijs, 2013, p.12). As David Cameron remarked in 2011 'we will remain in the European Union so long as it is in our interest to do so'. It is hard to imagine so ruthlessly pragmatic an utterance from the mouth of Angela Merkel or François Hollande. The discourse of British politicians has tended to extol the benefits of the market without much reference to the themes prevalent in the discourses present in other EU states, such as peace, values or the central Europeans' 'Return to Europe'.

The economics of EU membership is the longest running of all the themes that relate to British membership. In the 1950s, when the European Communities were being set up, not only was the great bulk of British trade with the Commonwealth, but the UK was comfortably the largest west European economy. By 1973, when the UK joined the EEC this position had reversed entirely, as Table 1 shows. At the nadir of Britain's relative decline in 1983 it had fallen to fourth place. Joining the Community was, therefore, almost

---

[6] See the Eurobarometer (1973–2014) surveys.
[7] We are grateful to Charlotte Galpin for help in clarifying our thinking on this point.
[8] *BBC News*, 4 May 2012. See also Shaw (2007).

Table 1: GDP of Four Largest Western European Economies
(Billions of 1990 International Dollars), 1950–2004

	United Kingdom	(West) Germany	France	Italy
1950	347 (1st)	265	220	164
1963	490 (2nd)	623	408	371
1973	676 (3rd)	945	683	582
1983	755 (4th)	1,119	852	758
1993	955 (3rd)	1,350	1,049	937
2004	1,331 (2nd)	1,573	1,329	1,107

Source: Maddison World Economics, historical GDP. Available at: «http://
www.worldeconomics.com/Data/MadisonHistoricalGDP/Madison%20Historical
%20GDP%20Data.efp».

a marker of economic and political defeat for a United Kingdom that had fallen on hard times. As the leading postwar British diplomat Nicholas Henderson put it in a valedictory telegram:

> Our decline in relation to our European powers has been so marked that we are not only no longer a world power but not in the first rank even as a European one. Income in Britain is now, for the first time for over 300 years, below that in France. We are scarcely in the same league as the Germans or French. (FCO, 1979)

Between the mid-1960s and the late-1990s the narrative in favour of European integration centred on the role of the common – and later single – market as a driver of economic modernization for a UK that had fallen so far behind its continental competitors. This also explains why the pro-business Conservative Party was the party of Europe during this 30-year period. It is no coincidence that it has been precisely in the period since the mid-1990s, when *mutatis mutandis*, the British economy has outperformed its west European competitors that the attractions of European integration have diminished in the eyes of the British elite[9] – a sentiment reinforced in recent times by the eurozone crisis. This interest-based calculation has not only tended to give opponents of integration the more appealing tunes to play to the electorate ('Love Britain', 'a Thousand Years of History', etc.), but most importantly it sets up Europe as a 'choice' (Daddow, 2013, p. 214). Choices can be made and unmade. As long as 'Europe' remains a choice rather than a fixed part of the political landscape, it remains open to ongoing contestation.

The root of Cameron's call for a referendum lies with the deal struck in Maastricht in December 1991. Although Margaret Thatcher had already articulated some fears of the emergent European super-state in Bruges in 1988, it was the Treaty on European Union agreed in Maastricht three years later that signalled that European integration was about more than just markets. This shift in the nature of European integration is key to explaining the Eurosceptic drift of the Conservative Party as the 'benefits' of the market get increasingly diluted by the 'costs' of integration in a whole host of other areas. In short, it is the changes and developments in European integration that matter as much as changes in the Conservative Party.

[9] With the exception of the early years of Blair's New Labour government when support for the single currency was high among business groups during economic good times (see Oppermann, 2008).

Although cues, cost–benefit analysis and party divisions have been continuities in Britain's position on the EU, three changes are crucial to explaining why Britain is now threatening exit: the Conservatives' return to government in 2010; the rise in support for UKIP; and the EU's response to the eurozone crisis. Since the fall of the Thatcher government and the ERM fiasco, the Conservatives have been perennially beset by divisions over Europe and it has featured as a central issue in a succession of leadership elections from the 1990s onwards (Bale, 2010). Cameron's promise to leave the centre-right grouping in the European Parliament, the European People's Party-European Democrats, for instance, was a key plank in his pitch for leadership. Although Cameron urged his party to stop 'banging on about' Europe when he became leader in 2006, there is a 'large element of the Conservative party which cannot imagine anything more important than banging on about Europe' (Gamble, 2012, p. 468). Nonetheless, the divisions abated while the party was in opposition, only to return when it ended its years in the opposition wilderness. In the first two years of the Cameron government, 93 Conservative MPs (30 per cent of the parliamentary party) rebelled on at least one of 29 votes on European integration issues (Lynch and Whitaker, 2013, p. 325), with a fifth of those rebelling at least ten times.

Rebellious behaviour was prompted by MPs responding to the compromises and deals governments of all political hues in the EU have to broker, and indeed to the novelty of a coalition government to which some Conservatives feel less loyalty, but also it owed something to the rise of UKIP. The anti-EU party has benefited from the inclusion of the usual repository of protest votes (and traditionally the most pro-European party), the Liberal Democrats, in the governing coalition. Europe is a lightning rod for Conservative protest about the nature of the coalition government, both in terms of natural Tory voters and the parliamentary party itself. It was here that its differences with its junior partner, the Liberal Democrats, were most obvious and to an extent the European issue also became the repository of complaints about the sacrifice of true blue Conservative principles on the altar of compromise. Again we return to the legacy of Margaret Thatcher. In office, as a skilful Prime Minister, Thatcher was amenable to compromise on many issues. But the folk memory of Thatcher in the Conservative Party centres more on episodes of resistance and long struggle – against the Argentinians in 1982, the miners in 1984, the Tory 'wets' and so on – followed by hard-won victories. In the context of an ongoing contest within the Conservative Party about who best represents the spirit of Margaret Thatcher, the European issue is a touchstone for all contenders.

Despite the ascent of the Eurosceptics in the Conservative Party, *Schadenfreude* at the eurozone's woes, the effective campaigning style of UKIP leader Nigel Farage and a steady beating of the anti-immigration drum have all contributed to UKIP's rise in the polls from around 4–10 per cent support in 2012 to 11–18 per cent in 2013 (UK Polling Report, 2014). And this increase in support for UKIP has changed the issue salience of the EU. Aware of internal divisions in their own ranks, both Conservatives and Labour have been keen to sweep the issue under the carpet, hoping that out of sight means out of mind. This consensus of silence was shattered by the rise of UKIP, who made the EU an issue of salience; it is, after all, the party's *raison d'être*. UKIP's success in the 2004 and 2009 EP elections (and expected success in May 2014) gave them a platform and a degree of respect. Once derided as a motley collection of 'fruitcakes, loons and closet racists'[10] by

---

[10] *Daily Telegraph*, 5 April 2006.

Cameron himself, UKIP had become by the time of the Prime Minister's speech a potentially major force in British politics which could no longer be ignored, aided in no small part by the return to the party leadership of Nigel Farage.

It is helpful to distinguish two different dynamics at work here. First, UKIP moved beyond its 'niche' anti-EU appeal (Lynch *et al.*, 2012). Although UKIP voters and potential voters harbour visceral dislike of the EU, their dislike is directed much more at the practical implications of European integration, especially the migration consequences of open labour markets. By opposing gay marriage, UKIP also tapped into a socially conservative strand missing from Cameron's metropolitan 'Notting Hill' conservatism. These factors fuelled support for the party and worried Conservative politicians. Nonetheless, much of the hard Eurosceptic core in the Conservative parliamentary party – which has been emboldened by the rise in support for UKIP – has been driven by a much more ideologically rooted critique of European integration, seeing the EU as a threat to the type of free market capitalism they wish to see in Britain. This threat is more imaginary than real. The *bête noire* of many Conservatives, the European Commission, is in fact a staunchly pro-market and liberalizing institution.

Calling a referendum for halfway through the next parliament has been a classic strategy of party management. From Harold Wilson's 1975 referendum, to the promises made by Blair on the euro and the constitutional treaty to Cameron's speech, British party leaders have used referendums as a means to manage dissent. It is, though, a high-risk strategy. Cameron's approach is built on the questionable premise that he will be able to persuade the other 27 heads of government around the European Council table to make enough concessions for him to sell the new renegotiated package as a success and the basis for Britain's continued membership of the club. This is a huge gamble. Cameron's own deputy Prime Minister, Nick Clegg, lambasted the idea of a 'grand, unilateral re-negotiation of Britain's relationship with the EU' as 'seductive' and likely to 'collapse under the weight of its own internal contradictions' (Clegg, 2013). Nevertheless, it would be wrong to suggest Cameron's tactics are purely defensive. He may have been boxed into a corner, but the pledge of a referendum offered him some breathing space, a chance to put clear blue water between the Conservatives and their coalition partners, and as elsewhere in Europe, to throw some offensive punches designed to 'reinforce their public prestige and to weaken the opposition' (Oppermann, 2013, p. 690). His promise helped provoke debate inside the Labour Party and contributed to Ed Miliband's speech on 12 March 2014 ruling out a referendum unless there were a further transfer of powers.

There is little enthusiasm at the EU level for extensive treaty reform, but necessity may be the mother of invention. The eurozone crisis has already led to an agreement on a fiscal compact and advanced discussions on banking union (Hodson, 2013; Howarth and Quaglia, 2013).[11] Ironically, Cameron and his finance minister George Osborne have become advocates of closer integration for the eurozone. They see the benefits of full fiscal union, banking union and the European Central Bank being lender of last resort because, as Andrew Gamble (2012, p. 471) noted, 'they fear that if the Eurozone disintegrates there will be catastrophic consequences for British banks and the British economy'. The echoes of Churchill's call for a United States of Europe are clear here. Churchill of course did not include Britain in his idea of a United States of Europe.

---

[11] See also Hodson's and Howarth and Quaglia's contributions to this volume.

Eurosceptic sentiments exist across the Union (indeed the UK was very far from being the most Eurosceptic country in the EU in 2013 – see Pew, 2013), so why have there not been similar in-or-out referendum pledges from others across Europe? Prominent politicians of similar ideological hues to Cameron such as Viktor Orbán or Václav Klaus in central Europe have lambasted the Union, as have a range of parties playing on very different themes including the *Front National* in France and *Alternative für Deutschland* in Germany in recent times, but in the political mainstream only Cameron has promised an in-or-out referendum. In addition to the adversarial nature of British politics, four factors here are key, all of which affect the discourse and actions of British Conservatives (and politicians in general): choice, vulnerability, leadership and hubris.

We mentioned 'choice' above with regard to cost-benefit analysis. Fuelled in part by nostalgia for the era of the Empire on which the sun never set, but linked to the knowledge that – even after 150 years of relative economic decline – the UK is the seventh largest economy in the world, a sizeable section of the Conservative opinion sees no need for Britain to be tied to Europe. Furthermore, it sees the EU as a hindrance rather than a help to economic development. This group of Conservative politicians envision a bright future for an economically liberal UK outside of the EU, often citing (bizarrely) the success of tiny city-states such as Singapore or Hong Kong as models for emulation. Shorn of the encumbrances of EU membership, Britons would be free to make their way in the world, living on their talents, wits and free-trading spirit. The British attachment to free trade is all the more striking given the country's decidedly lacklustre export performance. As with so much else, Britain's longstanding attachment to free trade itself is a historical legacy from its days of economic and political hegemony, rather than an objective assessment of what the optimal commercial policy of a medium-sized economy with a sizeable trade deficit and a weak manufacturing sector should be.

The gap between Britain's (or the British elite's) view of its place in the world, economically, politically and strategically, and the humdrum reality feeds through into the theme of vulnerabilities. The decision of states to pool sovereignty in the process of European integration is driven to a large extent by deep-seated concerns about their own capacity for action (and the perception of such vulnerabilities) (Copsey and Haughton, 2009; Haughton, 2010; Malová *et al.*, 2010). In part, this is a product of their size, geographical location and trading patterns, but it is also linked to cultural questions of identity and labelling. Some Britons, however, see an alternative to EU membership, albeit one rooted more in a grandiose, rose-tinted picture of the UK's self-importance, rather than one based on an objective assessment of its position.

Size and status feed through into questions of leadership. Although smaller states can provide direction on modest initiatives, as Finland did with its Northern Dimension, if more strategic leadership is to be offered by a specific Member State it needs to be one of the big three: Germany, France or the UK. Britain, however, has not only struggled to find a place in the Franco-German leadership tandem of the Union for 40 years, it has not made a positive contribution to European integration since Mrs Thatcher's single market drive in the 1980s with the possible exception of the European security and defence policy. In order to lead, one must be at the heart of Europe. But the UK is not in the eurozone; nor does it take part in the Schengen area of free movement. More recently, Britain refused to take part in both the fiscal compact and banking union. It has played the role of an awkward partner within the EU (George, 1990) for over 40 years. Just as would-be reformers of a socialist party need to wrap themselves in the red flag as they speak in favour of arms-length relations with trade unions and the benefits of the free market, it is only those who bear the most impeccable European credentials who are capable of making such an appeal for reform of the EU and radical change. The UK is emphatically not well-placed to lead the charge for reform in Europe (Copsey, forthcoming).

The final component is hubris. Cameron's referendum pledge was built on the hubristic notion that the British Prime Minister has the ability to persuade the other 27 Member States of the merits of a renegotiated package. Cameron's supporters can point to his success in the 2014–20 budget negotiations in which he secured an agreement favourable to the net contributors. Forging agreement on the budget, however, is a considerably simpler task than opening the Pandora's Box of a re-negotiated settlement which would probably have to amount to a new treaty. He also pledged to undertake this renegotiation in the run-up to a presidential election in France and a federal election in Germany. Reflecting again on Britain's overblown sense of self-importance, many Conservatives believe that the other Member States will acquiesce to Britain's wishes out of fear that the British could leave the Union. While it is true that there are many countries in the EU which would be keen for the British to stay, they would not support this at any price. Indeed, some Member States would be pleased to see the difficult British leave.

Central to any deal which would be acceptable to Cameron and would satisfy enough of his party is likely to be Angela Merkel. Although Germany may be the leading player in European politics, prompting some to label it the 'reluctant hegemon' (Paterson, 2011), and Merkel – the most powerful politician in the EU – has made it clear she would regret a British withdrawal, German power can be overemphasized and the willingness of Merkel to support actively Cameron's agenda and rally the troops remains to be seen. As Paterson (2014) has argued, the eurozone remains at the centre of Germany's EU priorities; that matters most for its domestic audience. Cameron's best hope may, therefore, rest on strong economic recovery in the eurozone which would accord – in the scheduled German federal election year of 2017 – Merkel more room for manoeuvre. But even that hope glazes over the fact that Germany's EU policy has become much less generous and idealistic and driven more by hard-headed calculations of the national interest (Bulmer and Paterson, 2013; Galpin, 2014).

Conclusions

This contribution has sought to explain why David Cameron took the radical step in January 2013 of committing the UK to an uncertain renegotiation of its terms of membership of the EU, to be followed by an in-or-out referendum on the deal that he hoped to conclude. In doing so, it termed the British domestic debate on the EU, and European integration more broadly, the politics of 'issue capture', which refers to a situation where a minority group takes near-total control of the terms of domestic political debate, to the near-exclusion of other voices. Subsequently, the contribution analysed UK public opinion on the EU in comparative context and concluded that the British public is perhaps rather less Eurosceptic in nature than Cameron's policy suggests. Nonetheless, we maintained there are deep-seated continuities in Britain's relationship with the EU that have underpinned the UK's scepticism, but a potent cocktail of the eurozone crisis, the rise in support for UKIP and the Conservatives' return to government in a coalition with the

Europhile Liberal Democrats all nudged Cameron in a more Eurosceptic direction. Despite the more pro-European noises in the first half, his speech illustrated the way in which debate in the UK has become subject to issue capture by the hardline Eurosceptics. Moreover, it also highlighted the British Prime Minister's belief in his own leadership and negotiating ability not just to extract a favourable settlement from the other 27 interlocutors around the European Council table, but also to sell any deal to the British electorate.

Cameron's announcement had significance not only for the practice of politics, but also for the study of it. Indeed, his speech prompts a series of questions requiring further research. First among these is the issue of the extent to which European integration is reversible (Webber, 2013). Cameron made clear that he wants – in line with the EU's commitment to subsidiarity – powers and responsibilities to flow back to Member States from Brussels. In other words, European integration should not be a one-way street. An assumption that underlies much of the scholarship on the EU, however, is that European integration is about deepening and widening. What if this were no longer true? What would it mean if the EU were to relinquish its powers in a given policy area? What would it mean for the study of the EU if some Member States were simply to leave?

The process of re-negotiating the terms of the UK's membership of the EU therefore poses a host of new research questions. What if other Member States seek a similar recalibration? Does Cameron's announcement presage a wider process of stocktaking about the pros and cons of EU membership in other European countries, as the Netherlands appeared to be doing? An issue of vital importance to those interested in the role of Member States in the policy-making processes that constitute the 'Brussels game' is the extent to which Cameron's policy of 'strategic disengagement' will affect the UK's capacity (positively or negatively) to achieve the outcomes that it wants in complex negotiations across a whole host of policy areas. We know that Brussels policy-making proceeds in package details and with a certain degree of horse-trading. Will the British be able to do this as effectively if the other Member States believe there is a good chance that they will not be members in a few years' time (and therefore unable to return favours)? As Herman Van Rompuy, President of the European Council put it: 'How do you convince a room full of people, when you keep your hand on the door handle? How to encourage a friend to change, if your eyes are searching for your coat?' (Van Rompuy, 2013).

More broadly, Cameron's speech reminds us of the need to understand the motors and breaks of domestic politics in the constituent Member States of the EU. Whatever supranational forces push along the process of European integration, ultimately it is Member State bargaining which forges the landmark deals and determines the course of integration. Yet the study of individual Member States and how domestic political dynamics interacts with EU-level politics remains surprisingly under-researched, with too much attention directed toward assessing top-down *Europeanization* (with some exceptions – notably Bulmer and Lequesne, 2013). The eurozone crisis has ensured the course and direction of the EU are far less clear than they were in previous decades. Many seeming certainties of European integration no longer hold. The keys to explaining the future development of the EU lie in the Member States and how domestic politicians respond to the consequences of crisis and the deep-seated vulnerabilities that pushed their states towards pooling sovereignty in the first place.

References

Allen, D. (2005) 'The United Kingdom: A Europeanised Government in a Non-Europeanised Polity'. In Bulmer, S. and Lequesne, C. (eds) *The Member States of the European Union* (Oxford: Oxford University Press).

Bale, T. (2010) *The Conservative Party: From Thatcher to Cameron* (Cambridge: Polity Press).

Bulmer, S. and Lequesne, C. (2013) *The Member States of the European Union* (Oxford: Oxford University Press).

Bulmer, S. and Paterson, W. (2013) 'Germany as the EU's Reluctant Hegemon? Of Economic Strength and Political Constraints'. *Journal of European Public Policy*, Vol. 20, No. 10, pp. 1387–1405.

Cameron, D. (2013) EU Speech at Bloomberg, 23 January. Available at: «https://www.gov.uk/government/speeches/eu-speech-at-bloomberg».

Clegg, N. (2013) 'A Richer, Stronger, Safer and Greener Europe'. Speech delivered on 8 October. Available at: «http://www.libdems.org.uk/nick_clegg_speech_on_a_richer_stronger_safer_greener_europe».

Copsey, N. (forthcoming) *Rethinking European Union* (Basingstoke: Palgrave Macmillan).

Copsey, N. and Haughton, T. (2009) 'The Choices for Europe: National Preferences in Old and New Member States', *JCMS*, Vol. 47, No. 2, pp. 263–86.

Crowson, N. (2007) *The Conservative Party and European Integration since 1945* (London: Routledge).

Crowson, N. (2010) *Britain and Europe: A Political History since 1918* (London: Routledge).

Curtice, J. (2014) 'Is It Really All Just about Economics?' Scottish Social Attitudes Survey. Available at: «http://www.natcen.ac.uk/media/265694/ssa_is-it-really-all-just-about-economics.pdf».

Daddow, O. (2012) 'The UK Media and "Europe": from Permissive Consensus to Destructive Dissent'. *International Affairs*, Vol. 88, No. 6, pp. 1219–36.

Daddow, O. (2013) 'Margaret Thatcher, Tony Blair and the Eurosceptic Tradition in Britain'. *British Journal of Politics and International Relations*, Vol. 15, pp. 210–27.

Eurobarometer (1973–2014). Available at: «http://ec.europa.eu/public_opinion/index_en.htm».

Foreign and Commonwealth Office (FCO) (1979) Diplomatic Report 129/79, 31 March. Available at: «http://fc95d419f4478b3b6e5f-3f71d0fe2b653c4f00f32175760e96e7.r87.cf1.rackcdn.com/D98F7773620F4D7EA92A697C0808A5FC.pdf».

Foreign and Commonwealth Office (FCO) (2012) 'Review of the Balance of Competences between the United Kingdom and the European Union'. White Paper. Cm 8415 (London: HMSO).

Galpin, C. (2014) 'Has Germany "Fallen out of Love" with Europe? The Eurozone Crisis and the "Normalization" of Germany's European Identity'. *German Politics and Societies*, forthcoming.

Gamble, A. (2012) 'Better Off Out? Britain and Europe'. *Political Quarterly*, Vol. 83, No. 3, pp. 468–77.

Geddes, A. (2013) *Britain and the European Union* (Basingstoke: Palgrave Macmillan).

George, S. (1990) *An Awkward Partner: Britain in the European Community*, 3rd edn (Oxford: Oxford University Press).

Haughton, T. (2010) 'Vulnerabilities, Accession Hangovers and the Presidency Role: Explaining New EU Member States' Choices for Europe'. Central and Eastern Europe Working Paper 68 (Cambridge, MA: Harvard University Center for European Studies). Available at: «http://aei.pitt.edu/14473/».

Hodson, D. (2013) 'The Eurozone in 2012: "Whatever it Takes to Preserve the Euro"?' *JCMS*, Vol. 51, No. s1, pp. 183–200.

Howarth, D. and Quaglia, L. (2013) 'Banking Union as Holy Grail: Rebuilding the Single Market in Financial Services, Stabilizing Europe's Banks and "Completing" Economic and Monetary Union'. *JCMS*, Vol. 51, No. s1, pp. 103–23.

Lynch, P. and Whitaker, R. (2013) 'Where There is Discord, Can They Bring Harmony? Managing Intra-Party Dissent on European Integration in the Conservative Party'. *British Journal of Politics and International Relations*, Vol. 15, No. 3, pp. 317–39.

Lynch, P., Whitaker, R. and Loomes, G. (2012) 'The UK Independence Party: Understanding a Niche Party's Strategy, Candidates and Supporters'. *Parliamentary Affairs*, Vol. 65, No. 4, pp. 733–57.

Malová, D., Rybář, M., Bilčík, V., Láštic, E., Lisoňová, Z., Mišík, M. and Pašiak, M. (2010) *From Listening to Action? New Member States in the European Union* (Bratislava: Comenius University Press).

Matthijs, M. (2013) 'David Cameron's Dangerous Game: The Folly of Flirting with an EU Exit'. *Foreign Affairs*, Vol. 92, No. 5, pp. 10–16.

Oppermann, K. (2008) 'The Blair Government and Europe: The Policy of Containing the Salience of European Integration'. *British Politics*, Vol. 3, No. 2, pp. 156–82.

Oppermann, K. (2013) 'The Politics of Discretionary Government Commitments to European Integration Referendums'. *Journal of European Public Policy*, Vol. 20, No. 5, pp. 684–701.

Paterson, W.E. (2011) 'The Reluctant Hegemon: Germany Moves Centre Stage in the European Union'. *JCMS*, Vol. 49, No. s1, pp. 57–75.

Paterson, W.E. (2014) 'Großbritannien und Deutschlands Führungsrolle'. In Harnisch, S. and Schild, J. (eds) *Deutsche Außenpolitik und internationale Führung: Ressourcen, Praktiken und Politiken in einer veränderten Europäischen Union* (Baden-Baden: Nomos Verlag).

Petrocik, J.R. (1996) 'Issue Ownership in US Presidential Elections, with a 1980 Case Study'. *American Political Science Review*, Vol. 40, No. 3, pp. 825–50.

Pew (2013) 'The New Sick Man of Europe: the European Union', 13 May 2013. Available at: «http://www.pewglobal.org/2013/05/13/the-new-sick-man-of-europe-the-european-union/».

Schmidt, V. (2006) 'Adapting to Europe: Is It Harder for Britain?' *British Journal of Politics and International Relations*, Vol. 8, pp. 15–33.

Schmidt, V. (2010) *Democracy in Europe* (Oxford: Oxford University Press).

Shaw, K. (2007) 'The End of the Beginning? Taking Forward Local Democratic Renewal in the Post-Referendum North East'. *Local Economy*, Vol. 22, No. 3, pp. 243–60.

UK Polling Report (2014) Poll of Polls. Available at: «http://ukpollingreport.co.uk/voting-intention-2».

Van Rompuy, H. (2013) 'Britain in Europe: Challenging Change Together'. Speech at the Annual Conference of Policy Network, London, 28 February.

Webber, D. (2013) 'How Likely is It that the European Union Will Disintegrate? A Critical Analysis of Competing Theoretical Perspectives'. *European Journal of International Relations*, forthcoming. Available at: «http://ejt.sagepub.com/content/early/2012/12/14/135406611246 1286.full.pdf+html».

JCMS 2014 Volume 52 Annual Review pp. 90–98   DOI: 10.1111/jcms.12165

In the Shadow of Austerity: Ireland's Seventh Presidency of the European Union

BRIGID LAFFAN
European University Institute

Introduction

Coinciding with the 40th anniversary of its accession to the European Union on 1 January 2013, Ireland assumed the Presidency of the Council for the seventh time. Ireland's first Presidency – a landmark for this small state in 1975 – marked the end of the country's apprenticeship in the then European Economic Community. As a small state and a net beneficiary of EU funding, successive Irish governments regarded the Presidency as an opportunity to make a constructive contribution to the management of European business for a six-month period (Laffan and O'Mahony, 2009). There was also awareness that the Presidency brought small states into the heart of the Union, reinforced bilateral relations with all Member States and gave welcome international exposure.

Ireland's seventh Presidency was unlike previous ones in two important respects (Laffan, 2013). First, Ireland found itself in the unenviable position of being a 'programme country' having had to request a bail-out in November 2010 (Donovan and Murphy, 2013). Prior to the Presidency, there was concern about how much Ireland could achieve given its weak economic position (Piedrafita, 2013; Barry, 2013a). In previous Presidencies, the government and administration tended to focus considerable energy on, and give priority to, the business of the EU. Domestic issues, other than very urgent ones, were put on the back burner. This time the core executive had no such luxury. The domestic economy required continuous attention and the Presidency provided a vital platform for the government in its continuing quest to repair the reputational damage that Ireland experienced as a result of the economic crisis. Second, Ireland's seventh Presidency was conducted under the rules of the Lisbon Treaty, which made substantial changes to the role and prerogatives of the rotating Presidency (Dinan, 2010). For long-serving diplomats and officials with extensive pre-Lisbon Presidency experience, there was a need to adjust to and prepare for the post-Lisbon world.

I. Planning and Priorities

Ireland has traditionally taken the business of the Presidency seriously, as demonstrated by its meticulous pre-planning of the priorities and the calendar (Humphries, 1997; Quaglia and Moxon Browne, 2006). This time was no exception. In its Presidency programme, the Irish government emphasized that its approach would 'reflect the best of our previous Presidencies: always an honest broker, open and transparent, striving for efficiency and with a firm focus on results' (Ireland, 2013a, p. 2). The established practice in Ireland is to run a Brussels-based Presidency, hence the key official was

Ireland's ambassador to the EU, Rory Montgomery, assisted by his deputy and other senior officials in the representation. The staffing level in Brussels was increased with the secondment of additional home-based officials and a large number of temporary contracts. Dublin played a crucial role as the ministers who chaired the Council formations were all Dublin-based and a large number of Presidency-related events were hosted in the capital. Official support for the ministers came from all of the domestic ministries with the central co-ordinating role exercised by the Prime Minister's office, which took over responsibility for the management of EU business in 2011. Given the domestic challenges, the final budget for the Presidency was €45 million – half of what had been spent in 2004. Rather than conduct meetings throughout the country which had been the practice previously, all informal Councils were held in Dublin Castle, as were most other Presidency events. It was not considered politic to have cavalcades of European politicians visible throughout the country given the depth of the domestic economic challenges.

All Member States seek to mould their Presidency programme in a manner that resonates with their domestic and EU priorities. Given the crisis that had bedevilled Ireland since 2008, the choice of priorities – stability, growth and jobs – was predictable. The emphasis on 'stability' was related to the complex package of issues and proposals concerning economic and monetary union (EMU). The other two priorities – growth and jobs – were about taking the EU agenda beyond the politics and policies of austerity to address the economic and social consequences of the crisis. Europe's low growth has made recovery considerably more difficult and continued to cast a shadow over Member State debt levels, particularly in the hardest hit countries. The identification of employment as a priority highlighted the devastating loss of jobs throughout the eurozone's troubled economies with particularly high levels of youth unemployment in the Mediterranean Member States. Ireland's unemployment rate at the onset of the Presidency was 14.6 per cent (Ireland CSO, 2013).

II. The Presidency in Numbers

The Irish administration kept detailed statistics on the conduct of the Presidency. These throw interesting light on the demands a Presidency places on a Member State. It is estimated that during the 181 days of the Irish Presidency, agreement was reached on 200 policy commitments, including 80 legislative proposals. This legislative and policy output forms the Presidency's central achievement in managing the business of EU negotiations to conclusion. Indeed, keeping the Union's negotiation engine going is the core responsibility of the Presidency. During the Presidency, Irish ministers chaired 54 Council meetings and together with Irish officials chaired a total of 2,477 events in all. The pivotal role of the Presidency in managing Council-European Parliament relations is brought sharply into focus by the following statistics. The Prime Minister, his deputy and sectoral ministers spent 111 hours at the European Parliament (EP) during the 181 days of the Presidency. During the EP session on 21–23 January, 20 Irish Ministers presented the Presidency priorities at 27 different EP committees. More significantly, 374 trilogues were held with the European Commission and the EP. Thus chairing Council meetings, which was at one time the central role of the Presidency, has been supplemented by the equally important role of managing interinstitutional relations, particularly those with the EP

(Ireland, 2013b). Long-serving officials, with extensive Presidency experience, identify this development as the most striking post-Lisbon shift in the Union's policy process and interinstitutional balance.

III. Negotiation Wins: Where Ireland Made a Difference

The Multiannual Financial Framework (MFF), 2014–2020

Following the failure to conclude negotiations on the MFF at the European Council in November 2012, getting agreement on the multiannual budgetary framework was a high priority. The European Council meeting of February 2013 reached agreement on a €960 billion budget in commitment appropriations (Laffan and Linder, 2014). Immediately following the February meeting, the Presidency took over responsibility for the critical next phase: negotiations with the EP designed to secure their consent. This proved to be the most contentious and controversial dossier and the most sensitive interinstitutional issue for the Presidency. It took until the morning of the 27 June European Council meeting to reach agreement with the EP and required the active engagement of Irish Prime Minister Enda Kenny, President of the Parliament Martin Schulz and President of the European Commission José Manuel Barroso to conclude the negotiations.

The Presidency was the conduit for negotiations between the Member States who had agreed a deal and an EP that was intent on flexing its new post-Lisbon powers.[1] At a sitting in March following the February European Council, the EP overwhelmingly rejected the MFF in the form agreed by the Heads of State and Government (HOSG) with 506 against and only 161 in favour (there were 23 abstentions) (European Parliament, 2013). The EP made a number of significant demands, though it did not press for an increase in the overall spending ceilings. Its demands related to the structure of the agreement and reflected longstanding preferences on the EU budget. The EP sought concessions on shortfalls in the 2013 budgetary allocation, flexibility on the use of unused financial resources, a mid-term review of the MFF and a reform of the own resources system.

From March to June, the EP continued its vocal opposition to the February deal and threatened a veto unless concessions were forthcoming. The two institutions engaged in a stand-off until the trilogue got underway on 13 May (Piedrafita, 2013, p. 1). Following ten rounds of lengthy and arduous negotiations between the Presidency, Commission and the EP delegation, Ireland's Deputy Prime Minister, Eamon Gilmore, announced prematurely on 19 June that agreement had been reached. The announcement evoked a furious response from the EP delegation. This was the first time during the Presidency that the substance of a negotiation became a matter of public controversy. This left the Presidency just one week to mend relations with the EP and reach agreement on one of its top priorities. Failure to sign off on the MFF would have been considered as a major Presidency failure. Right up to the end, it appeared as if agreement might not be forthcoming. A meeting of the leaders of the party groupings and intensive engagement by the Presidency finally delivered an outcome just in time for the European Council meeting.

[1] On the EP's assertiveness during 2013, see Dinan's contribution to this volume.

EMU and Related Issues of Economic Governance

There were a number of important dossiers related to the euro crisis and the challenge of ensuring that the single currency was based on sustainable foundations. These dossiers were important to all Member States, but particularly to the programme countries that were bearing the costs of the flawed EMU design. Central to this was banking union – an endeavour that was technically and politically very challenging.[2] The decision to embark on a banking union was welcomed in Ireland because its economic collapse was directly related to the problems of its banking system. The creation of a single supervisory mechanism (SSM) necessitated a package of measures relating to the supervisory authority of the European Central Bank (ECB) and changes to European Banking Authority (EBA) regulation. Agreement was reached with the EP on these measures at first reading. The second pillar of banking union was the establishment of a bank resolution and recovery (BRR) mechanism. Following two all-night negotiating sessions, the Presidency reached political agreement within the Council on how the BRR should work on 27 June (Piedrafita, 2013, p. 2).

Economic governance came to the fore at the beginning of the euro crisis. The incoming Irish Presidency presented its roadmap for the European Semester process to the General Affairs Council (GAC) in December 2012. Subsequently, the first phase of the Semester process culminated in country-specific recommendations for all Member States. Having already strengthened the regulatory environment in the field of economic governance, the Presidency reached agreement at first reading with the EP on the so-called 'Two-Pack' of legislative proposals designed to strengthen oversight of Member State public finances. Following the agreement with the EP, the two Regulations came into force on 30 May.

Youth Unemployment and the Growth Agenda

The extent and depth of youth unemployment in a number of Member States, including Ireland, pushed this issue up the political agenda during the Presidency. Increasing references to a lost generation and the social consequences of high youth unemployment demanded a European response (Radičová, 2013). In February, the Irish Minister for Social Protection led a discussion on the Youth Guarantee at an informal Council and then concluded negotiations on a recommendation. The focus of the Youth Guarantee was on a smooth transition between education and the world of work – a difficult transition for some young people with devastating consequences for their life chances. Concerning the growth agenda, the Presidency focused successfully on getting agreement to the Horizons 2020 programme on research and development, the new Erasmus programme, key infrastructural networks in transport and energy, the digital economy and a new funding programme for small and medium-sized enterprises. The last high-level Presidency meeting in Dublin was the annual Commission-sponsored Digital Agenda Assembly (DAA) – the first time that it had been held outside Brussels. For Ireland this was an important event as it enabled the country to showcase the presence in Dublin of all of the leading digital companies, including Google and Facebook.

---

[2] For details, see Howarth and Quaglia in this volume.

Agriculture and Fisheries

Reform of the common agricultural policy (CAP) and the common fisheries policy (CFP) were key priorities for the Presidency and gave rise to some of the most complex negotiations. As the same minister, Simon Coveny, was responsible for both policy fields in the Irish government, he carried a heavy burden and was involved in the long Council meeting and intensive interinstitutional negotiations that ran from 23–26 June. During this critical period, Council meetings were interspersed with trilogue meetings as the EP delegation went to Luxemburg so that the negotiations could conclude before the end of the Irish mandate. Both policy areas were also highly salient in domestic politics as Ireland continues to have a strong farming lobby and a small but vocal one in fisheries. The Irish government was determined to achieve reform, even in the face of domestic opposition. It also wanted to secure agreement during its term of office as it felt that it would have most influence over the direction of reform in the chair. A key priority was to ensure that Member States would have some flexibility in the allocation of payments at the domestic level rather than it being confined to the Commission's preference of a flat-rate payment, and Coveny achieved agreement on this. The Irish government considered CAP reform to be one of the key achievements of the Irish Presidency, and one that served both EU and domestic interests. Reform of the CFP – a very unpopular policy among Europe's fishermen – was also a top priority for the Presidency and was successfully achieved: the CFP underwent its first major re-form since 2002, including measures to combat overfishing and putting an end to the controversial policy of throwing fish back into the sea.

Europe in the World

The appointment of the High Representative and her responsibility for chairing the Foreign Affairs Council reduced but did not eliminate the role of the Presidency in Europe's external relations. As Ireland has a very open economy and relies for its economic wellbeing on trade, the Presidency was committed to furthering Europe's trade links. It was particularly committed to getting agreement in the Council for a Commission mandate so that the EU could open negotiations on a Europe–US transatlantic trade and investment partnership (TTIP).[3] Ireland regarded this as strategically important to the EU as well as to itself as it would build on its already strong economic and cultural links with the United States. Negotiations were stalled because of French demands for the exclusion of the audio-visual sector until a last-minute deal was crafted days before President Obama was due in Northern Ireland for a G8 summit on 17 June (Piedfafita, 2013, p. 2).

Process Innovation

Ever since Ireland's first Presidency in 1975, it has sought to be innovative by introducing small changes in an effort to make the rotating Presidency work better. Ireland's political and administrative culture is characterized by pragmatism, flexibility and adaptability, and this was again evident during the seventh Presidency. The Irish Permanent Representation reduced the length of COREPER meetings and held more informal breakfasts in an effort

---

[3] On TTIP and EU–US relations, see Hamilton in this volume.

to improve its work (Piedrafita, 2013, p. 2). Flexibility and innovation was also apparent in the response of Minister Coveney to the tortuous nature and lack of progress in trilogue negotiations. The traditional approach to trilogues was to work on the basis of four columns: the first three identified the proposed wording of the Commission, the Council and the EP, whereas the fourth was intended for a compromise text between the three institutions if that could be agreed. When it became apparent that this was not working in the negotiations on the CFP, Coveny (a former MEP) suggested that informal meetings should be used to agree the broad political outline, with these being followed up by the agreement being drafted into legal language (Barry, 2013b).

IV. A Presidency Reckoning

Ireland has always prided itself on running efficient and effective Presidencies and achieving tangible negotiating outcomes. Ireland's seventh Presidency was no different, but it had the added priority of completing the repair to Ireland's battered reputation. The assessment of the Irish Presidency was broadly favourable. In his speech to the EP on 2 July, when the Irish Prime Minister had delivered his final Presidency statement to the EP, Commission President Barroso concluded that:

> the Irish Presidency had all the elements of a successful one: a clear set of priorities, genuine political commitment, technical knowledge and drive, and a safe pair of hands to manage it all. And the capacity [. . .] to build and reinforce on the relation of trust and respect between the Presidency of the Council and the European institutions like the European Parliament and the European Commission. (Barroso, 2013)

The Centre for European Policy Studies review concurred with this assessment, stating that: 'For the most part, its Presidency rose to the challenge and was quite successful in the implementation with only a few shadows clouding the overall positive picture' (Piedrafita, 2013, p. 1). There were many dossiers upon which agreement was not possible, including a large set of issues concerning the digital agenda, which were handed over to Lithuania as the incoming Presidency.[4]

V. Domestic Challenges and Priorities

No account of the Presidency would be complete without an overview of the domestic challenges that faced the government holding the chair. During the Presidency, Ireland was in its fifth year of financial crisis that had mutated into an economic crisis and turned into a social crisis characterized by an unemployment rate of 13.6 per cent in June 2013, which was at least a reduction from the high of 15 per cent in March 2012 (Donavan and Murphy, 2013). The extent of the banking losses in Ireland had a major impact on the country's debt levels; taxpayer support to banks amounted to over €64 billion, or 39 per cent of gross domestic product in 2012. The International Monetary Fund estimated that only two banking crises over the last 40 years cost more. The staggering figure of €64 billion represented approximately €40,000 per household in the country. That Irish taxpayers shoulder the cost of the decisions of private banks and international bondholders

---

[4] On the Lithuanian Presidency (the second in the 18-month trio of Ireland, Lithuania and Greece), see Vilpišauskas in this volume.

was (and is) a source of considerable political controversy, social tension and disquiet. Irish society paid a very high price for the very poor regulation of the financial system not just in Ireland, but throughout Europe. When confronted with the crisis, the Irish state elite moved quickly to strengthen its core executive, bring new blood into key state institutions and get on with the business of being a programme country. An election in 2011 allowed the electorate to vent their anger on those in power (Little, 2011) and notwithstanding the severity of the crisis, Irish society did not implode and there was little evidence of the protests that characterized other hard-hit countries. The Presidency was just one more opportunity to promote recovery. During the Presidency, Ireland was intent on ensuring sufficient market confidence to enable it to exit the bail-out in December 2013, which was achieved.

A continuing problem for Ireland was the weight of the banking crisis on its economy and public finances. A major issue concerned what became known as 'promissory notes'. This issue was so important to the government that it was unwilling to forgo its search for a better deal until after the Presidency. Ireland's 'bad bank' – the Irish Bank Resolution Corporation (IBRC) – was funded by credit from the Irish Central Bank based on an Irish state guarantee with the approval of the ECB. This funding meant that international bondholders and creditors in other states did not suffer losses. The funding mechanism envisaged repayments of approximately €3 billion by the Irish state every year to 2022. This was highly controversial because the Irish public was furious at repaying international bondholders and the annual payment of €3 billion was on top of a programme of severe fiscal consolidation and austerity. Budgeted public expenditure in 2013 was €54.5 billion down from €62.4 billion in 2008.[5] Finding a solution to the promissory note problem was a major strategic aim of the Irish government and the Irish Central Bank. In the first half of the Presidency, Irish Finance Minister Michael Noonan continued to press for an agreement to alter the nature of the promissory notes. In the teeth of considerable opposition, including from Germany, the government succeeded in achieving an outcome in March when the promissory notes were replaced by long-term bonds ranging from 27 to 40 years maturity.

Conclusions

Ireland's 40th anniversary of EU membership and its seventh Presidency of the Council came at a very difficult time for Irish society. The shock of exclusion from the financial markets was deep as independent Ireland had never defaulted on its obligations. The reasons for the Irish crisis originated in the domestic economy, the eurozone and wider financial globalization. A historically poor country found itself with unlimited access to cheap money, and the government, regulators and the wider society did not display sufficient restraint and prudence. The state failed to regulate its banks so that a long boom turned into a bubble with catastrophic consequences. Dealing with the legacy of the bust may take the remainder of the decade, but Ireland has the institutional and cultural capital to return to prosperity. Irish society is resilient and the political system has managed the inevitable distributional conflicts thus far, but with considerable difficulty. Ireland's future depends on both a return to growth and a better design for the eurozone. Otherwise, the eurozone is a dangerous place to be.

[5] «http://budget.gov.ie/budgets/2013/Documents/Expenditure%20Report%202013%20Part%20I.pdf».

The Presidency was challenging and demanding given the complexity of the domestic agenda and the demands of the troika. However, the government and central administration saw it as offering a unique opportunity to regain credibility with its partners and EU institutions and to repair the damage to its international reputation. Nor was the Irish government willing to neglect domestic priorities. In its choice of Presidency priorities and attention to key dossiers such as agriculture, it set out to secure domestic benefit and to re-focus the European agenda on employment not just on austerity. Moreover, it was determined to get agreement on the promissory notes in March, notwithstanding the opposition of some of its partners. The Irish government used the Presidency to focus attention on some important issues notably youth unemployment and banking union. Given Ireland's difficulties since 2008, the year 2013 proved to be a good one, with a successful Presidency and a successful exit from the bail-out programme in December (Ireland, 2010–2013).

References

Baroso, J.M.D. (2013) Speech by President Barroso at the EP Plenary Debate on the Review of the Irish Presidency including the MFF Agreement, 7 July. Available at: «http://europa.eu/rapid/press-release_SPEECH-13-599_en.htm».

Barry, L. (2013a) *What to Expect from Ireland's Presidency of the Council of the European Union* (Stockholm: Swedish Institute for European Policy Studies).

Barry, L. (2013b) *Ireland's EU Presidency* (Dublin: Institute of International and European Affairs).

Dinan, D. (2010) 'Institutions and Governance: A New Treaty, a Newly Elected Parliament and a New Commission'. *JCMS*, Vol. 48, No. s1, pp. 95–118.

Donovan, D. and Murphy, A.E. (2013) *The Fall of the Celtic Tiger: Ireland and the Euro Debt Crisis* (Oxford: Oxford University Press).

European Parliament (2013) Resolution on the European Council conclusions of 7–8 February concerning the Multiannual Financial Framework of 13 March 2013. Available at: «http://www.europarl.europa.eu/sides/getDoc.do?pubRef=-//EP//TEXT+MOTION+B7-2013-0129+0+DOC+XML+V0//EN».

Humphries, P. (1997) *The Fifth Irish Presidency of the European Union: Some Management Lessons* (Dublin: Institute of Public Administration).

Ireland (2010–2013) Troika Reviews of the Irish Programme. Available at: «http://ec.europa.eu/ireland/economy/financial_assistance_programme_ireland/troika_review_reports/index1_en.htm».

Ireland (2013a) Programme of the Irish Presidency of the Council of the European Union, January–June 2013. Available at: «http://www.eu2013.ie/media/eupresidency/content/documents/EU-Pres_Prog_A4.pdf».

Ireland (2013b) Results of the Irish Presidency of the Council of the European Union, January–June 2013. Available at: «http://eu2013.ie/ireland-and-the-presidency/about-thepresidency/achievements-report/».

Ireland Central Statistics Office (CSO) (2013) Live Register. Available at: «http://www.cso.ie/en/media/csoie/releasespublications/documents/labourmarket/2013/lreg_jan2013.pdf».

Laffan, B. (2013) 'Irelands siebte EU-Ratsprasidentschaft: Starkung des Ansehnes und Wirtschafatliche Erholung'. *Integration*, Vol. 3, pp. 183–98.

Laffan, B. and Linder, J. (2014) 'The Budget: Who Gets What, When and How?' In Wallace, H., Pollack, M.A. and Young, A.R. (eds) *Policy-Making in the European Union* (Oxford: Oxford University Press).

Laffan, B. and O'Mahony, J. (2009) *Ireland in the European Union* (Basingstoke: Palgrave Macmillan).

Little, C. (2011) 'The General Election of 2011 in the Republic of Ireland: All Changed Utterly?' *West European Politics*, Vol. 34, No. 6, pp. 1304–13.

Quaglia, L. and Moxon-Browne, E. (2006) 'What Makes a Good EU Presidency? Italy and Ireland Compared'. *JCMS*, Vol. 44, No. 2, pp. 349–68.

Piedrafita, S. (2013) 'Ireland Gets the New Trio Presidency off to a Propitious Start'. *CEPS Commentary*, 28 August.

Radičová, I. (2013) 'Shock to the System: Division, Unemployment and the Common Sense of European Institutions'. *JCMS*, Vol. 51, No. s1, pp. 55–62.

JCMS 2014 Volume 52 Annual Review pp. 99–108   DOI: 10.1111/jcms.12164

Lithuania's EU Council Presidency: Negotiating Finances, Dealing with Geopolitics*

RAMŪNAS VILPIŠAUSKAS
Vilnius University

Introduction

Lithuania assumed the six-month rotating Council Presidency in July 2013, taking over from Ireland, which was the first in the Presidency trio comprising Ireland, Lithuania and Greece.[1] Domestically, the Presidency received significant attention from key political actors, even figuring in the debates regarding the appointments of the new ministers to the coalition government formed after the Lithuanian parliamentary elections in October 2012. At the same time, outside expectations of the Lithuanian Presidency were rather limited as the relatively unknown country was assuming this task for the first time, its administration was comparatively small and the budget allocated for the Presidency was rather modest (around €62 million). As Deputy Foreign Minister in charge of the Presidency Vytautas Leškevičius noted when assuming the mantle, 'underpromised – overdelivered, that's my motto' (Pop, 2013).

The Lithuanian Presidency proved to be unexpectedly effective in advancing negotiations on a number of dossiers, mediating between Member States and between the Council and the European Parliament (EP), and brokering agreements on a number of important files, including the multiannual financial framework (MFF) 2014–20, banking union, the posting of workers and others. There were, however, also disappointments – in particular the failure to sign an association agreement with Ukraine at the Eastern Partnership (EaP) summit in Vilnius, which was supposed to be a highlight of the Presidency. Nevertheless, the Lithuanian Presidency was positively assessed by the leaders of the EU institutions and Members of the EP, when on 15 January 2014, President Dalia Grybauskaitė reported:

> [W]ith pride [. . .] our small country, our young democracy, its statehood so recently regained, has shown that it too can carry out the tasks of an EU Presidency as well as any other Member State – large or small. (Grybauskaitė, 2014)

These assessments were also conveyed to the Lithuanian domestic audience as an indication that the country has established itself as a capable and respected Member State of the EU.

This contribution discusses the context, priorities and achievements of the Lithuanian Presidency. It first presents the domestic and European context, the capacities and

---

* I am grateful for reflections on the work of the Lithuanian EU Council Presidency to Dalia Grybauskaitė, Vytenis Andriukaitis, Petras Auštrevičius, Andrius Kubilius, Raimundas Karoblis, Jovita Pranevičiūtė, Arūnas Vinčiūnas, Darius Pranckevičius, Nerijus Aleksiejūnas, Eivilė Čipkutė, Julius Pranevičius, Inga Stanytė-Toločkienė, Neringa Majauskaitė, Ona Kostinaitė-Grinkevičienė, Martynas Barysas and Valdemaras Juozaitis. I am also grateful for comments to Tim Haughton, Nathaniel Copsey, Darius Žeruolis, Klaudijus Maniokas and Bruno Vandecasteele.

[1] See Laffan's contribution on Ireland's Presidency in this volume.

constraints of the Presidency. Then it reviews the priorities, placing them in the broader development of Lithuania's European policy since accession into the EU in 2004, especially the interplay between national interests and European priorities. Finally, by discussing the anticipated outcomes and the actual results of the Presidency in important policy areas, it presents the experience of the Lithuanian Presidency in terms of policies (agreements brokered) and politics (relations with other EU institutions and Member States). It concludes with more general observations on the experience of Lithuania's Presidency and the role of the rotating Presidency in the EU under the Lisbon Treaty.

I. Domestic and European Context

Early Preparations

Lithuanian institutions started their preparations for the Presidency soon after the country's accession into the EU. The centre-right coalition government formed in 2008 and headed by Prime Minister Andrius Kubilius included specific provision in its programme on the need to prepare for the forthcoming Presidency. In 2009, the government reformed the co-ordination of European affairs by assigning the main responsibilities to the Ministry of Foreign Affairs (MFA) and giving it the role of co-ordinating the preparations for the Presidency. Tasks included logistical preparations, extensive training of public sector officials working with EU affairs, strengthening institutions like the Permanent Representation to the EU by more than doubling its staff to 180 officials, aligning rotation schedules for the personnel working with EU affairs, working with the trio countries on the common programme and drafting of the Lithuanian Presidency programme (see Vilpišauskas *et al.*, 2013, pp. 20–7). Preparations for developing a working relationship with the EP were given particular attention, given its co-legislator's role under the Lisbon Treaty and growing institutional assertiveness.[2]

In 2010–11, the Lithuanian parliament and government adopted a number of resolutions and other documents providing the legal and financial basis for the preparatory work of the MFA and other institutions; parliamentary parties also signed an agreement on the need for continuity after the parliamentary elections of 2012. The smooth management of the EU Council activities and an increase of Lithuania's influence in the EU were defined as the main objectives of Lithuania's Presidency. It was also decided to opt for the 'Brussels-based' model characterized by the importance of the Permanent Representation to the EU where most of the responsibilities are placed on the chairs of the working groups and committees who co-operate with the Council Secretariat General and other institutions. The choice of this model located the most intensive daily activities of the Presidency in Brussels, allowing it more flexibility and effectiveness in reacting to unforeseen events.[3]

The President and Officials

The political importance of the EU Council Presidency was raised after the Lithuanian parliamentary elections in October 2012. The newly formed centre-left coalition was

---

[2] See Dinan's contribution to this volume.
[3] After the Presidency, the officials from the Permanent Representation of Lithuania to the EU maintained that the choice of the 'Brussels-based' model has been instrumental in the smooth running of the Presidency tasks (Interview with Lithuanian Permanent Representation to the EU, Vilnius, 15 February 2014).

challenged by President Grybauskaitė, who criticized some of the proposed ministers as being unfit for the Presidency tasks, including their knowledge of English. The fact that the new government was formed only half a year before the start of the Presidency did not help the process of preparations. However, changes of ministers and vice-ministers did not significantly affect the work of the Presidency given the choice of a Brussels-based model.

It should also be noted that the Lithuanian President decided to assume the role of the public face of the EU Council Presidency, leaving the Prime Minister sidelined. President Grybauskaitė's previous experience working as a European Commissioner responsible for the budget until 2009 made such a decision easy to explain, although domestic politics and impending presidential elections in May 2014 could also have contributed to her using this opportunity to strengthen her public visibility.

Forgotten Trio?

Lithuania's officials also worked with colleagues from the other two countries of the trio: Ireland and Greece. Although initially there were suggestions of extensive co-operation, eventually the work of the trio was limited mostly to the preparation of the joint programme. Greek officials showed little additional interest in trio co-operation, preferring instead to emphasize that with Italy following Greece, 2014 was the year of the Mediterranean. Co-operation between the Lithuanian and Irish Presidencies, however, was more intensive, although dependent on particular areas and constrained by interinstitutional dynamics and the desire of each Presidency to advance the legislative agenda. For example, although there was an idea circulated to invite Lithuanian representative to trilogues of the negotiations on MFF during the Irish Presidency, it was taken up only to a limited extent by Dublin because of fears that the EP might perceive this as a sign that the Irish Presidency did not intend to conclude agreements by the end of its term. It should also be noted that in some areas – for example, on advancing Eastern Partnership – officials from Lithuania co-operated closely with Polish colleagues during their Presidency in the second half of 2011 with a view to the forthcoming Lithuanian Presidency.[4] This is yet another example of coalitions between EU Member States based on similarity of their national priorities rather than formal arrangements such as the Presidency trio.

Working in the Shadow of Elections

The broader context of the Lithuanian Presidency was characterized by the approaching end of the term of the EU institutions. As European Commission President Barroso noted after the meeting with Lithuania's Prime Minister Algirdas Butkevičius in April 2013, 'the Lithuanian Presidency comes up against the backdrop of a challenging economic outlook and also in a particular moment of the democratic calendar' (Commission 2013, p. 2). The end of the EP's term and the 'exceptionally large amount of work' to be shared between the rotating Presidency and the EP was also mentioned by President Grybauskaitė in her speech presenting Presidency priorities (Mirguet, 2013). According to Lithuanian officials, since the adoption of the Lisbon Treaty 'no EU Presidency has had so many dossiers on their table' (there were 563) to be tackled (Pop, 2013). Finally, the parliamentary

[4] Interview with Lithuanian Permanent Representation to the EU, Vilnius, 17 February 2014.

elections in Germany in September 2013 affected negotiations on certain issues such as the agreement on the single resolution mechanism for the banking union.[5] They also increased the political sensitivity of some other items such as the run up to the Vilnius summit.

II. Priorities of Lithuania's Presidency

From National Priorities

The Lithuanian Presidency's four main priorities were first presented by the government in 2010: increasing energy security in the EU, advancing EU relations with Eastern Partnership countries, implementing the Baltic Sea strategy and strengthening external border control. It should be noted that the first two have been the key priorities of Lithuania's European policy since the country's accession (see Vilpišauskas, 2013). In this respect, they represent the use of instruments and opportunities provided by the EU to pursue national priorities.

To the European Agenda

The perception of the Presidency as an opportunity to further the country's national interests started to evolve in early 2013. The President's Office, working with the MFA and some members of the Lithuanian parliament, altered the debate about Presidency priorities among the political elites. The national priorities, some of which lacked substantive legislative content, were reformulated into three broadly defined European priorities: a credible, growing and open Europe. The preparation of the Presidency programme and the realization that the Lithuanian Presidency would be continuing the work started by previous Presidencies also contributed to this reframing of the priorities, especially the advancement of the EU legislative agenda through mediation and brokerage. In most of the Presidency reports and public presentations, the negotiations on the MFF and banking union were usually at the top of the list,[6] although the EaP summit in Vilnius attracted most media attention and was dubbed by outside analysts 'the most visible priority of Lithuanian Presidency' (Raik, 2013).

III. Assessing the Presidency

Although as soon as Lithuania took over the Presidency, unexpected events made it focus on allegations about phone tapping by the US National Security Agency, this assessment is structured around the broad priorities of a growing, credible and open Europe.

Concluding MFF (Growing Europe)

In early 2013, it seemed that the deal on the MFF would be finalized under the Irish Presidency. However, it soon reappeared on the Lithuanian Presidency agenda because

[5] On the banking union, see Howarth and Quaglia in this volume.
[6] Interview with Member of the Lithuanian parliament Vytenis Andriukaitis, Vilnius, 14 January 2014; Interview with President of Lithuania, Dalia Grybauskaitė, Vilnius, 16 January 2014; Interview with Lithuanian Permanent Representation to the EU, Vilnius, 15 February 2014.

MEPs were still unwilling to accept it. What took place afterwards looked more like a show of institutional strength with the EP testing the limits of its powers under the Lisbon Treaty than a debate about money.

On 3 July, the EP adopted a resolution stating that it would only vote on the MFF when the agreements on amendment of the 2013 budget and the draft 2014 budget were reached, and when there was sufficient progress in the work of the working group on own resources and significant progress in the negotiations of the MFF implementing legislation on agriculture and cohesion. The Presidency first focused on brokering an agreement on adjustments to the 2013 budget. Although the whole package requested by the EP was seen as highly problematic by the Council, the request for increasing the 2013 budget by €3.9 billion was seen as quite legitimate one.[7] But the problem was that it was reaching the ceilings of the payments set by the 2007–13 financial perspective due to additional expenses from the solidarity fund stemming from compensation for damage from unexpected disasters in central Europe. The European Commission supported by the EP requested additional funding for the solidarity fund, which was not acceptable to net payers (in particular Germany) as usually such compensation was granted through the regular budget. This debate delayed a deal by about a month and, finally, after reaching a compromise the United Kingdom tried to use procedural instruments to block voting in the Council, but did not succeed in preventing EP voting on this issue in October.

In parallel, intensive negotiations on the MFF implementing legislation (in particular cohesion and agricultural policy instruments) continued. On cohesion, the main sticking point was the so-called 'macroeconomic conditionality' – that is, the possibility to suspend funding in case a Member State does not follow financial discipline norms – which was important to the Council (in particular net payers), but was strongly opposed by the EP. After exhaustive trilogues and under growing time pressure, a breakthrough was reached at the end of October by modifying the application of conditionality. Agriculture negotiations were finalized at the beginning of October by reaching a deal on 'greening' and the application of delegated acts. On 11 November, the final agreement on amending the 2013 and 2014 budgets as well as preparatory discussion with the EP on the creation of the high-level group on own resources was reached allowing for the positive EP vote on the package on 19 November 2013.

The unpredictability of MEPs, who frequently distanced themselves from earlier agreements reached in trilogies, complicated these negotiations.[8] On the other hand, the tension between the political leadership of the EP, motivated to stage 'a political show', and the committees interested to get deals done helped to reach a compromise.[9] The agreement on the package and the vote of 19 November 2013 was also the turning point for other parts of the MFF, such as the external financial instruments, home and justice financing and advancement on fishery funds, and allowed agreement to be reached on the majority of programmes (59 out of 64) and MFF implementing legislation. As Deputy Foreign Minister Leškevičius observed on this occasion speaking in Strasbourg, 'the negotiations of unprecedented intensity and difficulty with the European Parliament were one of the biggest challenges of the Lithuanian and previous Presidencies' (Council of the EU, 2013b).

---

[7] Interview with Lithuanian Permanent Representation to the EU, Vilnius, 15 February 2014.
[8] Interview with Lithuanian Permanent Representation to the EU, Brussels-Vilnius, 21 February 2014.
[9] Interview with Lithuanian Permanent Representation to the EU, Vilnius, 15 February 2014.

Other issues under the priority of Growing Europe attracted much less public attention. Work progressed on particular dossiers under the Single Market Act (that is, a package of directives on public procurement, product safety) and deals on legislative proposals such as the posting of workers, the revised tobacco directive or the audit package were reached. One of the files, which attracted considerable media attention, was CO_2 emissions from cars. The Presidency was criticized for its unwillingness to put the issue to qualified majority voting (QMV) in the Council in order to avoid Germany (protective of its car industry) being outvoted. In the end, the Presidency brokered a compromise involving the extension of implementation schedules and changes to the CO_2 emissions credit system, which were agreed both in the Council and the EP.

Although no major legal initiatives were taken in the energy policy field, the Council endorsed two reports on the internal energy market and on EU external energy policy to frame further work. Similarly, attention to the single market in services and the use of the mutual recognition principle was expressed in the December 2013 Council (Competitiveness) conclusions and the Presidency also secured progress on e-identification to facilitate e-services.

Negotiating the Banking Union (Credible Europe)

While finalization of the legal norms implementing the MFF 2014–20 formed the basis of what was expected from the Lithuanian Presidency, the agreement on the banking union – in particular, the SRM – in the Council by December 2013 was, although called upon by the European Council in June, rather less certain due to strongly diverging positions of the Germany-led northern Member States and the southern eurozone countries. The initial proposal on the SRM presented by the European Commission in July immediately drew criticism from the German representatives, who disputed the choice of legal basis (Article 114 of the Treaty on the Functioning of the EU) and the content of the proposal – particularly the idea to pool together financial resources in a form of a single fully mutualized fund from the very beginning.[10]

The Lithuanian Presidency's work focused at bringing the initial proposal closer to the position of Germany, trying to accommodate the interests of the UK along the way and convince the rest of the Member States, mainly led by France, and EU institutions keen on setting up a common fund and pooling financial risks across the eurozone, that Germany was too important to be marginalized. For the latter reason, the option of submitting the proposal to a QMV vote was ruled out by the Presidency.[11]

The hard-fought agreement reached in December 2013 reflected these elements – the intergovernmental basis for the single resolution fund, the regulation comprising the establishment of the decision-making structure with the strengthened role of the single resolution board as the key player, giving the Council the final say, and the use of national funds which over a ten-year period would be merged into the single resolution fund reaching 1 per cent of covered deposits in participating Member States and pooling €55 billion. The SRM covered all banks in the participating Member States, with the board being responsible for the resolution of those directly supervised by the European Central Bank (some 130 banks), with national resolution authorities being responsible for all other

[10] Interview with Lithuanian Ministry of Finance, Vilnius, 21 February 2014.
[11] Interview with Lithuanian Ministry of Finance, Vilnius, 21 February, 2014.

banks (around 6,000). It also endorsed the bail-in rules established in the Bank Recovery and Resolution Directive as applicable to the use of a single fund with the aim of locking the agreed bail-in rules and unanimity-based intergovernmental agreement. It should be noted that the EU-wide deposit guarantee was left out for an unlimited term; only the harmonization of national deposit guarantee rules was agreed.

Four insights can be drawn from these negotiations. First, they re-confirmed the importance of the three biggest EU Member States, especially the centrality of Germany. Second, the Lithuanian Presidency proved to be effective partly because it had no particular pre-defined national interest in terms of the substance of the agreement, but rather acted as a broker aiming to find a consensus that would bring Germany on board by taking into account its concerns not to make ESM funding available for this purpose before EU Treaty change. Third, being outside the eurozone did not affect the ability of the Presidency to broker agreement on the SRM. Fourth, significant changes made to the initial proposal of the European Commission indicate the limits of the move in the direction of transfer union, at least under the current Lisbon Treaty provisions.

The final deal reached with the EP under the Greek Presidency in March 2014 involved giving more powers to the EU institutions and accelerated the process of setting up a single resolution fund, allowing the EP to claim that its negotiators 'rescued a seriously damaged bank resolution system' (European Parliament, 2014, p. 1). In contrast, Lithuanian Finance Minister Rimantas Šadžius described the March agreement reached in the trilogue as being 'within the framework of that compromise which we reached on 18 December'.[12]

Shaping the Geopolitical Map (Open Europe)

Although items such as launching of the transatlantic trade and investment partnership (TTIP) with the US,[13] concluding a free trade agreement with Canada, progressing with accession negotiations with Montenegro and re-launching talks with Turkey have all been included under the priority of Open Europe, it was the Eastern Partnership that attracted the particular attention of the Lithuanian Presidency. The EaP summit in Vilnius scheduled for 28–29 November 2013 was expected to be the Presidency's number one event. Initially the priorities for the EaP included the signing of an association agreement (AA) between Ukraine and the EU; the completion of negotiations on AAs and deep and comprehensive free trade agreements (DCFTAs) with Georgia, Moldova and Armenia; advancing tangibly in negotiations with Azerbaijan; progression in facilitating and eventually liberalizing the visa regime with EaP countries; and sectoral co-operation (Council of the EU, 2013a).

As some analysts maintained, the run-up to the Eastern Partnership summit in Vilnius was 'one of the most dramatic episodes in the recent diplomatic history of the EU' (Popescu, 2013, p. 1). It should be noted that Lithuanian officials had been actively working on the EaP from before the start of the Presidency, co-operating closely with EU institutions and other Member States.[14] Ukraine attracted most attention and concern due

[12] *Baltic News Service*, 20 March 2014.
[13] See Hamilton's contribution to this volume.
[14] Interview with President of Lithuania, Dalia Grybauskaitė, Vilnius, 16 January 2014; Interview with Lithuanian Permanent Representation to the EU, Vilnius, 17 February 2014.

to its complicated domestic situation and the difficulties with the implementation of EU conditionality set for Ukrainian officials. The efforts of Lithuanian diplomats and policy-makers were directed, on the one hand, at convincing Ukrainian authorities to make progress in meeting EU conditions, and on the other hand, to forge consensus among the EU Member States regarding the need for association with Ukraine. The latter task proved to be somewhat easier, knowing how far the EU was ready to go in accommodating the concerns of Ukrainian leaders at the start of Vilnius summit.

Soon after the beginning of the Lithuanian Presidency, the Russian authorities started exerting increasing pressure on some EaP countries, mostly by using targeted trade protection measures *vis-à-vis* goods originating from Ukraine and Moldova. Russian authorities also threatened to manipulate energy supplies. After experiencing additional pressure from Russia linked to the issue of Nagorno-Karabakh, Armenian leaders declared that they intend to join the Eurasian customs union, effectively shelving the association with the EU. In September and October, the Russian authorities applied protectionist measures towards Lithuania, first by intensifying inspections of transport carriers entering Russia from the country, then later by targeting dairy products originating from Lithuania.

The attempts at convincing the Ukrainian leadership to amend its legislation, address the problem of selective justice and implement other reforms continued until the first night of the Vilnius summit. Although the Ukrainian president declared his decision to suspend the preparations for the signing of AA with the EU just a week before the summit, the negotiations behind the scenes continued. On the first night, the EU offered a plan to postpone the adoption of the legal amendments on selective justice in Ukraine up to the February EU-Ukrainian summit. The plan also included mediation to ensure financial assistance from the International Monetary Fund, and to address fears of Ukrainian leadership in terms of trade provisions of the DCFTA, the plan outlined measures to support its implementation.[15] To facilitate the agreement, it was agreed that Tymoshenko's imprisonment should be treated separately from signing the AA. However, the same night President Yanukovych rejected the deal. Moreover, he surprised EU leaders next morning unexpectedly presenting them with a declaration written in Ukrainian which was quickly rejected by the EU. The main results of the Vilnius summit, therefore, were limited to initialing AAs (and DCFTAs) with Moldova and Georgia, noting the implementation of the visa facilitation plan in the case of Moldova, and the signing of visa facilitation with Azerbaijan (a similar agreement was signed before the summit with Armenia).

The suspension of the preparations for signing the AA of the Ukrainian President prompted some observers to declare the Vilnius summit 'a fiasco', referring to the EU's lack of strategic thinking and inadequate balance between incentives and obligations aimed at the EaP countries (Emerson, 2014). Arguably it increased the interest of EU Member States in the eastern neighborhood and made them better aware of the Ukrainian situation as well as the instruments Russian authorities are prepared to use to deter EaP countries from association with the EU. The negotiations with Georgia and Moldova actually progressed faster than many expected showing that EaP can be effective when there is sufficient political consensus in the partner countries and their elites are not just using the negotiations with the EU for their domestic rent-seeking and bargaining *vis-à-vis* Russia. The preparations for the summit aided by the energy and purpose of the

---

[15] Interview with Office of the President of Lithuania, Vilnius, 3 December 2013.

Presidency generated a powerful political dynamic, which contributed both to stronger consensus in the EU and more intense efforts in some EaP partners. The signature of the political part of the AA in March 2014 might be the first step towards Ukraine's integration with the EU and far-reaching domestic reforms, but the next steps are still extremely uncertain in light of Russia's annexation of Crimea and – at the time of writing – ongoing tensions in southeastern Ukraine.

Conclusions

Usually rotating Presidencies focus on the number of agreements adopted during their term as the key indicator of success. The Lithuanian Presidency is no exception, with its reports underlining that 147 legislative acts and 283 non-legislative acts were agreed during its term – more than twice of what has been the average during previous rotating Presidencies (Grybauskaitė, 2014). It has also been stressed that co-decision files agreed with the EP (that is, 92, with 87 first reading agreements and five second reading agreements) exceeded the number of those that have been agreed in the Presidencies in the run-up to previous EP elections in 2004 and 2009.

In addition to the number of agreements brokered, the Lithuanian Presidency advanced a number of important items on the EU agenda and 'exceed[ed] expectations' (Piedrafita and Renman, 2014). They include implementing norms and programmes of the MFF 2014–20, early agreement on EU budget for 2014, advancing work on the banking union, including the general agreement within the Council on the SRM and agreement with the EP on the Bank Recovery and Resolution Directive. On most of these issues the Presidency acted as a broker motivated mostly by advancing the European agenda. In some cases, mediation between the Council and the EP and the work in trilogues overshadowed the role of the representative of the former and consumed more efforts than mediation inside the Council.

The Lithuanian Presidency worked intensely with other EU institutions, although support from the Council Secretariat General depended on particular areas, while the European Commission sometimes pursued its own agenda and did not always help the Presidency and at times was even seen as creating obstacles in the negotiations with the EP.[16] Co-operation with the High Representative Catherine Ashton and European Council President Herman Van Rompuy was important. For example, in the run up to the Vilnius summit such innovative forms of co-ordination as kick-off meetings of all institutions concerned were held.[17] The Presidency also assisted the High Representative in representing the EU in the meetings with third countries. But it was mostly due to the active efforts of the Lithuanian Presidency in the field of EaP that some analysts concluded that under the Lisbon Treaty the 'country holding Council presidency can still make a difference to the EU's external relations' (Raik 2013, p. 2).

The EP was especially visible and active at exercising its powers and testing the limits of its competencies under the Lisbon Treaty. There still are areas where institutional relations are in the process of being defined. On the one hand, this creates incentives for

[16] Interview with Lithuanian Permanent Representation to the EU, Vilnius, 15 February 2014; Interview with Lithuanian Permanent Representation to the EU, Brussels-Vilnius, 21 March 2014.
[17] Interview with Lithuanian Permanent Representation to the EU, Vilnius, 17 February 2014.

institutional competition and uncertainty. It also allows the EP to exploit the desire of each rotating Presidency to advance as much as possible in terms of legislative work, although the approaching end of the term also motivates MEPs to accelerate the legislative process. On the other hand, it provides possibilities for the rotating Presidency to show initiative and be innovative in creating ad-hoc co-ordination forums involving all relevant actors.

References

Council of the European Union (2013a) Programme of the Lithuanian Presidency of the Council of the European Union 1 July to 31 December 2013. Available at: «http://static.eu2013.lt/uploads/documents/Presidency_programme_EN.pdf».

Council of the European Union (2013b) 'Lithuanian Presidency welcomes EP consent to EU multiannual financial framework'. Press Release, 19 November. Available at: «http://www.consilium.europa.eu/uedocs/cms_data/docs/pressdata/EN/genaff/139642.pdf».

Emerson, M. (2014) 'After the Vilnius Fiasco: Who is to Blame? What is to be Done?' CEPS Essay 8 (Brussels: Centre for European Policy Studies).

European Commission (2013) Statement by President Barroso following the meeting of the European Commission with the Prime Minister of Lithuania, Mr Algirdas Butkevičius. Speech/13/361, Press Point/Brussels, 24 April.

European Parliament (2014) 'Parliament negotiators rescue seriously damaged bank resolution system'. Press release, 20 March. Available at: «http://www.europarl.europa.eu/news/en/news-room/content/20140319IPR39310/html/Parliament-negotiators-rescue-seriously-damaged-bank-resolution-system».

Grybauskaitė, D. (2014) Speech by President Dalia Grybauskaitė to the European Parliament, 15 January. Available at: «http://www.eu2013.lt/en/news/statements/speech-by-president-dalia-grybauskaite-to-the-european-parliament».

Mirguet, O. (2013) 'Grybauskaite Presents Lithuania's Priorities to EP'. *Europolitics*, 3 July. Available at: «http://www.europolitics.info/grybauskaite-presents-lithuania-s-priorities-to-ep-artr353243-32.html».

Piedrafita, S. and Renman, V. (2014) 'Exceeding Expectations, Lithuania Moves the Trio Presidency Forward'. *CEPS Commentary*, 22 January.

Pop, V. (2013) 'Lithuania Faces Record Legislative Load for EU Presidency'. *EUObserver*, 4 June. Available at: «http://euobserver.com/lithuania/120299».

Popescu, N. (2013) 'After Vilnius'. Issue Alert 40 (Paris: European Union Institute for Security Studies).

Raik, K. (2013) 'Lithuania's Presidency Gamble'. FIIA Comment 14 (Helsinki: Finish Institute of International Affairs).

Vilpišauskas, R. (2013) 'Lithuanian Foreign Policy Since EU Accession: Torn between History and Interdependence'. In Braun, M. and Marek, D. (eds) *The New Member States and the European Union: Foreign Policy and Europeanization* (Basingstoke: Palgrave Macmillan).

Vilpišauskas, R., Vandecasteele, B. and Vaznonytė, A. (2013) 'The Lithuanian Presidency of the Council of the European Union Advancing Energy Policy and Eastern Partnership Goals: Conditions for Exerting Influence'. *Lithuanian Foreign Policy Review*, No. 29, pp. 11–37.

JCMS 2014 Volume 52 Annual Review pp. 109–124   DOI: 10.1111/jcms.12161

Governance and Institutions: The Unrelenting Rise of the European Parliament

DESMOND DINAN
George Mason University

Introduction

The year 2013 was an interregnum for the EU between the feverish events of the eurozone crisis and the impending institutional changes of 2014, beginning with the European Parliament (EP) elections in May. By late 2012 it seemed as if the crisis, though far from over, had peaked. The rapidly deteriorating situation in Cyprus in early 2013 was the sting in the tail of the crisis, but it seemed to be atypical because of the vast amount of Russian money that had flowed into the island's banks (Gros, 2013). Bad though the situation was, especially for ordinary Cypriot bank depositors, it did not detract from a general feeling of relief among politicians, officials and pundits that the EU was over the worst. As European Council President Herman Van Rompuy remarked in the opening paragraph of his report on the European Council in 2013:

> For Europe, 2013 was a year of 'in-between' – after the violence of the storm, but before the darkest clouds had cleared. [. . .] market tensions abated during the year, and we could safely say that the existential threats from the financial crisis were now firmly behind us. (Council of the European Union, 2014, p. 5)

Barring the unexpected, the next big development for the EU would be the institutional changes of 2014. In addition to a newly-elected EP, these would include a new Commission, a new President of the European Council and a new High Representative for Foreign Affairs and Security Policy/Vice-Commissioner. Ordinarily, routine institutional rearrangements, no matter how consequential, would not arouse much political interest more than 12 months beforehand. By mid-2013, however, Brussels was abuzz with speculation about the procedure for selecting the next Commission President and the implications of this for the nature of the Commission Presidency, the future of the Commission, and relations between the Commission, the EP and the European Council. Driving this speculation was the EP's determination to exploit seemingly minor modifications in the Lisbon Treaty.

The apparent demise of the eurozone crisis – or at least its passage from an acute to a chronic stage – and growing political attention to the institutional changes of 2014 may have given 2013 the appearance of an interregnum for the EU, but it hardly constituted an intermission. Far from slowing down, the pace of events – whether taking important legislative decisions or shoring up the wobbly edifice of economic and monetary union (EMU) – remained as rapid as ever before. In addition, difficult negotiations between the EP and the Council over the Multiannual Financial Framework (MFF) dragged on throughout the year. In all three areas – legislative decision-making, EMU reform (notably by means of establishing a banking union[1]) and concluding the MFF – the EP was particularly assertive and effective. Institutionally, 2013 was clearly a year in which the EP once again outshone the Commission and successfully stood up to the Member States, as represented not only in the Council (constituting ordinary ministers) but also in the European Council (constituting national leaders).

For the first year since the onset of the crisis, the European Council reverted to a normal, non-crisis mode of operation. As Van Rompuy (2013, p. 1) remarked at the end of the May 2013 European Council, the meeting 'was quite different from the crisis management meetings we have got used to'. Meetings of the Euro Summit in 2013 were also less frequent and less fraught than in previous years. A noteworthy development in 2013 was that the European Council adopted 'rules for the organisation of the proceedings of the Euro Summits', setting out how meetings were to be prepared, conducted and followed up. EU leaders adopted these rules in accordance with existing practices and treaty provisions, such as Article 12 of the Treaty on Stability, Co-ordination and Governance in the Economic and Monetary Union (the Fiscal Compact), dealing with the Euro Summit and the role of its President (European Council, 2013a).

As if to emphasize that 2013 may have been an interregnum but not an intermission, the EU once again expanded, with Croatia becoming the 28th Member State. As a small Member State (21st out of 28 in both population and gross domestic product), Croatia would hardly make a splash in the EU; it would be in neither the eurozone nor the Schengen area for some time to come. Yet Croatia's accession illustrated the institutional challenges of enlargement, especially for the Commission.[2]

The EP, by contrast, took enlargement in its stride. Though Croatia's accession generated a small influx of new Members of the European Parliament (MEPs), the EP would shrink slightly to 751 members following the 2014 elections, as mandated by the Lisbon Treaty. Whereas the vast majority of MEPs knew little and possibly cared less about the minutiae of parliamentary business, the EP's leadership proved adept in 2013 at positioning the institution at the forefront of EU affairs, ranging from 'ordinary' budgetary and legislative matters to EMU reform, transatlantic relations, foreign and security policy, and other important activities. As noted in last year's contribution, the EP owed its success in large part to the formidable leadership of President Martin Schulz (Dinan, 2013). Klaus Welle, the EP's politically astute Secretary-General, was equally influential, only slightly behind the scenes, in advancing the institution's interests and standing.

This contribution examines the EP's success during the 'in-between' year of 2013 not only in setting the agenda for the selection of the next Commission President but also, due partly to wide-ranging reforms, in continuing to master the inherently complicated legislative process. First, however, the article reviews the institutional implications of Croatia's accession.

I. Croatia's Accession

Compared to the formidable institutional impact of central and eastern enlargement in 2004–7, Croatia's accession sent small but nonetheless significant ripples throughout the

---

[1] See Howarth and Quaglia's contribution to this volume.
[2] On EU enlargement, see the contributions by Grabbe and Whitman and Juncos in this volume.

EU. Croatian became a new official language, bringing the total to 24, and raising translation and interpretation costs accordingly (European Commission, 2012). Croatian judges joined the Court of Justice and the General Court. Far from being burdensome, the appointment of an additional judge to each court would likely improve the courts' efficiency by reducing the workloads of the other judges, however slightly (Council of the European Union, 2012).

The addition of one more member to the European Council hardly mattered. The Council had long since lost the intimacy of its early days, when nine national leaders could engage in cozy fireside chats. Following successive rounds of enlargement and the European Council's growing political prominence, the institution has been dominated by the EU's most influential national leaders, coming from the largest Member States. Croatia's prime minister would not rock the boat.

Similarly, Croatia's impact on the Council was not profound: one more ministerial member; one more member of the Council preparatory committees. Croatia received seven votes in the Council, and the threshold for a qualified majority rose to 260 out of a total of 352 votes, cast by at least 15 countries. Croatia's small number of votes could make the difference between a qualified majority and a blocking minority on a key legislative proposal, but the outcome of Council decisions rarely hinged on such a small margin (Van Aken, 2012). In the event that a Member State requested verification that a qualified majority represented at least 62 per cent of the EU's population, the threshold in 2013 was around 315 million people out of a total of 508 million (Council of the European Union, 2013).

Croatia received an allocation of 12 seats in the EP. Elections for Croatia's MEPs took place on 14 April. The turnout was dismal – a mere 20.8 per cent of registered voters. This may have been due in part to the fact that EP elections would again take place in Croatia in May 2014, as part of the EU-wide elections for a new EP. On that occasion, Croatia's allocation of seats would fall to 11, in keeping with the reduction of the EP's size to 751 seats, under the terms of the Lisbon Treaty.

The Commission bore most of the institutional burden of Croatia's accession. The arrival of one more Commissioner was far more momentous for the Commission than was the arrival of one more minister in the Council or prime minister in the European Council. It was widely accepted that the Commission was already creaking under the weight of too many Commissioners, each of whom needed to have at least the appearance of a meaningful portfolio. Efforts to reduce the Commission's size to fewer members than there are Member States date back to the negotiations for the Amsterdam Treaty, in 1996–7. Following a breakthrough in the Nice Treaty of 2001 on reducing the Commission's size, the Lisbon Treaty provided that as of November 2014, with the formation of the first Commission following the entry into force of the Treaty, the Commission would consist of a number of members corresponding to two-thirds of the number of Member States, unless the European Council unanimously decided otherwise.

The European Council duly decided otherwise in May 2013: the Commission would continue to consist of a number of members equal to the number of Member States (European Council, 2013b). This was in line with the political agreements that the European Council reached in December 2008 and June 2009, noting the concerns of the Irish people with respect to the Lisbon Treaty and the Irish government's insistence, for the sake of holding (and winning) the second referendum on the Lisbon Treaty, on continuing the practice of having one commissioner per Member State. The European Council's May 2013 decision facilitated the appointment of a Croatian commissioner.

One month earlier, on 25 April, Croatia named Neven Mimica, a government minister with considerable experience in EU affairs, as its Commissioner-designate. Commission President José Manuel Barroso accepted the nomination and identified consumer policy as the Commissioner-designate's portfolio. This would be hived off from the portfolio of health and consumer protection, much to the chagrin of the Commissioner holding that portfolio, Tonio Borg, from Malta. The EP's Internal Market and Consumer Protection Committee (IMCO), together with the Environment, Public Health and Food Safety Committee (ENVI), held hearings on Mimica's nomination on 4 June. Despite some grumbling from MEPs, especially in the European People's Party, about Mimica's answers to their questions, he sailed through the hearing. On 12 June, the EP voted overwhelmingly in support of his nomination (565 votes in favour, 64 against and 64 abstentions) (European Parliament, 2013a). This paved the way for the Council to appoint Mimica to the Commission, by common accord with Barroso. Mimica took up his post on 1 July, when Croatia acceded to the EU.

Having one more participant in the weekly meetings of the Commission may seem as innocuous as having one more national leader in the European Council. Whereas the leaders of less influential Member States tend to be unassuming in the European Council, Commissioners are far less deferential at meetings of the college. Moreover, a new commissioner means a new head of cabinet (private office) and deputy-head of cabinet, which in turn means another voice in the weekly meetings of the heads of cabinet and deputy-heads of cabinet. The overall effect is to slow down deliberations at the top of the Commission's decision-making structure, which are already on the slow side because of Barroso's preference for reaching consensus.

The arrival of an additional commissioner and an additional head and deputy-head of cabinet, the proliferation of separate portfolios, and the increasing number of directorates-general and services highlights the difficulty of co-ordinating the work of the college and of the Commission as a whole. Jacques Delors, the most successful President in the Commission's history, managed a college of 18 commissioners, which he frequently complained was far too large, by having Pascal Lamy, his head of cabinet, ride roughshod over other cabinet heads and play a powerful co-ordinating role. With many more commissioners and cabinets, and a President (Barroso) whose management style is more accommodating and less combative than Delors's, the Commission is undoubtedly unwieldy and less effective than it otherwise might be.

Under these circumstances, the role of the Secretariat-General is particularly important, and Catherine Day, while extremely competent, was hamstrung by the enormous demands on her time, a tendency to micromanage and the fallout from the resignation in October 2012 of Commissioner John Dalli after an anti-fraud inquiry linked him to an attempt to influence tobacco legislation. Nevertheless, Day instituted a number of changes in the Secretariat-General to improve co-ordination among commissioners, directorates-general and services, and to improve co-ordination during the entire policy-making process. Perhaps the most significant of these changes is an increase to seven in the number of units involved in policy co-ordination.

Speaking to the Dutch parliament in December 2013, Schulz, who emerged during the year as a leading contender to succeed Barroso as Commission President (see below), voiced his dissatisfaction with the Commission's internal organization and suggested how he might change things in the Berlaymont:

> We have 28 Commissioners, whose portfolios all too often overlap and collide. And each one of these 28 Commissioners wants their moment of glory. So they produce more directives and regulations. Thousands more pages of legislation. In a way that is increasingly difficult to coordinate efficiently. This has to stop! If we want to change the way the Union is run, the next President of the Commission must lead by example – and start with the Commission. He may not be able to reduce the number of Commissioners as foreseen by the Lisbon Treaty. [. . .] But he or she can decide to [. . .] cut the 33 Commission departments and concentrate on priorities. (Schulz, 2013a)

The European Council noted in its decision of May 2013 that:

> In view of its effect on the functioning of the Commission, the European Council will review this decision well in advance of the appointment of the first Commission following the date of accession of the 30th Member State or the appointment of the Commission succeeding that due to take up its duties on 1 November 2014, whichever is earlier. (European Council, 2013b)

Implicit in the European Council's statement is that having 28 commissioners is detrimental to the Commission, and that a decision to reduce the Commission's size would be taken well before a new Commission is put in place in 2019. Presumably the European Council would decide on the Lisbon formula of a Commission corresponding to two-thirds of the number of Member States. Although the small Member States remain sensitive on the subject of the Commission's size, it is unlikely that one of them would veto such a decision. Nor is it likely that public opinion, even in Ireland, would strongly oppose such a development.

Apart from its impact on the college and on the institution's efficiency, the arrival of a new Member State upsets the Commission's recruitment and promotion system. Like any international organization, the Commission has to balance merit and national representation in the recruitment and promotion of officials. The Commission's recruitment targets with respect to Croatia were 149 officials at administrator level by July 2018, with one official at director-general level and three at director level. This may seem reasonable and fair, except to well-qualified officials from other Member States competing for these coveted positions.

II. The Ever More Assertive EP

Schulz's outspokenness about the Commission was not unusual. As noted in last year's review, Schulz is a new breed of EP President (Dinan, 2013). Unlike his predecessors in that office, Schulz is not a figurehead. He does not hesitate to assert the interests of the EP or to castigate the Commission, the Council and the European Council. The contrast between Schulz's opening speeches at meetings of the European Council and the opening speeches of former EP Presidents is striking. So is the feeling of frustration on Schulz's part that, by virtue of being EP President, he is unable to participate in the European Council proper (he must leave after making an opening speech).

Lecturing the European Council

This is what Schulz told the European Council in February 2013 about prospects for agreement on the MFF:

> I would strongly urge you to take account of both the financial and the more fundamental issues raised by the EP. You all have a wealth of experience in dealing with your national parliaments, so you know only too well that you have to take [MEPs'] views seriously if you want their consent to your proposals. [The current proposal] will not secure the approval of the EP. (Schulz, 2013b)

Following the EP's rejection of the European Council's proposed MFF on 13 March, Schulz told the European Council the following day that:

> This cannot have come as any surprise to you, because my fellow MEPs had set out their position in several resolutions [and because] at subsequent summits, I myself have repeatedly urged you to take the EP's priorities and red lines into account in your discussions. (Schulz, 2013c)

Six months later, with negotiations between the EP and the Council coming down to the wire, Schulz reminded the European Council that '[t]he EP showed that it was prepared to compromise when we accepted a lower budget for the forthcoming financial framework. Now it is up to the Council to fulfill its side of the bargain' (Schulz, 2013d).

Schulz was equally forthcoming in his criticism of the Council for its alleged tardiness and timorousness in shoring up EMU. 'The EP is extremely concerned at the delays in establishing a banking union,' he told the European Council in June 2013. Commenting on the ECOFIN agreement earlier that morning, 'after months of stalling tactics', on the resolution of failed banks, Schulz decried the ministers' 'lack of ambition' and warned that '[t]he Council can therefore look forward to tough negotiations with the EP, because we intend to make sure that no more banks have to be bailed out with taxpayer's money' (Schulz, 2013e). Schulz continued to inveigle against the finance ministers when addressing the European Council in December.

> If the ECOFIN decisions become a reality, then the Banking Union will not only fail to have positive effects, it could even have negative ones. [. . .] If we were to implement the ECOFIN decisions on a banking union in this way, it [. . .] would be the biggest mistake yet in the resolution of the crisis. [. . .] A Banking Union is something which must either be done right or not done at all. The EP will therefore not support the ECOFIN decisions in this form. (Schulz, 2013f)

Even more impressive was Schulz's forthrightness in attacking the European Council directly for its alleged subversion of the Community method.

> [MEPs] have a clear message which you should take with you into today's discussions [. . .] don't venture any further down the slippery slope towards intergovernmentalism! The Community method, as embodied in the relationship between the Community institutions, is not only more effective, it is also more democratic. [. . .] For some years now you have been taking an increasing number of legislative decisions at your level [. . .] and thus effectively reintroducing the unanimity principle. (Schulz, 2013c)

He returned to this theme when addressing the European Council in June:

> [The EP] should like to remind you once again that under the Treaties the European
> Council does not have the right to propose legislation. It is not your task to issue the
> Commission with instructions regarding the form and content of legislative proposals.
> This arrogation of rights by the European Council is undermining the division of powers
> within the European Union and, by extension, undermining our European democracy. Let
> me address these remarks directly to you, President Barroso: it is the Commission's task
> to put forward legislative proposals. (Schulz, 2013e)

These lengthy quotations are interesting not only in their own right, but also because of
Schulz's effort to change the way in which the next Commission President would
be selected, as well as his undisguised interest in getting the job himself. Yet it is difficult
to imagine that Schulz's unceasing criticism of national ministers won him many friends
in the European Council. His forthrightness also alienated some members of his own
Socialists and Democrats Group in the EP, and in the wider Party of European Socialists.
Indeed, his partisan and unapologetically assertive style as President of the EP seemed to
have ruffled feathers among parliamentarians of all persuasions.

Selecting the Next Commission President

Schulz's harsh words might come back to haunt him if, following the May 2014 elections,
the Socialists and Democrats seek to build a coalition in the EP to advance Schulz's
candidacy for the Commission Presidency. Even if Schulz won the support of an absolute
majority of MEPs, would the European Council agree to nominate him for the job? The
fact that a new selection procedure for the Commission President was even under consideration owed much to Schulz's assertiveness, and also to that of Klaus Welle,
Secretary-General of the EP.

    As Welle liked to point out in speeches that he gave in 2013, the Lisbon Treaty included
a number of changes with respect to the selection of the Commission President. On
the face of it, these changes were relatively small. They were intended to regularize the
practice that had developed over the previous few years whereby the EP approved the
European Council's nominee for Commission President. In 2004, for instance, the EP
voted narrowly in favour of Barroso's appointment. In 2009, Barroso won greater support
in the EP but only after he introduced a programme for the Commission's next term, at the
behest of the EP.

    Schulz and Welle exploited these relatively minor modifications in the Lisbon Treaty
to build a case for an entirely new approach to selecting and electing the Commission
President. As Welle mentioned in a speech in Brussels in September 2013:

> [P]eople are now finding out – to their astonishment – that [. . .] the Lisbon Treaty has
> very much changed the legal basis for the process on how to get the Commission into
> office. First, the EP 'elects' – not simply 'approves' – the Commission President. Second,
> the European Council selects its nominee for President based on the outcome of the
> European elections. (Welle, 2013a)

As Welle gleefully pointed out in another speech, in June 2013:

> This is complemented by [. . .] Declaration No. 11. [. . .] Nobody knows Declaration No. 11
> [of the Lisbon Treaty]! Well, I have asked our Legal Service, they did not know Declaration

No. 11 either. [. . .] Declaration No. 11 [says] that the President[s] of the European Council and the European Parliament have to set up a mechanism to consult on which name is to be proposed for [Commission] President by the European Council. That is something that should happen between the European elections [. . .] of May [2014] and the European Council making the proposal at the end of June. [This is] very important [. . .] because it is [. . .] public recognition that the outcome of the European elections matters and that the different political forces in the EP have to express themselves about which one of the potential candidates could also have a parliamentary majority. (Welle, 2013b)

Welle was alluding to one aspect of what he called the 'unused potential' of the Lisbon Treaty. His explanation reveals why the EP is so successful at enhancing its institutional and political power. It was the EP's President and Secretary-General, not the legal service, who appreciated the opportunity which the Lisbon Treaty presented to inject political competition into the selection of the Commission President, while in the process clipping the wings of the European Council, boosting the standing of the EP and possibly increasing voter interest (and therefore turnout) in the May 2014 elections.

The logical follow-on was for the European political parties to choose candidates for the Commission Presidency. By voting for the candidate of a particular European party in the EP election, a voter – regardless of the country in which he or she votes – would be voting as well for a particular candidate for Commission President. Schulz made it clear early in 2013 that he would be the candidate of the Party of European Socialists, though he would not officially secure the candidacy until a special congress took place in Rome in March 2014. Other European parties followed the Socialists' lead and decided to select their own candidates for Commission President, also in early 2014.

The outcome of the May 2014 elections and the formation of the new Commission will undoubtedly form the centrepiece of the article on governance and institutions in next year's *JCMS Annual Review*. What is important from the perspective of 2013 is how the EP set the agenda on this issue and, in the process, precipitated a showdown between the European Council and the EP over the choice of Barroso's successor. German Chancellor Angela Merkel and other national leaders voiced their disagreement with the EP's interpretation of the implications of the Lisbon Treaty changes. As a Christian Democrat, Merkel was an opponent of Schulz, a Social Democrat, though the Christian Democrats and the Social Democrats formed a grand coalition in Germany in December 2013. As a leading member of the European Council, Merkel did not like being told by the EP how the procedure for the selection of the next Commission President should unfold. Of course, no single member of the European Council is able to veto a nominee for Commission President as the European Council may decide the issue by a qualified majority vote.

Regardless of whether the EP's position prevails, the EP's interpretation of the Lisbon Treaty changes suggests an understanding of EU governance that is somewhat simplistic and at variance with the complexity of the EU system. Just as Schulz likened the EP's opposition to the European Council's proposed MFF to a national parliament's opposition to a national government's proposed budget, Welle compared European voters' choice of Commission President among the candidates presented by the European political parties in the EP elections to national voters' choice of national leaders among the candidates presented by national political parties in national elections. Inevitably, Welle took Germany as an example (Welle is German and the key national election within the EU in 2013 took place in Germany).

As he said in a speech in September 2013, the nomination by European political parties of candidates for Commission President

> is a very important change because it means that voters [will] have an idea about who would lead the Commission depending on the outcome of the European elections. That is something which on [a] national level is absolutely normal. Let's take the elections in Germany [. . .] the big [questions are]: Should it be Merkel? Should it be Steinbrück? Who is going to get the Executive? [. . .] If from now on, also in the EU, voters could know in advance who the personal alternatives are [. . .] then we also would have a much higher degree of legitimacy. (Welle, 2013c)

Schulz was emphatic when he addressed the European Council in March 2013:

> If we want a genuinely democratic European Union, one which has the ability to take effective action and which is accepted by ordinary people, then the Commission must be transformed into a proper European government which is elected by, and whose work is scrutinized by, the EP. (Schulz, 2013c)

Schulz and Welle were trying to appeal to voters, on the one hand, and to national leaders, on the other. Their strategy was to draw as close an analogy as possible between the unfamiliar EU system of governance and familiar national systems of governance. What could be simpler than to compare the EP to a national parliament, and to compare EP elections to national elections? In each case, elections result in the parliament (European or national) electing a leader (Commission President or chancellor/prime minister) to form the executive (Commission or government).

The problem is that the EU is markedly different from a national political system. The Commission has executive responsibilities, but is not analogous to a national government. The European Council plays a key governing role in the EU system, but is not the EU's government. The EP's legislative responsibilities resemble those of a national parliament, though the EP is not allowed to initiate legislation, among other differences. The EP's budgetary responsibilities are similar to those of a national parliament, and the EP is developing scrutiny powers similar to those of national parliaments. Still, the EP and other EU institutions are engaged in a system of governing and governance that defies easy categorization. For political purposes, however, it suits the EP to play down the EU's uniqueness and emphasize its ordinariness. In doing so, the EP aims to build popular support and legitimacy for the EU, while increasing its own power in the evolving EU political system.

Legislative Programming

Another aspect of the Lisbon Treaty's 'unused potential', frequently mentioned by Welle throughout 2013, concerned a core EP activity: legislative decision-making. Welle was referring not to the decision-making process following the submission of a Commission proposal to the Council, the EP and national parliaments (in most cases involving the ordinary legislative procedure), but to legislative programming during the pre-proposal stage.

Following on from the question 'Who knows Declaration No. 11?', Welle liked to ask 'Who knows the phrase on programming in Article 17 of the Lisbon Treaty?' The article in question includes a seemingly innocuous sentence: '[The Commission] shall initiate the

Union's annual and multiannual programming with a view to achieving interinstitutional agreements'. According to Welle, the Commission is familiar with the first part of the sentence but 'doesn't want to know' the second part. In other words, the Commission is happy to draft its annual and multiannual programs for legislative proposals but is uninterested in doing so on the basis of interinstitutional agreements, if that is, in fact, what the Treaty calls for. Welle thinks that it does:

> [I]t is not just that the Commission is invited to initiate [. . .] legislation. No. [The requirement] *to reach inter-institutional agreement* [. . .] means that we should have a consultative process, which should involve the two law-makers – the Council and the Parliament – to agree on the annual and on the multiannual legislative programme. (Welle, 2013b)

With the approval of the EP's Bureau, Welle reorganized the Presidency Directorate-General, giving the Deputy Secretary General special responsibility in the area of joint legislative programming. This was part of an effort to increase the EP's power by extending its legislative involvement from the post-proposal to the pre-proposal stage, thereby strengthening the EP's ability to influence the initiation of legislation, which is exclusively the Commission's prerogative. Welle was less interested in influencing the current Commission than in pressuring the next Commission to conclude interinstitutional agreements for legislative programming at the outset of its mandate. Such an outcome would significantly shift the interinstitutional balance in the legislative process in favour of the EP and the Council, to the detriment of the Commission.

An interinstitutional agreement on legislative programming, reached soon after the election of a new Parliament and formation of a new Commission, would undoubtedly expedite legislative decision-making early in the mandates of both institutions. Given the 2014 calendar – EP elections in May and the investiture of a new Commission in November (unless a showdown between the EP and the European Council delays the process) – little new legislation could be expected to pass before the end of 2014. Interinstitutional co-operation on legislative programming immediately after the investiture of the new Commission would help the Council Presidency in the first half of 2015 – the first full Presidency following the institutional changes – to be more productive in the legislative arena than the first full Presidencies following the turnover of the EP and the Commission usually are.

III. The Ever More Effective EP

Regardless of whether it succeeds in framing the EP elections as elections for the EU executive or in influencing legislative programming, the EP is increasingly effective in the conduct of everyday business. Perhaps because the monthly trek between Brussels and Strasbourg is so expensive and detrimental to the EP's image, the EP's leadership is adept at improving efficiency in the institution itself. The EP has a relatively new unit dealing with cost and quality control, under the direct supervision of the Secretary-General. The purpose of this unit and a key objective of the Secretariat-General more broadly is to improve the allocation of resources, especially qualified staff assistance and reliable information, to MEPs.

Accordingly, the EP has undertaken various in-house improvements, small and large. For instance, it reorganized committee meetings and plenary sessions in order to make better use of the interpreters' precious time. Setting up a 'one-stop-shop' for MEPs was another small improvement. In February 2013, following a wide consultation among MEPs aimed at finding ways to help them navigate the EP's complex bureaucracy, the EP Bureau (leadership) asked the Secretary-General to set up a facility to provide administrative support and assistance to MEPs at one location. The staff of the one-stop-shop let MEPs know exactly 'who does what' in the EP's labyrinthine administration. In cases where administrative matters require the involvement of different Directorates-General or services, the one-stop-shop identifies the leading service to assume responsibility for overall co-ordination. The new service came into operation in early 2014 (European Parliament, 2013b).

More substantively, work continued in 2013 on an ambitious, long-term EP project called 'Mapping the Cost of Non-Europe, 2014–19'. Consciously echoing Commission and EP efforts in the mid-1980s to calculate the costs of not pursuing deeper market integration, the current 'Cost of Non-Europe' exercise aimed to quantify the potential efficiency gains from deeper integration in a number of policy fields advocated by the EP, such as the digital single market, defence procurement and energy. Not surprisingly, the EP's analysis suggested massive gains, with the EU economy being 'boosted by some €800 billion – or six per cent of current GDP – by such measures over time' (European Parliament Research Service, 2014). The purpose of the mapping exercise was not only to bolster the case for deeper integration, but also to shape the legislative agenda during the mandate of the next Commission. By means of the mapping exercise, 'Parliament, through its own work, has thus put itself in a position to be able to shape the [legislative] agenda for the coming five years' (Welle, 2014).

At the same time, the EP is trying to improve the quality of its participation in the legislative decision-making process in a number of novel ways. Influenced by the work of the United States General Accounting Office, the EP hopes to nudge the Court of Auditors toward conducting assessments of the impact of EU legislation and spending programmes rather than simply accounting for the expenditure of EU funds, with a view to using the assessments to shape the EP's input into the procedure of amending existing legislation that constitutes the majority of EU legislation. Along the same lines, in 2013 the Commission negotiated an agreement with the EU's advisory bodies – the Committee of the Regions and the Economic and Social Committee – to ensure better co-ordination of the work of the three institutions during the legislative process (the agreement was signed in February 2014). Such co-operation would allow EP rapporteurs and shadow-rapporteurs to draw on the results of assessments of the impact of European directives and programmes, carried out by the two committees in Member States, thereby improving the quality of the EP's input into the legislative procedure (European Economic and Social Committee, 2014).

In November 2013, the EP inaugurated the Directorate-General for Parliamentary Research Service (DG EPRS). The new DG brought together two existing units – the library and the unit responsible for conducting impact assessment of legislative proposals as well as 'Mapping the Cost of Non-Europe' – and a new unit, the Members' Research Service, modelled on the US Congressional Research Service. The research service aims primarily at providing MEPs with reliable information on a wide range of issues coming before them in plenary sessions, especially in areas outside their areas of expertise and beyond the scope of their committee responsibilities. The combined output of the research service, the 'Cost of Non-Europe' exercise, and the impact assessments led the EP to claim that it

> could be seen as the biggest Think Tank in Brussels. The Think Tank section of the Europarl website is a self-conscious reflection of this fact and it will continue to be developed along these lines – providing a major contribution to public debate. (European Parliament, 2013c)

As well as providing high-quality information to MEPs via the Research Service, the EP has been improving the level of expertise available to assist MEPs in the conduct of their core business: 'politics and legislation' (Welle, 2013b). This includes strengthening both the policy departments and the committee secretariats of the EP, notably those that acquired a heavier workload as a result of changes in the Lisbon Treaty and the onset of the eurozone crisis. For instance, the EP increased the size of the international trade committee secretariat from four to 12 officials, commensurate with the launch of the negotiations for the Transatlantic Trade and Investment Partnership. Similarly, the EP is trying to improve the quality of draft amendments by using the expertise of the lawyer-linguists in the legislative procedure rather than exclusively in finalizing legislative texts.

The legislative output of the EU accelerated at the end of 2013, in the run-up to the 2014 elections. In a resolution of 4 July 2013, the EP called among other things for action to complete the Commission's current work programme before the end of the EP's mandate, particularly with respect to the single market in services, the digital agenda and the internal market in energy, promising 'to engage in intensive negotiation with the Council and Commission before the end of its mandate to complete as many dossiers as possible' (European Parliament, 2013d). Schulz told the European Council forcefully in October that:

> We need to identify the most important legislative files and work energetically to progress them. Hundreds of legislative procedures are due to be completed by the end of this electoral term. The European Parliament is willing and able to finish this work by May 2014. However, we consider it sensible to highlight a few particularly important projects. Priority must be given to addressing the creation of the banking union and adoption of the financial rules, economic policy governance including the social dimension, data protection, access to credit, and combating youth unemployment. [. . .] there must be an end to the stonewalling on some important legislative acts. (Schulz, 2013d)

The high legislative workload put the Lithuanian Council Presidency under considerable strain. During Lithuania's six months in office (July–December 2013), the Council and the EP adopted 147 legal acts, including several highly complex pieces of legislation[3]. According to one assessment of Lithuania's performance, the Presidency's 'overall success was only slightly marred by the haste with which a few agreements were negotiated' (Piedrafita and Renman, 2014).

Concerns about the quality of decision-making went beyond possible pressure on the Council Presidency to complete the Commission's annual and multiannual legislative

---

[3] See Vilpišauskas's contribution to this volume.

programmes and extended to the widespread practice of reaching decisions during the first-reading stage of the co-decision procedure, through the use of informal Commission–Council–EP trilogues, a point raised in last year's *Annual Review* (Dinan, 2013). Although many MEPs grumbled that these trilogues are too opaque and powerful, and rob the EP of its right – and duty – to examine and debate legislative proposals openly and fully, the pressure of so many proposals in the legislative pipeline makes recourse to trilogues early in the decision-making process too attractive for the EP's leadership to resist. Thus the EP's leadership, on the one hand, is trying to improve the quality of expertise and information available to help ordinary MEPs make informed decisions about complex legislative proposals, while, on the other hand, is facilitating a practice that arguably denies ordinary MEPs the opportunity to become extensively involved in the legislative process.

Often unstated in this discussion is that many – perhaps most – MEPs are not that interested in legislating to begin with. The EP is doing everything possible to provide MEPs with a first-class service and extensive resources, but the quality of MEPs themselves is highly variable. MEPs in leadership positions – the President and Vice-Presidents, party group leaders, committee chairs and vice-chairs, rapporteurs and shadow-rapporteurs – are almost always extremely competent and committed to their work. The quality of MEPs is a function of how the institution is regarded by politicians and the public in the Member States, and the process of selecting candidates for EP elections, which varies among Member States but does not generally favour the selection of first-rate candidates. Much to its frustration, especially in the run-up to the 2014 elections, the EP's leadership is unable adequately to influence either of these factors.

Conclusions

The eurozone crisis has been a wrenching experience for the EU. The fallout from it continued to have a profound impact on EU governance and institutions in 2013. The crisis turned the spotlight on the European Council, but other institutions were deeply affected as well. The European Semester, the main instrument of economic governance to emerge from the crisis, engaged the European Council, the Council, the Commission and the EP in an elaborate set of measures and procedures. It also further enmeshed the national and European levels of governance, through the intense involvement of national ministries and national parliaments.

Developments in EU governance and institutions in 2013 reflected the continuing impact of the eurozone crisis, as well as challenges such as the accession of another Member State, the quotidian demands of legislative decision-making and the perennial need for greater accountability and efficiency. Most striking was the ascendancy of the EP. Yet the rise of the EP is not new. Indeed, it is a recurring theme in the institutional history of the EU and of the Communities that preceded it (Rittberger, 2005). The EP owes its success over time to effective leadership, political opportunity (often because of treaty change) and the moral authority that comes from being the only directly-elected EU institution. In 2013, the EP had powerful leadership in the form of Schulz (its President) and Welle (its Secretary-General), and had political opportunity because of the 'unused potential' of the Lisbon Treaty. Schulz and Welle exploited a relatively minor treaty change, and used the political authority that derives from direct elections to try to bring about a major institutional realignment in the EU – one that would further advance the EP's position.

At the very least, the EP's determination to alter the process by which the Commission President is selected, and the European political parties' plans to nominate candidates for the position, injected considerable excitement into EU politics, notably among those already interested in the subject. Whether that excitement would be infectious, spread more widely throughout the EU and result in a significantly higher turnout in the EP elections remained to be seen as 2013 came to a close.

References

Council of the European Union (2012) Reform of the General Court, 14916/12, Brussels, 15 October 2013. Available at: «http://www.statewatch.org/news/2012/oct/eu-council-reform-ecj-14916-12.pdf».

Council of the European Union (2013) Factsheet: Changes within the European Union as from 1 July 2013 related to the accession of Croatia. Available at: «http://www.consilium.europa.eu/uedocs/cms_data/docs/pressdata/EN/genaff/137537.pdf».

Council of the European Union (2014) *The European Council in 2013* (Luxembourg: Publications Office of the European Union).

Dinan, D. (2013) 'Governance and Institutions: Stresses Above and Below the Waterline'. *JCMS*, Vol. 51, No. s1, pp. 89–102.

European Commission (2012) DG Translation Management Plan 2013, Directorate-General for Translation. Brussels, 18 December. Available at: «http://ec.europa.eu/atwork/synthesis/amp/doc/dgt_2013_mp_en.pdf».

European Council (2013a) European Council, 14/15 March 2013, Conclusions. Available at: «http://www.consilium.europa.eu/uedocs/cms_data/docs/pressdata/en/ec/136151.pdf».

European Council (2013b) The European Council decides on the number of members of the European Commission. Brussels, 22 May. Available at: «http://www.consilium.europa.eu/uedocs/cms_data/docs/pressdata/en/ec/137221.pdf».

European Economic and Social Committee (2014) Cooperation Agreement between the European Parliament, the European Economic and Social Committee, and the Committee of the Regions, 5 February. Available at: «http://www.eesc.europa.eu/?i=portal.en.eu-cooperation.31292».

European Parliament (2013a) Hearings on Commissioner-Designate Mimica. Available at: «http://www.europarl.europa.eu/croatiancommissionerhearing/».

European Parliament (2013b) Introducing the one-stop-shop for Members. Brussels, 16 December. Available at: «http://www.europarl.europa.eu/the-secretary-general/en/activities/recent_activities/articles/articles-2013/articles-2013-december/articles-2013-december-2.html».

European Parliament (2013c) Creating the European Parliament Research Service (DG-EPRS). Brussels, 14 November. Available at: «http://www.europarl.europa.eu/the-secretary-general/en/activities/recent_activities/articles/articles-2013/articles-2013-november/articles-2013-november-2.html».

European Parliament (2013d) Resolution of 4 July 2013 on the European Parliament's priorities for the Commission Work Programme, 2014 (2013/2679(RSP)). Available at: «http://www.europarl.europa.eu/sides/getDoc.do?type=TA&reference=P7-TA-2013-0332&language=EN».

European Parliament Research Service (2014) *Mapping the Cost of Non-Europe, 2014–19* (Brussels: European Parliament).

Gros, D. (2013) 'The Meaning of Cyprus: Moving towards Banking Union?' CEPS Commentary (Brussels: Centre for European Policy Studies). Available at: «http://www.ceps.eu/book/meaning-cyprus-moving-towards-banking-union».

Piedrafita, S. and Renman, V. (2014) *Exceeding Expectations: Lithuania Moves the Trio Presidency Forward* (Brussels: Centre for European Policy Studies). Available at: «http://www.ceps.eu/book/exceeding-expectations-lithuania-moves-trio-presidency-forward».

Rittberger, B. (2005) *Building Europe's Parliament* (Oxford: Oxford University Press).

Schulz, M. (2013a) Prepared Address by President Schulz to Tweede Kamer – The Netherlands, 2 December. Available at: «http://www.europarl.europa.eu/the-president/en/press/press_release_speeches/speeches/sp-2013/sp-2013-december/pdf/prepared-address-by-president-schulz-to-tweede-kamer–the-netherlands».

Schulz, M. (2013b) Speech to the European Council by Martin Schulz, President of the European Parliament, 7 February. Available at: «http://www.europarl.europa.eu/the-president/en/press/press_release_speeches/speeches/sp-2013/sp-2013-february/html/speech-to-the-european-council-on-7-february-2013-by-martin-schulz-president-of-the-european-parliament».

Schulz, M. (2013c) Speech to the European Council by Martin Schulz, President of the European Parliament, 14 March. Available at: «http://www.europarl.europa.eu/the-president/en/press/press_release_speeches/speeches/sp-2013/sp-2013-march/html/speech-to-the-european-council-by-martin-schulz-president-of-the-european-parliament».

Schulz, M. (2013d) Speech to the European Council by President of the European Parliament Martin Schulz, 24 October. Available at: «http://www.europarl.europa.eu/the-president/en/press/press_release_speeches/speeches/sp-2013/sp-2013-october/html/speech-to-the-european-council-24-october-by-the-president-of-the-european-parliament-martin-schulz».

Schulz, M. (2013e) Speech by President of the European Parliament Martin Schulz to the European Council, Brussels, 27 June. Available at: «http://www.europarl.europa.eu/the-president/en/press/press_release_speeches/speeches/sp-2013/sp-2013-june/html/speech-by-the-president-of-the-european-parliament-martin-schulz-to-the-european-council-of-27-june-2013».

Schulz, M. (2013f) Address to the European Council by President of the European Parliament Martin Schulz, Brussels, 19 December. Available at: «http://www.europarl.europa.eu/the-president/en/press/press_release_speeches/speeches/sp-2013/sp-2013-december/html/address-to-the-european-council-by-the-president-of-the-european-parliament-martin-schulz».

Van Aken, W. (2012) 'Voting in the Council of the European Union: Contested Decision-Making in the EU Council of Ministers (1995–2010). Report 2 (Stockholm: Swedish Institute for European Policy Studies).

Van Rompuy, H. (2013) Speech by President of the European Council Herman Van Rompuy at the European Parliament, Brussels, 28 May. Available at: «http://www.consilium.europa.eu/uedocs/cms_data/docs/pressdata/en/ec/137324.pdf».

Welle, K. (2013a) 'Democratic Progress, Citizen's Empowerment at the European Level'. ESPAS Experts Seminar, Brussels, 17 September. Available at: «http://www.europarl.europa.eu/the-secretary-general/en/secretary_general/strategic_thinking/strategic-2013/strategic-2013-september/strategic_thinking-2013-september-1.html».

Welle, K. (2013b) 'The EP in a Multi-Level Governance EU: Ways to Reduce the Democratic Deficit' (Brussels: Centre for European Policy Studies). Available at: «http://www.europarl.europa.eu/the-secretary-general/en/secretary_general/strategic_thinking/strategic-2013/strategic-2013-june/strategic_thinking-2013-june-1.html».

Welle, K. (2013c) 'Beyond Dialogue: Democratic Framework and Scrutiny for Banking Union and Deeper EMU' (Frankfurt: European Central Bank). Available at: «http://www.europarl.europa.eu/the-secretary-general/resource/static/files//2013/2013-09-20-ecb-seminar-speech-by-k.welle.pdf».

Welle, K. (2014) 'Total Quality Management along the Whole Legislative Cycle: A Fresh Look at Better Law-Making'. Paper presented at the Association of European Chambers of Commerce and Industry (Eurochambres) Conference, Brussels, 30 January. Available at: «http://www.europarl.europa.eu/the-secretary-general/en/secretary_general/strategic_thinking/strategic-2014/strategic-2014-january/strategic_thinking-2014-january-1.html».

JCMS 2014 Volume 52 Annual Review pp. 125–140   DOI: 10.1111/jcms.12178

The Steep Road to European Banking Union: Constructing the Single Resolution Mechanism

DAVID HOWARTH[1] and LUCIA QUAGLIA[2]
[1] University of Luxembourg. [2] University of York

Introduction

The construction of a European 'banking union' is one of the most significant developments in European integration since the agreement on Economic and Monetary Union in the Maastricht Treaty. Banking union was proposed by the European heads of government and state in June 2012 to restore confidence in European banking systems weakened by the double whammy of the international financial crisis and the sovereign debt crisis; break the sovereign debt-bank doom loop that plagued the eurozone periphery; counteract the growing fragmentation of European financial markets since the outbreak of the international financial crisis; and – in the words of Council President Herman Van Rompuy (2012) – 'complete' economic and monetary union, thus saving the euro and protecting it better from future shocks (Howarth and Quaglia, 2013; see also Donnelly, 2013). Banking union was to be based on five components: a single rulebook on bank capital and liquidity; a single framework for banking supervision; a single framework for the managed resolution of banks and financial institutions; a common deposit guarantee scheme; and a common backstop for temporary financial support (European Council, 2012b, c).

From June 2012, there were negotiations on four of the five elements of a banking union and, with the exception of the deposit guarantee scheme, agreements were reached by spring 2014. In September 2012, the European Commission proposed a regulation for the establishment of a single supervisory mechanism (SSM) (European Commission, 2012b), which was agreed in amended form by the December 2012 European Council (2012a) and adopted by the European Parliament (EP) and the Council in October 2013. The adoption of EU capital requirements legislation in early 2013 reinforced the single rule book – although many lacuna remained. A directive on banks' recovery and resolution (BRRD), proposed by the Commission on 6 June 2012 (European Commission 2012a), was agreed by the Council on 27 June 2013, approved in an institutional trialogue of Council, Commission and EP on 12 December 2013, and finally adopted by the EP in April 2014. The BRRD, which applies to all EU Member States, sets out rules for the 'bail-in' of struggling and failing banks that enable authorities to recapitalize a failing bank by writing-down liabilities and/or converting them to equity with the aim of continuing a bank as a going concern, decreasing financial system instability and giving authorities the opportunity to reorganize the bank or resolve it (European Commission, 2014).

In July 2013, the Commission proposed a regulation for the creation of the Single Resolution Mechanism (SRM) (European Commission, 2013a), which in a considerably modified form was agreed by government leaders in December 2013 (Council of

Ministers, 2013) and then adopted by the Council and the European Parliament in March 2014. The Commission had previously proposed a directive on deposit guarantee schemes (DGS) (European Commission, 2010), which was stalled. The European Stability Mechanism (ESM) began operation in September 2012 to replace eventually the temporary European Financial Stability Facility (EFSF) (Hodson, 2013). It was envisaged that, subject to certain conditions, the ESM could provide financial support to ailing banks and an amount was allocated specifically to Spanish banks via a national recapitalization fund (FROB).

However, despite these remarkable achievements, the move to a banking union was delayed in 2013 due to differences over the design and operation of the SRM, between the German government and a few northern European Member States, on the one hand, and the EU institutions, France and euro periphery Member States, on the other. While many had previously hoped that a banking union would be up and running in 2013, by the end of the year it was clear that the system would not be operational until 2015 and then in a much watered down form from what the Member States had called for in June 2012. Negotiations on the SRM centred around four specific issues: the scope and membership of the SRM, the centralization of decision-making authority, the sources of funding and the mechanism's legal basis.

The SRM, together with the SSM, was designed to address what we label the 'financial inconsistent quartet', which builds on the 'financial trilemma' outlined by Dirk Schoenmaker (2011; 2013). The trilemma examines the interplay of financial stability, cross-border banking and national financial policies, arguing that any two of the three objectives can be combined but not all three: one has to give way. While Schoenmaker presents an economic analysis to explain the existence of the trilemma, this contribution examines national preference formation with regard to the three objectives of the trilemma and how national preferences shaped one of the main elements of banking union: the SRM.

We argue that in the EU there is a fourth element to be considered: participation in the single currency. The effective absence of the 'lender of last resort' function at the national level in EMU and its legal elimination at the supranational level (Article 127, TFEU) created greater potential for financial instability, especially in the context of the growth in cross-border banking and the rapid expansion of bank balance sheets during the first seven years of the single currency. Hence, the trilemma became, for eurozone Member States, an 'inconsistent quartet'. We also argue that the analytical usefulness of this concept to explain national preferences on the SRM relies upon its nuanced application to individual countries, taking into account national policy-maker concerns regarding moral hazard, with preferences determined largely by Member State current account positions and national banking systems (and notably the internationalization of national banking systems). This contribution focuses specifically on one element of banking union – the SRM – although our argument also applies to the other elements (supervision, common deposit guarantee and the fiscal backstop).

Our analysis proceeds as follows. First, we summarize our understanding of the inconsistent quartet and how different EU Member States relate to this quartet given different positioning on moral hazard issues and very different national banking systems. Second, we seek to explain German reluctance on the SRM, which is important because of the significant German government influence in shaping the overall design of banking union. Third, we examine the intergovernmental debate on the SRM and the effort of three EU institutions – the European Parliament, the Commission and the European Central Bank (ECB) – to challenge German efforts to weaken the resolution mechanism and delay its coming into operation.

I. The 'Inconsistent Quartet' in EMU

In his seminal work, Dirk Schoenmaker (2011; 2013) points out the 'financial trilemma' based on the interplay of financial stability, cross-border banking and national financial policies. In the event that national governments want cross-border banking to continue, while maintaining financial stability, the logic runs, they have to accept 'supranational' prudential regulation and supervision. Schoenmaker focuses upon global bank govern-ance, but he dedicates a couple of pages in his conclusion to the need for a European banking union. We argue that for the large majority of EU Member States, there is a fourth element to be considered – namely the single currency. Hence, the trilemma becomes an 'inconsistent quartet'. We borrow from Padoa-Schioppa's (1982) use of the term, applied to the context of European monetary integration, just as Schoenmaker's trilemma borrows from Mundell-Fleming (Fleming 1962).

On the one hand, the single currency reinforced financial (including banking) integra-tion in the eurozone, with a massive rise in cross-border banking in the eurozone from 1999 (see Howarth and Quaglia, 2013). On the other hand, the single currency under-mined national financial policies because the function of lender of last resort – previously performed by the national central bank in providing liquidity – could no longer be performed effectively at either the national level or, legally at least, by the ECB. Moreover, national resolution powers were constrained by EU/eurozone fiscal rules. Consequently, national authorities had fewer tools at their disposal to safeguard financial stability, which encouraged them to look to supranational solutions.

The inconsistent quartet asserts that eurozone Member State governments sought but could not obtain all four objectives. We assume that the maintenance of the single currency was a prioritized goal for eurozone Member States – although the implications of membership for financial stability and control varied given that Member States were affected differently by lender of last resort concerns. The inconsistent quartet also leads to the hypothesis that in eurozone Member States where the banking system was less internationalized and domestic banks were less engaged in cross-border banking activi-ties, interest in the supranationalization of prudential regulation and supervision were likely to be more limited. Further, EU Member States unlikely to join the single currency in the near future – even those with highly internationalized banking systems and banks like the UK and Sweden – had less interest in joining banking union, in part because lender of last resort functions remained intact.

The interrelated global financial crisis that erupted in 2007 and the sovereign debt crisis that broke out in 2010 highlighted the difficulties arising from the inconsistent quartet within EMU – even if the ECB mitigated financial instability by providing liquidity and governments were, temporarily, permitted to break EU fiscal policy rules and bailed out a range of banks. The crisis was also necessary to overcome the entrenched opposition in a range of eurozone Member States reluctant to transfer prudential super-vision and bank resolution functions from the national to the supranational level. Prior to

2012, home country control of supervision dominated and financial support for failing banks came almost entirely from national fiscal authorities according to national priorities – proving Mervyn King's adage that banks are 'international in life but national in death' (see Turner Review, 2009, p. 36). The collapse or threatened collapse of a range of cross-border European banks in the context of the two crises and threats to other banking systems reinforced the logic of moving beyond unilateral or ad hoc arrangements. The sovereign debt-bank doom loop in the eurozone-periphery Member States further undermined the ability of their governments to rescue or resolve failing banks (for further details, see Howarth and Quaglia, 2013).

For these reasons, eurozone Member States decided (with reluctance in several cases) to explore the move to a banking union, thus replacing the third objective of Schoenmaker's trilemma – namely the maintenance of what he refers to as 'national financial policies'. Such policies in the context of the eurozone include regulation, which even prior to banking union was in part set at the EU level; supervision, which for large systemically important banks was to be undertaken by the ECB through its new supervisory board in the SSM; resolution, which was to be performed by the SRM (for banks subject to the SSM); a deposit guarantee scheme to be replaced by some kind of common European scheme; and even the lender of last resort function becoming – in addition to *de facto* ECB support – a European fiscal backstop for struggling and failing banks. Some argued that all of these elements were necessary in order to make banking union work (Gros and Schoenmaker 2014). However, eurozone Member State governments facing the inconsistent quartet had different preferences on the various elements of a banking union, depending on the concern of national policy-makers for the potential moral hazard created by BU-level financial support for banks and sovereigns and the configuration of their national banking system. Preoccupation with moral hazard depended on whether a Member State was more or less likely to be a net contributor to the proposed single resolution fund and the ability of national authorities to resolve banks headquartered in the Member State. While our inconsistent quartet allows us to predict interest in a banking union throughout the eurozone, it also helps us to explain German reluctance which stems, we argue, from moral hazard concerns but also the specific features of the German banking system – notably its limited internationalization.

II. Explaining German Reluctance: Moral Hazard, Legal Challenge and the *Sparkassen*

Germany – as the eurozone Member State with the largest economy and one of the largest banking system measured in total assets, the largest current account surplus and one of the more stable economic, financial and fiscal positions – would almost inevitably make net contributions through the support and resolution mechanisms of Banking union. Enjoying a kind of veto power – although one constrained by the threat of sovereign debt default in the euro periphery, contagion and eurozone disintegration – Germany had more influence on the design of banking union than other eurozone Member States. The German government's position thus merits further consideration and, specifically, its concern for moral hazard, the potential of legal challenge and the preoccupation with the impact of banking union on public sector savings banks (*Sparkassen*).

From November 2011, German Finance Minister Wolfgang Schäuble directly linked the use of ESM funds to help banks to the creation of the SSM in order to limit the effects of moral hazard, demanding that strong conditions be imposed on both sovereigns (supervisors) and banks that receive ESM funds (Boone and Johnson, 2011).[1] For sovereigns (supervisors), the potential availability of EU-level financial support for banks might effectively encourage them to loosen national regulation and/or supervision, allowing potentially riskier activities which in turn undermines the pursuit of Member State governments to discourage these activities given that national taxpayers and/or depositors will be less expected to pick up the tab for saving banks (Micossi *et al.*, 2011). To obtain ESM funds (potentially), according to this logic, Member State governments had to accept further constraints on their autonomy in financial regulation and supervision, and banks had to accept a potentially reinforced regulatory and supervisory framework.

The agreement to allocate ESM financial support to save struggling banks also created a moral hazard for banks – already a concern at the national level in the context of widespread bail-outs in the aftermath of the international financial crisis. The standard argument runs that banks are more likely to engage in riskier activities in the knowledge that they will be bailed out in the context of crisis. German preoccupation with the moral hazard created by EU-level support was demonstrated clearly in the intergovernmental debates over the Cyprus bail-out in March 2013 and in the German insistence on the significant bail-in of uninsured depositors (Pisani-Ferry, 2013).

The creation of an SRM with a single resolution fund also created moral hazard for both sovereigns and banks. The German government had already implemented its own bank restructuring and resolution mechanisms and urged other Member States to do so. German policy here contradicted the longstanding position of several other Member States, including France, the governments of which were previously hostile to national resolution mechanisms precisely on moral hazard grounds (Hardie and Howarth, 2009). With the SRM, the Germans (among others) were principally concerned that the creation of a large EU resolution mechanism could create perverse incentives for other Member State governments to be more lenient in the regulation and supervision of banks: at the end of the day, EU funds could be drawn upon to resolve the bank.[2] The funds would come from all EU banks (or at least those of a certain size) – not from governments. So the pressure on government resources (and national taxpayers) would be limited – especially following the creation of a single European fund. Thus, to limit this moral hazard, the German government insisted on the precondition of direct ECB supervision for systemically important banks, EU rules on 'bail-in' (that is, initial losses imposed on both private sector bond and shareholders – BRRD Article 37.51-52), with EU-level support only at the end of a relatively long process and difficult voting system. But these conditions and complexity led many observers to question the credibility of the mechanism and the likelihood of EU-level support, which created additional concerns about the resolution of banks and potentially undermined investor/international confidence in the long-term stability of eurozone periphery financial systems.

German policy-makers were also preoccupied with the compatibility of the SRM with the German Basic Law. Here, the German concern, as with the establishment of the ESM

---

[1] *New York Times*, 18 November 2011; *European Voice*, 16 February 2012.
[2] *Financial Times*, 29 April 2013.

and the proposed common deposit guarantee scheme was that German taxpayers would be required to step in to support the SRM without constitutionally required parliamentary approval. In particular, German policy-makers were concerned with the transition period when national resolution funds would exist, prior to the mutualization of these funds into a single EU fund. The German federal government favoured a two-step approach to the creation of the SRM, starting with a network of national authorities and creating a centralized authority in the future and only once EU treaties had been changed and appropriate measures enacted to protect national taxpayers.[3]

The BRRD and the SRM were to apply to all EU-headquartered banks. The directive was to enforce losses upon shareholders and bondholders of banks prior to a taxpayer-funded bail-out or resolution. However, it was highly unlikely that SRM funds would be needed to cover the resolution of smaller banks. The ECB was unlikely to be in a position to force resolution upon smaller German banks (notably the German co-operative banks or the publicly owned *Sparkassen*), except in the rare circumstance that the supervisory board of the SSM sought to extend direct control over the supervision of these institutions – a possibility created in the SSM regulation in the event that the board deemed (by a majority of its members) necessary to ensure the consistent application of 'high' supervisory standards. Member State finance ministers could also initiate the resolution through the SRM of any EU-headquartered bank, but again it was highly unlikely that this would involve smaller German institutions.

German reluctance on the SRM can thus be seen as stemming from the structural reality that very few of its banks would be covered. Approximately, 25 German banks were to be subject to direct ECB supervision: a range of commercial banks and all the remaining public sector regional banks (*Landesbanken*). The percentage of total bank assets covered by direct ECB supervision was the lowest of any eurozone (banking union) Member State given that the German banking system was the least concentrated in Europe.[4] Almost one-third of the eurozone's banks were German, including slightly more than 420 *Sparkassen* (publicly owned savings banks) and 1,200 co-operative banks (2011 figures) – none of which would be covered by direct ECB supervision.

Applying the 'inconsistent quartet' to Germany, we would expect less interest in banking union generally and, more specifically, in the creation of the SRM – despite German participation in the single currency – because the German banking system was one of the least internationalized in the eurozone both in terms of foreign bank penetration and the international presence of national banks.[5] The bulk of bank assets were nationally held with the exception of the biggest two and a small number of other much smaller

---

[3] *Wall Street Journal*, 10 July 2013.

[4] According the Herfindahl index, Germany is consistently the least concentrated banking system in the EU and has an index approximately one-fifth that of the eurozone average (ECB, 2013; ECB Statistical Warehouse: «http://sdw.ecb.europa.eu/»). The five largest credit institutions consistently have the lowest percentage of total bank assets of any national banking system in the EU (ECB Statistical Warehouse: «http://sdw.ecb.europa.eu/»).

[5] Foreign bank penetration (the branches and subsidiaries of foreign-headquartered banks) in Germany is 12.2 per cent of total assets versus the eurozone average of 17.8 per cent (ECB statistical warehouse, 2012 figures: «http://sdw.ecb.europa.eu/»). The international presence of German-headquartered banks reached 28 per cent of total bank assets (2007–11 average). When the largest three banks are excluded, only 16 per cent of German bank assets were held outside the country. The assets of German banks held outside the eurozone reached 14.6 and 5.5 per cent, respectively. Figures for British banks were 40 and 25.6 per cent, respectively. Figures for French banks were 25.2 and and 12.6 per cent, respectively. These figures are based on the authors' calculations, using data from national central banks.

commercial banks.[6] Although Germany was home to one very big, highly international-ized, commercial bank – Deutsche Bank – and a second very big commercial bank with a significant European presence – Commerzbank – almost all the other banks were nationally focused, with operations in nearly all cases limited to a small area in Germany. Negligible German interest in European-level funds stemmed from the fact that Germany as a comparatively large, rich and solvent Member State was unlikely to have financial difficulty bailing-out or resolving any of its banks – including the two largest commercial banks. The bank-assets-to-GDP ratio in Germany in 2013 was at 300 per cent of gross domestic product, below the EU average of 349 per cent, just above the EU median and far lower than the ratios in the Netherlands (397), France (423) and the UK (495).[7]

Systemic features of German bank liabilities also resulted in less preoccupation for lender of last resort type concerns. Notably, a possible collapse in bank liquidity – for example, through a freezing of interbank wholesale markets – was of marginal concern in Germany. Only 0.6 per cent of total bank funding was short-term wholesale market funding (less than two years) (3.9 per cent of total debt funding).[8] The comparison with French banks is revealing: 10.8 per cent of French bank funding was short-term wholesale market funding – 18 times the German level.[9] German public sector banks relied over-whelmingly on stable long-term wholesale market funding (*Pfandbriefe*) – nearly all of which was domestically held – and government held long-term debt ('silent participa-tions'), while the more traditional co-operative banks relied largely on deposits to fund bank lending. The bulk of German *Sparkassen* enjoyed a lower cost of capital compared to their commercial rivals because they relied disproportionately on high levels of funding through 'silent participations' and were under no obligation to make pay-outs to their local municipality investors.

German government concerns over the fate of the *Sparkassen* determined the contours of the banking union agreed between December 2012 and March 2014 and dictated the reach of ECB direct supervision, which ended up covering only one of the more than 420 savings banks. The *Sparkassen* banks were local or regionally based public sector banks with a vested interest in the local economy and a strong presence in local community life. They provided the bulk of external finance to the *Mittelstand* (small and medium-sized nonfinancial companies), the backbone of the German economy. In late 2012, the largest savings bank had a balance sheet of approximately €40 billion – about one-fiftieth that of Deutsche Bank – and more than 100 had less than a billion euros in assets.[10]

However, the *Sparkassen* also benefited from being part of a large closely linked network and collectively could be considered to be one of the largest financial groups in the world with more assets (€1 trillion) than Deutsche Bank, a collective 38 per cent share of German bank lending and almost 37 per cent deposits.[11] Furthermore, the *Sparkassen* (and *Landesbanken*) benefited from the German regulatory practice that considered loans between these banks as risk-free – which meant that no capital had to be held against such exposures. The *Sparkassen* were not required to file combined accounts as a single

[6] See the previous footnote.
[7] *The Banker* data base: «http://www.thebankerdatabase.com».
[8] Bundesbank statistics, end 2012.
[9] Bank of France statistics, end 2012.
[10] *Financial Times*, 2 December 2012.
[11] Bundesbank, end 2012 figures.

financial group and accounts were first overseen by auditors from within the saving bank group, not external auditors. The *Sparkassen* also benefited from a joint liability scheme (*Haftungsverbund*), which was to provide both bail-out funds and emergency liquidity for member banks (Simpson, 2013) – although such a scheme in place for the *Landesbanken* did not save German taxpayers from bail-outs and some *Sparkassen* did not contribute the level of aid that corresponded to their ownership stakes. Pointing to this joint liability scheme and competent management, the *Sparkassen* representative association, the VOB, vigorously denied the relevance of the Spanish *caja* precedent.[12] *Sparkassen* directors also appeared to be unanimous in their view that home regulators better understood their characteristics and way of doing business (Simpson, 2013).[13] Transferring control over their supervision and resolution to the supranational level was unacceptable.

III. The Negotiations on the SRM

In July 2013, the Commission issued a draft regulation to establish the SRM (European Commission, 2013a), designed to complement the SSM. The Commission envisaged the establishment of a single resolution board (SRB), consisting of representatives from the ECB, the European Commission and the national resolution authorities of the Member States where banks had their headquarters as well as their branches and/or subsidiaries. According to the initial proposal, the ECB, in its role in the SSM, would signal when a bank headquartered in a banking union Member State was in 'severe financial difficulties' and needed 'to be resolved' (European Commission, 2013a). The SRB would be 'responsible for the key decisions on how a bank would be resolved', with national resolution authorities 'closely involved in this work'. The Commission would then decide whether to enter a bank into resolution. The Commission, which drafted the proposal, argued that this decision could not rest with the SRB 'for legal reasons' – namely according to the Treaty, only an EU institution could take such a decision at the European level, precluding an agency (such as the European Banking Authority (EBA)) from fulfilling this role (European Commission, 2014).

National resolution authorities would retain responsibility for executing the resolution actions, with the SRB having an oversight role, monitoring implementation by national authorities. If the national authorities did not comply with SRB decisions, the SRB would have the power to 'directly address executive orders to the troubled banks' (European Commission, 2013a). A single bank resolution fund would be set up under the control of the SRB to provide financial support during the restructuring process (European Commission, 2013b). It was envisaged that this fund would be created from contributions from the banking sector, through the pooling of the resources of national funds of participating Member States. While these funds were being built up, however, the Commission proposed that the SRB should be able to borrow from the markets (European Commission, 2013a).

The draft legislation on the SRM was criticized from both sides. For some, it did not go far enough in that it failed to propose the establishment of a true single resolution authority, which would have required treaty revision. Hence, responsibilities were split

[12] *Financial Times*, 20 June 2013.
[13] *Financial Times*, 2 December 2012.

between several layers of decision-making (Deloitte, 2013). The Commission was assigned the ultimate decision-making power on whether or not to initiate a resolution. The SRB was tasked with planning resolutions, whereas national authorities were in charge of executing resolutions under national law. The actions of the SRB were contingent on the decision of the ECB/SSM to signal that a bank was in difficulty. Hence, the SSM's internal decision-making structure and its interaction with national authorities would form a further layer within the SRM (Deloitte, 2013). Numerous observers, the ECB and the Commission itself had argued with great regularity that during crisis, clarity and speed in decision-making were crucial for bank crisis management. Nonetheless, the Commission proposed a multilayered SRM with many veto points.

For other critics, the draft legislation gave too much power to the Commission, which would decide whether and when to place a bank into resolution. The head of a Bavarian banking association went so far as to liken the Commission's proposals to 'enabling acts', the laws that the Nazis used to seize power.[14] The German government challenged the Commission's draft on legal grounds, arguing that the Commission had overstepped its authority and that a treaty change was required for such a far-reaching reform.[15] German policy-makers feared that their country would be the main contributor to the resolution fund and that the Commission would take decisions that could have fiscal implications for the Member States. Should the single resolution fund not have enough financial resources to intervene, national governments (and ultimately taxpayers) would have to step in.

More specifically, German policy-makers demanded that resolution decisions should be taken by the European Council,[16] which operates by unanimity allowing each member state to retain its veto. German policy-makers also wanted to reduce the scope of the SRM: with their own *Sparkassen* (savings banks) in mind, they sought to exclude smaller banks from SRM coverage.[17] In this respect, Germany favoured a compromise that would mirror the deal reached with reference to the direct supervision of banks by the ECB in the SSM which deprived the ECB of involvement in the direct supervision of all but 130 banks – although the ECB retained the power to intervene in any bank if necessary subject to a majority vote in the SSM's supervisory board.

With reference to the resolution fund, German Finance Minister Wolfgang Schäuble opposed a single European bank rescue fund financed by levies on banks. This model was supported by the Commission, the ECB (as discussed below), the French government and southern eurozone Member State governments. German policy-makers favoured a network of national funds in the medium term and argued that the setting up of a common fund required treaty change.[18] According to the Commission's proposal, contributions to the fund would be lower for banks funded mainly through deposits and undertaking lower risk activities. However, the German position on fund contributions was more cautious than the French and southern European position – despite the large number of small banks engaged in 'traditional' banking activities in Germany. The two largest German commercial banks, Deutsche Bank and Commerzbank, fought a rear guard battle against the

[14] *Financial Times*, 11 July 2013.
[15] *Financial Times*, 6 December 2013.
[16] *Financial Times*, 6 December 2013.
[17] *Financial Times*, 6 December 2013; *European Voice*, 19 September 2013.
[18] *Financial Times*, 6 December 2013.

proposed funding scheme which would have hit them on both fronts (deposits and risk activities).[19] The German government also insisted on bringing forward rules to impose losses on senior creditors in banks to 2015. These bail-in measures, which were included in the BRRD, had been resisted by France, Italy and Spain.[20]

In the run up to the decisive Ecofin meeting in December 2013, Dutch policy-makers floated the idea of splitting the SRM proposal into two parts, to be discussed in parallel negotiations. One part concerned the scope and decision-making mechanism of the SRM, the other part concerned the single resolution fund.[21] With reference to the fund, a compromise solution proposed by Dutch policy-makers was a system whereby the reso-lution fund of the bank's home state would be used before other Member States' funds were utilized. The *Financial Times* also reported a possible compromise on the banks covered by the system, leaving national authorities in the lead in resolving smaller banks, as favoured by German policy-makers.[22]

Another contentious issue in the negotiations on the SRM was how to proceed if national resolution funds were insufficient to deal with a big bank's failure. German government officials argued that if the resolution funds were insufficient to resolve an ailing bank, the national authorities (and in the end, the taxpayers) of the home country should cover the costs. France and some southern European countries called for the use of the ESM as a common backstop. French Finance Minister Pierre Moscovici also called for the immediate creation of a single resolution fund with a 'unique backstop' to cover shortfalls while the fund was filled with levies on the banking industry.[23]

On 18 December 2013, an agreement was reached in the Council of Ministers on the draft regulation on the SRM (Council of Ministers, 2013). In addition, a decision was adopted by eurozone Member States that committed them to negotiating an intergovern-mental agreement on the functioning of the single resolution fund by March 2014. The draft regulation agreed by the Council established that 'upon notification by the European Central Bank that a bank was failing or likely to fail, or on its own initiative, the SRB would adopt a resolution scheme placing a bank into resolution'. It would decide on the application of resolution tools and the use of the single resolution fund. 'Decisions by the Board would enter into force within 24 hours of their adoption, unless the Council, acting by simple majority on a proposal by the Commission, objected or called for changes' (Council of Ministers, 2013). This was an important modification, advocated first and foremost by Germany, compared to the original Commission draft, which gave the Commission the power to decide on the resolution of a bank. It was agreed that the SRB would consist of an executive director, four full-time appointed members and the repre-sentatives of the national resolution authorities of all the participating countries. The Commission and the ECB would only have observer status. Any decisions with significant financial implications for the fund would be taken by a two-thirds majority of the board members representing at least 50 per cent of contributions. According to the version of the regulation agreed in December 2013, a decision to close down a bank would need the approval of a large number of actors including: the European Commission; the Council of

---

[19] *Wall Street Journal*, 10 July 2013.
[20] *Financial Times*, 6 December 2013.
[21] *Bloomberg*, 10 December 2013.
[22] *Financial Times*, 6 December 2013.
[23] *Bloomberg*, 10 December 2013.

Ministers; the supervisory board of the single supervisory mechanism (the ECB); as well as the executive board of the single resolution mechanism and its plenary council.

The SRM was to cover all banks in the participating Member States. However, the Germans succeeded in getting adopted their position that the board would be responsible for the resolution only of those banks directly supervised by the ECB. National resolution authorities would be responsible for the resolution of all other banks, except if a bank required access to the single resolution fund, which in the case of Germany was unlikely. National authorities would also be responsible for executing bank resolution plans under the control of the single resolution board (Council of Ministers, 2013). In order to guarantee Member State budgetary sovereignty, the SRM could not require governments to provide extraordinary public support to any bank under resolution (European Commission, 2013c).

The version of the regulation agreed by Member States in December 2013 created a single resolution fund that would be financed by bank levies raised at the national level. It would initially consist of national compartments that would be gradually merged over 10 years with the target funding level of €55 billion by 2026 or about 1 per cent of all insured depositions.[24] During this period, mutualization between national compartments would progressively increase (Council of Ministers, 2013). So while during the first year the cost of resolving banks (after bail-in) would mainly come from the compartments of the Member States where the banks are located, this share would gradually decrease and the contribution from other participating countries' compartments would increase. In the end, it was decided that during the building up of resolution funds, national governments would collectively have to provide the extra funding to resolve national ailing banks, if necessary by requesting a loan from the ESM. A fully shared backstop would be available only once national resolution funds reached their target level and were fully merged.[25] From this point on the SRM could no longer borrow from the ESM. The December version of the regulation also endorsed the bail-in rules set by the BRRD as applicable to the use of the single resolution fund.

The German government refused to include in the regulation the most sensitive elements of the SRM package: specific provisions on the transfer and pooling of Member State funded compartments into a single mutualized fund. These were placed in an intergovernmental side agreement. The Germans insisted upon subsequent intergovernmental agreements among participating Member States to permit the transfer of national funds towards the single resolution fund and the activation of the mutualization of the national compartments. The Germans sought an intergovernmental agreement in order to eliminate EP involvement on these matters and minimize the Commission's role.[26] Moreover, the December compromise ensured that the SRM regulation was not to apply before the intergovernmental agreement entered into force – which was to take place following ratification by participating Member States representing 80 per cent of contributions to the single resolution fund.

---

[24] *The Guardian*, 19 December 2013.
[25] *Wall Street Journal*, 18 December 2013; *The Guardian*, 19 December 2013.
[26] *European Voice*, 12 December 2013.

The EU Institutions Battle for the SRM

The EP, the ECB and the Commission joined forces in challenging elements of the regulation/intergovernmental agreement compromise of the December European Council. The EP questioned the need for an intergovernmental agreement to formulate the details on the functioning of the single resolution fund to be used in bank resolution (European Parliament, 2014a). In a letter sent to the EU's rotating presidency of the Council, the EP argued that the 'intergovernmental agreement on Single Resolution Fund is illegal because it bypasses the established legislative processes of the Union'.[27] The EP did not even formally recognize the Council text of the side agreement – regarding which it had no formal role. However, the EP retained some leverage on the side agreement because of its co-decision power on the SRM regulation.

To further complicate negotiations, the version of the regulation adopted by the EP in January 2014 was significantly different from that agreed by the Council. MEPs restated the requests that 'all banks must be treated equally, irrespective of which country they are established in, and that the system must be credible and efficient' (European Parliament, 2014a). They called for a simplification of the resolution decision-making process by creating a stronger, more centralized authority, with the supervisory board of the SSM possessing the final say over bank resolution without political interference. They also wanted to remove Germany's safeguards so that the single resolution fund would be available sooner, with access to a centralized/common credit line. A further EP demand was to accelerate the mutualization of the fund so as to complete it by 2018 rather than 2026. Informal 'trialogue' negotiations between the EP and the Council, assisted by the Commission, began in early 2014 with a view to reaching a first reading agreement on the proposal before EP elections in May 2014.[28]

Over a period of a fortnight in April 2013, all six of the ECB executive board members came out publicly in favour of a rapid move to a SRM even though this was clearly at odds with the German government's more gradualist version (see, for example, Mersch, 2013).[29] In November 2013, the ECB issued a 32-page opinion signed by Mario Draghi that the SRB should be, from the start, a single 'strong and independent' body, thus directly challenging the German position that the SRM should begin as a network of national authorities.[30] The ECB argued that 'co-ordination between national resolution systems has not proved sufficient to achieve the most timely and cost-effective resolution decisions, particularly in a cross-border context'.[31] The ECB also insisted that treaty change was unnecessary to create the new body.[32]

Following the December European Council compromise, Vitor Constâncio, a member of the ECB's executive board, expressed the ECB's fear that the markets would find the proposed resolution process insufficiently credible because it was too complex and involved too many policy-makers to work with the necessary speed in crisis situations

[27] *Financial Times*, 16 January 2014.
[28] *Febelfin*, 20 December 2013. Available at: «http://www.febelfin.be/en/eu-flash-single-resolution-mechanism-bank-recovery-and-resolution-brrd-deposit-guarantee-scheme-bank».
[29] *Financial Times*, 29 April 2013.
[30] *Financial Times*, 8 November 2013.
[31] *Financial Times*, 8 November 2013.
[32] *Bloomberg*, 17 December 2013. Available at: «http://www.bloomberg.com/news/2013-12-16/draghi-says-european-bank-resolution-plan-may-be-too-cumbersome.html».

(ECB, 2012). Constâncio also warned that to be credible, the national bank-resolution funds needed to have access to outside financing, especially in the period when national resolution funds were being built up.[33] He criticized the December agreement because it did not allow the resolution funds to borrow on the financial markets to raise extra funding:

> We are talking here not about a final backstop, we are talking here about a credit line, which is a system that exists for instance in the US. [. . .] You should flesh out the possibility of the fund borrowing in the markets to have bridge financing to complete the resolution process.[34]

Michel Barnier, the EU Commissioner responsible for financial services, remained concerned about the ability of the SRM to take difficult decisions to close a bank quickly or secretly enough. He argued that:

> decision-making within the SRM [was] still too complex with a consultation system which [slowed] down the process unnecessarily. What we are building is a single system and not a multi-storey intergovernmental network.[35]

Concerns similar to those expressed by the ECB and the Commission were also aired by policy-makers outside the EU. Jack Lew, the US Treasury Secretary stated: 'We don't think it's big enough. We don't think it's fast enough'.[36]

Conclusions

In 2013, most of the policy discussions on banking union focused on the issue of bank resolution, with the agreements on the BRRD in June and December and the publication of the Commission's draft SRM proposal in the summer of 2013. Two different amended versions of the regulation were adopted by the Council and the EP in December 2013 and January 2014, respectively. Afterwards, the main difficulty consisted of reconciling the two texts, with a view to adopting the new rules before the EP elections in May 2014. The text approved by the Council also envisaged an intergovernmental agreement to be reached by March 2014. The EP strongly opposed this side agreement, arguing that all the new rules concerning the SRM should be part of ordinary EU law and co-decided by the Council and Parliament.

The EP unsuccessfully attempted to bring the elements of the December intergovernmental side agreement into the regulation, winning only limited concessions in the 20 March 2014 compromise with the Council: a decreased period of eight years during which the national compartments would merge; an increased proportion of the fund shared at an earlier stage; and a marginally increased role performed by the Commission in the single resolution board – allowing the Council to reject resolution proposals only under certain conditions.[37] Although the Commission was to have a limited role in the SRM, Member State governments retained their vetoes on mutualization and an important say on the use

---

[33] *Wall Street Journal*, 18 December 2013; *The Guardian*, 19 December 2013.
[34] *The Telegraph*, 18 December 2013.
[35] *The Telegraph*, 18 December 2013.
[36] *Financial Times*, 16 January 2014.
[37] *Financial Times*, 20 March 2014.

of resolution funds. A messy compromise was reached on triggering the resolution process. It was agreed that the ECB (the SSM's supervisory board) would hold the trigger, being responsible for deciding whether or not a bank should be resolved. The single resolution board would ask the ECB take such a decision and if the ECB declined to do so, then the board itself would take the decision. The ECB was therefore to be the main 'triggering' authority but the board might also play a role if the ECB was reluctant or hesitated to act (European Parliament, 2014b).

The main issues in the negotiations on the SRM concerned the centralization of decision-making power, the scope of the SRM, the sources of funding and the legal basis of the new mechanism. German opposition to the Commission's draft directive on the SRM stemmed from concerns over moral hazard both for banks and for sovereigns, legal difficulties and the structure of the Germany banking system. More crudely put, the German government disliked both having to pay for the closure of foreign banks and empowering foreigners to close German banks. The Commission proposal envisaged that decision-making power would be assigned to the Commission itself. Some Member States, first and foremost Germany, argued that decision-making power should rest with national resolution authorities individually and then collectively in the EU Council of Ministers. The Commission pushed for SRM coverage of all EU banks, whereas the Germans insisted upon coverage of only the largest systemically important cross-border banks. As for funding the new mechanism, the Commission proposed the creation of a common resolution fund, funded by banks, but some Member States, particularly Germany, opposed this idea. The fourth issue concerned the legal basis of the SRM, in particular whether it required treaty revision, as requested by German policy-makers, or not, as argued by the Commission, the ECB, France, Italy and Spain, which were keen to speed up the establishment of the SRM.

By March 2014, banking union Member States had agreed a complicated set of bank resolution procedures. In the space of less than two years, all the main elements of banking union – except the common deposit guarantee system – had been agreed. Yet most observers were highly sceptical of the institutional design of the nascent banking union – and in particular the single resolution mechanism – and its potential contribution to banking and financial system stability (see, for example, Münchau, 2014). For the eurozone periphery, the delayed and complex SRM agreed failed to provide the clear backstop that they sought to prevent doubts about the solvency of national governments from undermining confidence in their domestic banks. In other words, it remained unlikely that the institutions and procedures agreed would significantly undermine the sovereign debt-bank doom loop. The process of 'squaring' the inconsistent quartet was and would continue to be highly contentious and complicated. Future institutional and procedural modifications were almost inevitable and the road to an effective banking union remained a steep ascent.

References

Boone, P. and Johnson, S. (2011) 'Europe on the Brink'. *Policy Brief PB* 11–13 (Washington, DC: Peterson Institute for International Economics).
Council of Ministers (2013) 'Council agrees general approach on Single Resolution Mechanism'. 17602/13, 18 December. Available at: «http://www.consilium.europa.eu/uedocs/cms_data/docs/pressdata/en/ecofin/140190.pdf».

Deloitte (2013) 'EU Commission Sets Out Plans for Single Resolution Mechanism in Banking Union/New Single Resolution Board Proposed'. Available at: «http://blogs.deloitte.co.uk/financialservices/2013/07/eu_commission_sets_out_plans_for_srm_in_banking_union.html».

Donnelly S. (2013) 'Power Politics and the Undersupply of Financial Stability in Europe'. *Review of International Political Economy*, DOI: 10.1080/09692290.2013.801021.

European Central Bank (ECB) (2012) 'Introductory Statement to the Press Conference (with Q&A) Presented by Mario Draghi, President of the ECB and Vítor Constâncio, Vice-President of the ECB at Frankfurt am Main, 6 December. Available at: «http://www.ecb.int/press/pressconf/2012/html/is121206.en.html».

European Central Bank (ECB) (2013) Banking Structures Report, November. Available at: «http://www.ecb.europa.eu/pub/pdf/other/bankingstructuresreport201311en.pdf».

European Commission (2010) Proposal for a Directive on deposit guarantee schemes [recast]. COM/2010/0368 final, 12 July.

European Commission (2012a) Proposal for a Directive establishing a framework for the recovery and resolution of credit institutions and investment firms. COM(2012) 280/3, 20 June.

European Commission (2012b) Proposal for a Council Regulation conferring specific tasks on the European Central Bank concerning policies relating to the prudential supervision of credit institutions. COM(2012) 511 final, 12 September.

European Commission (2013a) Proposal for a Regulation establishing uniform rules and a uniform procedure for the resolution of credit institutions and certain investment firms in the framework of a single resolution mechanism and a single bank resolution fund. 10 July.

European Commission (2013b) Commission proposes single resolution mechanism for the Banking Union. IP/13/674, 10/07/2013. Available at: «http://europa.eu/rapid/press-release_IP-13-674_en.htm».

European Commission (2013c) Commissioner Michel Barnier's remarks at the ECOFIN Council press conference. Memo/13/1186, 19/12/2013. Available at: «http://europa.eu/rapid/press-release_MEMO-13-1186_en.htm?locale=en».

European Commission (2014) EU Bank Recovery and Resolution Directive (BRRD): Frequently asked questions. Memo/14/297 15/04/2014. Available at: «http://europa.eu/rapid/press-release_MEMO-14-297_en.htm».

European Council (2012a) 'Council Agrees Position on Single Supervisory Mechanism'. 17739/12, PRESSE 528, 13 December. Available at: «http://www.consilium.europa.eu/uedocs/cms_data/docs/pressdata/en/ecofin/134265.pdf».

European Council (2012b) 'The European Council Agrees on a Roadmap for the Completion of Economic and Monetary Union', 14 December. Available at: «http://www.european-council.europa.eu/home-page/highlights/the-european-council-agrees-on-a-roadmap-for-the-completion-of-economic-and-monetary-union?lang=en».

European Council (2012c) 'Conclusions on Completing EMU', 14 December. Available at: «http://www.consilium.europa.eu/uedocs/cms_data/docs/pressdata/en/ec/134320.pdf».

European Parliament (2014a) 'MEPs' Statement on the Work on the Single Resolution Mechanism for Banks'. Economic and Monetary Affairs Press Release, 09-01-2014.

European Parliament (2014b) 'Parliament Negotiators Rescue Seriously Damaged Bank Resolution System', 20 March. Available at: «http://www.europarl.europa.eu/news/en/newsroom/content/20140319IPR39310/html/Parliament-negotiators-rescue-seriously-damaged-bank-resolution-system».

Fleming, J.M. (1962) 'Domestic Financial Policies under Fixed and Floating Exchange Rates'. *IMF Staff Papers*, Vol. 9, pp. 369–79.

Gros, D. and Schoenmaker, D. (2014) 'European Deposit Insurance and Resolution in the Banking Union'. *JCMS*, Vol. 52, No. 3, pp. 529–46.

Hardie, I. and Howarth, D. (2009) 'Die Krise but not La Crise? The Financial Crisis and the Transformation of German and French Banking Systems'. *JCMS*, Vol. 47, No. 5, pp. 1017–39.

Hodson, D. (2013) 'The Eurozone in 2012: "Whatever It Takes" to Preserve the Euro?' *JCMS*, Vol. 51, No. s1, pp. 183–200.

Howarth, D. and Quaglia, L. (2013) 'Banking Union as Holy Grail: Rebuilding the Single Market in Financial Services, Stabilizing Europe's Banks and "Completing" Economic and Monetary Union'. *JCMS*, Vol. 51, No. s1, pp. 103–23.

Mersch, Y. (2013) 'Europe's Ills Cannot Be Healed by Monetary Innovation Alone'. *Financial Times*, 24 April.

Micossi, S., Carmassi, J. and Peire, F. (2011) 'On the Tasks of the European Stability Mechanism'. CEPS Policy Brief 235 (Brussels: Centre for European Policy Studies).

Münchau, W. (2014) 'Europe Should Say No to a Flawed Banking Union'. *Financial Times*, 16 March.

Padoa-Schioppa, T. (1982) 'Capital Mobility: Why is the Treaty Not Implemented?' In Padoa-Schioppa, T. (1994) *The Road to Monetary Union in Europe* (Oxford: Clarendon Press).

Pisani-Ferry, J. (2013) 'The Politics of Moral Hazard'. *Project Syndicate*, 30 March. Available at: «http://www.project-syndicate.org/commentary/cyprus-and-the-politics-of-moral-hazard-in-europe-by-jean-pisani-ferry».

Schoenmaker D. (2011) 'The Financial Trilemma'. Tinbergen Institute Discussion Paper (Amsterdam: Duisenberg School of Finance).

Schoenmaker D. (2013) *Governance of International Banking: The Financial Trilemma* (Oxford: Oxford University Press).

Simpson, C. (2013) *The German* Sparkassen *(Savings Banks): A Commentary and Case Study* (London: Civitas Institute for Civil Society).

Turner Review (2009) *A Regulatory Response to the Global Banking Crisis* (London: Financial Services Authority).

Van Rompuy, H. (2012) 'Towards a Genuine Economic and Monetary Union'. Speech delivered on 5 December. Available at: «http://www.consilium.europa.eu/uedocs/cms_Data/docs/pressdata/en/ec/134069.pdf».

JCMS 2014 Volume 52 Annual Review pp. 141–156

DOI: 10.1111/jcms.12160

Justice and Home Affairs

JÖRG MONAR
College of Europe

Introduction

After several years which had been marked more by difficult negotiations than by substantive progress of the EU's area of freedom, security and justice, 2013 saw the completion of four major projects: the remaining legislative acts needed for the completion of the Common European Asylum System (CEAS) were adopted, the second-generation Schengen Information System (SIS II) as well as the border surveillance system Eurosur started to operate, and the Schengen governance reform initiated under the pressure of the 2011 Arab Spring refugee movements ended with a legislative compromise which – contrary to some initial concerns – strengthened rather than weakened the Schengen system overall. Some legislative progress was also achieved in the fields of migration policy and judicial co-operation. However, there were also a number of implementation challenges identified, and negotiations on several other legal instruments again proved to be difficult.

I. Developments in Individual Policy Areas

Asylum Policy

After a period of relative stability in the numbers of asylum applications during the first few months of the year, applications started to rise from April onwards. With 117,800 applications in the third quarter, the numbers exceeded those of the same period the year before by 32.4 per cent (Eurostat, 2013), with the sharp increase in the number of Syrian refugees being a major contributing factor. While these increasing numbers meant already increased pressure on the EU's Common European Asylum System (CEAS), a special momentum of political and public pressure was added in October with the tragic loss of over 500 lives as a result of the shipwrecks of two refugee boats: on 3 October close to the Italian island of Lampedusa, and on 11 October in Maltese territorial waters. The incidents not only provoked a national day of mourning in Italy and a visit by Commission President José Manuel Barroso to Lampedusa, but also sharp criticism from Maltese Prime Minister Joseph Muscat who spoke about an emerging 'cemetery within our Mediterranean sea' and the rest of Europe only providing 'empty talk'.[1]

The Mediterranean incidents and the increasing application numbers, however, overshadowed a number of notable legislative advances in the asylum policy field: on 13 March, a Decision of the European Parliament and the Council was adopted which – by amending an earlier EC Decision – increased the co-financing rate of measures supported

---

[1] *BBC News Europe*, 12 October 2013.

by the European Refugee Fund, the European Return Fund and the European Fund for the integration of third-country nationals. The Union contribution was increased by a further 20 per cent beyond the maximum of 75 per cent for Member States experiencing or threatened with serious difficulties with respect to their financial stability (European Parliament/Council of the European Union, 2013a). This Decision was aimed at providing additional liquidity to asylum projects carried out by Member States particularly affected by the deepening financial crisis (especially Greece) to ensure the continued implementation of ongoing measures. It indicated further recognition by the Union of asymmetric pressures and capabilities of Member States in the asylum field and the need for corresponding solidarity measures. The fact, however, that it had taken six months from the original Commission proposal of September 2012 to the adoption of this ultimately rather simple and not exceedingly costly adjustment showed again that rapid financial solidarity is not the Union's forte.

After years of negotiation the Council and Parliament were able to reach a package compromise on the four remaining legislative acts needed for the completion of the CEAS. The original 2012 deadline set by the Stockholm Programme (see Monar, 2012, 2013) was missed, but after a first reading approval by the Parliament on 12 June the recast Asylum Procedures and Reception Conditions Directives as well as recast Dublin II and Eurodac Regulations were formally adopted on 26 June: the recast Asylum Procedures Directive (European Parliament/Council of the European Union, 2013b) enhances the coherence of EU asylum policy by introducing a single 'international protection' procedure with identical basic principles and guarantees the granting and withdrawing of both asylum and subsidiary protection status (Articles 6–29). The recast Directive enhances a range of guarantees for the applications while at the same time redefining and clarifying procedures with a view to reaching decisions earlier – normally within six months (Article 31(3)) – and with a greater legal quality, which is expected to reduce the number of appeals. Among the enhanced guarantees are mandatory personal interviews in all international protection cases (Article 14), the possibility for the applicant to request interviews to be conducted by a person of the same sex (Article 15(b)), tighter rules on the reporting and recording of these interviews (Article 17), and free legal assistance and representation in appeals procedures (Article 21). Also of importance is the obligation for Member States to ensure that their personnel are properly trained, taking into account the relevant training standards established and developed by the European Asylum Support Office (EASO) and the need for a general knowledge of problems that could adversely affect applicants' ability to be interviewed, such as indications that they may have been tortured in the past (Article 4(3)). The conditions for applying 'accelerated procedures' with reduced guarantees are defined more restrictively, and Member States can 'prioritize' applications in case they appear particularly well-founded or applicants being vulnerable or in need of special procedural guarantees, such as in the case of unaccompanied minors (Article 31).

While it was generally recognized that the recast Asylum Procedures Directive brings progress on a range of points, the often complex political compromises it reflects also attracted criticism. The UNHCR thus regretted the problematic provisions of Article 25(6) on the applicability of border procedures to unaccompanied minors (UNHCR, 2013) and the European Council on Refugees and Exiles (ECRE, 2013) the continuing applicability of 'accelerated procedures' to vulnerable groups and the range of conditions to which free legal assistance remains subject.

The recast Reception Conditions Directive (European Parliament/Council of the European Union, 2013c) provides for partially enhanced and more harmonized living standards of applicants for both asylum and subsidiary protection. One of the most contentious issues in the negotiations had been the detention of asylum seekers, and the provisions on detention are the most detailed of the recast legal instruments. Article 8 of the Directive provides that an applicant can only be detained on the basis of an individual assessment in six defined situations – such as the verification of an applicant's identity or nationality – and if less coercive alternative measures, such as regular reporting to authorities, cannot be applied effectively. This excludes any systematic detention of applicants. The detention has also to be for 'as short a period as possible', must be based on a written order stating the reasons for it in fact and in law and is subject to a 'speedy' judicial review, which if not initiated *ex officio* can also be requested by the applicant (Article 9). As a rule, detention has to take place in special facilities, and if prison accommodation has to be used instead the detained applicants have to be kept separately from ordinary prisoners, with access to open air spaces and representatives from the UNHCR and relevant nongovernmental organizations (NGOs) being guaranteed in all cases (Article 10). There is a range of new provisions in favour of vulnerable persons, and unaccompanied minors can only be detained in exceptional circumstances (Article 11(3)). Another controversial issue during the negotiations – access to the labour market – ended with the compromise of a shortening of the currently applicable 12 months waiting period to a maximum of nine months after the lodging of the application – an arguably rather small concession as Member States can, for reasons of national labour market policy, still give priority to EU nationals or legally resident third-country nationals (Article 15).

The recast Dublin II Regulation (European Parliament/Council of the European Union 2013d), which defines the criteria and mechanisms for determining the Member State responsible for processing an asylum application, was marked both by a (mostly northern) majority of Member States securing an almost unchanged continuation of the existing criteria and transfer system, which puts the primary 'burden' on the (mostly southern) first countries of irregular entry, and by an at least partially successful effort by the European Parliament to extricate from the Council a number of additional guarantees for applicants for international protection. As regards the sharing (or rather non-sharing?) of responsibilities under the Dublin system, the recast Regulation arguably even increases the pressure on the first countries of irregular entry by providing for a new 'mechanism for early warning, preparedness and crisis management' that obliges Member States facing a major surge of applications and/or capacity problems to submit first a Commission monitored 'preventive action plan' and then, in case of a deteriorating situation, at the request of the Commission a 'crisis management action plan' – all of this under the 'political guidance' of the Council, which extends also to potential solidarity measures with the Member State(s) concerned (Article 33).

This solidarity counterpart was given some substance during the year not only by the above mentioned co-financing rates of the relevant EU funds, but also by the agreement reached during the negotiations on the new 2014–20 EU Financial Framework on a substantial increase of spending on solidarity measures in the context of the new €3.1 billion Asylum, Migration and Integration Fund (AMIF). This will from 2014 onwards replace the existing funding instruments that, for instance, provided in October the basis of an emergency support operation by the EASO in Bulgaria after the country experienced a surge in asylum applications (EASO, 2013). Although still amounting for only 3.1 per cent of total EU budget appropriations for the seven-year programming period, EU funding support for measures in the field was increased by nearly 50 per cent with increased funding opportunities of a total of €360 million also for the resettlement of refugees within the EU (European Parliament, 2014a). Given the large numbers of refugees seeking shelter in the EU this is hardly more than a small step towards an effective solidarity system. It should be added, however, that the mandatory personal interview of applicants foreseen by the recast Asylum Procedures Directive has at least the potential of enhancing the fuller consideration of other of the Dublin criteria, such as the existence of family links (Articles 7 and 8), before an applicant is sent back to the Member State of first irregular entry, which would contribute to both more fairness to the applicants and a less uneven distribution among Member States.

The fourth and final of the legal instruments still needed to complete the CEAS – the recast Eurodac Regulation (European Parliament/Council of the European Union, 2013e) – was adopted together with the other parts of the package in June, although it dealt with the much more technical issue of the biometric database for comparing fingerprints needed for the effective application of the Dublin Regulation. The main contentious issue had been the access of law enforcement authorities to the fingerprints of applicants. While the Parliament could not prevail against the Council's determination to render this access possible, the assembly was able to secure a number of important restrictions and conditions to this use of biometric refugee data for law enforcement purposes.

Indeed Article 1(2) of the recast Regulation introduces as a new additional purpose of Eurodac: the possibility for designated national authorities and Europol to request, for law enforcement purposes, the comparison of fingerprint data with those stored in the Eurodac central system. There are, however, numerous restrictions and conditions: the designated national authorities must be responsible for the prevention, detection or investigation of terrorist offences or of other serious criminal offences. They cannot include authorities exclusively responsible for national security intelligence (Article 5) and must act under the supervision of specifically designated 'verifying authorities' (Article 6), which have to make sure that all necessary conditions for sending a comparison request to Eurodac are met. These include cumulatively: a last resort provision (requests can only be made if the necessary data could not be found in the databases of the requesting Member State or any other Member State as well as the EU Visa Information System); an overriding public security concern that makes the searching of the database proportionate; a necessity to carry out the comparison only in specific cases (that is, not as part of a systematic search); and reasonable grounds to consider that the comparisons will substantially contribute to the prevention, detection or investigation of a terrorist offence or other serious criminal offence (Article 20). Requests from Europol, which has to identify within its own structure an independent verification authority (Article 7), are subject to the same conditions plus an authorization of Europol by the Member State of origin for the processing of information obtained from Eurodac data (Article 21). There are also a range of enhanced rules as regards data protection and the information rights of persons entered into the Eurodac system (Article 29).

While, among other NGOs, ECRE took the view that the recast Regulation still raised 'important questions relating to the possible stigmatization of an already vulnerable group' (ECRE, 2013), it was generally recognized that a serious effort had been made to balance internal security considerations with the duty to protect those seeking refuge in the EU. The protracted debate about the access of law enforcement authorities somewhat obscured the fact that the recast Regulation is also aimed at improving the efficiency and effectiveness of the system by passing responsibility for the database to the European Agency, for the operational management of large-scale information technology systems in the area of freedom, security and justice (EU-Lisa) in Tallin (Article 4), a mandatory maximum processing time of request of requests of 24 hours and a number of provisions aimed at improving both transmission speeds and data quality (Articles 24 and 25).

While the legislative (and political) effort to finalize the CEAS package has surely been considerable and progress addressing many existing weaknesses is undeniable it still remains to be seen how well the now at least officially 'completed' system will work in practice when all the instruments will have become fully applicable in 2015. Quite a few of the new rules are of greater complexity than the existing ones, and the inevitable political compromises have also left some wide margins of interpretations that can still result in significant implementation problems and persisting major differences between national systems. The functioning of the CEAS will also depend very much on the further development of solidarity between the Member States and the so far still limited but evolving role of the EASO in terms of analysis and emergency support. The main message in the joint statement issued by 11 leading NGOs on the occasion of the final vote in the Parliament on 10 June that the new CEAS has 'still a long way to go' therefore appears to be a healthy caveat (NGO Statement, 2013).

Migration Policy

In comparison with legislative progress on asylum, there were again rather meagre changes in the domain of legal immigration. Only on the Directive for non-EU seasonal workers – originally proposed by the Commission back in 2010 – did the Council and Parliament reach a political agreement in October that made the adoption of the instrument in early 2014 very likely. According to this agreement, Member States will retain large margins for national implementation: not only will they keep the right to determine volumes of admission and reject applications if EU workers are available, but it will also be left to them, in particular, to determine a period of stay between five and nine months in any 12-month period. Non-EU seasonal workers will benefit from equal treatment with EU nationals in terms of employment and working conditions, including pay and dismissal, working hours and holidays, as well as to several social security benefits such as those linked to sickness, invalidity and old age. However, because of the temporary nature of the stay of seasonal workers, Member States will not be obliged to ensure equal treatment regarding unemployment and family benefits, and can also limit equal treatment on tax benefits and education and vocational training. The European Parliament successfully insisted on seasonal workers having their pay and working hours specified in a contract before applying to enter the EU, on guarantees by employers regarding appropriate accommodation and on sanctions for employers in breach of the obligation who will also have to compensate the seasonal workers concerned (European Parliament, 2013).

The Council had its own internal problems during the negotiations with the Parliament as two Member States, the Czech Republic and Poland, continued to question the legitimacy of EU action on this matter on subsidiarity grounds, and Bulgaria was having difficulties with the granting of certain equal rights to third-country nationals at a time when there were still restrictions in place regarding the free movement of Bulgarian (and Romanian) workers inside the EU. This highlighted again the extent to which legal immigration for work purposes remains a minefield of national political sensitivities and competence concerns. Given the current debates on immigration in many Member States, the granting of at least some equal rights to non-EU seasonal workers can be regarded as quite an achievement.

The other Commission proposal on legal migration under negotiation between the Council and the European Parliament already since 2010, a Directive on non-EU intra-corporate transferees, continued to be delayed mainly by disagreements between the Council and Parliament over equal treatment rights of the non-EU intra-corporate trans-ferees. On 25 March the Commission added to the negotiation agenda a proposal for a new Directive on the conditions of entry and the residence of third-country nationals for the purposes of research, studies, pupil exchange, remunerated and unremunerated training, voluntary service and au pairing (European Commission, 2013a). This proposal did not cover entirely new ground as its main aim is to merge Directive 2005/71/EC of 12 October 2005 on a specific procedure for admitting third-country nationals for the purposes of scientific research and Directive 2004/114 of 13 December 2004 on the conditions of admission of third-country nationals for the purposes of studies, pupil exchange, unremunerated training or voluntary service into a single instrument while at the same time addressing a number of weaknesses of both existing instruments. The proposed new Directive covers admission conditions for two groups of third-country nationals currently not covered by EU immigration rules – au pairs and remunerated trainees – and improves admission conditions for third-country national researchers as regards family reunifica-tion, access to the labour market by family members and intra-EU mobility. It provides that an applicant who satisfies all admission conditions to a Member State shall be granted a long-stay visa or residence permit. It also facilitates and simplifies intra-EU mobility for students and researchers, particularly for those under the Erasmus Mundus/Marie Curie programmes, which will be expanded under the 2014–20 Multiannual Financial Framework.

With access to the labour market always being a sensitive issue,the Commission showed some political courage by proposing that students and researchers should be allowed after the end of their studies and/or research to stay within the Member State in order to look for work or set up a business, indicating rightly that the possibility to stay on for such a purpose is often an important factor for students and researchers to choose their destination. The Commission proposal received a broadly favourable initial reaction within the Parliament but – unsurprisingly – a more mixed one in the Council.

Given the slow and patchy advances of the EU's 'common immigration policy' (the ambitious term used in Article 79 TFEU), the Commission felt it necessary in its Annual Report on Immigration and Asylum published in June to stress again that the working-age population's (15–64 year-old age group) share of total EU population already reached its peak in 2006, Moreover, the old-age dependency ratio reached 26.8 per cent in 2012 – and is projected to increase sharply up to 52.6 per cent by 2060 – and that well-managed legal migration can play a positive role in boosting growth and addressing labour market shortages (European Commission, 2013b). With 0.18 per cent of the total population (0.9 million, 2012 figures) net legal immigration into the EU appeared still to be at a very moderate level. This figure, however, does not include illegal immigration, and the reported 20.7 million third-country nationals living in the EU (4.1 per cent of the population total) already make a more substantial figure if compared to the only 13.7 million EU citizens living in other Member States. It remains an unpleasant fact that higher concentrations of non-nationals in certain cities and regions and (often false) perceptions about enhanced labour market competition can fuel xenophobic reactions among EU citizens and be instrumentalized by populist or even extremist political forces. The Commission was therefore surely right in its annual report to underline the need for effective measures to promote integration. It did not, however, propose any major new initiative on this front, and it clearly does not help that Member States' sensitivities in this field have limited EU competences on integration to purely supporting measures (Article 67(4) TFEU).

Although Frontex (2013) reported in its 2013 Annual Risk Analysis a sharp fall in detected illegal border crossings into the EU in 2012 by 49 per cent to 72,437, other indicators of illegal immigration pressure such as detected illegal stays (344,928) and refusal of entry (115,305) remained nearly unchanged, and for the third quarter of 2013 Frontex reported a massive 93 per cent increase of detected illegal border crossings into the EU in comparison to the same period in 2012, mainly due to a significant increase of illegal immigrants from Syria and Eritrea (Frontex, 2014). Illegal immigration pressure, therefore, remained very much on the EU's migration policy agenda.

Apart from the by now traditional focus on external border management responses to this challenge (see next section), the EU also continued its external action on this side by the conclusion of readmission agreements with Armenia and Cape Verde in April and made much progress in the negotiations with Azerbaijan. As usual the Union combined this with – as a counterpart – nearly parallel progress on visa facilitation agreements. On 13 June Commissioner Cecilia Malmström also signed on behalf of the Union a Mobility Partnership with Morocco that, while providing for negotiations on visa facilitation and other measures facilitating temporary stays of Moroccan vocational trainees, students, researchers and businessmen within the EU, also foresees co-operation in the combat against illegal immigration, networks involved in the trafficking and smuggling of human beings as well as the promotion of an effective return and readmission policy (Council of the European Union, 2013a). A similar Mobility Partnership was signed with Azerbaijan on 5 December (Council of the European Union, 2013b) and another was in advanced preparation with Tunisia at the end of the year, highlighting the continuing effort of the Union to strengthen the external (protective) dimension of its migration policy. The need for more co-operation with third-countries to manage migration flows was also strongly highlighted in the Commission's December report on the work of the 'Task Force Mediterranean', which had been set up as a result of the aforementioned boat incidents off Lampedusa and Malta (European Commission, 2013c).

Border Policy

The EU's border policy continued to be driven primarily by the migratory pressures on its external borders. Most of the aforementioned surge of detected illegal border crossings in the third quarter of the year (reaching a total of 42,618) affected the southern Italian sea borders, but there was also a 600 per cent increase of detections compared to the same period the year before, which was at least partially ascribed to a diversionary effect due to the enhanced surveillance of the nearby land borders between Greece and Turkey that had been a major problem area in the preceding years (Frontex, 2014). This highlighted not only the continuing pressure on EU external borders, but also the constant evolution of the situation and the resulting need for comprehensive intelligence and analysis to enable border guards – be it at the national level only or in the form of Frontex initiated joint operations – to react fast and flexibly to situation changes at the external borders. The adoption on 22 October of the Regulation establishing the European Border Surveillance System (Eurosur) marked a significant step forward for the improvement of the situational awareness and reaction capability of Member States and Frontex (European Parliament/Council of the European Union, 2013f).

The Eurosur system, which has been in preparation since 2008, covers information exchange and co-operation with regard to the surveillance of external land and sea borders, including the monitoring, detection, identification, tracking, prevention and interception of unauthorized border crossings for the purpose of detecting, preventing and combating illegal immigration and cross-border crime and contributing to ensuring the protection and saving the lives of migrants. It consists of: (a) national co-ordination centres (NCCs) co-ordinating national border-control activities; (b) 'national situational pictures' established and maintained by the NCCs; (c) a secure communication network maintained by Frontex to allow for the exchange of bilateral and multilateral information in near-real-time on a round-the-the clock basis; (d) a 'European situational picture' established and maintained by Frontex on the basis of the national situational pictures as well as a range of additional information sources, including Frontex itself, the European Commission, Union delegations and other Union bodies and international organizations; (e) a common pre-frontier intelligence picture established and maintained by Frontex in order to provide the NCCs with effective, accurate and timely information and analysis on the pre-frontier area outside of the EU; and (f) a common application of surveillance tools co-ordinated by Frontex using ship reporting systems in accordance with their respective legal bases, satellite imagery and sensors mounted on any vehicle, vessel or other craft.

The national and European situational pictures comprise an events layer regrouping data on unauthorized border crossings, incidents relating to the risks of migrants, cross-border crime and crisis situations, and an operational layer regrouping data on operational means, including military means assisting law enforcement missions, information on the position, status and type of these means and on the authorities involved as well as information on terrain and weather conditions at the external borders. This is completed by an analysis layer containing key developments and indicators, analytical reports, risk rating trends, regional monitors, intelligence analysis, reference imagery, background maps, earth observation imagery based change analysis, geo-referenced data and external border permeability maps.

One of the main purposes of Eurosur is the attribution by Frontex of impact levels to each of the external land and sea border sections of Member States, ranging from 'low impact', where the incidents related to illegal immigration or cross-border crime occurring at the relevant border section have an insignificant impact on border security, through 'medium impact', where they have a moderate impact on border security, to 'high impact' where they have a significant impact on border security (Article 15 of the Regulation). In the case of the attribution of a 'high impact level' the Member State concerned must not only ensure that its authorities operating at that border section are given the necessary support and that reinforced surveillance measures are taken but it may also request support from Frontex (and via Frontex other Member States) in the form of priority treatment as regards the common application of surveillance tools, the deployment of European Border Guard Teams and the deployment of technical equipment at the disposal of Frontex (Article 16).

With its standardization of border situational information, the provision for a constantly updated and analytical enriched European *situational* picture and the justification it provides for requesting operational solidarity measures in case of a 'high impact' assessment by Frontex, Eurosur goes clearly beyond a simple information exchange network towards a common threat assessment and response system, even though it does not make common responses mandatory. Before the background of the tragic refugee boat incidents in the Mediterranean, Commissioner Cecilia Malmström also emphasized on 3 October that Eurosur will help Member States to better track, identify and rescue small vessels at sea thanks to much improved co-ordination between national authorities, appropriate channels of communication and improved surveillance technology (European Commission, 2013d). The system's targeting of EU external border challenges was reflected in the fact that it became initially operational on 2 December only for the 18 Schengen countries and one Schengen associated country (Norway) in charge of most of the EU's external borders. The other eight Schengen Member States (Austria, Belgium, Czech Republic, Denmark, Germany, Luxembourg, Netherlands and Sweden) and three associated countries (Iceland, Liechtenstein and Switzerland) are expected to join on 1 December 2014, with only Ireland and the United Kingdom as non-Schengen Member States staying outside. The full development of the system obviously requires enhanced technical capabilities of both Frontex and national border authorities. The European Commission has estimated the full cost of establishing the system for the 2014–20 EU Financial Framework at €244 million, with the Member States being able to request up to 75 per cent of EU-co-funding for the establishment of the NCCs (European Parliament, 2014b). Yet critics have argued that the highly complex system has not been developed on the basis of adequate technological risk assessments and could eventually easily cost the EU three times as much (Hayes and Vermeulen, 2012).

The potential for large-scale EU border management technology projects to run considerably over initial time and cost plans was demonstrated by the much delayed start of the second generation Schengen Information System (SIS II), which finally became operational on 9 April 2013. Allowing national authorities both to issue and consult 'alerts' on persons who may have been involved in serious crime or may not have the right to enter or stay in the EU as well as on stolen or lost objects (such as cars and passports), the system remains crucial to the effective functioning of the Schengen border regime. The initial target delivery date for the SIS II had been March 2007, and the costs for putting it into place rose from an initial 2001 estimate of €23 million to €167.8 million, with delays being due both to initial design flaws and changing legal, technical and political requirements. Yet in the end the enhanced technical specifications were met, with the system now allowing for the linking of alerts on persons, objects and vehicles, the processing of biometric data, European Arrest Warrants and information on misused identity as well as the placing of alerts regarding stolen aircrafts, boats, boat engines, containers, industrial equipment, securities and means of payment. The capacity of the system (which currently contains 45 million alerts, of which over 39 million are on stolen identity documents) was increased to 70 million alerts on entry into operation. The system was prepared and tested, however, for later capacity increases up to 100 million alerts so that the EU may not have to go through another laborious and costly upgrade process very soon (European Commission, 2013e).

After months of difficult negotiations between Council and Parliament a compromise was finally also found on the Schengen governance reform package that was triggered by the Arab Spring refugee 'crisis' of 2011 and subsequent debate about the temporary re-introduction of internal border controls. The substantively more important of the two legislative instruments – Regulation (EU) 1051/2013 on common rules for the temporary re-introduction of border control at internal borders in exceptional circumstances – was adopted on 22 October (European Parliament/Council of the European Union, 2013g). The Regulation re-affirms the already existing right of Schengen Member States to re-introduce controls at internal borders in case of a serious threat to public policy or internal security, but does so with a number of new conditions and procedural require-ments that amend the Schengen Borders Code of 2006 (Regulation (EC) 562/2006).

While the time limits for the *planned re-introduction of controls* are quite generous – renewable periods of 30 days up to six months (amended Article 23 of the Schengen Borders Code), the conditions under which Member States are allowed to proceed with a re-introduction have been toughened. Controls can only be re-instated as a 'measure of last resort' and Member States must assess the extent to which the re-introduction is likely to adequately remedy the threat to public policy or internal security as well as the proportionality of the measure in relation to that threat (new Article 23a of the Code). On the procedural side, the Regulation requires the respective Member State in case of planned re-introductions of controls to notify the other Member States and the Commis-sion at the latest four weeks before those will take effect and to specify the reasons, including all relevant data detailing the events that constitute a serious threat to its public policy or internal security, the scope of the proposed re-introduction, specifying at which part or parts of the internal borders controls are to be re-introduced and the duration of the planned re-introduction. This information also has to be submitted to the Parliament and the Council, and the Commission can request supplementary information. The Commis-sion or any other Member State can then issue an opinion, and the Commission should in any case do so if it has concerns as regards the necessity or proportionality of the planned re-introduction of controls. These opinions will then trigger 'consultations' between the notifying Member States, the Commission and all other affected Member States (amended Article 24 of the Code). This could generate significant political pressure when the Commission and/or other Member States disagree with the notified measure. In *cases requiring immediate action*, a Member State is allowed to re-introduce controls immedi-ately but initially only for up to ten days and with a possibility of prolongation of up to a maximum of two months and with the same information obligations applicable in case of a planned re-introduction (amended Article 25 of the Code).

Entirely new is the 'specific procedure' under the amended Article 26 of the Borders Code 'where exceptional circumstances put the overall functioning of the area without internal border control at risk' and that provides for the re-introduction of controls for a period of up to six months with possible prolongation up to two years. This procedure is in two respects quite innovative. First, the reason to activate is not a threat to public policy or internal security of a Member State, but a risk to the functioning of the Schengen border system as such – which is thus for the first time recognized as a common security interest whose potential endangering can justify a prolonged re-introduction of internal border controls. Second, the new procedure is innovative in that it is up to the Council to recommend that one or more Member States decide to re-introduce border control at all or at specific parts of their internal borders 'as a last resort and as a measure to protect the common interests [. . .] where all other measures are ineffective in mitigating the serious threat identified'. This takes the decision on a general threat to the functioning of the system and a resulting prolonged re-introduction of internal controls out of the discretion of individual Member States – which French President Nicolas Sarkozy and Italian Prime Minister Silvio Berlusconi had wanted to strengthen with their 2011 call for an overhaul of the Schengen system (see Monar, 2012) – and makes it subject to collective decision-making. The Commission, however, suffered a defeat as it had tried in its original legislative proposal to make the re-introduction dependent on its own authorization, which had been fiercely resisted by most of the Member States. Under the new Article 26(2) of the Borders Code its power is now limited to making a proposal, which can also be requested by the Member States.

The second legislative instrument of the Schengen governance reform – the Regulation also adopted on 22 October – is the Council Regulation (EU) 1053/213 on the Schengen evaluation and monitoring mechanism, which is essentially a peer review process aimed at identifying any deficits on the Member States side as regards the effective application of the Schengen border managements rules and standards. There had been a major clash between the Parliament and Council over the latter's change of the legal base for the instrument to Article 70 TFEU (measures on the evaluation of the implementation of EU measures within the 'area of freedom, security and justice') as this required only the information of the Parliament about the results of evaluations. The Parliament relented, however, after the Council accepted to consult the Parliament formally and to also do so in the case of a future amendment.

The four main innovative elements of the Council Regulation are the Commission's task to propose, after consulting Frontex and Europol, both a five-year evaluation programme and annual programmes to implement it (Articles 5 and 6), the linking of the evaluations with Frontex border risk analyses (Article 7), in addition to the already existing evaluation questionnaires and announced on-site inspection visits the introduction of the possibility of announced inspection visits (Article 13) and a much enhanced monitoring and follow-up on recommendations to Member States as a result of their evaluation (Articles 15 and 16). Member States now not only have to draw up a national action plan to address identified deficiencies and report on its implementation, but the Commission can also schedule revisits for verification purposes and alert the Council and Parliament in case of 'serious deficiencies' constituting 'a serious threat to public policy or internal security within the area without internal border controls' (Article 16(7)), which could then trigger the aforementioned procedure under amended Article 26 of the Schengen Borders Code for the re-introduction of internal controls.

Overall the Schengen governance reform arguably ended with an general strengthening of the rules and mechanisms that safeguard the Member States' right to take protective measures in special circumstances but at the same time provides substantial guarantees against an uncontrolled and/or generalized re-introduction of internal border controls and is likely to add to more implementation effectiveness and mutual trust among the Member

States because of the much enhanced evaluation mechanism. The 2011 Schengen crisis has thus resulted in a strengthening rather than weakening of the Schengen system.

Judicial Co-operation

Compared to the major legislative progress of the year before, judicial co-operation in civil matters evolved more modestly with the adoption of only one new instrument on 12 June: Regulation (EU) 606/2013 on mutual recognition of protection measures (European Parliament/Council of the European Union 2013h). The Regulation covers orders issued by national authorities to protect a person's physical and psychological integrity by prohibiting or regulating the entering of this person's residence and workplace and/or any forms of contact (telephone or other) and or approaching of the protected person (Article 2). It provides for any such measure ordered in a Member State to be recognized in the other Member States without any special procedure being required and shall be enforceable without a declaration of enforceability being required (Article 3), thus constituting a further (small) extension of the principle of mutual recognition.

In the field of criminal justice co-operation the rights of defendants were strengthened by the adoption on 22 October of Directive 2013/48/EU on the right of access to a lawyer in criminal proceedings (European Parliament/Council of the European Union, 2013i), which can be regarded as most important measure of the 2009 Council Roadmap on criminal procedural rights. Core provisions include the Member States' obligation to ensure access to a lawyer without undue delay before and during questioning, upon the carrying-out of investigative or evidence-gathering acts, after deprivation of liberty and prior to appearing in court (Article 3). Member States must also ensure the respecting of the confidentiality of communication between a suspect and lawyer, including in meetings, correspondence and telephone conversations (Article 4) as well as ensure that suspects have the right to have someone of their choosing being informed of their arrest and to communicate personally with at least one person of their choice, such as a relative or employer (Article 5). The Regulation also provides for suspects arrested under a European Arrest Warrant to have the right to a lawyer in both the country of the arrest and the country that issued the warrant (Article 10). These provisions make it the most important measure adopted as part of the 2009 Council Roadmap on criminal procedural rights and a highly necessary corollary of repressive instruments such as the European Arrest Warrant.

On 17 July the Commission made its long announced proposal for the establishment of a European Public Prosecutor's Office (EPPO) aimed at improving the EU-wide prosecution of cases of fraud against the financial interests of the EU which it combined with proposals also for the reform of Eurojust (European Commission, 2013f). According to the EPPO legislative proposal, the office would have the powers and the resources necessary to investigate, prosecute and bring its cases, whether national or cross-border, to courts, and ensure both higher speed and effectiveness of fraud prosecution cases whose current (that is, 2011) success rate the Commission rated at only 43 per cent. In most cases, delegated European prosecutors would carry out the investigations and prosecutions in the respective Member State, using national staff and applying national law. Yet there would also be a strong element of centralization and hierarchy as the European delegated prosecutors would be co-ordinated and work under the instructions of the

European Public Prosecutor to ensure a uniform approach throughout the EU, which would be of crucial importance particularly in cross-border cases. In particularly serious and complex cases the European Public Prosecutor, who would appointed by the Council with the consent of the European Parliament for a non-renewable term of eight years, could also take over the investigation (European Commission 2013g).

As regards Eurojust – whose prosecution co-ordination functions would continue to apply to all criminal cases not falling within the remit of the EPPO and would provide administrative and technical support to the latter – the Commission's legislative proposal focuses primarily on a clear distinction between the operational tasks of the Eurojust College (consisting of one National Member per Member State) and administrative tasks – to be handled by a new Executive Board – in order to enable the College and the National Members to focus on their operational tasks (European Commission, 2013h). Not unexpectedly the United Kingdom, Ireland and Denmark decided to opt-out of the proposed EPPO Regulation, and a majority of the other Member States indicated a preference for a more decentralized collegial structure of the EPPO, which suggests that the negotiations might take quite some time.

Internal Security Co-operation

The implementation of the initial three-year reduced policy cycle for organized and serious international crime was completed during the year. The Commission submitted in January an evaluation report that identified a range of both programming and implementation weaknesses and made a number of suggestions for improvement, including a more precise definition of priorities and strategic goals, specific threat assessments, a strengthening of the operational planning, more flexibility on the implementation side, and improved quality and accuracy of the data provided by Member States to Europol (European Commission, 2013i). The June Council Conclusions on setting the EU's priorities for the fight against serious and organized crime between 2014 and 2017 – the next and this time full 'policy cycle' in the field – took the Commission's recommendations partially into account as regards enhanced precision and operational objectives. It put the disruption of organized crime groups involved in the facilitation of illegal immigration and of those involved in intra-EU human trafficking and human trafficking from the most prevalent external source countries for the purposes of labour exploitation and sexual exploitation at the top of the list of priorities (Council of the European Union, 2013d). It was noteworthy, however, that Europol's Serious and Organized Crime Threat (SOCTA) Assessment for 2013 identified drug trafficking and trade in counterfeit goods as the two highest listed crime areas (Europol, 2013), so that the Council Conclusions clearly reflected a higher political preoccupation with illegal immigration and human trafficking than Europol's law enforcement data assessment would have suggested.

Conclusions

This fourth full year of the implementation of the 2010–14 Stockholm Programme saw the EU making much progress on asylum and border management issues, but less so on legal immigration – where its record remains patchy – and internal security co-operation – where there seemed to be more programming than substantive progress. As in previous years, substantive progress appeared to depend on the Member States most immediate concerns, such as responding to refugee and illegal migration pressures, rather than on longer term strategic considerations, such as the need to put a more comprehensive solidarity system into place or reconsider a global approach to migration giving full weight to the EU's economic and demographic challenges. The fact that the initial debate on the establishment of Eurojust was almost exclusively focused on its role with regard to the protection of the financial interests of the EU with only slight consideration of its wider implications for an common EU law enforcement area also showed that this is not a time in which both the Member States and the Commission are willing to pursue major ambitions – and accept commensurate political risks – in the justice and home affairs domain. At the end of the year the question remained open whether, in the light of unequal policy dynamics in the different fields and the obvious priority changes over time, the five-year programming practice that the Stockholm Programme had continued was still a useful framework for ensuring the further development of the 'area of freedom, security and justice' and whether a new programme to follow on after its expiry in 2014 would still make sense. There seemed to be a growing consensus among European policy-makers that if such a new multi-annual programming effort were beneficial, consolidation and better implementation rather than adding many new objectives should be the guiding rationale.

References

Council of the European Union (2013a) Joint Declaration establishing a Mobility Partnership between the Kingdom of Morocco and the European Union and its Member States. 6139/13, 3 June.

Council of the European Union (2013b) Joint Declaration on a Mobility Partnership between the Republic of Azerbaijan and the European Union and its participating Member States. 16399/13, 26 November.

Council of the European Union (2013d) Council Conclusions on setting the EU's priorities for the fight against serious and organised crime between 2014 and 2017. 12095/13, 26 July.

European Asylum Support Office (EASO) (2013) 'EASO to Provide Support to Bulgaria', Valetta, October.

European Commission (2013a) Proposal for a Directive [. . .] on the conditions of entry and residence of third-country nationals for the purposes of research, studies, pupil exchange, remunerated and unremunerated training, voluntary service and au pairing. COM(2013)151, 25 March.

European Commission (2013b) Annual report on immigration and asylum (2012). COM(2013)422, 17 June.

European Commission (2013c) Communication [. . .] on the work of the Task Force Mediterranean. COM(2013) 869, 4 December.

European Commission (2013d) Tragic accident outside Lampedusa: Statement by European Commissioner for Home Affairs, Cecilia Malmström. MEMO/13/849, 3 October.

European Commission (2013e) Questions and answers: Schengen Information System (SIS II). MEMO/13/309, 9 April.

European Commission (2013f) Communication [. . .]. Better protection of the Union's financial interests: Setting up the European Public Prosecutor's Office and reforming Eurojust. COM(2013) 532, 17 July.

European Commission (2013g) Proposal for a Council Regulation on the establishment of the European Public Prosecutor's Office. COM(2013) 534, 17 July.

European Commission (2013h) Proposal for a Regulation of the European Parliament and of the Council on the European Union Agency for Criminal Justice Cooperation (Eurojust). COM(2013) 535, 17 July.

European Commission (2013i) Evaluation of the EU policy cycle on serious and organised crime, 2011–2013. SWD(2013) 17, 24 January.

European Council of Refugees and Exiles (ECRE) (2013) *Common European Asylum System: The Real Job Still Needs to be Done* (Brussels: ECRE).

European Parliament (2013) Non-EU seasonal workers: EP/Council deal on better social rights and conditions. Luxemburg, 29 October.

European Parliament (2014a) European Parliamentary Research Service: EU funds for asylum, migration and borders. Luxembourg, February 2014.

European Parliament (2014b) Joint answer given by Ms Malmström on behalf of the Commission Written Questions E-011817/13 and E-011908/13. E-011817/13 and E-011908/13, Luxembourg, January.

European Parliament/Council of the European Union (2013a) Decision 258/20123/EU [. . .] of 13 March 2013 amending Decisions 573/2007/EC and 575/2007/EC of the European Parliament and of the Council and Council Decision 2007/435/EC with a view to increasing the co-financing rate of the European Refugee Fund, the European Return Fund and the European Fund for the Integration of Third-Country Nationals as regards certain provisions relating to financial management for certain Member States experiencing or threatened with serious difficulties with respect to their financial stability. OJ L 82, 22 March.

European Parliament/Council of the European Union (2013b) Directive 2013/32/EU [. . .] of 26 June 2013 on common procedures for granting and withdrawing international protection (recast). OJ L 180, 29 June.

European Parliament/Council of the European Union (2013c) Directive 2013/33/EU [. . .] of 26 June 2013 laying down standards for the reception of applicants for international protection (recast). OJ L 180, 29 June.

European Parliament/Council of the European Union (2013d) Regulation (EU) 604/2013 [. . .] of 26 June 2013 establishing the criteria and mechanisms for determining the Member State responsible for examining an application for international protection lodged in one of the Member States by a third-country national or a stateless person (recast). OJ L 180, 29 June.

European Parliament/Council of the European Union (2013e) 'Regulation (EU) 603/2013 [. . .] of 26 June 2013 on the establishment of "Eurodac" for the comparison of fingerprints for the effective application of Regulation (EU) 604/2013 establishing the criteria and mechanisms for determining the Member State responsible for examining an application for international protection [. . .]. OJ L 180, 29 June.

European Parliament/Council of the European Union (2013f) Regulation (EU) 1052/2013 [. . .] of 22 October 2013 Establishing the European Border Surveillance System (Eurosur). OJ L 295, 6 November.

European Parliament/Council of the European Union (2013g) Regulation (EU) 1051/2013 [. . .] of 22 October 2013 amending Regulation (EC) 562/2006 in order to provide for common rules on the temporary reintroduction of border control at internal borders in exceptional circumstances. OJ L 295, 6 November.

European Parliament/Council of the European Union (2013h) Regulation (EU) 606/2013 [. . .] of 12 June 2013 on mutual recognition of protection measures in civil matters. OJ L 181, 29 June.

European Parliament/Council of the European Union (2013i) Directive 2013/48/EU [. . .] of 22 October 2013 on the right of access to a lawyer in criminal proceedings and in European arrest warrant proceedings, and on the right to have a third party informed upon deprivation of liberty and to communicate with third persons and with consular authorities while deprived of liberty. OJ L 294, 6 November.

Europol (2013) 'Europol SOCTA 2013'. The Hague, September.

Eurostat (2013) 'Asylum Applicants and First Instance Decisions on Asylum Applications: Third Quarter of 2013'. *Data in Focus* 16/2013.

Frontex (2013) 'Annual Risk Analysis 2013', Warsaw, April.

Frontex (2014) 'FRAN Quarterly: Quarter 3, July-September 2013', Warsaw, January.

Hayes, B. and Vermeulen, M. (2012) *Borderline: The EU's New Border Surveillance Initiatives* (Berlin: Heinrich-Böll-Stiftung).

NGO Statement (2013) 'Establishing a Common European Asylum System: Still a Long Way to Go – NGO Statement', Brussels, 10 June. Available at: «http://www.ecre.org/index .php?option=com_downloads&id=752».

Monar, J. (2012) 'Justice and Home Affairs', *JCMS*, Vol. 51, No. s2, pp. 116–31.

Monar, J. (2013) 'Justice and Home Affairs', *JCMS*, Vol. 52, No. s1, pp. 124–38.

United Nations High Commissioner for Refugees (UNHCR) (2013) 'Moving Further toward a Common European Asylum System: UNHCR's Statement on the EU Asylum Legislative Package', Brussels, June.

JCMS 2014 Volume 52 Annual Review pp. 157–169   DOI: 10.1111/jcms.12171

Challenging Events, Diminishing Influence? Relations with the Wider Europe

RICHARD G. WHITMAN[1] and ANA E. JUNCOS[2]
[1] Global Europe Centre, University of Kent. [2] University of Bristol

Introduction

The EU's wider European neighbourhood moved from a condition of challenges to one of disarray in the course of 2013. Excepting the bright spots of the accession to the EU of Croatia and the opening of accession negotiations with Serbia, the enlargement policy of the Union to its neighbours remained largely static. The Vilnius summit of the Eastern Partnership (EaP) of November 2013, intended as a moment to mark a deepening of the EU's relationship with its eastern neighbours through the agreement of a new set of bilateral relations, was unsettled and an already negotiated and initialled association agreement with Ukraine remained unsigned. The EU struggled to develop a coherent collective response between its Member States to the civil war in Syria and was a largely irrelevant actor in the post-Arab Spring transitions taking place in other southern neighbours – most notably Egypt and Libya.

The overall assessment of the EU's policies towards the neighbourhood is that 2013 was a period largely of unravelling of its already meagre influence within the neighbourhood. This comes on the back of a disappointing policy performance in the preceding three years (Whitman and Juncos, 2011, 2012, 2013). The EU's policies for its neighbourhood are largely irrelevant to the transition processes in its southern neighbourhood. Furthermore, they are now being challenged directly and actively in its eastern neighbourhood by Russia, which has developed a competing model of economic integration to that on offer from the EU.

The slow recovery of the eurozone economies in the course of 2013 has, however, had a locomotive effect for the economies of the EU's neighbours in the Western Balkans. Assuming that the pace of growth continues, and the eurozone continues its move into what appeared to be a period of post-crisis stabilization, there may be grounds for optimism that the EU's economic and political capital can be more fully engaged with the multiple challenges of its wider neighbourhood.

I. Enlargement

The year 2013 marked two important anniversaries in the EU's enlargement history: it was 20 years since the adoption of the Copenhagen criteria and ten years since the Thessaloniki summit.[1] The Copenhagen criteria adopted in 1993 laid out the conditions

---

[1] For a reflection of the EU's 'transformative power' in the decade since the 2004 enlargement, see Grabbe's contribution to this volume.

for the accession of new members into the EU and guided the transition and the eventually successful accession of the central and eastern European countries. Ten years later, at the European Council in Thessaloniki in June 2003, EU leaders acknowledged that the 'future of the Balkans is within the European Union' and endorsed a clear perspective of EU membership for the Western Balkan countries (European Council, 2003). This constituted a crucial shift in the EU's strategy after the devastating wars in the region.

Far from being a year of celebrations, however, 2013 can be better described as a year of 'highs' and 'lows' as far as the EU's enlargement policy was concerned. The successes included the accession of Croatia to the EU on 1 July 2013 as the 28th EU Member State and the momentous political agreement between Serbia and Kosovo negotiated in the spring. The latter led the way to the decision of the European Council to open accession negotiations with Serbia in June, followed by the Council's decision to authorize the opening of negotiations for a Stabilization and Association Agreement between the EU and Kosovo. As the Council noted in December 2013, both Croatia's accession and the agreement between Serbia and Kosovo 'are a strong and visible testimony of the transformative and stabilising effect of the enlargement and stabilisation and association process' (Council of the EU, 2013b). There was also some good news with the opening of a negotiating chapter on regional policy with Turkey after a three-year lapse and the signing of a re-admission agreement between the EU and Turkey.

By contrast, lack of progress regarding political reform in Bosnia and Herzegovina and the unresolved name dispute between Greece and Macedonia provided an illustration of the problems that continued to hamper EU enlargement policy. For its part, the newly elected Icelandic government decided to put accession negotiations on hold in May 2013.[2] The decision followed the victory of the eurosceptic Independence and the Progressive parties in April 2013, which was widely seen as a vote against continuing negotiations on EU membership. The decision also provides evidence of the lack of the EU's transformative power in cases where the asymmetric interdependence between candidate countries and the EU is not so pronounced and where the economic costs are perceived to outweigh the benefits of enlargement (Moravcsik and Vachudova, 2003).

Overall, the EU's enlargement strategy remained unchanged in 2013 as summarized in the Commission's strategy report unveiled in October (Commission, 2013c). Over the last two decades the enlargement strategy has remained firmly based on the Copenhagen criteria through the use of conditionality. However, as stated in the Commission's report, the accession process has been refined over the years, becoming 'more rigorous and comprehensive than in the past' (Commission, 2013c, p. 2).[3] This is not just a reflection of the EU's own evolution and increase in competencies, but also the result of the lessons learned from previous enlargement rounds. One the key lessons of this process has been 'the importance of addressing the *fundamentals first*', meaning compliance with conditions in the areas of the rule of law, democracy and economic governance (Commission, 2013c, p. 2; emphasis in the original). Hence, 20 years after Copenhagen, the enlargement strategy has come full circle. Given the legacies of conflict, but also the impact of the financial and economic crisis, these conditions are particularly relevant in the case of the Western Balkan countries.

[2] In February 2014, a decision was taken to officially withdraw the country's application to join the EU (*EUObserver.com*, 25 February 2014). At the time, 27 of the negotiating chapters had been opened and 11 provisionally closed.
[3] See also Commission (2013b) for a summary of the key stages in the enlargement process.

In line with this new approach to the accession negotiations and lessons from the 2007 enlargement, the EU has also prioritized chapters 23 (on the judiciary and fundamental rights) and 24 (on justice, freedom and security) in the negotiation with candidate countries. This approach has been implemented in negotiations with Montenegro[4] and has also been integrated into the negotiating framework for Serbia. The assumption is that '[t]ackling these areas early in the negotiations gives maximum time to enlargement countries to ensure that reforms are deeply rooted and irreversible' (Commission, 2013c, p. 7). The EU is also keen to deal with these issues before accession. As the 2004 and 2007 enlargements have demonstrated, it is before accession that the EU's leverage is the greatest (Schimmelfennig and Scholtz, 2008; Vachudova, 2009). For instance, one of the lessons from the 2004 enlargement and the Cyprus issue is that candidate countries should 'avoid importing significant bilateral disputes into the EU' (Commission, 2013c, p. 13). While this approach means that conditionality becomes more rigorous, the addition of new benchmarks and 'goalposts' along the way provides for new opportunities for the EU Member States to block the process as we have witnessed in the past. The new approach to accession negotiations also means that countries are expected to have adopted not only the relevant legislation in these areas, but also to demonstrate 'solid track records of reform implementation to be developed throughout the process' (Commission, 2013c, p. 7). In sum, as aptly summarized by Vachudova (2014, p. 132):

> EU actors have learned three things: that leverage works well only *before* accession, that a longer period for exercising conditionality is needed, and that fostering the rule of law and independent state institutions takes finer-grained requirements that are also better enforced.

Throughout 2013, it also became clear that Germany is emerging as key actor not just on economic and monetary affairs, but also in enlargement issues (Paterson, 2011). However, this might be more by default than design as other key actors such as Italy or France have lost interest in enlargement issues or are preoccupied with dealing with the effects of the eurozone crisis at home (Judah, 2013). German politicians were instrumental in pushing negotiations between Serbia and Kosovo as a condition for opening negotiations with the former.[5] German internal politics also explained the timing of the decisions as German policy-makers were keen to delay any decision on negotiations with Serbia until after the general election in September as parliamentary approval is now required for decisions concerning EU enlargement (ECFR, 2014). With the accession of Croatia to the EU, one might also see a strengthening of the pro-enlargement coalition as Croatia takes the opportunity to lobby on behalf of its neighbours from the inside. In fact, the accession of Croatia can provide much needed incentives to other candidates, particularly in the Balkans. However, this will very much depend on how Croatia benefits both in material (increasing economic growth thanks to EU funds, trade and direct foreign investment) and political terms (increasing influence inside and outside the Union) from EU membership in the years to come as Croatia's performance will be closely watched by those 'outside' (Nič, 2013). This will be a real test for the EU's enlargement policy and its future success.

---

[4] Montenegro has been required to prepare comprehensive action plans as a basis for opening negotiations in these chapters.
[5] BalkanInsight.com, 20 March 2013.

The candidate and potential candidate countries still face key challenges in the areas of economic development (with the exception perhaps of Turkey), democracy and the rule of law, and dealing with the legacies of conflicts and bilateral disputes. The following issues, highlighted in the Commission's report on Bosnia, are illustrative of the issues faced by *all* the enlargement countries:

> Increased attention is needed on the rule of law, including judicial reform and the fight against corruption and organised crime, public administration reform, freedom of expression, including to address [sic] intimidation of journalists, and on tackling discrimination, including of Roma. Further economic reforms are needed to improve the weak business environment. (Commission, 2013c, p. 20)

Yet it is worth discussing some of these challenges here in more detail starting with challenges in the economic sector. In this area, there are important differences between the Western Balkan countries and Turkey. While the latter has a growing and dynamic economy,[6] none of the Western Balkan countries lining up for enlargement is yet a functioning market economy. These countries have also proven more reliant on exports to, and foreign direct investment from, the EU and hence were particularly affected by the negative consequences of the eurozone crisis (Bechev, 2012; Whitman and Juncos, 2012). As a result of the level of integration into the EU economy and domestic policy failures, the economies of the region suffered a double-dip recession in 2012, with high unemployment rates averaging over 20 per cent, particularly among the youth (World Bank, 2012). The return to positive figures in the eurozone area has brought much needed economic recovery to the region in 2013, although growth rates are still modest at around 2 per cent (Commission, 2013c, p. 3). The recovery is also hindered by structural problems regarding the labour market, inadequate infrastructures and the low competitiveness of the Western Balkan economies. For this reason, from 2014 onwards the Commission is intending to intensify the dialogue on economic policy with the Western Balkan governments, who will be now 'invited' to prepare a national economic reform strategy, including a macroeconomic and fiscal programme as well as structural reforms and a competitiveness programme.

The second area where challenges remain refers to the rule of law and the democratization of candidates and potential candidate countries. There is evidence that the enlargement process has had a 'democratizing effect' on its neighbours (Vachudova, 2005; Schimmelfennig and Scholtz, 2008) and this has also been the case in Turkey and the Western Balkans. For instance, in March 2013, EU mediation led to the return of the opposition party (the Social Democrats) to the Macedonian parliament after three months of boycott, with an agreement to participate in the local elections.[7] Moreover, the smooth conduct of parliamentary elections in Albania in June had a lot do with the country's ambition to gain candidate status. Given the history of electoral irregularities and polarization between the two main Albanian political parties, the peaceful transfer of power from Sali Berisha's Democratic Party of Albania to the Socialist Party led by Edi Rama was especially remarkable (Barbullushi, 2013) and gained the country another recommendation to open negotiations from the Commission. A decision on the opening of negotiations, however, was postponed by the Council to June 2014, in part because of

---

[6] Turkey returned to rates of growth of 4 per cent of gross domestic product in 2013 after a slowdown in 2012.
[7] *European Voice*, 2 March 2013.

concerns among the Member States of Denmark, France, Germany, the Netherlands and the UK about corruption and organized crime (Council of the EU, 2013b; ECFR, 2014).

Generally, problems regarding corruption and organized crime were still high on the agenda in 2013 and provide evidence of the challenges that the EU still faces in the region. Even in the new Member State of Croatia there remain problems relating to organized crime and corruption (Commission, 2013a). Corruption issues are particularly worrying in the case of Montenegro – now the most advanced country in the race for membership – where Prime Minister Milo Djukanović has remained in power since 1989. Here, the decision of the EU to begin accession negotiations with the most demanding chapters of the *acquis* on the judiciary – organized crime and corruption – came as no surprise. Djukanović has been hit by several high-profile corruption accusations in the past year, including accusations of misusing public funds to fix the presidential elections, and the country will be closely monitored by the Commission.[8] Linked to these issues is the need for judicial reform and a professional and independent civil service. A more transparent and depoliticized judiciary and administration should go some way in not only addressing these problems, but also in helping with the implementation of the *acquis*.

Civil society continues to be weak in the candidate countries and in some cases fragmented along ethnic lines, for instance, in Bosnia. However, even in this case, there were some signs for optimism in 2013 when people took to the streets to protests against their predatory and incompetent political elites. The 'baby revolution' was the result of popular anger at the failure of Bosnian politicians to agree on a new law on identity card numbers, which prevented newborn children from travelling abroad as they could not get passports. However, as pointed out by Florian Bieber (2013), while these protests have the potential to transcend current monoethnic politics that have led to political stagnation, they still face the difficulty of how to create a cross-ethnic or country-wide political platform capable of challenging the *status quo*. Popular protests were also held in Turkey over the summer, prompted by the decision to redevelop Gezi Park in Istanbul. These protests were also animated by opposition to the increasingly perceived authoritarian style of Prime Minister Recep Tayyip Erdoğan. The heavy-handed crackdown by the authorities brought a widespread condemnation in European capitals and by the European Commission in its October report. However, the adoption of the democratization package (including provisions on linguistic rights and the rights of persons belonging to minorities) in September mended some of the relations and helped re-launch the accession negotiations (ECFR, 2014).

When it comes to dealing with past conflicts and bilateral disputes, the record has been rather mixed in 2013. On the one hand, the EU can claim to have achieved significant success by brokering the deal between Serbia and Kosovo earlier in the year. As mentioned in the Commission's report: 'The historic agreement reached by Serbia and Kosovo in April is further proof of the power of the EU perspective and its role in healing history's deep scars' (Commission, 2013c, p. 1). This is a remarkable success for European foreign policy and particularly for High Representative Catherine Ashton, who had invested a lot of personal capital in mediating between the parties in recent years. The agreement means that Serbia accepts that the north of Kosovo remains part of Kosovo under Kosovan law in exchange for extensive autonomy for the ethnic Serb communities in areas such as

---

[8] *The Economist*, 17 August 2013.

policing and justice. The deal, however, does not imply a formal recognition of Kosovo's independence by Serbia. The agreement was also facilitated by the arrival of the Nikolić/Vučić coalition government in Serbia led by the Progressive and Socialist parties in 2012. Despite the fact that many feared a eurosceptic turn in Serbia after their victory, the Progressive Party has been able to push for more progress towards accession than its predecessor, Boris Tadić from the Democratic Party. According to Vachudova (2014, p. 131), this shows that 'sometimes it is the post-authoritarian parties that enact the most difficult reforms, in part to lend credence to their new identity'.

There was also some progress in facilitating high-level contacts between the countries of the region, and in February Kosovo was welcomed as a full participant in the Regional Co-operation Council – something which had been blocked by Serbia in the past. In Turkey, there were also some positive signs with the launch of a peace process aimed at finding a solution to the Kurdish issue, with the call by Abdullah Öcalan (the imprisoned leader of the Kurdistan Workers Party [PKK]) to PKK fighters to end the armed struggle and the adoption of the democratization package (see above). However, this package of reforms has been criticized for not going far enough to meet the expectations of the Kurdish minority and hence endangering the fragile peace process (Kurban, 2013).

However, in other cases, the EU has not been that successful. For the fifth consecutive year, the Council delayed opening accession negotiations with the former Yugoslav Republic of Macedonia because of the name dispute with Greece. The Council asked (again) the Commission to report in 2014 'on tangible steps taken to promote good neighbourly relations and to reach a negotiated and mutually accepted solution to the name issue' (Council of the EU, 2013b, p. 8). Similarly, no progress was achieved in 2013 in bringing about a solution to the Cyprus conflict: the UN-mediated talks, which were due to take place in October, had to be postponed because of the banking and financial crisis that affected Cyprus in March. Informal talks between the two Cypriot leaders in November did not yield any results. For its part, the EU continued to insist that Turkey has to implement the 2004 Ankara Protocol and allow Cypriot vessels and aircraft into Turkish ports and airports as a condition to open negotiations on new chapters. In Bosnia, ethnic politics continued to stall the implementation of EU reforms. Ethnic tensions were particularly palpable during the first postwar census, which took place in 2013 and which could provide evidence of a change in the balance between the different ethnic communities, with a predicted decline of the Bosnian Croat population (the first results will be made public in mid-2014). In particular, Bosnian politicians failed to agree on the implementation of the two key conditions set out in the roadmap of June 2012: the implementation of the Sejdić–Finci decision of the European Court of Human Rights (ECHR) and the establishment of a co-ordination mechanism to adopt EU-related legislation. This time, however, the EU responded with a punitive measure, freezing funds from the Instrument for Pre-accession Assistance (IPA) programme.

II. The EU's Southern Periphery: What is Left of the Arab Spring?

Two years on, the EU was still hesitant about how to respond to the Arab Spring and its aftermath. The year 2013, however, was more akin to an 'Arab Winter' in view of developments in the region, with Libya struggling to find a transitional path to democracy, the return of the military in Egypt and civil war worsening in Syria. Perhaps the most serious lesson for the EU continues to be the inadequacies of the European neighbourhood policy (ENP) as a framework to deal effectively with events in the Middle East and North Africa. In a communication reflecting on the first two years after the Arab uprisings, the EU acknowledged that 'these transitions will of course be difficult and will take time – measured in years instead of months – and setbacks may well occur'. But it also reiterated its commitment to the long-term goal of a democratic and prosperous southern neighbourhood. This goal, according to this statement, would require 'strategic patience and timely support measures' (European Union, 2013). After the Arab uprisings in 2011, the EU made clear that it was going to support democratizing forces in the region ('deep democracy') and that it was going to reward those performing better with more resources (the 'more for more' approach). However, in 2013, there were still many inconsistencies between the EU's rhetoric and its practice. In particular, the EU was still struggling to deal with the stability versus democracy dilemma, and was unsure about how to deal with Islamic movements in the region.

A case in point was that of Egypt, where the EU's response to the military coup ousting President Mohammed Morsi in July was anything but resolute. This was followed by the massacre of hundreds of Muslim Brotherhood supporters and the imprisonment of over 2,000 of them. Former President Mubarak was released in November, and in August Mr Morsi faced his first trial, alongside other senior leaders of the Muslim Brotherhood movement. Although Catherine Ashton initially tried to mediate in the crisis, she was soon side-lined and could not exercise any influence on the military regime of General Abdel Fattah al-Sisi. For their part, the Member States avoided using the term 'coup' to refer to Morsi's removal of power (Blockmans, 2013, p. 2) in order to preserve a stance of neutrality with the hope of being able to maintaining some leverage over the regime and a future transition to democracy. Moreover, the EU chose to maintain the non-military assistance provided by the ENP to avoid hurting the most vulnerable people in Egypt. The risk is that by adopting a wait-and-see approach and by engaging with the military interim regime, the EU might go back to its pre-Arab Spring policy of favouring stability and hence further undermining its legitimacy *vis-à-vis* pro-democracy movements across the region. As summarized in a ECFR report, the EU's response to the events in Egypt 'sent a strong signal to other neighbouring countries that the EU had little commitment to supporting human rights, democracy, and the rule of law' (ECFR, 2014, p. 86). The case of Egypt also shows that the 'more for more' approach of the ENP failed to produce any meaningful results. As noted by Blockmans (2013, p. 1), 'the sums of conditional aid (offered mainly in the form of loans) have proved too small and the prospects of increased trade and investment too elusive to entice the Egyptian leadership to sign up to the EU's reform agenda'.

The conflict in Syria appears, if anything, more complex than the situation in Egypt and so far the EU has been pushed to the margins. The EU has not played any meaningful diplomatic role so far and no other (military) role is envisaged for the EU, beyond the provision of humanitarian assistance for the Syrian refugees. The only instruments that the EU has been able to deploy (unsuccessfully) in the case of Syria are those of economic sanctions and an arms embargo (see Whitman and Juncos, 2013). Yet, the arms embargo basically fell apart in May after France and the UK refused to support it further and decided to arm the rebels. Although France and the UK were still very active during the first half of 2013 and pushed for military intervention in response to the alleged use of chemical weapons by the Assad regime,[9] it was the US and Russia who brokered the deal on the destruction of chemical weapons by the Syrian government. The conflict in Syria was also having a negative impact across the region in the form of refugee flows to Jordan and Turkey and causing growing instability in Lebanon and Iraq.

As far as the Middle East peace process was concerned, 2013 did not see much progress towards the achievement of the two-state solution despite efforts by US State Secretary John Kerry. However, there were some positive developments like the adoption in July of the EU's guidelines on financing to settlements which will deny grants, prizes and financial instruments to Israeli entities base in the Occupied Territories.[10] The December European Council also offered 'an unprecedented package of European political, economic and security support' to Israel and Palestine if they agreed on a two-state solution. Israel and Palestine were also offered a 'special privileged partnership' status in the event of a final peace agreement, which would include increased access to the single market (Council of the EU, 2013a). The Commission continued to deepen EU relations with Israel, including the signature of an Open Skies agreement between the EU and Israel that should facilitate direct flights between Europe and Israel and the inclusion of Israel in the EU's Global Navigation Satellite System (GNSS).

The only countries that seemed to be escaping from the worst of the violence affecting the region are Morocco and Tunisia. The former signed a mobility partnership with some EU Member States in June,[11] a fisheries agreement on 18 November 2013 and began negotiations on a Deep and Comprehensive Free Trade Agreement (DCFTA). The EU-Morocco Association Council also adopted a new Action Plan for 2013–17. Morocco remains the largest recipient of EU assistance in the southern neighbourhood with €580.5 million for the period 2011–13. Tunisia, for its part, is still facing a challenging political situation. On 6 February 2013, the opposition leader Chokri Belaid was shot dead, sparking a political crisis and the resignation of Prime Minister Hamadi Jebali.[12] The EU has sought to support the transition in the country through the implementation of the three Ms: 'money, markets and mobility'. Tunisia concluded some preliminary discussions on a DCFTA and a mobility partnership and was also one of the main recipients of EU funds, reflecting on the progress achieved by the country and in line with the 'more for more' principle. Between 2011 and 2013, Tunisia received €485 million, and it was the first recipient of additional funds under the SPRING programme. It is also still unclear whether the deal with Iran on its nuclear programme – undoubtedly one of the greatest diplomatic successes of the year for European foreign policy – might also have a positive impact at the level of regional politics.[13]

III. The Eastern Neighbourhood

The EaP summit that took place in Vilnius from 28–29 November was the central event guiding the EU's policy towards its eastern neighbours in 2013. It provided the EU with the opportunity to both reflect upon the broad policy approach and to use the summit as

---

[9] The UK Parliament voted against military intervention in Syria.

[10] *EUObserver.com*, 16 July 2013.

[11] The agreement was signed only by nine Member States: Belgium, France, Germany, Italy, the Netherlands, Portugal, Spain, Sweden and the UK.

[12] *BBC News*, 6 February 2013.

[13] On Europe's relations with countries beyond the neighbourhood, see Hadfield and Fiott's contribution to this volume.

a deadline to refresh and upgrade the EU's policy towards its eastern neighbours. Some Member States were keen to see the EaP summit as signalling more than a destination, a point of departure for a deepening of relations. In a joint note to the EU's High Representative of the Union for Foreign and Affairs and Security Policy/Vice-President of the European Commission (HR/VP), Catherine Ashton, from the German, Polish, Czech and Swedish governments in February, the case was made for the objective of a combined European economic area-type relationship between the EU and all of its EaP countries. The Polish government went further calling again for a promise of future accession to be made at the EaP summit.[14] Such longer term objectives were set alongside the 'very mixed picture', in the words of the European Commission and High Representative's annual reports on the progress of the implementation of the EaP and its participating states (Commission and HR/VP, 2013).

Assessing each country's national action plans agreed with the European Commission against the implementation in the areas of democracy, improvements in governance, reform of judiciary and the rule of law, open markets and the movement of people, and aligning with EU legislation, Moldova and Georgia were assessed as the most advanced pupils. The EU's assessment on democracy broadly concurred with that of Freedom House, which ranked Georgia and Moldova as being 'partly free' (alongside Armenia and Ukraine) and ranked Azerbaijan and Belarus as 'not free' on the basis of political rights and civil liberties (Freedom House, 2014).

The autumn of 2013 saw Georgia go through a period of considerable political transition. A new President was inaugurated on 17 November, on the same day that a new constitution entered into force, changing Georgia from a presidential to a parliamentary system. Furthermore, Prime Minister Bidzina Ivanishvili stepped down on 24 November and handed over the post of Prime Minister to the former Interior Minister, Irakli Garibashvili. All of these processes were completed in an orderly fashion, were welcomed by the EU and appear to offer Georgia a higher degree of political stability.

The collapse of the government in Moldova in March 2013 to be replaced by the 'Pro-European Government Coalition' brought to an end an immediate political crisis. Although these events did not alter the subsequent direction of Moldova's European policy in 2013, the country remains politically fragile.

The Commission's assessment of Armenia was rather lukewarm and the declaration by Armenian President Sargsyan on 3 September 2013 that his country intended to join the Eurasian customs union effectively curtailed the EU's Armenia policy. This step was widely seen as the result of pressure by Russia, which is the main security guarantor of Armenia in its ongoing territorial dispute with Azerbaijan.

The Commission's evaluation of Azerbaijan was noteworthy for marking the country as being a poor performer and most especially for the continuing condition of political prisoners, a lack of a free and open civil society, independent judiciary or a political system meeting internationally acceptable standards. Relations between the countries in the South Caucasus remained hostage to their own political instability and the unresolved frozen conflicts of South Ossetia/Abkhazia and Nagorno-Karabakh.

Belarus remained the unwavering constant in the neighbourhood impervious to EU attempts to encourage reform. Belarus sits outside the bilateral track of the EaP, although

---

[14] *EUObserver.com*, 20 February 2012.

some engagement continues along the sector co-operation and visa/readmission issues. Sanctions against members of the Lukashenka regime were renewed by EU foreign ministers for a further 12 months in October 2013 banning 232 Belarusian officials, business people and associates of the regime from travel to the EU and imposing an assets freeze. In addition, 25 businesses linked to the regime are subject to sanctions. There was a modest opening to Belarus in mid-2013 when Foreign Minister Vladimir Makey had his visa ban suspended to allow for the first visit of a regime official to Brussels since 2010, which was a prelude to his attendance at the EaP Vilnius summit representing Belarus.

The EU's evaluation of Ukraine was marked by the ongoing gap between the government's declared ambition to comply with agreements made with the EU and its failure to act to address the EU's concerns and conditions. During 2013, the EU continued to press Ukraine to comply with the conditions set out in the Foreign Affairs Council conclusions of 10 December 2012 (Council of the European Union, 2012a) to allow for the signature to be applied to the association agreement initialled in 2012. These conditions were the compliance of the 2012 parliamentary elections with international standards and follow-up actions; Ukraine's progress in addressing the issue of selective justice and preventing its recurrence; and in implementing the reforms defined in the jointly-agreed association agenda. Despite the EU's desire to end the downturn in relations that had characterized 2012, and the first cancellation of an EU-Ukraine summit in 15 years, there was a determination on the EU side to see the Yanukovych-led government sign the association and DCFTA agreements with the EU at the earliest opportunity. The EU signalled that it wished to see progress on 'selective justice' and the freeing of former Prime Minister Yulia Tymoshenko 'at the latest by May'.[15] Ukraine's response was not to deliver on these conditions, but rather to deliver a further complication in the relationship with the EU by signing a memorandum to deepen co-operation with the Russian-led Eurasian customs union on 31 May 2013. The EU position was that there was a fundamental incompatibility between membership of the Eurasian customs union and a DCFTA with the EU. In order to work around the impasse on the release of Yulia Tymoshenko in June and July, an attempt was made by the German government via bilateral diplomacy with Ukraine to allow for her to be released from prison to allow for medical treatment in Germany. This initiative failed and Tymoshenko embarked on a hunger strike in prison from 25 November in protest at the subsequent failure of the Ukrainian government to sign the association agreement.

The Vilnius summit itself did not set a substantive future direction for the EaP, postponing this as a topic for their next summit in two years (Council of the European Union, 2013c). Aside from acting as a focal point for the signature of upgraded bilateral relationships it became a rather pointed illustration of the limits of some EaP countries to deepen their relationships with the EU. At the summit, Georgia and Moldova both initialled association agreements, including DCFTAs. Azerbaijan signed a visa facilitation agreement following in the footsteps of the other EaP states (except Belarus). The government of Armenia, although concluding its negotiations with the EU for its association agreement and DCFTA, demurred from initialling the agreement at the summit. The EU sought to maintain a brave face by issuing a joint statement with the government of Armenia regarding the commitment to an updated ENP action plan but also making

---

[15] *EUObserver.com*, 25 February 2013.

clear that the association agreement and the DCFTA were now frozen (EEAS, 2013). More dramatically, in the days leading up to the summit the government of Ukraine decided to suspend its preparations for the signing of its own agreement, for which negotiations had been concluded and initialled in 2012, but with a full signature on the agreement delayed due to the imposition of conditionality by the EU. The 'non-signature' of both of these agreements gave the Vilnius summit an unexpected tone. A number of EU Member State governments and Presidents Barroso and van Rompuy were unambiguous and directed approbation at Vladimir Putin and the government of the Russian Federation for having applied pressure on both the Armenian and Ukrainian governments not to formally deepen their relationships with the EU.[16]

The domestic political consequences in Ukraine of the decision not to sign the association agreement were significant. Demonstrations started on the streets of Kyiv on 21 November opposing President Viktor Yanukovych's perceived sell-out. These were the largest anti-government protests since the 2004 Orange Revolution. Demonstrations and the occupation of Independence Square in the centre of the Ukrainian capital continued in the aftermath of the Vilnius summit, with protestors occupying the city hall and other government buildings and seeking the resignation of Yanukovych and his government and the signing of the association agreement with the EU. The protests, which became known as the 'Euromaidan' (Euro Square protests), continued until the end of the year. Widespread condemnation came from the EU and its Member States following unsuccessful attempts to clear the Square by force on the 30 November and on 11 December – with the latter attempt taking place during a visit to Kyiv by Baroness Ashton for meetings with President Yanukovych. At the year's end the protestors were still in occupation of central Kyiv. At the final European Council of 2013, the EU's heads of state and government made clear their support for the protestors and saw President Yanukovych's failure to resign from power as being the obstacle to reviving the association agreement (European Council, 2013).[17]

Conclusions

In 2013, the EU's neighbourhood was a region in which the EU's political and economic influence was under considerable stress. Despite the accession of Croatia to the EU in July and the historic agreement between Serbia and Kosovo, progress by the candidate and potential candidate countries to meet the EU conditions was undermined by serious political and economic problems. In Turkey and the Western Balkans, the EU faces key challenges in the area of rule of law, democracy and supporting economic development. While economic recovery across the EU might provide some much needed boost to the EU's transformative power, the task ahead for the EU will remain a colossal one – particularly in countries such as Bosnia and Kosovo.

The EU's policy towards its eastern neighbours was experiencing a bifurcation between states seeking a deepening of relationship with the EU and other EaP states seeking a more restricted relationship with the EU due to economic and political pressure being exercised by the Russian Federation. The EU's policy to the east was further

---

[16] *EUObserver.com*, 29 November 2013.
[17] *EUObserver.com*, 20 December 2013.

complicated by the lack of a substantive political reform process in a number of the partner countries. In the southern neighbourhood, the EU was largely a spectator in the political and economic transition processes of the states affected by the Arab Spring. The political and economic fragility of the majority of its southern neighbours, the quasi- and active-civil wars of, respectively, Libya and Syria represented active diplomatic and security challenges for the EU, for which it had not yet formulated a sufficient response. The revamped ENP remained an ineffective tool to promote reforms, particularly, democracy, in the EU's eastern and southern flanks. The EU remained inconsistent and hesitant in reacting to developments in its neighbourhood and where it did act, the incentives provided by the ENP through the 'more for more' approach did not prove to be attractive enough to change the policies and behaviours of the recipient countries.

As the EU slowly pulled out of its economic and eurozone crises, a heightening of the EU's response to the substantive challenges in its neighbourhood needed to be a priority. The new leadership of the EU's institutions due to take office in autumn 2014 faced a substantial workload on the wider Europe.

References

Barbullushi, O. (2013) '2013 Albanian Post-Election Report: The Quick, Quiet Albanian Elections and the End of Transitional Politics'. *The Monkey Cage*, 7 August. Available at: «http:// themonkeycage.org/2013/07/08/2013-albanian-post-election-report-the-quick-quiet-albanian-elections-and-the-end-of-transitional-politics/».

Bechev, D. (2012) 'The Periphery of the Periphery: The Western Balkans and the Euro Crisis'. ECFR Policy Brief (London: European Council on Foreign Relations).

Bieber, F. (2013) 'Is Change Coming to Bosnia?' *Balkan Insight*, 12 June. Available at: «http:// www.balkaninsight.com/en/blog/is-change-coming-to-bosnia».

Blockmans, S. (2013) 'Egypt and the EU: Where Next?' *CEPS Commentary*, 4 November.

Council of the European Union (2012a) Council conclusions on Ukraine 3209th Foreign Affairs Council meeting Brussels, 10 December. Available at: «http://www.consilium.europa.eu/ uedocs/cms_data/docs/pressdata/EN/foraff/134136.pdf».

Council of the European Union (2013a) Council Conclusions on the Middle East Peace Process, Foreign Affairs Council meeting, Brussels, 16 December.

Council of the European Union (2013b) Council Conclusions on Enlargement and Stabilisation and Association Process, General Affairs Council meeting, Brussels, 17 December.

Council of the European Union (2013c) Eastern Partnership: The Way Ahead – Joint Declaration of the Eastern Partnership Summit, Vilnius, 28–29 November. 17130/13 PRESSE 516.

European Commission (2013a) Monitoring report on Croatia's accession preparations. COM(2013) 171 final, 26 March.

European Commission (2013b) Steps towards joining. Available at: «http://ec.europa.eu/ enlargement/policy/steps-towards-joining/index_en.htm».

European Commission (2013c) Communication from the Commission to the European Parliament and the Council on enlargement strategy and main challenges, 2013–2014. COM(2013) 700 final, 16 October.

European Commission and HR/VP (2013) Joint Staff Working Document on implementation of the European Neighbourhood Policy in 2012 regional report: Eastern Partnership. SWD(2013) 85 final, 20 March. Available at: «http://eeas.europa.eu/enp/pdf/docs/2013_enp_pack/2013 _eastern_pship_regional_report_en.pdf».

European Council (2003) EU-Western Balkans Summit Declaration. C/03/163, 10229/03 (Presse 163), Thessaloniki, 21 June.

European Council (2013) Conclusions: European Council, 19–20 December. 20 December. Available at: «http://www.consilium.europa.eu/uedocs/cms_Data/docs/pressdata/en/ec/140245 .pdf».

European Council of Foreign Relations (ECFR) (2014) *European Foreign Policy Scorecard 2014*. Available at: «http://ecfr.eu/page/-/ECFR94_SCORECARD_2014.pdf».

European External Action Service (EEAS) (2013) Joint Statement between the European Union and the Republic of Armenia as agreed by High Representative Catherine Ashton and Foreign Minister Edward Nalbandian, Vilnius, 29 November. 291113/03. Available at: «http://www .eeas.europa.eu/statements/docs/2013/131129_03_en.pdf».

European Union (2013) EU's response to the Arab Spring: State-of-play after two years', 8 February. Available at: «http://www.eu-un.europa.eu/articles/en/article_13134_en.htm».

Freedom House (2014) *Freedom in the World, 2013*. Available at: «http://www.freedomhouse.org/ report-types/freedom-world#.U2IzboFdWSp».

Judah, T. (2013) 'Germany and the Balkans: The Pivot in the Balkans' EU Ambitions'. *The Economist*, 26 February. Available at: «http://www.economist.com/blogs/easternapproaches/ 2013/02/germany-and-balkans».

Kurban, D. (2013) 'Not a Roadmap for Peace'. *SWP Comments*, November. Available at: «http:// www.swp-berlin.org/fileadmin/contents/products/comments/2013C35_kun.pdf».

Moravcsik, A. and Vachudova, M.A. (2003) 'National Interests, State Power and EU Enlargement'. *East European Politics and Societies*, Vol. 17, No. 1, pp. 42–57.

Nič, M. (2013) 'The EU's Role in the Western Balkans after Croatian Accession'. Policy Brief (Bratislava: Central European Policy Institute). Available at: «http://www.cepolicy.org/ publications/eus-role-western-balkans-after-croatian-accession».

Paterson, W.E. (2011) 'The Reluctant Hegemon? Germany Moves Centre Stage in the European Union'. *JCMS*, Vol. 49, No. s1, pp 57–75.

Schimmelfennig, F. and Scholtz, H. (2008) 'EU Democracy Promotion in the European Neighbourhood'. *European Union Politics*, Vol. 9, No. 2, pp. 187–215.

Vachudova, M.A. (2005) *Europe Undivided: Democracy, Leverage and Integration after Communism* (Oxford: Oxford University Press).

Vachudova, M.A. (2009) 'Corruption and Compliance in the EU's Post-Communist Members and Candidates'. *JCMS*, Vol. 47, No. s1, pp. 43–62.

Vachudova, M.A. (2014) 'EU Leverage and National Interests in the Balkans: The Puzzles of Enlargement Ten Years On'. *JCMS*, Vol. 52, No. 1, pp. 122–38.

Whitman, R.G. and Juncos, A.E. (2011) 'The Arab Spring, the Eurozone Crisis and the Neighbourhood'. *JCMS*, Vol. 49, No. s1, pp. 187–208.

Whitman, R.G. and Juncos, A.E. (2012) 'The Arab Spring, the Eurozone Crisis and the Neighbourhood: A Region in Flux'. *JCMS*, Vol. 50, No. s1, pp. 147–61.

Whitman, R.G. and Juncos, A.E. (2013) 'Stasis in Status: Relations with the Wider Europe'. *JCMS*, Vol. 51, No. s1, pp. 155–67.

World Bank (2012) 'South East Europe: Regular Economic Report 3'. 18 December. Available at: «http://www.worldbank.org/content/dam/Worldbank/document/SEERER_3_Report _FINAL_eng.pdf».

JCMS 2014 Volume 52 Annual Review pp. 170–185   DOI: 10.1111/jcms.12167

Relations with the Rest of the World: From Chaos to Consolidation?

AMELIA HADFIELD[1] and DANIEL FIOTT[2]
[1] Canterbury Christ Church University. [2] Vrije Universiteit Brussels

Introduction

Our 2012 review painted a picture of an EU pulled between a seemingly inexorable series of internal crises, on the one hand, and myriad external demands, on the other (Hadfield and Fiott, 2013). The year 2013 largely continued the theme of balancing slow-paced internal consolidation with increasingly demanding diplomatic requirements arising from within the Eastern Partnership, and specifically Ukraine. Despite the tentative recovery of the Eurozone, the challenges of confirming its own budget (the Multiannual Financial Framework, or MFF) and the continuing difficulties in its neighbourhood, the EU arguably gained greater confidence in diplomatic terms in 2013.

Our retrospective begins by scrutinizing the European External Action Service's (EEAS) Mid-Term Review. The portents thus far remain mixed. Deemed by the General Affairs Council in December to represent 'a modern and operational foreign policy service, equipped to promote EU values and interests' (Council of the European Union, 2013, p. 1) and by the European Parliament to represent an unprecedented 'new body of hybrid nature' (EP, 2013, p. 4), the institutional stasis of the EEAS appears to have receded. Yet the goal of establishing comprehensive policy coherence remains elusive. EEAS strategy is still typified by an indiscriminate labelling of policies, both old and new, as equally capable vehicles of the much-vaunted 'comprehensive approach',[1] which we termed the EU's 'newly discovered foreign policy "trademark"' in last year's *Annual Review* (Hadfield and Fiott, 2013, p. 174). More positively, the High Representative of the Union for Foreign Affairs and Security Policy/Vice President of the European Commission (HR/VP), Catherine Ashton, began to gather the fruits of some particularly effective high-level policy-making in securing the Serbia–Kosovo agreement and leading the E3+3 negotiations with Iran: a season of proactive engagement that will round out, rather than characterize her tenure.

Moving out concentrically from Brussels, we examine events in the European neighbourhood area (covered in more detail in this issue by Whitman and Juncos), moving from North Africa, the Middle East and the sub-Sahara, to consider the significant geopolitical rifts in EU–Russia relations as a result of upheavals in Ukraine. Next, we examine the EU's Asian and American relations, as well as the continued unrolling of various free trade agreements (FTAs). As illustrated, the range of current and potential FTAs being organized by the EU speaks to what Damro (2012) has termed 'Market

---

[1] For more on the comprehensive approach, see Hadfield and Fiott (2013, pp. 174–5).

Power Europe', especially as these FTAs seek not only to establish mutual economic benefits, but also to further institutionalise the proliferation of EU regulatory standards and norms. Indeed, what emerges from the analysis is that despite the energy currently put into constructing a global diplomatic presence – as evidenced by the EEAS Mid-Term Review – the EU retains a clear preference for economic tools that literally under-write its presence, allowing it to maintain both political and economic influence, and on occasion, strategic depth. Despite the internal tensions stemming from the management of the Eurozone crisis, and fraught debates over the international impact of the EEAS, FTAs and other economic tools (for example, sanctions and development aid) remain the dominant features of the EU's external relations. Nevertheless, given that 2013 marks the ten-year anniversary of both the European security strategy (ESS) and the European neighbourhood policy (ENP), as well as witnessing the EEAS' first major review, it is worth analysing whether the EU is living up to the objectives outlined in the ESS – namely, 'to react less and do more strategically to command the world agenda' (Allen and Smith, 2009, p. 215).

I. The High Representative and the EEAS: Mid-Term or Half-Time?

The EEAS Mid-Term Review, published in July, was the key internal development of 2013.[2] Preceded by remarks to the EP by HR/VP Ashton in June, and then subsequently publicized as a 'top story', anticipation was high among supporters and critics alike regarding the first real opportunity to examine the service in detail since the fraught days of its inception. From the end of 2012 onwards, the EEAS received a slew of recommendations to increase its legitimacy by taking the 2013 review process seriously. Seen as lacking in both efficiency and accountability, the main message was that EEAS executives take a more professional attitude to improving 'the rigour and hence legitimacy, credibility and usefulness' of the EEAS, thereby enhancing the 'relevance of European external action on the global stage' (ECDPM, 2012, p. 1).

Within the plethora of recommendations for the Mid-Term Review, one can detect a variety of common expectations; principally the need to promote cross-policy coherence via further refinement and implementation of the comprehensive approach. Other suggestions directed the EEAS towards a more efficacious division of labour, chiefly to counteract the failure of the HR/VP to make viable use of the 'VP' aspect of her position (as noted last year: Hadfield and Fiott, 2013, p. 171), due to inadequate convening of the External Affairs Commissioners (the Relex Group). This observation emerged alongside suggestions to nominate junior Commissioners as deputies to represent EEAS strategy in the Commission and the European Parliament (EP). Furthermore, on the basis of the infamous EEAS organogram, there were robust demands for more streamlined co-operation between the HR/VP, the corporate board and management heads, as well as between Heads of Delegations and Member State foreign ministries, and the long overdue integration of the Commission's service for foreign policy instruments.

---

[2] Established in 2010 to halt the growing incoherence of EU external policy following a Council Decision that set out the organization and functions of the EEAS, as well as the roles of the HR/VP, the EEAS was bound by the same Decision to present a self-evaluation in the form of a review by mid-2013.

In June, HR/VP Ashton provided the EP in Strasbourg with a preview (EP, 2013) of the July review (EEAS, 2013a), beginning with a firm commitment to the continued use of the comprehensive approach. Frequently seized upon by Ashton in 2013 as 'the central concept' upon which the EEAS's 'main strength' is founded, this trademark now underwrites the rationale of many EEAS' strategic documents (EEAS, 2013a, p. 5). Perhaps in anticipation of persistent criticism over the imbalance between the 'HR' and 'VP' aspects of her role, Ashton then outlined her misgivings on working more co-operatively with the Commission (stating that 'there is already extensive joint working between me and my Commission colleagues'), but conceded the need for deputizing Commissioners 'in parliamentary matters and internationally' (Ashton, 2013, p. 4). The overall message to Strasbourg was summed up in the following terse statement, which could be interpreted either as a reassurance to Member States wary of the growing ambitions of the EEAS, or a rebuke to those who had previously attempted to curtail the EEAS:

> But we should not delude ourselves – Lisbon left [the] CFSP as intergovernmental and subject to unanimity decision making: in situations where there is an absence of political will or an agreement amongst the Member States there are limits to what the Service can deliver. (Ashton, 2013, p. 3)

The European Parliament's response, adopted the following day, acknowledged the 'good progress in setting up the EEAS', but ultimately felt 'that more can be achieved in terms of synergy and coordination between institutions' (EP, 2013, p. 3). This includes enhancing 'political leadership and visibility' which pave the way to 'a more rational and efficient structure for 21st century diplomacy' (EP, 2013, p. 3). Alongside the predicted calls for reformed budgets, enhanced training and representative recruitment, the EP argued simply for a sharper sense of the 'appropriate structure for ensuring a comprehensive approach' (EP, 2013, p. 3). A negative reading of this response suggests that the EEAS is not yet fit for purpose. In other words, its current form prevents it from leveraging the strategic vision leveraging the strategic vision entailed in the comprehensive approach and that consequently 2014 will be the defining year for the EEAS. A more constructive viewpoint suggests that the EP broadly supports the comprehensive approach as both the hallmark of EU external relations and the EEAS's own 'in-house style' by which to implement genuine coherence across a range of policies (despite their divided institutional heritage). The EEAS needs simply to complete its internal organisation in order to provide the carrying capacity for this ambitious objective. The latter viewpoint is largely echoed in the Mid-Term Review that followed in July.

Divided into four parts, the review enumerates the current and proposed transformations of the EEAS in terms of organization, function, the HR/VP post, and hiring and performance. The review also outlines the unique selling points of emergent EU diplomacy that contextualize the report, principally by providing the EEAS with a rationale for the entirety of its requisite transformations, and deepens the commitment of the service to its primary objective of policy coherence in pursuance of an effective comprehensive approach.

Similar to the composition of the Mid-Term Review itself, the hallmarks of EU external engagement are divided into *geopolitical, thematic and institutional* dimensions. Geopolitical scope is entailed in the EU's global coverage, with the review identifying the EU's southern and eastern neighbourhood as areas 'where the EU has influence and leverage to promote and to deliver change' (EEAS, 2013a, p. 5). Having determined the general theatre of policy engagement, the EU's *thematic* instruments are understood to flow almost exclusively from a comprehensive approach that coherently promotes a 'triple-D' policy of defence, diplomacy and development. Finally, all ensuing *institutional transformations* must be undertaken with a view to rendering efficacious, reliable and enduring support for both the geographic and thematic components of EU diplomacy, which in turn will ultimately secure the EEAS's role as both architect and manager of multiple policy areas as they become increasingly interconnected. As such, the vast majority of the Mid-Term Review includes *organizational* recommendations, *functioning* changes and *staffing* measures – all designed to significantly strengthen the EEAS' ability to manage common security and defence policy (CSDP) operations, and restore a better working balance with the Commission on external assistance programmes, in pursuance of 'optimal coherence with EU foreign policy priorities' (EEAS, 2013a, p. 20).

Apart from the surprising paucity of published responses to the review, both positive and negative consequences flow from its reflections and recommendations. The harshest judgement suggests that very little has changed within the EEAS. Interviews with various EEAS staff suggest that while much international organization has taken place and bedded down, little of this activity has promoted genuine 'cooperation between us [the EEAS] and national diplomacies', with Member State support for the EEAS seen as 'lukewarm at best and downright oppositional at worst'.[3]

The EEAS review also conspicuously failed as a catalyst for national foreign ministries 'to review the functioning of their own services and to develop the division of work between the various elements of the post-Lisbon system' (Lehne, 2012, p. 1). Indeed as the British Parliamentary response made clear, while many of the review's recommendations appeared 'sensible and would increase the efficiency of the EEAS', particularly those measures 'embedding the Comprehensive Approach to crisis management', both its consular cost-cutting ideas, and its ambitions over the external aspects of EU policies appeared inherently provocative. Indeed, upon these two points, the British response stated bluntly that 'the EEAS should not have a role in providing consular assistance', that Member State competence should instead remain the bulwark against proliferating EU defence engagements, thus making explicit the need to 'remain vigilant against any threat of competence creep on the part of the EEAS' (Parliament of the United Kingdom, 2013, p. 5). In this respect, little institutional learning appears to have taken place within the EEAS. Indeed, the EEAS's attempt to maintain an 'active influence on programming of EU external assistance, within the existing legal framework' is a itself a double-edged sword: necessary in pursuance of the comprehensive approach, but not yet managed by the service with any real insight with either acumen or authority, and as such bound to provoke turf wars with the Commission and Member States (EEAS, 2013a, p. 16).

The positive outcome of the review however, is a clear understanding of the need to ensure that the institutional distribution of labour mirrors the functional needs inherent in constructing and implementing genuine cross-policy coherence implicit in the comprehensive approach. If the post-review EEAS can indeed produce structures and strategies that efficaciously blend 'diplomacy with development aid, rule of law support, military

---

[3] Interview with a senior EEAS staff member, Brussels, 22 November 2013.

and civilian operations' and build bridges with the Commission that reinforce its capacity for managing 'external aspects of EU key policies (energy security, environment, migration, fight against terrorism, external economic issues' (EEAS, 2013a, p. 16), it may well emerge as a 'streamlined, results-orientated, efficient structure, capable of providing support for political leadership' (EP, 2013, p. 2). From this perspective, the MTR captures both the geopolitical and thematic components of the EEAS' emergent identity, and illustrates the degree to which its internal transformations have enabled EU diplomacy to take hold around the world.

II. The Southern Neighbourhood: The Arc of Instability?

Crisis and democratic transition marked the year in North Africa, the Sahel and the Sahara. In North Africa, the EU attempted to consolidate the political transitions in Libya and Tunisia, despite the rise of extremist elements and attacks in both countries. Indeed, the EU continued its financial and technical support for Tunisia, deploying a border assistance mission (EUBAM) to Libya in May with the aim of supporting Libyan authorities through the provision of technical expertise on land, sea and air border management. There was further evidence of the EU moving from its reactive engagement with the region to a more proactive stance; with a view to addressing the extant instability in Libya and the burning crises in the Sahel, the EU engaged with regional powers in order to ensure no further descent into crisis, commencing negotiations. For example, not only did it start negotiations for a deep and comprehensive FTA with Morocco in April, and re-engaging in Algeria after years of strained relations.

Given the historical animosity felt by Algeria towards Europe, the EU's steps to normalize relations was a disregarded success. Following the hostage crisis at a BP plant in January 2013, in which *Al Qaeda* militias connected to a network in Mali attacked and killed British workers, Algeria–EU relations began to thaw. Mutual rapprochement was strengthened when Algeria's government announced that it was revising its constitution, subsequently taking the decision to move closer to the ENP. The EU was quick to offer assistance on anti-corruption measures and the rule of law. By organizing the first ministerial dialogue with the five countries of the Maghreb (Algeria, Libya, Mauritania, Morocco and Tunisia) in September, the EU attempted to build further regional relations between Algeria and its immediate neighbours.

The root of the increasing instability in the Sahel Region emanated from the crisis in Mali. Following the seizure of towns by *Al Qaeda* and *Tuareg* rebels, the French decided to launch a military mission of 4,500 troops to the country. Even though the campaign was a success, France stepped aside from the core political problems facing the country over the long term. Nevertheless, the January intervention was important for the continued health of the CSDP. France's decision moved from a national strategy to an EU mode of engagement, with a number of countries assisting with logistics and intelligence. Despite growing, the mission gave rise to growing French impatience with EU co-operation through the CSDP, EUTM Mali 2013 was launched in February to provide assistance to the Malian armed forces. This operation saw 550 people deployed for an initial period of 15 months; that they were not directly involved in combat operations (EEAS, 2013b) was regarded by France as a less than ideal level of ambition. This issue was further highlighted during France's military deployment to the Central African Republic (CAR), which saw 1,600 troops deployed to the country in December 2013 under a United Nations mandate to separate groups engaged in ethnic strife. Again, France did not wait for an EU response before intervening on its own.

While the crises in Mali and CAR appeared to endorse the EU's new-found penchant for regional strategies, they also demonstrated that France remained largely unconcerned about launching unilateral missions in the neighbourhood in the absence of a specific EU framework in which to do so. Each recent crisis in the Sahel – in Libya, Mali and the CAR – have highlighted France's willingness to launch military missions under a 'coalitions of the willing' approach rather than under the CSDP. The French interventions in the Sahel Region also highlight the geostrategic importance of the region to French foreign policy, and formed a basis for discussions at the December European Council on defence. Following such experiences, one crucial change in France's relationship to the CSDP was manifested in the country's shift from a concerted belief in a *l'Europe de défense* to – as indicated in France's 2013 security and defence White Paper on security and defence – a more pragmatic engagement with the policy. Accordingly, while much collective energy has gone into establishing the EEAS and making the case for the continued relevance of the CSDP, France regularly reverts to a brand of impatient exceptionalism, one that waits neither for the EU nor NATO in those situations it deems to be in its national interest.

Elsewhere in Africa there were signs of row back, with the closure of the CSDP mission (EUAVSEC) to protect Juba International Airport in South Sudan in a context where, after two years of independence, South Sudan would become home to routine humanitarian aid blockages, human displacement and human rights violations; particularly in the east of the country. Perhaps most crucially, the EU took an important step towards building on its relatively successful anti-piracy mission (EUNAVFOR) off the Horn of Africa. Seeing the importance of naval capacity-building, and attempting to isolate Africa's eastern and western access points for piracy, terrorism and narcotics, the EU initiated a programme tackling critical maritime routes in the Gulf of Guinea (CRIMGO) in January with Benin, Cameroon, Equatorial Guinea, Gabon, Nigeria, São Tomé and Príncipe and Togo to help governments in the Gulf secure shipping routes through information exchange and coastguard training.

Events in Egypt were largely out of EU hands, as July saw the removal of Mohamed Morsi and the suspension of the constitution by the Egyptian military. Morsi was taken into military custody following a new wave of protests in Tahrir Square, which led to an interim government under the protection of General Abdul-Fattah el-Sisi and provoked clashes between the opposing groups. Among the chaos, Ashton met with Morsi in July, the first diplomat to do so since his ousting. The meeting was symbolically pertinent not only for Ashton's own initiative, but in illustrating the EU's difficulty in taking sides in the crisis. Only a year earlier, Ashton had spoken of the 'major milestone in Egypt's transition to democracy' following Morsi's election; now support was required without simultaneously endorsing a military coup. EU diplomacy in this respect thus attempted to reflect its support for the 'Egyptian people' rather than any political party (Ashton, 2012). Although the debate about Syria had turned shifted from civilian crisis to chemical weapons, the EU was still engaged with events on the ground mainly through humanitarian aid to Syria and surrounding countries.

The EU's humanitarian response was rolled out in a regional fashion in order to deal with the serious crisis of the approximately two million Syrian refugees dispersed across in Egypt, Iraq, Jordan, Lebanon, Turkey and other parts of North Africa, as well as the 4.25 million internally displaced persons in Syria itself. Despite the restrictions that derive from providing assistance to a civil war, the EU was subsequently overshadowed as an important actor in the region. Such efforts would, however, be overshadowed by the EU's internal controversy about relaxing the full arms embargo on Syria in place since May 2011. While Britain and France pushed to have the embargo lifted as a way to arm anti-Assad factions in Syria, they failed to convince other EU Member States of the merits of their argument (the Czech Republic, the Netherlands and Sweden remained sceptical about British and French assurances that arms would reach only democratic opposition forces in Syria) and succeeded merely in allowing a routine review of the embargo to lapse.

III. EU–Russia Relations

As examined elsewhere in this issue, 2013 was a defining year for the EU.[4] Tensions came to a head at the November summit of the Eastern Partnership (EaP) in Vilnius. In dispensing with the previously agreed EU Association Agreement, Ukrainian President Yanukovych crossed a Rubicon by making plain the need to resume 'an active dialogue with the Russian Federation and other countries of the Customs Union. With the geopolitical stakes both permanently and publicly raised, negotiations at Vilnius swiftly spiralled into the comprehensive breakdown of relations between the EU, the United States and Russia.[5] As 2013 drew to a close, the EU and the international community alike appeared unable to explain the swift purposiveness of Russia's own neighbourhood ambitions, the robust divisiveness resounding from an increasingly fractured Ukraine and, after the ousting of Yanukovych, the subsequent annexation of the Crimea in spring 2014. The year 2013 thus saw a worrying increase in EU–Russia tensions that, taken together, indicate a serious erosion of their broader historical relations.

Russian Minister of Foreign Affairs Sergey Lavrov's perspectives on EU–Russia relations published in last year's *JCMS Annual Review* are instructive in more fully understanding these events. Major initiatives like the partnership for modernization (PFM) are cited by Lavrov as evidence of decent EU–Russia relations, intersectoral success stories flagged up and the critical mass of interdependent energy trade and investment made clear. Yet Lavrov suggests that the 'long-term vision' and even the 'very close overall cooperation' publicly espoused by Barroso in the March 2013 EU–Russia summit was neither a 'clearly visualized goal' held by Russia, nor one convincingly shared with the EU, and that accordingly 'the strategic goals of Russia–EU relations have not yet become reality affecting daily affairs' (Lavrov, 2013, p. 7). Chief among Lavrov's concerns are the legal unbundling of vertically integrated energy companies necessitated by the EU's third energy package, poor progress towards visa-free travel, serious differences of opinion over Syria, and the EU's inability to recognize the unification rationale behind either the Eurasian Customs Union (ECU) or Russia's self-proclaimed need for 'close integration based on different values, with a new political and economic foundation' (Lavrov, 2013, p. 10).

---

[4] See the contributions by Menon, Hamilton, and Whitman and Juncos.
[5] *EurActiv*, 17 December 2013.

Statements assuaging EU anxieties about Russian intentions 'to restore the Russian Empire or the Soviet Union in any shape or form' appear, with the passage of 2013, eerily prophetic (Lavrov, 2013, p. 10). They run alongside Lavrov's subsequent statement that '[i]t is only natural to take advantage of economic, infrastructural, logistic and transport connections we inherited from the time when our countries were all parts of the same state', which – in his words – simply make 'common sense' (Lavrov, 2013, p. 10). The question is whether this hard-edged perspective regarding a leveraged neighbourhood constitutively explains Russian foreign policy regarding Ukraine in late 2013 and early 2014.

The answers are inconclusive. One the one hand, as articulated by Lavrov, Russian proposals merely offer a more attractive financial package to Ukraine than the EU, easing it into the new Eurasian Customs Union:

> When we will achieve all our plans regarding the Customs Union and the future Eurasian Union, I'm convinced that we will move toward putting in place the common economic space between Eurasia and the EU on conditions which are mutually beneficial.[6]

Putin's own argument however that 'Ukraine and its leadership will yield to pressure or will be able to resist it and take a pragmatic stance in line with national interests'[7] indicates an abiding ethos of *realpolitik* underlying contemporary Russian foreign policy, brutally evidenced in the subsequent seizure of Ukrainian territory by a combination of force and an enforced plebiscite. The outcome has produced increasing fractures between an intractable Russia convinced of its proprietorship over eastern Ukraine, and EU and American diplomats resorting to an increasingly touch but ineffective series of economic measures. That there was no major gas disruption to accompany the diplomatic fallout in 2013 may in hindsight be seen as the only positive outcome of news of this fractious season.

Higher tension levels arose much earlier in 2013 over energy security, with Russia retaining its prominent role as the largest supplier of natural gas and crude oil to the EU. In March, Energy Commissioner Günther Oettinger and Russian Minister for Energy Alexander Novak signed the EU–Russia Energy Roadmap 2050, covering large areas of energy security complementarity. Drawn up in the language of interest convergence, though still largely symbolic, the roadmap outlines key priorities, including market integration, interconnections and interoperability of various power systems, which if effected, could create a common, pan-European energy space (Commission for Energy, 2013).

The year 2013 also saw protracted energy wrangling between both sides, with Russian gas-exporting giant Gazprom facing a year-long antitrust investigation by the European Commission into its conduct in central and eastern Europe. Gazprom stands accused of using its dominant market position to hinder competition, which runs counter to the market methodology of unbundling, instituted (with limited success) across the EU energy sector by the European Commission. The Commission remains unrelentingly confident that such unbundling will accelerate the establishment of the internal energy market. Gazprom remains unconvinced. Ever pragmatic however, both sides remained at the bargaining table in 2013.

---

[6] *EurActiv*, 21 November 2013.
[7] *Aljazeera*, 22 November 2013.

Any positive or pragmatic quality in 2013 EU–Russia relations faded quickly however against the increasingly severe strains on such relations brought about by the geopolitical upheavals of 2014. Looking ahead, the differential expectations regarding neighbourhood, clashing understandings of integration, incommensurate approaches to the use of power and authority that characterized 2013 will arguably illuminate, and indeed contextualise the problems and potential solutions arrived at in 2014. Lavrov's use of Barroso's explanation of the EU–Russia relationship may be the most instructive in decoding 2013 and discerning the events of 2014:

> [T]he situation will only change if Russia–EU interaction goes from a 'partnership of necessity' to a 'partnership of choice'. And this means that our relationship needs strategic trust as a strong foundation. (Lavrov, 2013, p. 7)

Russia will have to work hard to regain lost trust, but the EU too must move swiftly to consolidate and implement a strategy for an increasingly fragmented Ukraine as the linchpin between two very different economic and political unions, without spiralling into zero-sum tactics with Russia.

IV. Asia: Europe's Pivotal Moment?

While our 2012 review focused on the impact of the Eurozone crisis on the EU's relationship with China, 2013 was marked by the new leadership of Xi Jinping and a deepening of the EU's and China's trade and security relationship. However, the EU–China relationship was not without tension, as evidenced by ongoing trade disputes. In October, the World Trade Organization (WTO) ruled in favour of the EU, Japan and the United States in the longstanding dispute over Chinese export restrictions on the export of rare earths minerals. In the trade dispute on solar panels, however, the EU and China jointly addressed the issue by agreeing to a minimum price for China's exports to the EU. This seemingly mature response – designed to avoid another WTO enquiry – came only after reports that China was considering its own investigation into the selling practices of European wine producers and governmental support for the German automobile sector (European Voice, 2013).

In addition to human rights issues, discussed in June at the 32nd EU–China dialogue on human rights, economic relations formed the core of discussions at the 16th EU–China summit on 20–21 November. The summit also launched the EU–China 2020 strategic agenda for co-operation, in which both parties pledged to enhance peace and security, prosperity, sustainable development and people-to-people exchanges over the next six years.

In the same month as the summit, however, EU–China relations were overshadowed by a decision taken by the Chinese government to unilaterally establish an 'East China sea air defence identification zone' (the 'ADIZ'). The ADIZ represents a Chinese response to recent disputes with Japan over the Senkaku/Diaoyu Islands, permitting China to react militarily to any unauthorized aircraft encroaching the zone, its announcement was met with chagrin for countries in the region including Japan and South Korea. The HV/VP responded by calling for caution and restraint, signalling that the EU itself had significant interests in the region. This claim was put to the test the following month when Ashton intervened to help lessen regional tensions after Japan's

Prime Minister Abe visited the Yasukuni Shrine, which celebrates Japan's war dead from the Second World War.

Tensions in East Asia yet again posed the question of the EU's strategic interest in the region. Some have claimed that the EU could also pivot towards Asia in 'economic, monetary, technological and soft-power' terms rather than with a security or military focus (Casarini, 2013). The question is whether any such European pivot could be seen to complement or balance the American pivot to the Asia-Pacific region. Clearly EU interests in the region will continue in importance, both bilaterally with China, but also via FTA negotiations with Japan, the 'EU's other major traditional "strategic partner"' (Allen and Smith, 2011, p. 227). Nor should relations with South Korea, which already has an FTA with the EU, be overlooked. South Korea is now seeking to build security relations with the EU, and has as such signed a framework participation agreement to allow it to engage with the EU in CSDP initiatives.

Relations with countries in Asia remained largely commercial in nature, with the EU pushing forward with free trade in the region by initiating investment agreements with ASEAN countries including Cambodia, Indonesia, Laos, Malaysia, Myanmar, Philippines, Singapore, Thailand and Vietnam – a process that will itself be boosted by the WTO's first global trade deal, agreed in December. The EU initiated both FTA and partnership and co-operation agreements talks with Thailand, continued FTA negotiations with Vietnam, signed partnership and co-operation agreements with Mongolia and inked a deal with Indonesia to curb the illegal trade in timber.

A strictly commercial policy however, does not always serve wider purposes of building constructive relations with prospective partners; a case in point being that of EU–India relations. The January EU–India ministerial meeting proved difficult in moving forward to anything strictly beyond trade policy. Indeed, even in the area of trade there has been no real departure from Allen and Smith's (2012, p. 171) observation that 'India does not see the need for an agreement that would give away cherished areas of control over market access'. The result is something of a diplomatic impasse: with 'no immediate crises to address, just the continuing divergence of views (Allen and Smith, 2011, p. 223). Moving beyond trade relations is crucial for both sides as 'long drawn [out] negotiations soak up most of the attention and risk pegging the entire relationship to their success or failure' (Khandekar, 2013, p. 1). Thus while the EU has designated India a 'strategic partner', 'it is [still] open to question how much strategy is reflected in its policies towards' India (Allen and Smith, 2009, p. 223).

A number of other regional security issues demanded EU attention. Myanmar's continued democratic transition saw the EU open a new delegation and lift further sanctions. The first EU–Myanmar task force met on 13–15 November to discuss EU political and financial support for the country's authorities. In Bangladesh, the planned EU election observation mission was suspended following widespread violence and party boycotts. The EU did however successfully deploy observation missions to Pakistan in May, and Nepal in October. The EU also succeeded in prolonging its EUPOL mission to Afghanistan until the end of 2014. Following the earthquake that struck the country in October and the devastation left by Typhoon Haiyan in November, the EU donated approximately €40 million in aid to the Philippines.

Moving further east, the EU's first EU–Central Asia high level security dialogue proved significant in building relations between the EU and Kazakhstan, the Kyrgyz

Republic, Tajikistan, Turkmenistan and Uzbekistan, in which the two sides discussed counter-terrorism, border management and drug policy, underlining the EU's growing interest in the region as a transit route for energy, goods, people and narcotics. The dialogue was also an important feature of the ongoing EU–Russia relationship *vis-à-vis* Central Asia. As argued above, Russia, through its Eurasian Customs Union (ECU), and the EU, through its association agreements, are both vying for regional influence. However, while the association agreements remain attractive to many Central Asia states, 'the emergence of the ECU means that the EU is no longer the only actor promoting deep economic integration premised on regulatory convergence in the post-Soviet space' (Delcour and Wolczuk, 2013, p. 180).

V. The Americas: The Economic Ties that Bind

South America remained on the EU's radar during 2013. MERCOSUR trade ministers met with EU representatives in January for an exchange of offers on customs duties and quotas, and in March the EU's FTAs with Peru and Colombia came into force. Two events in particular, the sixth EU–Brazil summit and the EU–Community of Latin American and Caribbean States, organized within two days of each other, so that the EU and Brazil could 'counter – on the symbolic level at least – accusations of "privileging" their bilateral partnership over their commitment to inter-regionalism and regional cooperation' (Lazarou, 2013, p. 2). While it is perhaps unfair to say that the EU now completely neglects the promotion of regionalism in Latin America, it should be noted that the EU–Brazil relationship is the main strategic relationship that has emerged out of Latin America in the recent years. As stated above, with the case of the EU–India partnership, the EU will have to try and move beyond trade issues if the EU–Brazil partnership is really to mature – especially as Brazilian imports of EU goods have been on the decline since 2011.

'A new era in EU-Canada relations' (EU, 2013) was heralded in October as Canadian Prime Minister Stephen Harper, alongside European Commission President Jose Manual Barroso, together announced the Canada–EU economic and trade agreement (CETA). Harper declared it 'the biggest deal our country has ever made' and considered it to be 'a historic win for Canada' (Canada–European Union, 2013). While in some respects the win appeared greater for Canada, in securing a decent EU deal well 'ahead of its major competitors'[8] the EU itself reaped the benefits of nailing down its first agreement with a G8 country and gained sufficient traction for the renewed bout of negotiations on the transatlantic trade and investment partnership (TTIP) with the United States. The next five years will therefore be the acid test as to whether CETA is truly a '21st century, gold-standard agreement' (European Commission, 2013a).

Certain expectations have certainly been made clear. Even prior to tariff dismantling, the Commission recognized that the unprecedented concessions that Canada had offered constitute a stepping stone for future negotiations with other partners (European Commission, 2013b). Equally, the United States will expect conditions for its own TTIP to be no less favourable than those granted to Canada. EU–Canadian Arctic relations, on the other hand, were far chillier. From their rock bottom 2009 status after the EU ban on seal

---

[8] *Reuters*, 18 October 2013.

products imports, May 2013 saw Canadian misgivings scupper the EU's second application for observer status to the Arctic Council, while applications from China and five other countries for full and observer membership were granted (Arctic Council, 2013).

The year also yielded a great degree of promise and strain for EU–US relations,[9] highlighting the schizophrenia that sometimes surrounds such relations. On the one hand, in the context of global economic uncertainty and extant concerns about the health of the eurozone, the TTIP is a good example of the United States and the EU attempting to bolster their already strong economic relationship. It is true however that there are disagreements over regulatory standards and initiatives (Fiott, 2013),[10] and political relations remain strained in some areas. On dossiers such as Iran's nuclear policy, the EU and the United States stand side-by-side in their diplomatic activities. In contrast, however, the 'Snowden revelations' highlighted the extent to which America's National Security Agency (NSA) had comprehensively undermined security relations with Europe with news that it had been conducting habitual surveillance on European political partners, leaders, diplomats, citizens, and institutions.

Beyond the TTIP negotiations and the NSA scandal, however, the EU and the United States had a number of crises to address jointly. Following the August chemical attacks on civilians in the Ghouta suburbs of Damascus, President Obama felt obliged to honour a previously drawn 'red line' on the use of chemical weapons, which subsequently raised the spectre of military action in Syria. The 'red line' affected the British and French by association, and by September the three countries looked for a UN Resolution that provided for a robust mandate for military action. Meanwhile the HR/VP called the chemical attack an appalling 'war crime', but urged caution against a military response and instead called for time for UN weapons inspectors to investigate the alleged attack site. Ashton's perspective would ultimately prevail, but not on the strength of any diplomatic rationale. Instead, it took a vote in the British House of Commons and debate in the United States Congress and French *Sénat* to scupper the proposed combined military response as retribution for the chemical attacks.

While the United States and France still maintain that military action in Syria over chemical weapons is possible, and given that there is an ongoing civilian crisis in the country and region, the western response to Syria's chemical arsenal was unco-ordinated, which can be seen in contrast to the relative harmony seen over action in Libya in 2011. France had diplomatically over-invested in military action to such a degree that when American and British involvement became untenable the French had to scale-back on its initial bullish tone. President Hollande had to tell the *Sénat* that the French would not get involved in Syria unless the United States did, but by this time the diplomatic damage had been done. This political dynamic allowed Russia to take an upper hand in the crisis as it brokered a deal on dismantling Assad's chemical weapons capability. The United States, Britain and France embarrassingly had no choice but to follow the path laid by Moscow (Mead, 2014).

Perhaps most significantly, November negotiations between Iran and the 'EU3+3" (China, France, Germany, Russia, the UK and the US) over the country's nuclear

---

[9] See Hamilton's contribution to this volume.
[10] For example, the April 2013 decision by the EU to suspend its emissions trading system on airlines as a result of EU–US and international disagreement, and the exemptions for the audio-visual and defence sectors.

programme yielded a six-month agreement that saw Iran freeze the most contentious elements of its nuclear activities with the EU3+3 easing sanctions. While secret talks between the United States and Iran had taken place since March, and given the relative openness of the new government in Tehran when compared to Ahmadinejad's tenure, Ashton's role in the deal was seen by many as a defining moment in her role as HR/VP. Many of the newspapers that had criticized her at the beginning of her posting either fell silent on the back of her diplomacy over Iran, or undertook a public *volte-face*. On this occasion, Ashton's brand of 'quiet diplomacy' reverberated globally. As one newspaper put it, she was lauded to be 'as indefatigable as she is low profile and discreet'.[11] The Iran deal demonstrated that if the conditions are right, Ashton can indeed play an effective role, even if the claim that she has failed 'to get an overall grip on all aspects of EU external relations' remains valid of key aspects of her tenure (Allen and Smith, 2012, p. 176).

Examining the overall reasons for the diplomatic breakthrough, it is clear that the EU's determination in leading the talks certainly created the right conditions for a deal. Indeed, the EU's success in brokering a deal with Iran is seen as a combination of dogged persistence by the six powers to avert conflict with Iran in lieu of an agreement, and Ashton's leadership of this effort with her own brand of down-to-earth diplomacy. As one of her former senior advisors in the EEAS put it: 'All involved pay tribute to her patience, her handling of people, her ability to be frank but never aggressive: those elusive qualities we now call "emotional intelligence"'.[12] The EU will surely have to maintain this persistence and 'intelligence' to ensure that Iran keeps to its side of the bargain. In this regard, much depends on the EU maintaining a united front. Finally, the paradox surrounding the EU and Iran is that Ashton will step down as HR/VP by the end of 2014, making a deal before then essential; a change in personnel could impact the future discussions between the EU3+3 and Iran.

Conclusions

The year 2013 had a degree of diplomatic exit velocity for the EU that did not go unnoticed. From a positive perspective, EU soft power in 2013 translated into formidable normative pull that caused major divisions in a variety of neighbourhood countries between civil societies still vocal and restive over unforthcoming rights, witnessed so saliently in Ukraine in December 2013. From a cynical perspective, the EU's growing soft power expertise has yet to translate its laudable, if unwieldy policies into substantive, and effective actorness. This lack of proven reliability could unnerve the EU's strategic neighbours who have come to rely on EU support. The question is whether the EU can construct a foreign policy relationship with them that extends beyond soft power platitudes, beyond partial trans-border tactics, into a strategic series of dependable, regional relations. Andrew Rettman's observation that 'the EU this year lost a battle for Ukraine, but nobody is laughing at its soft power any more' may turn out to be a double edged sword (2013).

A great deal rests on the much-vaunted potential of the comprehensive approach. While the comprehensive approach has had initial outings in the Horn of Africa, and the

---

[11] *The Observer*, 30 November 2013.
[12] *Financial Times*, 11 December 2013.

Sahel, the 2014 EU neighbourhood will be the testing ground by which it, and the EEAS as its guardian, ensures a systematic approach to actually implementing join efforts between the European Commission and the EEAS in the categories of conflict prevention and crisis resolution. The EU has long possessed a wide array of policies and instruments, and been mindful of the need for a 'joined-up deployment' of those instruments (European Commission and HR/VP, 2013, p. 3). However, the EU has yet to fully appreciate – in the wake of a lacklustre ENP – what is materially entailed in avoiding the temptation to reach for 'blue-prints or off-the-shelf solutions' but operating instead within a foreign policy construct whose central philosophy is a paradox of hybridity (European Commission and HR/VP, 2013, p. 3).

The range of FTAs analysed in this review gives one pause for thought about the precise nature of the EU's global power. Indeed, for all the developments in the EEAS and the promotion of the comprehensive approach, the EU is still a largely economic and market power. There can be no doubt that a well-functioning EEAS will, in time, help to streamline the implementation of EU foreign policy decisions. However, the EU is still deadlocked on a number of issues because of the diverging interests of Member States.[13] While one must acknowledge differences of opinion between the Member States on the TTIP, it is reasonable to say that the FTA has become as much a part of the EU foreign policy toolbox as, say, economic sanctions, development aid and, to a lesser extent, CSDP missions. In many ways this was to be expected. Indeed, just as the political conditionality attached to EU accession or association agreements can help transform countries, so too can mutually agreeing FTAs with states beyond the neighbourhood draw these countries nearer to the EU's internal market and its regulatory and norm-setting power.

How has the EU fared in its capacity to act strategically? After ten years of the ESS, has the EU transformed into an actor that can command the global agenda or is it still too reactive to events? The picture is mixed. The TTIP negotiations, the maturing of relations with China, the Iran deal and its continued development of the EEAS shows that, on the one hand, the EU is, in certain areas, thinking strategically. In this regard, the EU's main concern is to sustain interdependent and healthy relations with the United States and China – this is wise and to be lauded. On the other hand, the crises in Syria, Ukraine and Central Africa highlight the continued divisions between Member States when it comes to deciding on joint action for major international crises. Where there is division, the EU can only be labelled a 'non-reactive power'. Nevertheless, the EEAS has made important steps to 'get ahead of the game', but it will take time before the EU has the capacity to comprehensively deal with crises. While the 'comprehensive approach' is still essentially a reactive concept, it is the EU's economic and market resources that overwhelmingly ensure that one can still refer to the EU as a 'strategic actor'. Challenging times await.

References

Allen, D. and Smith, M. (2009) 'Relations with the Rest of the World'. *JCMS*, Vol. 47, No. s1, pp. 213–32.

Allen, D. and Smith, M. (2011) 'Relations with the Rest of the World'. *JCMS*, Vol. 49, No. s1, pp. 209–30.

---

[13] See Menon's contribution to this volume.

Allen, D. and Smith, M. (2012) 'Relations with the Rest of the World'. *JCMS*, Vol. 50, No. s2, pp. 162–77.

Arctic Council (2013) 'Observers'. Available at: «http://www.arctic-council.org/index.php/en/about-us/arctic-council/observers».

Ashton, C. (2012) 'Remarks by EU High Representative Catherine Ashton Following Her Meeting with President Morsi'. Available at: «http://www.consilium.europa.eu/uedocs/cms_Data/docs/pressdata/EN/foraff/131877.pdf».

Ashton, C. (2013) 'HR/VP Statement on EEAS Review'. SPEECH/13/530, 12 June. Available at: «http://europa.eu/rapid/press-release_SPEECH-13-530_en.htm».

Canada–European Union (2013) 'Canada Reaches Historic Trade Agreement with the European Union'. Available at «http://www.actionplan.gc.ca/en/news/ceta-aecg/canada-reaches-historic-trade-agreement-european».

Casarini, N. (2013) 'The European "Pivot"'. *EU Institute for Security Studies Alert*, No. 3.

Commission for Energy (2013) 'Roadmap EU–Russia Energy Cooperation until 2050'. Available at: «http://ec.europa.eu/energy/international/russia/doc/2013_03_eu_russia_roadmap_2050_signed.pdf. Accessed: 25 January 2014».

Council of the European Union (2013) 'Council conclusions on the EEAS Review', 17 December. Available at: «http://www.consilium.europa.eu/uedocs/cms_data/docs/pressdata/EN/genaff/140141.pdf».

Damro, C. (2012) 'Market Power Europe'. *Journal of European Public Policy*, Vol. 19, No. 5, pp. 682–99.

Delcour, L. and Wolczuk, K. (2013) 'Eurasian Economic Integration: Implications for the EU Eastern Policy'. In Dragneva, R. and Wolczuk, K. (eds) *Eurasian Economic Integration: Law, Policy and Politics* (Cheltenham: Edward Elgar).

European Centre for Development Policy and Management (ECDPM) (2012) 'Gearing Up for the 2013 EEAS Review: Opportunities, Challenges and Possible Approaches'. Briefing Note 44 (Brussels: ECDPM).

European Commission (2013a) 'Declaration by the President of the European Commission and the Prime Minister of Canada: "A new era in EU-Canada relations"'. MEMO/13/914, 18 October. Available at: «http://europa.eu/rapid/press-release_MEMO-13-914_en.htm».

European Commission (2013b) 'CETA summary of negotiating results following the break-through on 18 October'. Available at: «http://www.tradejustice.ca/wp-content/uploads/2013/08/CETA-Summary-of-negotiating-results-following-the-break-through-on-18-October.doc».

European Commission and High Representative of the European Union for Foreign Affairs and Security Policy (European Commission and HR/VP) (2013) 'Joint Communication to the European Parliament and the Council entitled "The EU's comprehensive approach to external conflict and crises"'. JOIN 30 final, 11 December.

European External Action Service (EEAS) (2013a) 'EEAS Review 2013'. Available at: «http://eeas.europa.eu/top_stories/2013/29072013_eeas_review_en.htm».

European External Action Service (EEAS) (2013b) 'Fact Sheet: EU Training Mission in Mali'. Available at: «http://eeas.europa.eu/csdp/missions-and-operations/eutm-mali/pdf/01092013_factsheet_eutm-mali_en.pdf».

European Parliament (EP) (2013) 'Recommendation to the High Representative of the Union for Foreign Affairs and Security Policy and Vice President of the European Commission, to the Council and to the Commission on the 2013 review of the organisation and the functioning of the EEAS'. Procedure file 2012/2253 (INI), 13 June.

European Union (EU) (2013) 'Declaration by the President of the European Commission and the Prime Minister of Canada: "A new era in EU-Canada relations"'. Available at: «http://europa.eu/rapid/press-release_SPEECH-13-817_en.htm».

European Voice (2013) 'EU, China Settle Solar-Panel Dispute'. *European Voice*, 28 July. Available at: «http://www.europeanvoice.com/article/2013/july/eu-china-settle-solar-panel-dispute/77994.aspx».

Fiott, D. (2013) 'The "TTIP-ing Point": How the Transatlantic Trade and Investment Partnership Could Impact European Defence'. *International Spectator*, Vol. 48, No. 3, pp. 15–26.

Hadfield, A. and Fiott, D. (2013) 'Europe and the Rest of the World'. *JCMS*, Vol. 51, No. s1, pp. 168–82.

Khandekar, G. (2013) 'Building a Sustainable EU–India Partnership'. Policy Brief 9 (Brussels: European Strategic Partnerships Observatory).

Lavrov, S. (2013) 'Russia–EU: Prospects for Partnership in the Changing World'. *JCMS*, Vol. 51, No. s1, pp. 6–12.

Lazarou, E. (2013) 'The Sixth EU–Brazil Summit: Business beyond the Usual?' Policy Brief 8 (Brussels: European Strategic Partnerships Observatory).

Lehne, S. (2012) *The Review of the European External Action Service in 2013* (Brussels: Carnegie Europe). Available at: «http://carnegieeurope.eu/publications/?fa=50020».

Mead, W. (2014) 'The 10 Biggest Winners of 2013'. *American Interest*, 4 January. Available at: «http://www.the-american-interest.com/wrm/2014/01/04/the-10-biggest-winners-of-2013/».

Parliament of the United Kingdom (2013) 'Review by the High Representative of the European External Action Service'. FCO 35271, 27 August.

Rettman, A. (2013) 'EU to Yanukovych: You are Taking Ukraine Nowhere'. *EUObserver*, 28 November. Available at: «http://euobserver.com/foreign/122292».

JCMS 2014 Volume 52 Annual Review pp. 186–201   DOI: 10.1111/jcms.12170

Eurozone Governance: Recovery, Reticence and Reform

DERMOT HODSON
Birkbeck College, University of London

Introduction

When it came to eurozone governance, the year 2013 was lucky for some. As discussed in last year's review, fears mounted in 2012 that Spain and Italy would face the same fiscal fate as Greece, Portugal and Ireland until European Central Bank (ECB) President Mario Draghi promised to do 'whatever it takes' to save the euro (Hodson, 2013). The feel-good factor from this decision did not fade in 2013 but instead was enhanced as the eurozone exited recession and Ireland ended its EU-IMF (International Monetary Fund) programme. Fortunate though the eurozone was in these respects, there were limits to its good luck. In May 2013, Cyprus became the fifth eurozone member in three years to seek external financial assistance after its fiscal crisis spiraled out of control. Other worrying developments for the eurozone in 2013 included unacceptably high levels of unemployment and an increased risk of deflation. Talk of a currency war also arose on the international stage and, closer to home, plans for a genuine economic and monetary union (EMU) progressed with only varying degrees of success.

This contribution takes stock of these and other developments in eurozone governance in 2013. The first section gives an update on the euro crisis, focusing on Cyprus's entry to the euro crisis club and Ireland's exit from it. The second section looks at the economic outlook in 2013 and the factors driving the eurozone's tentative recovery. The third section explores key developments in eurozone monetary policy, including moves towards a more transparent approach to decision-making. The fourth section focuses on financial surveillance in the eurozone and ongoing efforts to the get the single supervisory mechanism up and running. The fifth section turns to economic policy co-ordination and reviews the Six-Pack's second year in operation. The sixth section examines the eurozone's global role and gauges its response to concerns over currency wars. The sixth section discusses ongoing reforms to eurozone governance, including the entry into force of the Two-Pack and patchy progress in 2013 towards the realization of a 'genuine' EMU.

I. The Euro Crisis in 2013

The nightmare scenario for 2013 was that the sovereign debt crisis that began in Greece in early 2010 before spreading to Ireland and Portugal, would engulf Spain and Italy. Spain had negotiated a €100 million loan from the eurozone in 2012 to cover the costs of bank recapitalization, but full-scale financial support for this country or Italy, it was feared, would be sufficient to stretch the resources of the EU beyond breaking point. That this scenario did not come to pass was due to Mario Draghi's promise in July 2012 to engage in unlimited bond purchases (see below). The willingness of the Rajoy, Monti and

Letta administrations to take tough decisions also made a difference here, as did a large measure of good luck. The sovereign debt crisis subsided in 2013 as a result, but it by no means disappeared. By the end of the year, Spain and Ireland had exited their adjustment programmes, but Portugal and Greece struggled on. Cyprus, meanwhile, became the latest eurozone member to secure financial assistance from the EU and IMF in May 2013.

The reasons behind Cyprus's fiscal predicament reflect a combination of bad luck and ill judgement.[1] The former ranged from the country's high degree of exposure to Greece's sovereign debt crisis to a fire that caused widespread power and water shortages and ended up costing the economy an estimated 17 per cent of gross domestic product (GDP) (Apostolides, 2011). The latter included a combination of lax fiscal policies after Cyprus joined the eurozone in January 2008 and a banking system that was disproportionate in size as a result of offshore deposits by wealthy Russians and Eastern Europeans (see Stephanou, 2011). In May 2013, the government of Cyprus concluded a three-year package of loans worth €10 billion from the EU and IMF. This was small by the standards of the euro sovereign debt crisis, but negotiations leading up to this deal proved problematic. The Cypriot government's reluctance to do a deal before a general election in February 2013 was a complicating factor here. So too was the eurogroup's support for an emergency levy on all depositors in Cypriot banks. These terms were rejected by the House of Representatives (the Cypriot parliament) and the final package, which was approved, imposed an emergency levy only on those savers with deposits in excess of €100,000. Politically, the original levy owed much to eurozone leaders' desire to take a hard line against a Member State that was perceived as profligate and a tax haven to boot. Economically, the move was a costly one as it created uncertainty as to whether governments, bondholders or savers would foot the bill in future financial support packages (Begg, 2013).

Ireland's exit from its EU-IMF programme in December 2013 is a test case for a Member State's ability to return to economic normality after the euro crisis. Negotiations and deliberations over Ireland's exit centred on two politically contentious issues. The first involved a change to the terms of the Irish government's emergency financial support to Anglo-Irish Bank in 2009. This support took the form of a €30.6 billion promissory note, which the Irish government financed by means of a loan plan that required it to pay an eye-watering 2 per cent of its GDP per year over ten years.[2] In February 2013, by which time the promissory note affair had become a lightning rod for public discontent in Ireland, the governor of the Central Bank of Ireland won the tacit approval of the ECB Governing Council to reschedule the repayment of this loan over 40 years, saving around €20 billion in the process.[3] The second sticking point was whether Ireland would exit the EU-IMF programme without a precautionary credit line, which would have provided loans if the country struggled to borrow on financial markets. Such loans would have come with conditions attached that the Irish government was keen to reassert control over its economic policy after three years of oversight by the troika. In the end, Ireland chose not

---

[1] For an insider account of this issue, see *The Economist*: 'Interview with Athanasios Orphanides: What Happened in Cyprus?', Free Exchange Blog, 28 March 2013. Full text available at: «http://www.economist.com/blogs/freeexchange/2013/03/interview-athanasios-orphanides».
[2] See Whelan (2013) for a detailed discussion of the promissory note affair.
[3] The operative word here is 'tacit' as the ECB still has reservations at the time of writing over whether the Central Bank of Ireland's actions in this affair may have amounted to monetary financing of government borrowing, which is prohibited under the Treaty. See ECB (2014, p. 110).

to apply for a precautionary credit line, leaving it dependent once again on financial markets when it comes to managing its public finances.

Spain also exited its European stability mechanism programme in December 2013. The country's bank recapitalization efforts went more smoothly than expected and, in the end, the government requested less than half of the €100 billion that had been set aside for it by other eurozone members.

II. A Tentative Economic Recovery

The eurozone entered a deep recession in 2009 – the first in its history and the worst in memory for its members – before bouncing back in 2010. This recovery was built, in part, on the effects of a co-ordinated fiscal stimulus package in the EU and other parts of the world. Once this stimulus faded, it fell to monetary policy to provide cheap credit, but the ECB offered too little too late and the eurozone economy slowed in 2011 before entering a double-dip recession in 2012. Real GDP contracted by 0.4 per cent in 2013 (see Table 1) but a tentative economic recovery began in the second quarter of the year. This recovery was mainly due to international factors. Although the pace of economic growth slowed in two of the eurozone's key trading partners – the United States and China – in 2013, increasing exports to the rest of the world helped to counteract this effect. Domestic demand, in contrast, continued to serve as a drag on economic growth. The effects of a modest recovery in private and public consumption were offset here by declining investment in the eurozone.

Table 1: Real GDP Growth (% Annual Change): Eurozone, 2010–14

	2010	2011	2012	2013	2014[f]
Belgium	2.3	1.8	−0.1	0.2	1.4
Germany	4.0	3.3	0.7	0.4	1.8
Estonia	2.6	9.6	3.9	0.7	2.3
Ireland	−1.1	2.2	0.2	0.3	1.8
Greece	−4.9	−7.1	−6.4	−3.7	0.6
Spain	−0.2	0.1	−1.6	−1.2	1.0
France	1.7	2.0	0.0	0.3	1.0
Italy	1.7	0.5	−2.5	−1.9	0.6
Cyprus	1.3	0.4	−2.4	−6.0	−4.8
Luxembourg	3.1	1.9	−0.2	2.1	2.2
Malta	3.3	1.7	0.9	2.0	2.1
Netherlands	1.5	0.9	−1.2	−0.8	1.0
Austria	1.8	2.8	0.9	0.3	1.5
Portugal	1.9	−1.3	−3.2	−1.6	0.8
Slovenia	1.3	0.7	−2.5	−1.6	−0.1
Slovakia	4.4	3.0	1.8	0.8	2.3
Finland	3.4	2.8	−1.0	−1.5	0.2
Eurozone	2.0	1.6	−0.7	−0.4	1.2
EU	2.0	1.7	−0.4	0.1	1.5

Source: European Commission AMECO data base (updated 27 February 2014).
Note: Forecasts are denoted by *f*.

Table 2: Unemployment (% of the Civilian Labour Force): Eurozone, 2010–14

	2010	2011	2012	2013	2014[f]
Belgium	8.3	7.2	7.6	8.4	8.5
Germany	7.1	5.9	5.5	5.3	5.2
Estonia	16.9	12.5	10.2	8.8	8.3
Ireland	13.9	14.7	14.7	13.1	11.9
Greece	12.6	17.7	24.3	27.3	26.0
Spain	20.1	21.7	25.0	26.4	25.7
France	9.7	9.6	10.2	10.8	11.0
Italy	8.4	8.4	10.7	12.2	12.6
Cyprus	6.3	7.9	11.9	16.0	19.2
Luxembourg	4.6	4.8	5.1	5.9	6.0
Malta	6.9	6.5	6.4	6.5	6.4
Netherlands	4.5	4.4	5.3	6.7	7.4
Austria	4.4	4.2	4.3	4.9	4.8
Portugal	12.0	12.9	15.9	16.5	16.8
Slovenia	7.3	8.2	8.9	10.2	10.8
Slovakia	14.5	13.7	14.0	14.2	13.9
Finland	8.4	7.8	7.7	8.2	8.3
Eurozone	10.1	10.1	11.4	12.1	12.0
EU	9.7	9.7	10.5	10.9	10.7

Source: European Commission AMECO data base (updated 27 February 2014).
Note: Forecasts are denoted by *f*.

As always, the economic performance of eurozone members varied. Real GDP in France and Germany increased by 0.3 and 0.4 per cent, respectively, in 2013. For France, this was an improvement on the preceding year but only just, adding to the pressure on the country's embattled President, François Hollande. For Germany, the economy slowed further in 2013, although increased expenditure by consumers and a modest fiscal stimulus helped to counteract the effects of declining investment. Fiscal austerity continued to take its toll in the eurozone members worst hit by the sovereign debt crisis but there was a modicum of good news in Greece, Spain and Portugal – all of which saw GDP contract in 2013 but by less than in 2012. The common factor between these three countries was the positive contribution of net exports to economic growth. Ireland's economy continued to gain momentum in 2013. An increase in private consumption helped to counteract the effects of fiscal consolidation here, alongside increasing investment and a relatively strong export performance. Cyprus, meanwhile, saw its real GDP contract by 6.0 per cent in 2013 as the effects of its fiscal crisis began to bite.

In the eurozone as a whole, the unemployment rate exceeded 12.0 per cent in 2013 (see Table 2). This was the fifth consecutive year in which the rate of joblessness either rose or remained constant. Within the eurozone, nine members recorded unemployment rates in excess of 10 per cent in 2013. Spain and Greece continued to give most cause for concern with more than a quarter of the civilian labour force in these countries without work in 2013. Of the two, Spain's prospects seemed a little less bleak. This was not only because the scale of fiscal adjustment expected of this country was less, but also because it had made more progress in reforming its labour market. Spain has long had a segmented

Table 3: Inflation Rates (% Change on Preceding Year):
Eurozone, 2010–14

	2010	2011	2012	2013	2014[f]
Belgium	2.3	3.4	2.6	1.2	0.9
Germany	1.2	2.5	2.1	1.6	1.4
Estonia	2.7	5.1	4.2	3.2	1.8
Ireland	−1.6	1.2	1.9	0.5	0.8
Greece	4.7	3.1	1.0	−0.9	−0.6
Spain	2.0	3.1	2.4	1.5	0.3
France	1.7	2.3	2.2	1.0	1.2
Italy	1.6	2.9	3.3	1.3	0.9
Cyprus	2.6	3.5	3.1	0.4	0.4
Luxembourg	2.8	3.7	2.9	1.7	1.5
Malta	2.0	2.5	3.2	1.0	1.2
Netherlands	0.9	2.5	2.8	2.6	1.1
Austria	1.7	3.6	2.6	2.1	1.8
Portugal	1.4	3.6	2.8	0.4	0.8
Slovenia	2.1	2.1	2.8	1.9	0.8
Slovakia	0.7	4.1	3.7	1.5	0.7
Finland	1.7	3.3	3.2	2.2	1.7
Eurozone	1.6	2.7	2.5	1.3	1.0
EU	2.1	3.1	2.6	1.5	1.2

Source: European Commission AMECO data base (updated 27 February 2014).
Note: Forecasts are denoted by *f*.

labour market in which workers on temporary contracts have been much easier to hire and fire than those in permanent positions (Bentolila *et al.*, 1994). Reforms enacted by the Rajoy administration have, *inter alia*, extended the trial period for permanent workers and reduced dismissal costs for those on long-term contracts. Research by the Organization for Economic Co-operation and Development (OECD) suggests that the number of permanent contracts being signed in Spain has increased by as much as 25,000 per month as a result (OECD, 2013, p. 7).

High unemployment dampened inflationary pressures in the eurozone in 2013. Other contributory factors here included falling energy prices and an appreciation in the external value of the euro. In the eurozone as a whole, the consumer price index rose by 1.3 per cent in 2013, compared with an increase of 2.5 per cent in 2012 (see Table 3). Within the eurozone, the Netherlands, Austria, Finland and Estonia recorded inflation rates in excess of 2 per cent, while Spain, Greece, Ireland, Portugal and Cyprus experienced rates of close to or below zero. Such inflation differentials are in stark contrast to developments in the first ten years of the single currency, which saw those in the periphery of the eurozone record relatively high price increases while those in the core showed greater restraint. As a result, the periphery saw its external competitiveness deteriorate sharply during this period and it was harder hit by the global financial crisis as a result. That Spain, Greece, Ireland, Portugal and Cyprus have embarked on a strategy of competitive disinflation since 2010 is welcome from the point of view of macroeconomic adjustment in the eurozone. It comes, however, at a high and potentially prohibitive price for the countries concerned, insofar as deflation increases the real costs of borrowing and adds to the real burden of paying down government debt (see Bernanke, 2002).

Table 4: Net Lending (+) or Net Borrowing (−) General
Government Balance (% of GDP): Eurozone, 2010–14

	2010	2011	2012	2013	2014ƒ
Belgium	−3.7	−3.7	−4.0	−2.7	−2.6
Germany	−4.2	−0.8	0.1	−0.1	0.0
Estonia	0.2	1.1	−0.2	−0.4	−0.4
Ireland	−30.6	−13.1	−8.2	−7.2	−4.8
Greece	−10.7	−9.5	−9.0	−13.1	−2.2
Spain	−9.6	−9.6	−10.6	−7.2	−5.8
France	−7.1	−5.3	−4.8	−4.2	−4.0
Italy	−4.5	−3.8	−3.0	−3.0	−2.6
Cyprus	−5.3	−6.3	−6.3	−5.5	−5.8
Luxembourg	−0.8	0.1	−0.6	−0.2	−0.5
Malta	−3.5	−2.8	−3.3	−3.0	−2.7
Netherlands	−5.1	−4.3	−4.1	−3.1	−3.2
Austria	−4.5	−2.5	−2.5	−1.7	−2.1
Portugal	−9.8	−4.3	−6.4	−5.9	−4.0
Slovenia	−5.9	−6.3	−3.8	−14.9	−3.9
Slovakia	−7.7	−5.1	−4.5	−2.5	−3.3
Finland	−2.5	−0.7	−1.8	−2.4	−2.5
Eurozone	−6.2	−4.2	−3.7	−3.1	−2.6
EU	−6.5	−4.4	−3.9	−3.5	−2.7

Source: European Commission AMECO data base (updated 27 February 2014).
Note: Forecasts are denoted by *f*.

Fiscal consolidation continued apace in 2013. In the eurozone as a whole, the budget deficit as a percentage of GDP fell from 3.7 to 3.1 (see Table 4). Spain, Ireland and Portugal posted deficits of 7.0 per cent or more, which is well above the 3.0 per cent deficit ceiling for the stability and growth pact but a significant improvement on the double-digit deficits that precipitated sovereign debt crises in these countries. Greece saw its budget deficit increase from 9.0 per cent in 2012 to 13.1 per cent in 2013. This deterioration was due to a significant extent to the one-off costs of recapitalizing Greek banks under the terms of the second financial support package with the EU and IMF. Government debt as a percentage of GDP remained above 120 in Greece, Ireland and Portugal in 2013 – this threshold having come to be seen (somewhat arbitrarily) as a proxy for fiscal sustainability. Posting a primary surplus is a more conventional indicator of a country's ability to reduce its government debt. In 2013, Greece, Ireland, Portugal, Spain and Cyprus all posted primary deficits. Slovenia, meanwhile, saw of its budget deficit as a percentage of GDP increase from 3.8 in 2012 to 14.9 in 2013. This, too, reflected the costs of bank recapitalization. Slovenia almost found itself turning to the EU and IMF in 2013 as a result, but it narrowly avoided this fate.

III. Transparency and Accountability in Eurozone Monetary Policy

The ECB has, on balance, been slow to react to the global financial crisis and its after effects. It was slow to cut interest rates after liquidity shortages in mid-2007, slow to embrace unconventional monetary policies once interest rates reached record lows and slow to engage in the purchase of government bonds as the sovereign debt crisis escalated.

Such caution is partly the product of the ECB's idiosyncratic institutional design. The Treaty requires the ECB to pursue price stability above all other goals, and a concern for inflationary pressures has been evident in the Bank's reticence about cutting interest rates and embracing unconventional monetary policy over the last five years. In July 2012, ECB President Mario Draghi finally bit the bullet by agreeing to do 'whatever it takes' to save the euro. This commitment gave rise to the so-called 'outright monetary transactions programme', under which the ECB agreed, in principle, to the unlimited purchase of government bonds on secondary markets for Member States facing fiscal crises. Draghi's move was a major success, as evidenced by the falling risk premia on government debt issued by Spain and Italy in the second half of 2012.

Risk premia on Italian and Spanish debt continued to fall in 2013. In Spain, the interest rate on ten-year government bonds fell from 5.27 per cent at the end of 2012 to 4.14 per cent at the end of 2013. In Italy, this rate fell from 4.50 to 4.04 per cent. Because government debt is, by definition, more sustainable at lower long-term interest rates, the outright monetary transactions programme was not activated in 2013, which is just as well given the serious economic and legal doubts that surround it. As regards economic doubts, the ECB's decision to make access to financing under this scheme conditional on compliance with a strict programme of economic and fiscal adjustment is problematic because Member States most in need of outright monetary transactions could well struggle to meet such conditions. As regards legal doubts, the compatibility of outright monetary transactions with EU and German law was challenged before Germany's Federal Constitutional Court in June 2013 and this case had not been settled at the time of writing.

Faced with concerns over deflation, the ECB Governing Council responded by cutting interest rates in May and November 2013. These cuts brought the interest rates on the ECB's three policy rates – the main refinancing rate, the deposit facility and the marginal lending facility – to historic lows of 0.25, 0.00 and 0.75 per cent, respectively. Also significant was Mario Draghi's announcement in July 2013 that 'the Governing Council expects the key ECB interest rates to remain at present or lower levels for an extended period of time' (Draghi, 2013a). This was an unusual move for the ECB, which typically avoids tying its hands through policy pre-announcements of this sort and a sign that eurozone monetary authorities were taking the threat of deflation seriously. The ECB was not alone in providing such 'forward guidance' at this time. In August 2013, the new Governor of the Bank of England, Mark Carney, ruled out interest rate increases until the UK's unemployment rate had fallen below 7.0 per cent. The fact that the ECB's forward guidance was more circumspect than that of the Bank of England speaks to the idea that Frankfurt is less transparent than London when it comes to monetary policy (Eijffinger and Geraats, 2006).

Those who criticize the ECB for lacking transparency have pointed in the past to the Bank's reluctance to publish minutes of meetings in which monetary policy decisions are taken (Buiter, 1999). Under current rules, details of what is discussed in the ECB Governing Council are published only after 30 years. This contrasts with standard operating procedures in other central banks; minutes of the Bank of England's Monetary Policy Committee, for example, are published after just six weeks. Minutes matter here because they reveal whether monetary authorities were in agreement over policy moves and whether they changed their mind over time. Publishing such information in real time (or after a short delay) provides valuable information to financial markets about the possible future direction of interest rate changes. Such information can also be advantageous for accountability because it gives politicians and the public a better understanding of how monetary policy decisions are reached and where individual central bankers stood on particular issues. The ECB has traditionally resisted pressure to publish minutes of ECB Governing Council meetings for fear that such information could draw disproportionate attention to the question of whether national central bank governors act in the interest of the eurozone or the Member State from which they come (Issing, 1999). In December 2013, Mario Draghi broke from this tradition by announcing that the ECB Executive Board was a preparing a proposal to publish meetings of the ECB Governing Council (Draghi, 2013b).

IV. Building the Single Supervisory Mechanism

Further details emerged in 2013 about the ECB's new role in financial supervision. In June 2012, eurozone heads of state or government agreed to take forward plans for a single supervisory mechanism as part of efforts to create a European banking union. The Commission duly presented draft legislation in September 2012, which was finally adopted by EU finance ministers and the European Parliament in November 2013. Under this legislation, the ECB will assume overall responsibility for the supervision of banks and other credit institutions in all eurozone members and in those EU Member States that have agreed to participate in the single supervisory mechanism from November 2014. The ECB has been entrusted here with responsibility for 'contributing to the safety and soundness of credit institutions and the stability of the financial system within the EU and each Member State'.[4] In carrying out this mandate the ECB is required to show due regard for the integrity of the single market – this qualification seeking to reassure non-euro area members, most notably the UK, that the single supervisory mechanism will not put their financial institutions at a competitive disadvantage.

Once the single supervisory mechanism is up and running, the ECB will have three key policy instruments at its disposal. First, it will have responsibility for licencing more than 6,000 credit institutions. Second, it will have the power to enforce prudential standards and rules concerning governance arrangements in credit institutions. The third policy instrument concerns the right to carry out supervisory reviews of credit institutions. This includes the conduct of an asset quality review of credit institutions or 'stress test' as it has come to be known. Taken together these policy instruments provide for the single most important transfer of economic competences to the EU since the launch of EMU's third stage in January 1999. Although the ECB has played a prominent role in EU financial supervision since the creation of the European Systemic Risk Board in December 2010, this watchdog relied on peer pressure in its efforts to promote financial stability in the EU and its Member States. The single supervisory mechanism, in contrast, turns the ECB into a regulatory agency backed by extensive hard law powers.

EU Member States do not cede sovereignty easily in this domain (or any other) and so national supervisors will play a key role in the governance of the single supervisory mechanism. Responsibility for planning and executing the ECB's new tasks has been

---

[4] Council Regulation (EU) 1024/2013 of 15 October 2013 conferring specific tasks on the European Central Bank concerning policies relating to the prudential supervision of credit institutions, *Official Journal*, L 287/63, 29 October 2013.

entrusted to a newly created Supervisory Board rather than the ECB Executive Board. The Supervisory Board will include a chair, vice-chair, four representatives of the ECB and an official from each of the national supervisors. Provision is also made for representatives of national central banks to attend in cases where these banks do not have responsibility for financial supervision. This is a more streamlined arrangement than the Governing Council of the European Systemic Risk Board, which involved up to 65 members in a voting and non-voting capacity, but its membership will still reach double digits. The Financial Policy Committee of the Bank of England, in contrast, has ten members. As with the ECB Governing Council, this raises concerns that the ECB Supervisory Board will be slow to react to changing circumstances.

The Supervisory Board's governance structures are not only crowded, they are also designed in a way that constrains the power of the ECB President. Whereas the Financial Policy Committee is led by the Governor of the Bank of England, the ECB President will not sit on the Bank's Supervisory Board. Instead, it falls to the ECB Governing Council to nominate candidates for the chair and vice chair of the Supervisory Board on the basis of an open recruitment process and subject to the approval of the European Parliament. National central bank governors are in a majority on the ECB Governing Council and so it is not entirely unsurprising that they nominated an ECB outsider, Danièle Nouy, to lead the ECB Supervisory Board. Nouy was formerly Secretary General of the French Prudential Supervision and Resolution Authority and before that an official at the Banque de France.

V. Room for Manoeuvre under the Six-Pack

The stability and growth pact has led a curious existence since the global financial crisis struck. By mid-2008 all eurozone members were deemed to have reduced their government borrowing below 3.0 per cent of GDP for the first time since euro notes and coins had been introduced in 2002. Within two years, all eurozone members had breached this threshold after the costs of bank bail-outs and a very steep recession caused government borrowing to soar and, in the case of Greece, significant inaccuracies in the reporting of public finance statistics came to light. At this point, eurozone members might have been expected to set aside the stability and growth pact – this is what happened, after all, when France and Germany found themselves in breach of the EU's fiscal rules in 2003 (Heipertz and Verdun, 2010) – but instead national authorities charted a course to get government borrowing below 3.0 per cent of GDP once again.

The reasons for this somewhat surprising show of support for the stability and growth pact were threefold. First, reforms to the pact adopted in 2005 provided for a large measure of flexibility already, which the European Commission and EU finance ministers used to the full in monitoring Member States' fiscal consolidation plans. Second, demonstrating compliance with the stability and growth pact was one of the few ways in which heavily indebted eurozone members could seek to reassure financial markets as to the sustainability of public finances. And third, a commitment to fiscal discipline became part of the political *quid pro quo* for providing financial support to eurozone members once these efforts failed. Germany was both golden goose and fiscal hawk here, and Chancellor Angela Merkel insisted on the need for stringent fiscal rules in return for providing financial support to other eurozone members.

If the stability and growth pact survived the global financial crisis, therefore, through a combination of fiscal flexibility and fortitude, a pair of reforms discussed in last year's review of eurozone governance, pose a *prima facie* challenge to this formula. The first is the Six-Pack: a set of six legislative measures that extend the scope of economic and fiscal surveillance in the eurozone and shift the emphasis from peer pressure to pecuniary sanctions. The second is the fiscal compact: an intergovernmental treaty signed by all EU Member States with the exception of the UK and the Czech Republic and designed to reinforce the provisions of the Six-Pack. A key question for the future of eurozone governance is whether these reforms reduce the scope for discretion when it comes to enforcing limits on government borrowing. To the extent that they do, membership of the eurozone will restrict the scope for macroeconomic management by Member States yet further and/or sow the seeds for periodic political crises between Brussels and national capitals over enforcement.

Last year's review of the eurozone suggested that the Six-Pack made surprisingly little difference to fiscal surveillance and this conclusion still stands in 2013. Eleven eurozone members began the year in a state of excessive deficit. One member of this group, Italy, exited the excessive deficit during the course of the year after EU finance ministers, acting on a recommendation from the Commission, agreed that government borrowing had been reduced below 3.0 per cent of GDP. That finance ministers took this decision in spite of Italy's burgeoning debt-to-GDP ratio shows that political discretion over the application of the EU's fiscal rules is alive and well. In its decision on Italy, EU finance ministers took note of the fact that the country's debt-to-GDP ratio was forecast to rise to 131.4 per cent of GDP in 2013, but they did not explain why this situation was permissible. The pact, it should be recalled, prohibits government debt in excess of 60 per cent of GDP and one of the aims of the Six-Pack was to threaten Member States that failed to make sufficient progress towards meeting this goal with the possibility of financial penalties. To this end, a new formula was adopted which requires Member States with government debt in excess of 60 per cent of GDP to reduce this shortfall by an average of 0.05 per cent over a three-year period. That this formula was not invoked here can be explained by the fact that the Six-Pack provided a 'transition period' for Member States facing excessive deficits at the time of its adoption.

The implication is that Italy and other heavily indebted eurozone members will be held to a higher standard in due course but it does not mean that pecuniary sanctions are inevitable. An early test case in this context occurred in November 2013 in a Commission report on Finland's fiscal policy. Finland exited an excessive deficit procedure in 2011 and its budget deficit remained below 3.0 per cent of GDP in the two years that followed but its debt-to-GDP ratio was forecast to rise to 61 per cent of GDP in 2014. In its report, the Commission concluded that the pace of debt reduction in Finland was insufficient but nonetheless permissible, *inter alia*, because of cyclical conditions and the country's contribution to financial support for other eurozone members. Economically, this decision was defensible since Finland's debt was just a percentage point above the debt criterion. Politically, however, it sets a precedent that suggests that the enforcement of the stability and growth pact will not be as severe as some hoped and others feared.

Of the ten eurozone members that remained in a state of excessive deficit in 2013, Spain, France, the Netherlands, Malta and Slovenia were deemed to have taken effective action in response to earlier recommendations. Greece, Ireland and Portugal either faced additional recommendations to bring their excessive deficits to an end or carried over recommendations from previous years, but none of these Member States faced a threat of financial penalties in 2013. This left Belgium, which moved a step closer to financial penalties after EU finance ministers agreed in June 2013 to give notice to this Member State to undertake specific measures to reduce government borrowing below 3.0 per cent of GDP. In November 2013, EU finance ministers concluded that Belgium had taken sufficient steps in this direction and that further disciplinary measures were not envisaged at this stage. The EU, in other words, did not rush headlong into imposing financial penalties – a conclusion which fits with the claim that the Six-Pack is more flexible than often appreciated.

VI. The Eurozone and Currency Wars

The year 2013 was a comparatively calm one for global economic governance not least because fears over the eurozone receded to a significant degree. This provided an opportunity for members of the Group of Twenty (G20) to explore other issues of international economic importance. Among the more urgent matters on the G20's agenda concerned the risk of a currency war among economies seeking to gain a competitive advantage by devaluing their currencies. Although concerns over China's exchange rate regime tend to capture the headlines in such debates it was Japan's exchange rate policy that provided the talking points in 2013. Over the course of the year, the Japanese yen depreciated by around 16 per cent against the euro and by approximately 14 per cent against the dollar, providing a major boost to Japan's exporters. For some commentators, this fall in the yen was the result of a deliberate policy of competitive devaluation borne of the loose monetary policy initiated by Prime Minister Shinzo Abe after his election in December 2012.

Concerns over a currency war were discussed at a meeting of G20 finance ministers and central bank governors in Moscow in February 2013. No specific mention was made in the summit's communiqué of the yen, but participants agreed to 'refrain from competitive devaluation' and not to 'target [. . .] exchange rates for competitive purposes' (G20 Finance Ministers and Central Bank Governors, 2013). The stakes in this debate were not quite the same for the US and the eurozone. For the former, a key question was whether the unconventional monetary policies pursued since the global financial crisis could be unwound without triggering an unwelcome appreciation of the dollar. For the eurozone, the concern was rather that the already high value of the euro could bring the nascent economic recovery to a sudden end. Traditionally, the eurozone has adopted a policy of benign neglect towards the external value of the single currency, but the ECB's decision to cut interest rates in May and November 2013 were seen by some as being driven by a desire to engineer a depreciation of the euro. If so, the ECB's actions were far from being a success. The euro appreciated in 2013 not only against the yen, but also against a weighted basket of the eurozone's most important trading partners (see Figure 1).

On previous occasions, the eurozone has responded to concerns over currency regimes through bilateral diplomacy (Hodson, 2011a). No such efforts materialized in 2013 and ECB President Mario Draghi, for his part, sought to downplay talk of a currency war (Emmott, 2013). For critics of eurozone external representation, Draghi's dovishness will provide further proof of the limits of European monetary power on the international stage. An alternative reading, however, is that eurozone authorities were reluctant to talk tough against Japan at a time when the ECB was weighing up the possibility of unconventional

Figure 1: The External Value of the Euro in 2013

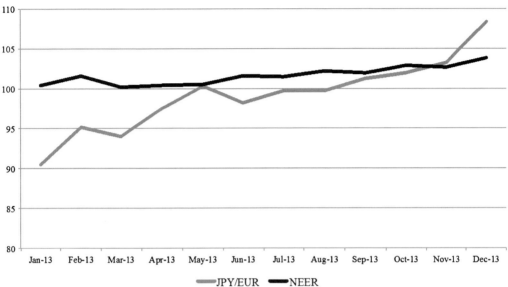

Source: ECB Statistical Warehouse and Pacific Exchange Rate Service.
Note: Nominal effective exchange rate measured against the so-called 'EER-20' group of trading partners. Both series are expressed as an index in which the first quarter of 1999 is set to 100.

monetary policies of its own. Such policies could cause a significant depreciation of the euro against the dollar and so all eyes are on the ECB to see whether deflation in the eurozone could set in motion a round of competitive devaluations in the international monetary system.

VII. The Two-Pack and Patchy Progress towards a Genuine EMU

There has been a succession of reforms to eurozone governance since the global financial crisis struck. Recent reviews have discussed the European Systemic Risk Board (Hodson, 2010), the Six-Pack (Hodson, 2011b), the European semester, the European stability mechanism and fiscal compact (Hodson, 2012), and plans for European banking union and a genuine EMU (Howarth and Quaglia, 2013; Hodson, 2013). Taken as a whole these reforms can be seen in functional, strategic and political terms. A functional view sees EU Member States as addressing the shortcomings in eurozone governance that either contributed to or amplified the effects of the euro crisis. This helps to explain the focus on, say, fiscal discipline and macroeconomic imbalances in the Six-Pack but it struggles to make sense of why some reforms have gone in different directions, with the contrast between the soft-law approach of the European Systemic Risk Board and the hard-law logic of European banking union a case in point. A strategic perspective sees reforms as sending a signal to financial markets that EU policy-makers are managing the crisis. This helps to explain why the frequency of reforms intensified as the euro sovereign debt crisis worsened, but it does not account for Member States' apparent preoccupation with preventing future crises rather than dealing with the current one. A political perspective, finally, emphasizes the importance of asymmetric bargaining between eurozone members. Germany, as always, remains the key player in relation to EMU and it has been fairly transparent in its willingness to show financial solidarity to other Member States only in exchange for more credible commitments to fiscal discipline. What is downplayed in this story is the fact that the commitments contained in reforms such as the Six-Pack are, as noted above, less stringent than they appear at first glance.

With the de-escalation of the eurozone sovereign debt crisis, the strategic case for continued reform may have dissipated but the functional and political arguments in favour have not. Thus, the running reforms to eurozone governance continued in 2013. A key development in this respect was the entry into force of the Two-Pack in 2013. Adopted under Article 136 of the Treaty on the Functioning of the European Union (TFEU), the Two-Pack codifies further changes to the EU fiscal surveillance calendar and provides for enhanced surveillance of Member States experiencing financial difficulties or at risk thereof. Under the regulation dealing with the first of these points, eurozone members are required to submit a draft budget for the year ahead to the Commission and eurozone finance ministers in October of each year with a view to adopting the final budget by December. As with the European semester, the Two-Pack's bark looks worse than its bite since the regulation neither specifies sanctions against Member States that fail to comply with these requests nor challenges the fact that Member States have first and final say over national budgets.

The second regulation in the Two-Pack allows the Commission to go beyond the monitoring requirements of the stability and growth pact for those Member States facing, or at risk of, financial difficulties. Under this enhanced surveillance, which will be mandatory for Member States in receipt of external financial assistance from the EU or elsewhere, the Commission will conduct an ongoing, intensive review of economic and financial developments. Where further action is warranted, EU finance ministers, acting on the basis of a Commission proposal, can recommend that the Member State address financial difficulties or prepare a draft macroeconomic adjustment programme to be approved by EU finance ministers. Member States are expected to comply with this programme, but the Two-Pack specifies no sanctions for failing to do so other than an obligation to seek 'technical assistance' from the Commission in some cases.

Progress was also made 2013 on certain aspects of Herman van Rompuy's plan for a genuine EMU, which was presented to the European Council in December 2012. Stage 1 of this plan envisaged the creation of a single supervisory mechanism and a deal to allow the direct recapitalization of banks by the European stability mechanism. As the building blocks of the single supervisory mechanism were being put in place in 2013, eurozone finance ministers agreed that the European stability mechanism could bail-out banks rather than simply lending to Member States. Under such circumstances, it was agreed, the Member State concerned would typically bear some of the cost of this bail-out. This proviso did not fully satisfy financial markets, but they were a *sine qua non* for Germany. Financial markets were keen here for future European stability mechanism recipients to avoid the fate of Ireland and Spain, which borrowed to bail-out domestic banks and found themselves in a sovereign debt crisis as a result. Germany was insistent, however, that Member States pay a price for failing to ensure financial stability for fear that access to European stability mechanism funding could incentivize excessive risk-taking in the regulation of eurozone financial institutions.

The second stage of van Rompuy's plan involved the creation of a single bank resolution mechanism for the eurozone and financial support for Member States implementing structural reforms. In July 2013, the European Commission tabled its proposal for the creation of a single resolution mechanism, but negotiations progressed slowly in the remainder of the year. Key sticking points here included the question of who should decide whether a bank is failing, what degree of autonomy should be retained by national authorities over bank resolution, and whether financial contributions to the fund would be pooled or earmarked for particular Member States. Germany, once again, emerged as defender in chief of a minimalist, intergovernmentalist vision of banking union. It was opposed here by the European Parliament, which sought to pool Member States' resources for the purposes of bank resolution and to minimize the involvement of national representatives in what has the potential to be a highly politicized process of decision-making. A compromise between the two sides was eventually hammered out, but not before the end of 2013.

Discussions over financial support for structural reforms proved less fruitful still. In March 2013, the Commission put forward preliminary plans for a convergence and competitiveness instrument. Under this arrangement, eurozone Member States would set out plans for specific reforms in a contractual arrangement to be approved by eurozone finance ministers and monitored by the Commission and receive financial support for these reforms in exchange for compliance. At the European Council in December 2013, the heads of state or government expressed support for the idea of contractual arrangements but agreed that further work was needed on the modalities of financial support and agreed to return to this issue in October 2014. Given the lack of progress over the convergence and competitiveness instrument, it is not surprising that the idea of a fiscal capacity for the eurozone – the third stage of van Rompuy's plan – stalled in 2013. Lack of political support for this idea was already evident at the European Council in December 2012, and this fact did not change in 2013.

Conclusions

In summary, 2013 was the year in which the eurozone experienced a tentative economic recovery, pressed ahead with governance reforms and responded to pressing policy challenges with a degree of political reticence that is, by now, all too familiar. The economic outlook in 2013 gave no grounds for celebration, but it was still a significant improvement on recent years. The most encouraging development in this respect was the eurozone's exit from the double-dip recession that began in 2012. Greece, Portugal and Spain remained in recession, meanwhile, but the prospects for recovery were a little brighter in these countries and better still in Ireland. There were signs of recovery, too, from the sovereign debt crisis as the ECB's promise of unlimited bond purchases held good for financial markets and Ireland and Spain exited adjustment programmes with the IMF and/or the EU.

Among the key policy challenges to confront the eurozone in 2013 was the fiscal crisis in Cyprus. Although eurozone members saw this crisis coming they were no less hesitant in their response. Cypriot authorities must take some of the blame here for their lack of urgency in securing external financial assistance. So, too, must the eurogroup for its failure to foresee the problems posed by proposing an emergency levy on all depositors in

Cypriot banks. Reticent too was the eurozone's response to concerns over an international currency war. Although the ECB showed a concern over the euro's appreciation against the yen, it was reluctant to press Japanese authorities on this issue, mindful perhaps that the unconventional monetary policies pursued by the Bank of Japan in 2012, or a European version thereof, could be coming soon to the eurozone.

Eurozone governance remained in a state of flux in 2013 as recent reforms took hold and negotiations over further changes continued. In the monetary sphere, questions remained over the credibility of the outright monetary transactions, but financial markets continued to give the ECB's bond buying programme the benefit of the doubt. The ECB's forward guidance was less successful in this regard, although the Bank's willingness to talk about future interest rate decisions and its discussions over the publication of Governing Council minutes were welcome moves from the point of view of transparency. In the financial market sphere, key building blocks for the single supervisory mechanism were put in place in 2013, but progress over other aspects of European banking union was slower than anticipated. In the economic sphere, the entry into force of the Two-Pack helped to reinforce EMU's fiscal rules yet further, although early experiences of the Six-Pack suggest that a large measure of flexibility has been retained in how these rules will be enforced. As regards plans for a genuine EMU, discussions over financial incentives for structural reform progressed slowly and the prospects for a eurozone fiscal capacity seemed ever more remote.

References

Apostolides, A. (2011) '2nd estimate on "best case" cost estimate: 2.9 bn euro'. *Thoughts of Cyprus and Malta Blog*. Available at: «http://econcyma.blogspot.co.uk/2011/07/2nd-estimate-on-best-case-cost-estimate.html».

Begg, I. (2013) 'The Cypriot banking crisis shows that Europeans have yet to work out the answer to the question, "who pays?"'. LSE European Politics and Policy (EUROPP) Blog, 26 March. Available at: «http://blogs.lse.ac.uk/europpblog/2013/03/26/the-cypriot-banking-crisis-shows-that-europeans-have-yet-to-work-out-the-answer-to-the-question-who-pays/».

Bentolila, S., Dolado, J.J., Franz, W. and Pissarides, C. (1994) 'Labour Flexibility and Wages: Lessons from Spain'. *Economic Policy*, Vol. 18, pp. 55–99.

Bernanke, B.S. (2002) 'Deflation: Making Sure "It" Doesn't Happen Here'. Remarks before the National Economists Club, Washington, DC, 21 November.

Buiter, W.H. (1999) 'Alice in Euroland'. *JCMS*, Vol. 37, No. 2, pp. 181–209.

Draghi, M. (2013a) Introductory Statement to the Press Conference (with Q&A), 4 July (Frankfurt am Main: European Central Bank).

Draghi, M. (2013b) Introductory Statement to the Press Conference (with Q&A), 5 December (Frankfurt am Main: European Central Bank).

Eijffinger, S.C. and Geraats, P.M. (2006) 'How Transparent are Central Banks?'. *European Journal of Political Economy*, Vol. 22, No. 1, pp. 1–21.

Emmott, R. (2013) 'Draghi Dismisses Talk of Currency War, but Watching Euro'. *Reuters*, 18 February.

European Central Bank (ECB) (2014) *Annual Report 2013* (Frankfurt am Main; European Central Bank).

G20 Finance Ministers and Central Bank Governors (2013) Communiqué, Moscow, 16 February.

Heipertz, M. and Verdun, A. (2010) *Ruling Europe: The Politics of the Stability and Growth Pact* (Cambridge: Cambridge University Press).

Hodson, D. (2010) 'The EU Economy: The Eurozone in 2009'. *JCMS*, Vol. 48, No. s1, pp. 225–42.

Hodson, D. (2011a) *Governing the Euro Area in Good Times and Bad* (Oxford: Oxford University Press).

Hodson, D. (2011b) 'The Eurozone in 2011'. *JCMS*, Vol. 49, No. s1, pp. 231–50.

Hodson, D. (2012) 'The Eurozone in 2012'. *JCMS*, Vol. 50, No. s2, pp. 178–94.

Hodson, D. (2013) 'The Eurozone in 2012: "Whatever It Takes to Preserve the Euro"?' *JCMS*, Vol. 51, No. s1, pp. 183–200.

Howarth, D. and Quaglia, L. (2013) 'Banking Union as Holy Grail: Rebuilding the Single Market in Financial Services, Stabilizing Europe's Banks and "Completing" Economic and Monetary Union'. *JCMS*, Vol. 51, No. s1, pp. 103–23.

Issing, O. (1999) 'The Eurosystem: Transparent and Accountable or "Willem in Euroland"'. *JCMS*, Vol. 37, No. 3, pp. 503–19.

Organization for Economic Co-operation and Development (OECD) (2013) *The 2012 Labour Market Reform in Spain: A Preliminary Assessment* (Paris: OECD).

Stephanou, C. (2011) 'Big Banks in Small Countries: The Case of Cyprus'. *Cyprus Economic Policy Review*, Vol. 5, No. 1, pp. 3–21.

Whelan, K. (2013) 'ELA, Promissory Notes and All That: The Fiscal Costs of Anglo Irish Bank'. *Economic and Social Review*, Vol. 34, No. 4, pp. 653–73.

JCMS 2014 Volume 52 Annual Review pp. 202–218   DOI: 10.1111/jcms.12168

Developments in the Economies of Member States Outside the Eurozone

RICHARD CONNOLLY[1] and CHRISTOPHER A. HARTWELL[2]
[1] University of Birmingham. [2] Kozminski University

Introduction

After a turbulent 2012, during which many economies of the region experienced recession or stagnation at best, the European economy began to show signs of recovery in the second half of 2013. While growth across the region remained negative or subdued during the first half of the year, most major economies began to register growth in exports and output in the second half. Importantly, many of the smaller economies of the region located on Europe's 'periphery' continued to make progress in rebalancing their economies away from growth models based on debt-driven consumption towards export-led growth. Such a model, however, requires expansion in demand for European goods and services. Unfortunately, the global picture was mixed. Growth in China – the fastest growing major economy in the post-crisis period – slowed considerably as policy-makers attempted to reduce excessive growth in investment (Pettis, 2014). Growth in Europe's largest neighbour, Russia, also decelerated as fears mounted that significant economic reform would be required to generate a resumption of pre-crisis growth rates (Connolly, 2013; Mau, 2013). Growth in other so-called 'emerging markets', such as Brazil and Turkey, also slowed as financial markets were affected by the prospect of a tightening of monetary policy in the US. It was in the US, however, where prospects looked brightest. Economic activity accelerated even as government spending was cut, suggesting that optimism in the private sector had returned.

It was against this mixed backdrop that the economies of the Member States outside the eurozone continued their unsteady and multispeed recoveries from the global recession of 2008–09. This year's *JCMS AR* contribution is comprised of three sections. The first gives an overview of key economic performance indicators, while the second summarizes key developments in each of the European economies outside the eurozone. The third section examines the state of financial sector stability in central, east and southeastern Europe – a salient issue due to the role that financial vulnerabilities played in causing the severe recession in 2008–09. Indeed, the reduction of financial vulnerabilities was a key policy aim in the period immediately after the financial crisis in 2008. It is therefore vital to examine the progress made in this area of fundamental economic importance.

I. Economic Performance Outside the Eurozone: Main Economic Indicators

Economic Growth

Although economic activity in the eurozone continued to slow in the first half of the year, gross domestic product (GDP) growth rates in the non-eurozone were considerably faster than rates recorded in 2012, albeit with significant variation observed within the group.

Table 1: Real GDP Growth (% Annual Change): Non-Eurozone, 2009–13

	2009	2010	2011	2012	2013[e]
Bulgaria	−5.5	0.2	1.7	0.8	0.5
Croatia	−6.9	−2.3	0.0	−2.0	−0.7
Czech Republic	−4.7	2.7	1.9	−1.3	−1.0
Denmark	−5.2	1.7	0.8	0.6	0.3
Latvia	−17.7	−0.3	5.5	4.3	4.0
Lithuania	−14.8	1.4	5.9	2.9	3.4
Hungary	−6.8	1.3	1.6	−1.2	0.7
Poland	1.6	3.9	4.3	2.4	1.3
Romania	−6.6	−1.9	2.5	0.8	2.2
Sweden	−5.2	5.6	3.9	1.1	1.1
UK	−4.4	1.8	0.9	−0.3	1.3
Eurozone	−4.2	1.9	1.4	−0.4	−0.4
EU average	−4.2	2.0	1.5	−0.3	−0.0

Source: European Commission (2013, p. 138, Table 1).
Note: Estimates are denoted by e.

The data presented in Table 1 reveal the heterogeneity of the recovery across the countries outside the non-eurozone.[1] Latvia, Lithuania and Romania were the fastest growing economies from within the group, with all three economies growing significantly faster than the EU and eurozone averages. The richest economies – Denmark, Sweden and the UK – all registered positive growth rates, with growth speeding up in the second half of the year in all three. Elsewhere, and in line with performance in the eurozone, both Croatia and the Czech Republic experienced a contraction in annual GDP. As in previous years, the fact that many of the countries with the lowest levels of per capita income in the EU (that is, the countries of central and eastern Europe) were experiencing such sluggish growth rates was a source of concern.

Employment

Compared to pre-crisis levels, unemployment remained high in all non-eurozone economies (Table 2). Moreover, unemployment continued to grow in many countries, with significant declines in unemployment levels observed in only Denmark, Latvia and Lithuania. Significantly, unemployment in the two Baltic economies of Latvia and Lithuania reached the lowest levels since 2010. While the pre-crisis lows remained some way off, unemployment was moving in the right direction. Within the non-eurozone economies there are two distinct groups. The first group, comprising Bulgaria, Croatia, Hungary, Latvia and Lithuania, all exhibited unemployment rates significantly higher than the EU average. This was a concern as it suggested the worst effects of the prolonged period of economic uncertainty continued to be felt by the newest and poorest of the Member States. The second group of countries, which included the rest of the non-eurozone, registered unemployment rates that were lower than the eurozone and overall EU averages. In the

[1] Unless otherwise stated, all data are taken from European Commission (2013).

Table 2: Unemployment (% of the Civilian Labour Force):
Non-Eurozone, 2009–13

	2009	2010	2011	2012	2013ᵉ
Bulgaria	6.8	10.8	11.3	12.7	12.9
Croatia	9.1	11.8	13.5	15.9	16.9
Czech Republic	6.7	7.3	6.7	7.0	7.1
Denmark	6.0	7.4	7.6	7.7	7.3
Latvia	17.1	18.7	16.2	15.2	11.7
Lithuania	13.7	17.8	15.4	13.5	11.7
Hungary	10.0	11.2	10.9	10.8	11.0
Poland	8.2	9.6	9.7	10.1	10.7
Romania	6.9	7.3	7.4	7.4	7.3
Sweden	8.3	8.4	7.5	7.5	8.1
UK	7.6	7.8	8.0	7.9	7.7
Eurozone	9.5	10.1	10.1	11.3	12.2
EU average	8.9	9.7	9.7	10.5	11.1

Source: European Commission (2013, p. 143, Table 23).
Note: Estimates are denoted by *e*.

Table 3: Inflation Rate^a (% Change on Preceding Year):
Non-Eurozone, 2009–13

	2009	2010	2011	2012	2013ᵉ
Bulgaria	2.5	3.0	3.4	2.5	0.5
Croatia	2.2	1.1	2.2	3.4	2.6
Czech Republic	0.6	1.2	2.1	3.6	1.4
Denmark	1.1	2.2	2.7	2.4	0.6
Latvia	3.3	−1.2	4.2	2.4	0.3
Lithuania	4.2	1.2	4.1	3.4	1.4
Hungary	4.0	4.7	3.9	5.6	2.1
Poland	4.0	2.7	3.9	3.8	1.0
Romania	5.6	6.1	5.8	3.5	3.3
Sweden	1.9	1.9	1.4	1.0	0.6
UK	2.2	3.3	4.5	2.7	2.6
Eurozone	0.3	1.6	2.7	2.5	1.5
EU average	1.0	2.1	3.1	2.7	1.7

Source: European Commission (2013, p. 140, Table 17).
Notes: ^{a} Harmonized index of consumer prices. Estimates are denoted by ^{e}.

one country that defies this simple categorization, Poland, unemployment rose for the fifth consecutive year despite the country experiencing better GDP growth rates than nearly all of its neighbours.

Inflation

Between 2009 and 2012, inflation rose across the economies of the non-eurozone (Table 3). This was supported by a rise in global commodity prices throughout the period, fuelled by political instability in major energy producing regions as well as by loose

Table 4: Net Lending (+) or Net Borrowing (−), General
Government Balance (% of GDP): Non-Eurozone, 2009–13

	2009	2010	2011	2012	2013[e]
Bulgaria	−4.7	−3.1	−2.0	−1.5	−2.0
Croatia	−5.3	−6.4	−7.8	−5.0	−5.4
Czech Republic	−5.8	−4.8	−3.3	−3.5	−2.9
Denmark	−2.7	−2.6	−1.8	−3.9	−1.7
Latvia	−10.2	−8.3	−3.4	−1.7	−1.4
Lithuania	−9.2	−7.0	−5.5	−3.2	−3.0
Hungary	−4.4	−4.2	4.3	−2.5	−2.9
Poland	−7.2	−7.8	−5.0	−3.4	−4.8
Romania	−8.6	−6.9	−5.5	−2.8	−2.5
Sweden	−0.9	0.2	0.4	0.0	−0.9
UK	−11.4	−10.3	−7.8	−6.2	−6.4
Eurozone	−6.3	−6.2	−4.1	−3.3	−3.1
EU average	−6.8	−6.6	−4.4	−3.6	−3.5

Source: European Commission (2013, p. 149, Table 36).
Note: Estimates are denoted by e.

monetary policy in the world's major economies (including the eurozone, where monetary policy was formulated by the European Central Bank). While commodity prices remained high in 2013, the rate of growth was more moderate than in previous years. However, due to the widespread deceleration of growth across the continent, and against the backdrop of rising unemployment in many countries, price inflation slowed sharply in every country, reflecting a wider tendency across the region. In countries such as Bulgaria, Hungary, Latvia, Lithuania, Romania and the UK, this moderation in price rises was welcome as concerns had been expressed that inflation was approaching excessive levels in 2011–12. Nevertheless, the sudden and sharp nature of price declines observed in 2013 did suggest that deflation, rather than excessive inflation, was becoming a danger.

Public Finances

The state of public finances, and the issue of sovereign debt, continued to be particularly important around the world in 2013 – not least in Europe, where concerns over the solvency of Greece, Italy, Portugal and Spain were responsible for the persistence of gloomy economic sentiment across the region.[2] As Table 4 illustrates, government balances across the non-eurozone varied significantly in 2013, although the average for the group was slightly lower than in the previous year.

Every country from within the non-eurozone registered budget deficits, although these ranged from the very small, as in Bulgaria, Denmark, Latvia and Sweden, to substantially larger than the EU and eurozone averages, as in Croatia, Poland and the UK. Of perhaps more importance than the levels of government borrowing was the change in trajectory for some countries from within the non-eurozone. While budget deficits continue to narrow in the Czech Republic, Denmark, Latvia, Lithuania and Romania, budget deficits grew in Bulgaria, Hungary, Poland, Sweden and the UK.

[2] On developments in the eurozone, see Hodson's contribution to this volume.

Table 5: Gross General Government Debt (% of GDP):
Non-Eurozone, 2009–13

	2009	2010	2011	2012	2013ᵉ
Bulgaria	14.7	16.3	16.3	19.5	19.4
Croatia	36.6	44.9	51.6	55.5	59.6
Czech Republic	35.3	37.6	40.8	45.1	49.0
Denmark	41.5	43.7	46.6	45.4	44.3
Latvia	36.7	44.7	42.2	41.9	42.5
Lithuania	29.5	38.0	38.5	41.6	39.9
Hungary	78.4	81.3	81.4	78.4	80.7
Poland	50.9	54.9	56.4	55.5	58.2
Romania	23.9	31.0	33.4	34.6	38.5
Sweden	41.9	39.7	38.4	37.4	41.3
UK	68.2	79.9	85.0	88.7	94.3
Eurozone	79.1	85.6	88.1	92.9	95.5
EU average	74.0	80.3	83.0	86.8	89.7

Source: European Commission (2013, p. 168, Table 42).
Note: Estimates are denoted by *e*.

Mixed success in reducing government deficits resulted in the stock of government debt declining in just three of the ten countries of the non-eurozone in 2013: levels of gross government debt declined in Bulgaria, Denmark and Lithuania (Table 5). Government debt grew in the seven other countries. Nevertheless, only in the UK did the stock of debt exceed the eurozone and EU averages. However, stocks of private debt remain high across much of the non-eurozone, including in the high-income countries of Denmark, Sweden and the UK. Therefore, while sovereign default risk did not appear especially high, most economies retain significant financial vulnerabilities (see Section III).

Competitiveness

Competitiveness – that is, the potential to increase exports due to lower comparative production costs – remained an important consideration for policy-makers in 2013. With substantial private and public sector debt burdens dampening domestic demand, faster economic growth sufficient to reduce overall debt-to-GDP ratios tended to come from rapid net export growth, especially in the countries of central and eastern Europe. For the countries of the non-eurozone, depreciation of the nominal exchange rate was a short-term mechanism to increase competitiveness. Improvements in cost competitiveness were observed in Croatia, Czech Republic, Hungary and the UK. However, unit labour costs adjusted for nominal exchange rate movements increased in the six other countries of the non-eurozone. Although some countries, such as Romania and Sweden, experienced brisk appreciation of the real effective exchange rate (REER), it was significant that no country from the non-eurozone registered a rate of REER appreciation faster than the eurozone average (Table 6). This indicated that the competitive position of non-eurozone economies improved relative to their trading partners despite significant cost increases.

Table 6: Real Effective Exchange Rate (% Change on Preceding Year): Non-Eurozone, 2009–13

	2009	2010	2011	2012	2013ᵉ
Bulgaria	10.6	3.0	1.8	−0.2	2.6
Croatia	1.6	−2.0	−1.8	−3.4	−0.5
Czech Republic	−5.6	3.1	3.0	−1.6	−1.1
Denmark	3.9	−4.4	−1.3	−3.7	2.2
Latvia	−9.3	−11.6	2.5	−1.6	2.0
Lithuania	−2.1	−8.1	−1.0	−1.3	2.4
Hungary	−9.6	−1.0	−0.4	−0.2	−3.6
Poland	−19.3	8.1	−3.2	−3.5	0.3
Romania	−13.0	6.6	1.3	−4.4	5.2
Sweden	−8.0	5.1	3.4	1.2	5.1
UK	−9.4	2.2	−0.6	6.7	−2.3
Eurozone	3.9	−7.6	0.0	−4.8	5.8
EU average	−3.4	−7.8	0.3	−5.0	7.6

Source: European Commission (2013, p. 148, Table 33).
Note: Estimates are denoted by *e*.

II. Economic Developments in Non-Eurozone Countries

Bulgaria

Bulgaria's economic performance in 2013 was, as in the previous year, extremely frail. GDP grew by an estimated 0.5 per cent over the year. This modest rate of growth was driven by net exports (contributing 0.3 per cent to GDP growth) and increased public expenditure, which grew by 3 per cent. However, domestic consumption, which accounts for nearly two thirds of GDP in Bulgaria, contracted by 0.3 per cent. While growth was weak, the fact that net exports grew and public consumption shrank did at least indicate that the country was undergoing much-needed economic rebalancing. Indeed, after registering some of the largest current account deficits in Europe prior to the 2008–09 recession, Bulgaria recorded a current account surplus in 2013 of 0.3 per cent. The news for Bulgarian households was, despite the reduction in aggregate consumption, not all bad: the purchasing power of consumers was boosted by growth in real wages as inflation dropped to just 0.5 per cent – a decade-long low.

Croatia

On 1 July 2013, Croatia became the 28ᵗʰ Member State of the EU. While EU membership may offer improved economic prospects in the long term, Croatia has continued to suffer through a prolonged economic downturn. Economic performance continued to be poor, with GDP declining by around 0.7 per cent in 2013 (continuing a streak of negative growth that stretches back to 2008). Several specific factors, some of them linked to EU accession, affected economic performance throughout the year. First, purchases in anticipation of higher excises on EU entry pushed up private consumption. Second, imports increased on the back of expected changes in the system of excises and the effects of the common EU foreign trade policy on the prices of some imported goods. Third, domestic producers increased exports to trading partners covered by the central European free trade agreement (CEFTA) in anticipation of the change in trade regime with these countries. Together, these factors provided a boost to the economy that caused an improvement in performance compared to the previous year. Thus, while nearly all components of GDP declined in 2013, the rate of decline was slower than in 2012.

Czech Republic

With a contraction in GDP of 1 per cent in 2013, the Czech Republic continued to struggle to achieve even modest sustained growth. While the International Monetary Fund (IMF) attributed this decline to sluggishness in the eurozone, the Czech export-led recovery seemed to remain solid in 2013: exports increased 7.4 per cent from November 2012 to 2013, with exports to Germany (the main market for Czech goods) hitting new highs of over 95 billion koruna in the fourth quarter of the year. Moreover, the unemployment rate was comparatively low by the end of the year, reaching 6.9 per cent at the end 2013 – a decline from a high of 7.4 per cent earlier on in the year. The driver of the continued Czech stagnation appeared to be weak investment levels, especially in fixed capital formation which, driven by construction, declined 5.3 per cent year-on-year for the third quarter. Investment itself seemed to be highly affected by the government's decision to raise the rate of value-added tax from 20 to 21 per cent at the beginning of the year, as well as introducing a 'solidarity tax' that penalized earners of more than 100,000 CZK per month, with a 7 per cent tax on the amount above this threshold. With monetary policy holding the benchmark interest rate at so-called 'technical zero' (0.05 per cent), it appeared that the fiscal consolidation in Prague, driven almost entirely by revenue expansion measures and no reduction in spending, continued to weigh on the economy.

Denmark

After slipping back into recession during 2012, the Danish economy experienced positive, albeit modest (0.3 per cent), real GDP growth in 2013. This performance meant that output in Denmark had, to all intents and purposes, stagnated for a period of four years. Nevertheless, because of an increase in the growth rate in the second half of 2013 that suggested gathering momentum, a sense of cautious optimism emerged. Increasingly positive results from business confidence indicators, growing industrial production and a return to house price growth all contributed to the strongest six-month period of output growth since 2010. Growth in households' real disposable income, caused by a combination of the 2012 tax reform, lower interest rates and a decline in inflation (at nearly half the rate of inflation in 2012), all helped deliver a solid boost to domestic demand which grew by around 0.3 per cent. In addition, the 'investment window' tax breaks – which ended at the end of 2013 – along with the public investment projects that formed part of 'Growth Plan DK', caused a build-up of inventories that formed the bulk of the overall annual rise in investment. On the downside, there was little sign that a rebalancing away from domestic consumption-led growth was occurring, with net exports again exerting a drag on overall growth.

Hungary

After the *annus horribilis* that Hungary faced in 2012, economic performance improved somewhat in 2013. As the IMF (2013, p. 1) politely noted, the 'government [. . .] continued to pursue an unconventional strategy for economic recovery'. As a result, growth resumed in the second half of the year, with an estimated annual growth rate of 0.7 per cent. As in the Czech Republic, investment fell in Hungary by 0.4 per cent, while the unemployment rate grew to 11 per cent. Nevertheless, the public finance picture began to improve as the budget deficit, which had run as high as 4.5 per cent of GDP in 2009, stabilized in 2013 at below 3 per cent. However, public debt rose slightly to 80.7 per cent of GDP. A second threat to the Hungarian recovery came from the monetary side, as the Hungarian Central Bank continued its own monetary easing throughout 2013. The benchmark interest rate stood at a historic low of 3 per cent in December 2013 after 16 consecutive months of easing. The continual monetary easing did, however, cause the forint to weaken, falling to nearly 300 forint/euro from its high position of 287.23 forint/euro in May 2013.

Latvia

As of 1 January 2014, Latvia became the 18th member of the eurozone. The economic recovery in Latvia proceeded apace, with GDP growth for the year projected at 4.0 per cent after 5.0 per cent growth in 2012. More impressively, unemployment fell sharply throughout the year, reaching an estimated 9 per cent by the end of the year, compared to 13.9 per cent at the end of 2012. Consumer prices also declined by 0.4 per cent over 2013, driven mainly by declines in the price of housing, transport and food as well as lower primary commodity prices worldwide. General government debt grew slightly, reaching 35 per cent of GDP, but the overall downward decline and anticipated further declines in 2014 and 2015 meant the government's debt load was perceived as manageable. The one weakness in the Latvian economy was in gross fixed capital formation, which was estimated to have grown at an anemic 0.3 per cent in 2013.

Lithuania

Like fellow Baltic States, Lithuania continued a relatively strong growth performance in 2013, with GDP growth of 3.4 per cent, a slight drop from 2012 (3.7 per cent). While net exports drove growth in 2011 and 2012, the return of household demand (increasing 4.8 per cent in 2013) appeared to be underlying Lithuania's continuing growth. Moreover, investment also recovered after a dismal contraction in 2012 of 3.6 per cent, growing just under 5 per cent in 2013 (although this was augmented by one-time public investments). Inflation was a mere 0.4 per cent higher in December 2013 than it was in 2012, and the labour market also showed signs of recovery, dropping to just above 11 per cent from 13.4 per cent at the end of 2012. Public debt remained constant at around 40 per cent of GDP, and the government's deficit was projected to reach 3 per cent of GDP in 2013 due mainly to an increase in public sector wages and poor tax collection efforts. While Lithuania was urged by the IMF to increase property taxes to compensate for the tax revenue shortfall, the government of Prime Minister Algirdas Butkevičius (despite earlier campaign promises) made no changes to the tax system in 2013 and announced in January 2014 that there would be no radical changes in the tax system to come. Lithuania's financial sector, the least scarred of the Baltic countries' by the global financial crisis, also saw modest and sustainable growth in domestic credit, with loan portfolios growing by 1 per cent in 2013 (in line with the growth of deposits).

Poland

After a relative slowdown in 2012, Poland's growth prospects in 2013 picked up steadily throughout the year. An annual GDP growth rate of 1.6 per cent was achieved in 2013; however, investment fell by 5 per cent over 2012 and ended the year at only 18.4 per cent of GDP (against 19.1 per cent in 2012), with household consumption the only bright spot with a gain of 0.8 per cent. Unemployment also remained stubbornly and unexpectedly high, peaking at 13.4 per cent in December 2013. Perhaps because of this relative lack of economic activity and general prudent management by the National Bank of Poland, inflation was a mere 0.9 per cent. Moreover, the general government deficit deteriorated to 4.6 per cent of GDP in 2013 (from 3.9 per cent in 2012). Much-needed spending cuts looked unlikely to materialize. Perhaps most troublingly, while Poland had been a poster boy for prudent financial sector policies, dark clouds were on the horizon. A planned pension reform indicated the intention of the government to confiscate 150 billion złoty of government bonds from privately managed funds back to the state and immediately cancel them. While the reform was projected to reduce public debt by 9 per cent of GDP (from its 2013 level of 58 per cent), it threatened to shatter the image of Polish financial stability.

Romania

Romania continued to experience relatively slow GDP growth in 2013 (annual growth of 1.8 per cent) as the economy rebalanced from the consumption-based pre-crisis growth model to a model based on net exports. The rebalancing was driven by a rapid and sustained expansion of exports (11.9 per cent) – most notably in the automobile industry. This helped compensate for nearly-flat private consumption (0.3 per cent growth) and actually flat public consumption. Most worryingly, investment fell by 2 per cent in 2013, threatening the sustainability of the recovery. Nevertheless, investment was projected to increase in the future, facilitated by enhanced absorption of EU funds to fund major infrastructure projects. The most significant risks, however, continued to remain in the fiscal sector. After falling to 3 per cent of GDP in 2012, the budget deficit was estimated to have shrunk to 2.5 per cent in 2013.

Sweden

The year 2013 saw the Swedish economy continue to grow, although in more balanced fashion than in previous years. Whereas the comparatively (that is, relative to other high-income EU economies) strong performance in 2012 (real GDP growth of 1 per cent) was driven primarily by consumption growth, the 2013 performance saw both consumption and investment make roughly equal contributions to an overall growth rate of 1.1 per cent. Measures to reduce the tax burden on businesses as well as significant public investment in infrastructure helped generate broad growth across the economy. The positive contribution of investment, along with a reduction in inflation, allowed the household savings rate to rise from the previous year (from 14.7 to 15.4 per cent of total household disposable income), hinting that the Swedish recovery might not be accompanied by a further rise in the already high level of household debt. However, wider regional economic turbulence and a strong Krona weighed down on Swedish export performance during the year. After net exports grew at 1.3 per cent in 2012, net exports were flat in 2013 as both imports and exports declined by over 2 per cent.

United Kingdom

Following the weak economic performance in 2012 when annual GDP growth contracted by 0.3 per cent, 2013 saw the UK economy experience an increase in the rate of growth. Estimates suggested that annual output growth reached 1.3 per cent in 2013, with most of this improved performance due to robust growth in domestic demand, primarily from household consumption, which grew at a rate of 1.6 per cent – the fastest annual growth rate since the 2008–09 recession. By the end of 2013, private consumption had grown for seven consecutive quarters, indicating that household confidence was growing. This improvement in sentiment was helped by falling inflation, with the rate of consumer price inflation falling for the second consecutive year to an annual rate of increase of 2.6 per cent, down from a post-recession peak of 4.5 per cent in 2011. This was accompanied by a decline in the unemployment level from 7.9 per cent in 2012 to 7.7 per cent in 2013.

The modest good news of 2013 was, however, tempered by worrying signs that the weak recovery was anything but durable. Gross fixed capital formation fell by 0.8 per cent, with the real (that is, adjusted for inflation) level of investment at levels last observed in 2005. It is notable that previous Commission forecasts for the British economy predicted significant growth in UK investment in each year from 2011 onwards. By the end of 2013, this growth had yet to materialize. Household consumption growth – the driver of UK growth in 2013 – was not based on any increase in household disposable incomes. Instead, rapid private sector credit growth fuelled household expenditure. Aided by a permissive monetary policy, as well as supportive government policies, consumer credit grew in real terms by 4.9 per cent, even as lending to businesses declined by 3.4 per cent (Bank of England, 2014). This increase in the aggregate household debt burden threatened to stretch the already overburdened UK consumer, suggesting that a recovery based on a sustained rise in household consumption would be subject to any shift in borrowing conditions.

III. Financial Volatility in Central, Eastern and Southeastern Europe: Is the Worst Finally Over?

This section examines if financial volatility in central, eastern and southeastern Europe (CESEE) has moderated since the global financial crisis. The build-up of extreme financial vulnerabilities across the region prior to 2008 accounted for its poor performance during the 2008–09 recession (Connolly, 2009, 2012). If financial sector weakness is observed elsewhere – whether due to the resumption of eurozone worries, or because of

Figure 1: Daily Stock Market Price Index Volatility in the Austrian Traded Index (ATX), 2011–13

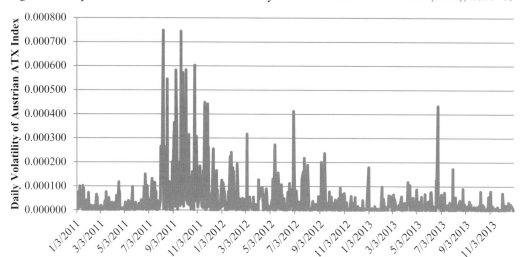

Source: Author's calculations from data series obtained on Bloomberg (underlying data provided by Wiener Börse). 'Volatility' is defined here as the sum of squared log daily price changes.

'tapering' by the US Federal Reserve – financial stability in the economies of CESEE will be essential to shield the region from another severe recession. A key point for this region is that there is a tough balancing act between avoiding destabilizing credit growth, like the expansion that contributed to the financial crisis, while at the same time providing the burgeoning enterprises with the capital necessary to succeed. This is made more difficult by the variation in economic conditions across the region.

As shown in previous sections, economic performance in the eurozone and, to a certain extent, outside it, continued to be affected by the sovereign debt crisis in the eurozone periphery. However, the financial volatility (including widening bond spreads and extreme fluctuations in stock markets) that characterized 2012 for the most part moderated in the western European financial markets in 2013, reaching more 'normal' levels than in the waning days of 2011 and the summer of 2012.[3] Indeed, there was a definite return to normality for much of Europe, even in the CESEE region, with the exception of a handful of countries still suffering from the lingering effects of the debt crisis. In particular, as Figure 2 shows, Croatia, Hungary and Slovenia were still perceived by the markets as being disproportionately risky, whereas other countries in the region such as Poland and especially the Czech Republic were seen as less likely to relapse into crisis.

While financial volatility may have generally subsided in 2013, there were continuing worrying trends elsewhere in the financial systems of the region, with the largest of these being the deleveraging of banks in western Europe. The CESEE region as a whole has depended on the developed banking systems of western Europe for capital. Evidence from the European Commission (Voegel and Winkler, 2010) shows that the high level of foreign

---

[3] Figure 1 shows the stock market volatility in Austria – a country that is both highly exposed to eurozone issues and the problems facing CESEE.

Figure 2: Sovereign Credit Default Swap (CDS) Spread, CESEE Region, 2013

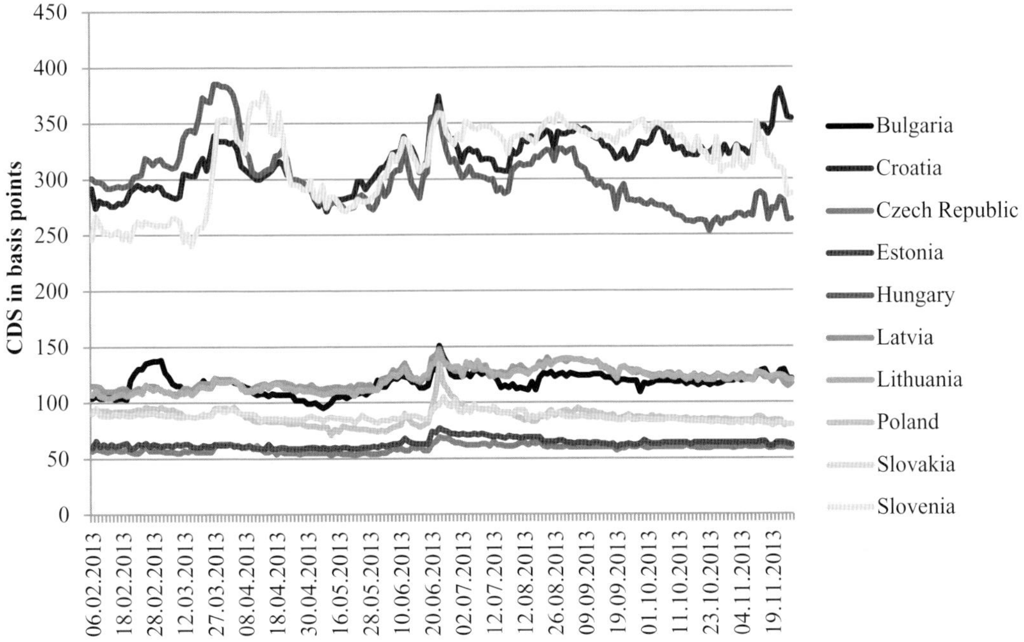

Source: Bloomberg (see Figure 1)

bank shares in CESEE actually mitigated the credit crunch of the global financial crisis after September 2008 – a result that did not hold for other developing countries. However, the eurozone crisis had a more prolonged effect and possibly deleterious effect, savaging credit lines repeatedly in addition to the wounds inflicted by the global financial crisis. Beginning at the end of 2011 and accelerating through 2012 and 2013, western banks' funding for the whole of CESEE declined by 6 per cent of GDP, 'more than during the height of the financial global financial crisis in late 2008 and 2009' (Vienna Initiative, 2013, p. 2). A look at the progression of external loans and deposits in emerging Europe since 2005 (Figure 3) clearly shows the stagnation of these flows, with lending in September 2013 at the same level as March 2007 but below that of March 2011, when the worst of the global financial crisis had passed.

The result of this cessation of flows was predictable, and manifested itself in anemic growth in credit to the private sector across the region. Of course, the issue of credit in the CESEE countries is a complex one; at the time, it was assumed that much of the credit expansion was part of the 'catching up' process, as research from the European Central Bank (Égert *et al.*, 2007) and from within the region (Kiss *et al.*, 2006) claimed that the levels of credit were justified by macroeconomic fundamentals or even were undershooting. However, the substantial increase in credit across the region prior to the global financial crisis (hitting levels of nearly 100 per cent of GDP in Latvia and up to 60 per cent of GDP in Estonia and Lithuania) was generally agreed *ex post* to be a key driver for the collapse in growth during the crisis. As Becker *et al* (2010, p. 12) note:

Figure 3: External Loans and Deposits of Banks in Emerging Europe, December 2005–September 2013

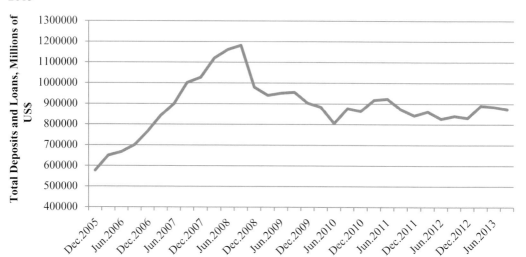

Source: BIS Statistics (Table 7a). [as above] Emerging Europe includes: Albania, Belarus, Bosnia and Herzegovina, Bulgaria, Croatia, Czech Republic, Hungary, Latvia, Lithuania, Macedonia, Moldova, Montenegro, Poland, Romania, Russia, Serbia, Turkey and Ukraine.

> [W]hile the level of credit as a percentage of GDP remained well below the EU15 average even at the peak of the pre-crisis credit boom [. . . it was] the *speed* at which the equilibrium level of credit is reached that matter[ed] for macroeconomic stability.

This increase was seen most vividly in the Baltic economies, where credit growth averaged 44 per cent per year (compared to 14 per cent per annum in Poland, Hungary, Czech Republic and Slovakia), but was felt throughout the CESEE region and was weighted heavily towards household lending.

Since the global financial crisis and the subsequent deleveraging from western Europe, credit in the CESEE region showed a nominal growth rate of 1.2 per cent from June 2012 to June 2013 (which is actually a contraction in real terms). The situation was worst for those countries with the highest reliance on the banks in Austria and Italy: Croatia, Hungary and Slovenia saw nominal and real credit contractions throughout 2013. The question remains if the continuing dearth of credit in the region is merely a slow wringing out of the liquidity of the system, or if there are actually deeper structural issues regarding credit creation. As Coudert and Pouvelle (2010) have pointed out, the credit increase prior to the global financial crisis was the most 'excessive' in precisely the same countries that saw the deepest contractions (Croatia, Hungary and Slovenia, as well as Bulgaria). Moreover, as previously noted, the Baltic States had the highest rates of credit growth pre-crisis, and Latvia and Lithuania saw nominal and real rates of credit to GDP decline continuously since 2009, reaching a nadir in 2013. Thus, it was difficult to tell if the CESEE countries were still experiencing a natural correction or an artificial drought.

Regardless of the source, the credit contraction in the region has been notable in that, while the boom was concentrated in household lending, the contraction was felt most deeply in corporate lending. Even in countries such as Slovakia, which had shown solid

Figure 4: Non-Performing Loans in CESEE, 2012–13

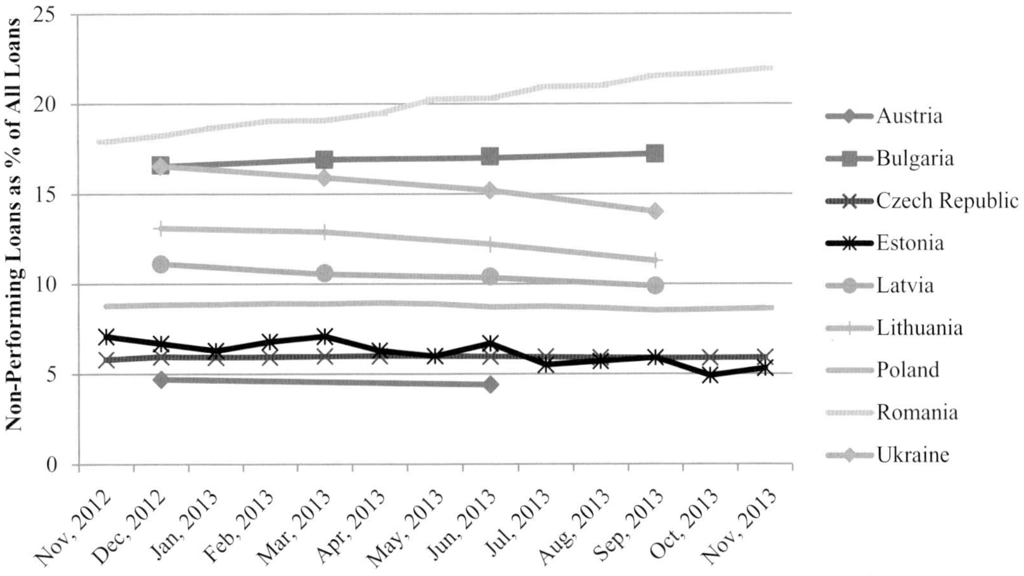

Source: CEIC Database, from National Authorities' Data (see above).

growth and resilience to global economic conditions, corporate lending was barely above levels seen in December 2010 and has been on a slow decline ever since its post-crisis high in November 2011. Other, more troubled countries such as Hungary saw a 6.4 per cent year-on-year decline from Q2 2012 to 2013, with a further 3.5 per cent contraction in Q3. Lending to small and medium-sized enterprises (SMEs) has also stagnated in the region, although there have been some policy moves to cushion the impact (as with the national bank's 'Funding for Growth' scheme in Hungary at the end of 2013, which is intended to lower the cost of borrowing for SMEs). In general, the trend in the region has been for corporates to rely on their own internal sources of funding – an approach that favours larger firms over SMEs, but a reality in a 'credit-less' environment. And again, while the slower credit growth may be welcome in contrast to the destabilizing rise pre-crisis, it is important to note that one cannot have capitalism without capital.

Apart from these issues on the supply of capital, there also remained a real demand problem in CESEE as the level of non-performing loans (NPLs), especially for households, remained at high levels. There are data issues regarding what actually constitutes an NPL as Jakubík and Reininger (2013, p. 51) note: '[T]here is, so far, no internationally harmonized definition that has been applied in all or most countries of the world for a considerable period of time.' Most countries in the CESEE region keep some form of data on NPLs, and the results were not encouraging. As Figure 4 shows, Romania faced a situation where nearly a quarter of all its loans were non-performing, while in Bulgaria NPLs remained at an uncomfortably high level throughout 2013. Poland was also consistent in the level of NPLs, albeit at not as high a level as other countries. In a bank survey conducted by the Vienna Initiative in Q3 2013, the banks polled noted that the high levels of NPLs at both the subsidiary (that is, in the CESEE region) and the group (that is, western Europe) levels was the most important factor weighing on credit supply (Vienna Initiative, 2013).

Table 7: External Vulnerability Indicators, Select CESEE
Countries, 2012–14

	2012	2013[f]	2014[f]
Bosnia	78	77.3	76.5
Bulgaria	130.3	111.5	109.6
Croatia	193.8	173.1	170.1
Czech Republic	85.7	71.8	87.4
Hungary	158.8	135.6	138.2
Latvia	313.1	283.3	243.1
Lithuania	186.2	183.4	159.3
Poland	129.7	115.8	122.9
Romania	102.4	101.7	93.1
Ukraine	350.1	386.0	454.3

Source: Moody's Statistical Handbook on Country Credit, May 2013.
Note: Forecasts are denoted by *f*.

In sum, the CESEE countries did see a reduction in the very short-term financial volatility in 2013 that characterized 2011 and 2012, but there were still signs of financial weakness throughout the region that did not abate over the year. These weaknesses looked unlikely to materialize into a region-wide conflagration as seen in 2009, but still threatened to act as a drag on growth and recovery in many of the CESEE countries. The threat was not evenly distributed, however, based on the divergent characteristics of the countries in the region. As Table 7 shows, the extent of vulnerability was projected to vary widely in 2014.[4] While it is debatable that Latvia's vulnerability was actually two-and-a-half times higher than Poland's, this did give a sense of the post-crisis variation in economic and financial performance across the CESEE region.

Perhaps it was this point that was the most crucial in assessing the CESEE region and its financial weaknesses in 2013: the region itself is not monolithic, and the countries are by no means uniform in terms of their financial development, volatility, risk profiles or even linkages to the rest of Europe. Moreover, the headline numbers of credit growth or foreign bank penetration in some sense obscure the country differences that are the deliberate result of domestic political movements, economic policies and local economic conditions. Perhaps the fluctuations in Slovenia and Hungary over the past three years demonstrate this most vividly, as markets have reacted to poor economic planning (such as Hungary's continued taxation of the financial services sector or Slovenia's state-owned banks and their continued lack of corporate governance) and this has manifested itself in both poor macroeconomic and financial performance.

Vulnerability and volatility were thus in reality outcomes of past decisions, and not just exogenously given conditions. The global financial crisis and its effects on the CESEE region was an external event that hit the entire region simultaneously, mainly because there were global conditions that led to a convergence of outcomes amongst CESEE countries. Credit growth was rapid in each country, although, even here, there were differences in pace and breadth. As previously noted, however, this 'perfect storm' looked

---

[4] The indicator is defined as the sum of short-term external debt, currently maturing long-term external debt, and total nonresident deposits over one year, divided by official foreign exchange reserves.

unlikely to repeat itself, and thus from the standpoint of 2013, it appeared that a return to normality similar to that in the financial markets noted at the beginning of this section was the more likely outcome.

Conclusions

While instability in the eurozone and beyond moderated in 2013, the economies of the non-eurozone continued to make an uncertain and unsteady recovery from the severe recession of 2008–09. The pace of recovery continued to be much slower than is usual after a recession, with many countries yet to achieve levels of GDP observed in 2008. Unemployment was still either high or rising (in some cases, both), and a number of countries saw government debt rise, with little progress made in reducing private sector debt. On the bright side, the gains in cost competiveness achieved between 2009 and 2011 were further augmented in 2013 in most cases. With such a weak recovery evident across the continent, it was important to note that while the economic recovery remained weak, the existence of financial vulnerabilities, especially across the CESEE countries, remained a serious problem threatening the long-term growth prospects of many economies of the region.

References

Bank of England (2014) *Trends in Lending*, London: Bank of England.

Becker, T., Daianu, D., Darvas, Z., Gligorov, V., Landesmann, M., Petrovic, P., Pisani-Ferry, J., Rosati, D., Sapir, A. and Di Mauro, B.W. (2010) *Whither Growth in Central and Eastern Europe: Policy Lessons for an Integrated Europe*. Blueprint Series Volume XI (Brussels: Bruegel).

European Commission (2013) *European Economic Forecast, Autumn 2013* (Brussels: Directorate General for Economic and Financial Affairs).

Connolly, R. (2009) 'Financial Vulnerabilities in Emerging Europe: An Overview'. Institute for Economies in Transition (BOFIT) Research Paper 3 (Helsinki: Bank of Finland).

Connolly, R. (2012) 'The Determinants of the Economic Crisis in Post-Socialist Europe'. *Europe-Asia Studies*, Vol. 64, No. 1, pp. 35–67.

Connolly, R. (2013) 'Strategies for Economic Development in Russia'. *Russian Analytical Digest*, July, 2013, No. 133.

Coudert, V. and Pouvelle, C. (2010) 'Assessing the Sustainability of Credit Growth: The Case of Central and Eastern European Countries'. *European Journal of Comparative Economics*, Vol. 7, No. 1, pp. 87–120.

Égert, B., Backé, P. and Zumer, T. (2007) 'Private Sector Credit in Central and Eastern Europe: New (Over) Shooting Stars?' *Comparative Economic Studies*, Vol. 49, No. 2, pp. 201–31.

International Monetary Fund (IMF) (2013) 'Hungary Staff Report for the 2013 Article IV Consultation and Third Post Program Monitoring Discussions' (Washington, DC: IMF).

Jakubík, P. and Reininger, T. (2013) 'Determinants of Nonperforming Loans in Central, Eastern and Southeastern Europe'. *Focus on European Economic Integration*, No. 3, pp. 48–66.

Kiss, G., Nagy, M. and Vonnák, B. (2006) 'Credit Growth in Central and Eastern Europe: Convergence or Boom?' Working Paper 2006/10 (Budapest: Magyar Nemzeti Bank).

Pettis, M. (2014) *Avoiding the Fall: China's Economic Restructuring* (Washington, DC: Carnegie).

Mau, V. (2013) 'Between modernization and stagnation: Russian economic policy and global crisis'. *Post-Communist Economies*, Vol. 25, No. 4, pp. 448–64.

Vienna Initiative (2013) CESEE Develeraging and Credit Monitor, 31 October. Available at: «http://www.imf.org/external/np/pp/eng/2013/102813.pdf».

Voegel, U. and Winkler, A. (2010) 'Cross-Border Flows and Foreign Banks in the Global Financial Crisis: Has Eastern Europe Been Different?' In 'Capital Flows to Converging European Economies: From Boom to Drought and Beyond?' Occasional Paper 75 (Brussels: Directorate General for Economic and Financial Affairs). Available at: «http://ec.europa.eu/economy_finance/publications/occasional_paper/2011/pdf/ocp75_en.pdf».

JCMS 2014 Volume 52 Annual Review pp. 219–224   DOI: 10.1111/jcms.12166

Chronology: The European Union in 2013

FABIAN GUY NEUNER
University of Michigan

At a Glance

Presidencies of the EU Council: Ireland (1 January–30 June) and Lithuania (1 July–31 December).

January

1	The Treaty on Stability, Co-ordination and Governance in the Economic and Monetary Union, commonly known as the 'Fiscal Compact Treaty', enters into force.
1	The Commission launches the 'European Year of Citizens'.
8	The European Investment Bank announces that the Member States have unanimously approved a €10 billion capital increase.
9	The Commission adopts the Entrepreneurship 2020 Action Plan.
11	The European Cybercrime Centre (EC3) is officially opened. The organization is tasked with assisting Member States in cross-border enforcement activities.
20	Austrians vote against ending conscription and introducing a professional army in a non-binding referendum.
21	Dutch Finance Minister, Jeroen Djisselbloem, is appointed President of the Eurogroup.
22	The eurozone finance ministers agree upon the principle of introducing a financial transaction tax.
23	British Prime Minister, David Cameron, outlines his plans for a referendum on Britain's EU membership.
24	EU–Brazil summit.
25–26	Miloš Zeman is elected President of the Czech Republic, becoming the country's first directly elected President.
26–27	EU–CELAC (Community of Latin American and Caribbean States) summit.

February

3	The Progressive Citizens' Party gains the most votes in the Liechtenstein general election and Adrian Hasler is designated Prime Minister.
5	The Commission proposes legislation to enhance co-operation on anti-money-laundering activities.
7–8	In the European Council, leaders reach agreement on the Multiannual Financial Framework (MFF) for 2014–2020. Further discussions concern trade policy and external relations, particularly concerning southern Mediterranean partners and Mali.

14	The Commission tables a proposal on the implementation of a financial transaction tax.
15–16	G20 Finance Ministers meet in Moscow.
18	Serzh Sargsyan is re-elected President of Armenia.
20	The Bulgarian government resigns amid popular protests over austerity measures and high electricity prices.
24	Nicos Anastasiades is elected President of Cyprus in a second-round run-off election.
24–25	The centre-left alliance Italy Common Good, led by the Democratic Party, obtains a majority of seats in the Italian Chamber of Deputies. Enrico Letta, the Democratic Party's deputy secretary, is designated Prime Minister.
25	EU–Ukraine summit.
26	The Council reaches informal agreement on reform to the EU's fisheries policy concerning the protection of endangered stocks and the termination of the practice of discarding unwanted fish.
27	The Slovenian government, led by Janez Janša, is ousted in a vote of no-confidence.
28	The Council reaches agreement on the Youth Guarantee Scheme – a measure to ensure that all young people under the age of 25 are offered employment or further training within four months of exiting school or becoming unemployed.

March

4	The Commission launches the 'Grand Coalition for Digital Jobs' initiative aimed at training an increased number of information and communication technology professionals.
9	Parliamentary elections in Malta see the Labour Party winning a majority of the seats and Joseph Muscat designated as Prime Minister, thereby ending a 15-year period of rule by the Nationalist Party.
10–11	Falkland Islanders vote in favour of remaining an Overseas Territory of the United Kingdom in a referendum. Turnout is 92 per cent, with 99.8 per cent voting in favour.
11	The end of the phasing-out period for the policy banning the marketing of cosmetic products that were tested on animals.
14–15	The European Council meeting is primarily concerned with economic and social policy as well as measures to deepen integration of the economic and monetary union.
20	Adoption of the 2013 European Neighbourhood Policy Package.
25	A €10 billion EU–IMF bail-out for Cyprus is announced.
25	The Commission launches a green paper on the long-term financing of the European economy.
27	The Commission launches a green paper on the 2030 energy and climate framework.

April

| 14 | Croatia holds a special EP election to elect the country's first 12 MEPs. |

15	The EU Anti-Trafficking Directive enters into force.
19	Serbia and Kosovo sign an agreement on normalizing relations in Brussels.
25–26	The Commission holds executive talks with the African Union.
27	Parliamentary elections in Iceland see victories for the Independent Party and the Progressive Party, who form a centre-right coalition government with Sigmundur Davíð Gunnlaugsson as Prime Minister.

May

2	The European Central Bank (ECB) decreases the interest rate on the main refinancing operations of the eurozone and the marginal lending facility to 0.50 per cent and 1.0 per cent, respectively.
12	Parliamentary elections in Bulgaria see the Citizens for European Development of Bulgaria (GERB) remain the largest party, but fail to command a majority. The Socialist Party subsequently forms a minority government with Plamen Oresharski as Prime Minister.
15	Inauguration of the Emergency Response Centre, which provides the Commission with a central platform for disaster response.
21	The European Parliament (EP) adopts offshore oil and gas drilling safety standards.
22	In the European Council, the main debate focuses on the EU's energy policy as well as measures to counter the problems posed by tax fraud and tax evasion.
28	The EU lifts the arms embargo against Syrian rebels.
30	The 'Two-Pack' reform package enters into force in all eurozone Member States. The policies are aimed at strengthening monitoring budgetary cycles and improving economic governance.

June

3	EU–Russia summit.
5	The Commission convergence report for Latvia indicates that the country fulfills the conditions for adopting the euro.
5	Edward Snowden first leaks information about mass surveillance activity of citizens by intelligence agencies including the National Security Agency (NSA).
9	The Swiss vote in favour of amendments to the country's asylum law in a referendum, but vote against a proposal to directly elect the members of the Federal Council.
17	Czech Prime Minister Petr Nečas resigns amid a corruption scandal.
17	G8 summit in Lough Erne, United Kingdom. As part of the meeting, the EU and the US launch negotiations on the transatlantic trade and investment partnership (TTIP).
23	The Socialist Party wins a majority of the seats in the Albanian parliamentary elections and Edi Rama is designated Prime Minister.

27–28   In the European Council, leaders agree to new comprehensive measures to tackle youth unemployment and discuss financial stability. The Council further opens accession negotiations with Serbia and confirms that Latvia has met the convergence criteria needed to join the euro.

28   The Commission proposes legislation aimed at reducing carbon dioxide emissions in maritime transport.

28   The ECB suspends Cypriot bonds as collateral.

July

1   Croatia becomes the European Union's 28th Member State. Neven Mimica becomes the Commissioner for Consumer Protection.

1   Portuguese Finance Minister Vítor Gaspar resigns.

3   Egypt's military removes the country's first democratically elected President, Mohamed Morsi, from office and suspends the constitution.

3   The EP elects Emily O'Reilly as the European Ombudsman. She takes up the post on 1 October.

4   The EP launches an inquiry into the systematic electronic surveillance of EU citizens following the revelations of widespread spying by international intelligence agencies including the NSA.

5   The ECB reactivates the eligibility of Cypriot bonds as collateral.

9   The Economic and Financial Affairs Council gives final approval for Latvia's adoption of the euro.

11   Luxembourg Prime Minister, Jean-Claude Juncker, submits his resignation following a wiretapping scandal.

18   EU–South Africa summit.

21   Crown Prince Philippe is sworn in as the new Belgian king after his father, Albert II, abdicates.

August

1   NSA leaker Edward Snowden is granted asylum by Russia.

13   Czech Prime Minister Jiří Rusnok announces his resignation after his caretaker government loses a vote of confidence but remains in power until a new government is formed.

September

5–6   G20 summit in Saint Petersburg.

11   Commission President José Manuel Barroso delivers his annual State of the Union address.

16   New Deal for Somalia conference held in Brussels.

22   Parliamentary elections in Germany see incumbent Angela Merkel's Christian Democratic Union/Christian Social Union win nearly 50 per cent of the seats, while her coalition partner, the Free Democrats, fail to cross the electoral threshold. The CDU/CSU enters into a grand coalition with the Social Democrats with Merkel continuing as Chancellor.

22   The Swiss vote against the abolition of compulsory military service in a referendum.

23   Start of 68th United Nations General Assembly in New York.

| 29 | Parliamentary elections in Austria see the Social Democratic Party win the most seats and form a grand coalition with the People's Party, with Werner Faymann continuing as Chancellor. |

October

4	In two simultaneous constitutional referendums, the Irish reject abolishing the upper house of the Oirechtas and voted in favour of establishing a Court of Appeals.
9	Ilham Aliyev is re-elected President of Azerbaijan.
15	The first pillar of Europe's banking union – the single supervisory mechanism (SSM) – is established.
16	The Commission publishes the annual enlargement package and progress reports, including the recommendation to grant candidate status to Albania.
20	Parliamentary elections in Luxembourg see Jean-Claude Juncker's Christian Social People's Party retain the largest share despite losing three seats. Following government formation talks, Xavier Bettel of the Democratic Party is designated Prime Minister after forming a coalition with the Socialist Workers' Party and the Greens.
22	The Council adopts the European Border Council Surveillance System (EUROSUR) aimed at reinforcing the EU's external borders and co-ordinating actions between Member States.
24–25	In the European Council, discussion centres on the digital economy, innovation and services, as well as increased economic policy co-ordination and completion of economic and monetary union.
25–26	Early legislative elections in the Czech Republic see the Social Democratic Party winning the most seats. They form a coalition government with the Christian Democrats and the recently formed ANO. Subsequently, Social Democrat Bohuslav Sobotka becomes Prime Minister.
27	Giorgi Margvelashvili is elected President of Georgia.

November

7	The ECB further decreases the interest rate on the main refinancing operations of the eurozone and the marginal lending facility to 0.25 per cent and 0.75 per cent, respectively.
8	EU–Republic of Korea summit.
13	The Commission publishes the 2013 Annual Growth Survey.
19	EU–Japan summit in Tokyo.
20	The EP awards the 2013 Sakharov Prize for Freedom of Thought to Malala Yousafzai.
21	The Ukrainian government announces plans to suspend signing association agreement with the EU amid fears of Russian trade sanctions.
21	EU–China summit in Beijing.
24	Mass protests erupt in Kyiv against the Ukrainian government's delay in signing an association agreement with the EU.
28–29	Eastern Partnership summit in Vilnius. Moldova and Georgia sign association agreements.

December
1	Croatians vote in a referendum in favour of a constitutional amendment defining marriage as between a man and a woman.
2	The Council adopts the 2014–2020 budget (the MFF) following prolonged negotiations.
15	Ireland becomes the first country to exit its bail-out package.
15	The EU suspends trade agreement talks with Ukraine.
16	Danièle Nouy is appointed chair of the supervisory board of the ECB's SSM.
18	Switzerland signs co-operation agreement to participate in the Galileo programme.
19–20	In the European Council, discussion centres on the common security and defence policy. Other topics of discussion include economic policy, banking union and migration policy. As part of the discussion on external relations, leaders assess the political situation in Ukraine and call for restraint and democratic solutions to the political crisis.

Index

Note: Italicized page references indicate information contained in tables.

ENABLE
DISCOVERY

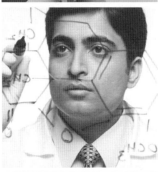

Make:

Handy-Dandy
BOARD GUIDE
2017 EDITION

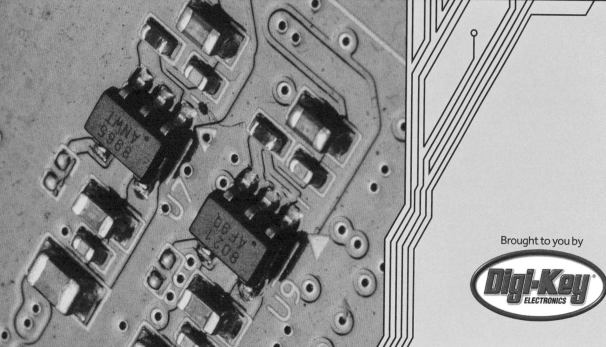

Brought to you by

Table of Boards

Written by Matt Stultz

Welcome to our second Board Guide, a curated sampling of tools available for wiring a brain — be it a microcontroller or single-board computer — into your project. We've compiled the important specs you need to find the right board for you. This list incorporates many of the classics you'll still find in the market along with newcomers that look to be important for years to come.

Knowing what you and your creation require from the start is the key to finding the best solution. Need real time control with precise signal timings? Look for a microcontroller with a fast processor. Is the basis of your project internet-connected? Your choice should include Wi-Fi or Ethernet. This table splits out these specs, making it easy for you to pinpoint your selection.

While this list may not incorporate every feature found on every board, it represents the key elements makers are interested in. If we missed an important metric, let us know — just like the boards in this list, our process is always evolving! ⊘

MICROCONTROLLERS (MCU)

Board Name	Price	Dimensions	Software	Clock Speed	Processor
Adafruit Circuit Playground	$20	2.0" dia.	Arduino	8MHz	8-bit ATmega32U4
Adafruit Circuit Playground Express	$25	2.0" dia.	Arduino/C/MicroPython/PXT/Typescript	48MHz	32-bit ATSAMD21
Adafruit Feather 32u4 BLE	$30	2.0"×0.9"	Arduino/C	8MHz	8-bit ATmega32U4
Adafruit Feather 32u4 RFM96 LoRa Radio - 433MHz	$35	2.0"×0.9"	Arduino	8MHz	8-bit ATmega32U4
Adafruit Feather Huzzah	$17	2.0"×0.9"	Arduino/C/MicroPython/JavaScript/Lua	80MHz	32-bit ESP8266
Adafruit Flora	$15	1.8" dia.	Arduino	8MHz	8-bit ATmega32U4
Adafruit Gemma	$10	1.0" dia.	Arduino	8MHz	8-bit ATtiny85
Adafruit Gemma M0	$10	1.1" dia.	Arduino/C/MicroPython	48MHz	32-bit ATSAMD21
Adafruit Metro Express	$25	2.8"×2.0"	Arduino/C/MicroPython	48MHz	32-bit ATSAMD21
Adafruit Trinket 3.3V & 5V	$7	1.1"×0.6"	Arduino	8MHz or 16MHz	8-bit ATtiny85
Arduino 101	$30	2.7"×2.1"	Arduino	32MHz	32-bit Intel Curie
Arduino Mega	$46	4.0"×2.1"	Arduino	16MHz	8-bit ATmega2560
Arduino MKR1000	$35	2.6"×1.0"	Arduino	32MHz	32-bit SAMD21 Cortex-M0+
Arduino Uno	$25	2.7"×2.1"	Arduino	16MHz	8-bit ATmega328PU
Arduino Yún	$69	2.7"×2.1"	Arduino	16MHz	8-bit ATmega32U4
Arduino Zero	$50	2.7"×2.1"	Arduino	16MHz	32-bit ATSAMD21G18
Arrow SmartEverything	$118	2.7"×2.1"	Arduino	32MHz	32-bit SAMD21 ARM Cortex-M0+
Bare Conductive Touch Board	$62	3.3"×2.4"	Arduino	16MHz	8-bit ATmega32U4
BBC micro:bit	$18	1.97"×1.57"	Other	16MHz	32-bit ARM Cortex-M0
BITalino (r)evolution	$150	3.94"×2.56" (all-in-one board)	OpenSignals; APIs for MaxMSP, Python, Matlab, C++, Unity, etc.	12MHz	8-bit Atmel ATmega328p
Blend Board	$33	2.9"×2.1"	Arduino	16MHz	8-bit ATmega32U4
ChipKIT Lenny	$25	2.7"×2.1"	Arduino IDE with chipKIT-core	40MHz	PIC-32MX270F256D
ChipKIT uC32	$30	2.7"×2.1"	Arduino IDE with chipKIT-core	80MHz	PIC32MX340F512H
ChipKIT Wi-FIRE	$80	3.5"×2.1"	Arduino IDE with chipKIT-core	200MHz	PIC32MZ2048E-FG100
DFRobot Leonardo with Xbee	$20	2.8"×2.2"	Arduino	16MHz	8-bit ATmega32U4
Espruino	$40	2.1"×1.6"	Espruino JavaScript Interpreter	32MHz	32-bit STM32F103RCT6 ARM Cortex-M3
Espruino Pico	$30	1.3"×0.6"	Espruino JavaScript Interpreter	84MHz	32-bit ARM Cortex-M4
Espruino Puck.js	$39	1.4" dia.	Espruino JavaScript Interpreter	64MHz	32-bit ARM Cortex-M4

Memory	Digital Pins	Analog Pins	Radio	Video	Ethernet On Board	Input Voltage	Operating Voltage	Website
32KB flash, 2KB RAM, 1KB EEPROM	1–10	7–12	–	–	–	3V–6V	3.3V	adafruit.com
256KB	8	8 (1 DAC)	–	–	–	3V–6V	3.3V	adafruit.com
32KB flash, 2KB RAM	20	6	Bluetooth	–	–	3.7V–5V	3.3V	adafruit.com
32KB flash, 2KB RAM	20	10	–	–	–	5V	3.3V	adafruit.com
4MB flash	9	1	Wi-Fi, Bluetooth	–	–	3.7V–5V	3.3V	adafruit.com
32KB flash	1–10	4–6	–	–	–	3.5V–16V	3.3V	adafruit.com
8KB flash	1–10	1–3	–	–	–	4V–16V	3.3V	adafruit.com
256KB	3	3 (1 DAC)	–	–	–	3V–6V	3.3V	adafruit.com
256KB	24	6 (1 DAC)	–	–	–	6V–12V	3.3V	adafruit.com
8KB flash	5	3	–	–	–	3.3–16V	3.3V or 5V	adafruit.com
196KB flash, 24KB SRAM	11–20	4–6	Bluetooth	–	–	7V–20V	3.3V	arduino.cc
256KB flash	50+	7–12	–	–	–	6V–20V	5V	arduino.cc
32KB flash	1–10	7–12	Wi-Fi	–	–	5V–6V	3.3V	arduino.cc
32KB flash	11–20	4–6	–	–	–	6V–20V	5V	arduino.cc
32KB flash	11–20	7–12	Wi-Fi	–	–	5V	5V	arduino.cc
256KB flash	1–10	4–6	–	–	–	7V–12V	3.3V	arduino.cc
256KB flash	11–20	4–6	Bluetooth	–	–	5V–45V	3.3V	smarteverything.it
32KB flash, microSD	11–20	7–12	–	–	–	3V–5.5V	5V	bareconductive.com
16KB RAM	11–20	4–6	Bluetooth	–	–	1.8V–3.3V	3.3V	microbit.org
32KB flash, 1KB EEPROM, 2KB SRAM	10	7	Bluetooth	–	–	3.0V–5.5V	3.3V	bitalino.com
32KB flash	14	6	Bluetooth	–	–	6.5V–12V	5V	redbearlab.com
256KB flash, 64KB RAM	27	6	Bluetooth	–	–	6.5V–12V	3.3V	chipkit.net
512KB flash, 32KB RAM	47	12	–	–	–	7V–15V	3.3V	chipkit.net
2MB flash, 512KB RAM	43	12	Wi-Fi	–	–	7V–15V	3.3V	chipkit.net
32KB flash	11–20	7–12	Wi-Fi, Bluetooth	–	–	6V–12V	5V	dfrobot.com
256KB flash	21–50	13+	–	–	–	3.6V–15V	3.3V	espruino.com
384KB flash, 96KB RAM	22	9	–	Composite and VGA	–	3.3V–16V	3.3V	espruino.com
512KB flash, 64KB RAM	17	5	–	–	✓	1.7V–3.6V	3V	espruino.com

MICROCONTROLLERS (MCU)

Board Name	Price	Dimensions	Software	Clock Speed	Processor
Espruino WiFi	$35	1.2"×0.9"	Espruino JavaScript Interpreter	100MHz	32-bit ARM Cortex-M4
LilyPad Arduino USB - ATmega32U4 Board	$25	2.0" dia.	Arduino	16MHz	8-bit ATmega32U4
LinkIt One	$59	3.3"×2.1"	Arduino	100MHz	32-bit ARM7EJ-STM
MicroPython pyboard	$45	1.7"×1.66"	MicroPython	100MHz	32-bit STM32F405RG ARM Cortex-M4
Netduino 3	$70	3.3"×2.1"	.Net Micro Framework 4.3	100MHz	32-bit STM32F427VI
Parallax Propeller Activity Board	$50	4.0"×3.05"	SimpleIDE, Propeller Tool, XBee Ready	80MHz	32-bit Octo-core P8X32A-Q44
Particle Electron	$49 for 2G / $69 for 3G	2.0"×0.8"	Arduino	100MHz	32-bit STM32F205
Particle Photon	$19	1.44"×0.8"	Arduino	100MHz	32-bit STM32F205 ARM Cortex-M3
PJRC Teensy 3.2	$20	1.4"×0.7"	Arduino	32MHz	32-bit MK20DX256 ARM Cortex-M4
Punch Through LightBlue Bean	$35	1.8"×0.8"	Arduino	100MHz	8-bit ATmega328
Realtek 8710	$4	0.945"×0.63"	Other	32MHz	32-bit ARM Cortex-M3
RFduino	$29	1.51"×0.9"	Arduino	16MHz	32-bit ARM Nordic Cortex-M0
Seeed Studio RePhone	$59	1.0"×0.8"	Arduino	260MHz	32-bit ARM7EJ-STM
Seeed Studio Xadow	$130 for kit	1.0"×0.8"	Arduino	16MHz	8-bit ATmega32U4
SparkFun Blynk Board	$30	2.0"×1.66"	Blynk App	16MHz	32-bit ESP8266
SparkFun ESP32 Thing	$20	2.35"×1.0"	ESP-IDF toolchain or Arduino	240MHz	32-bit ESP32
SparkFun ESP8266 Thing	$16	2.18"×1.02"	Arduino	80MHz	32-bit ESP8266
SparkFun MicroView	$40	1.05"×1.04"	Arduino	16MHz	8-bit ATmega328P
SparkFun RedBoard	$20	2.7"×2.1"	Arduino	16MHz	32-bit ATmega328 MCU with Optiboot (UNO) Bootloader
SparkFun RedStick	$20	2.6"×0.7"	Arduino	16MHz	8-bit ATmega328P
Texas Instruments Tiva C TM4C1294	$25	4.9"×2.2"	Other	100MHz	TM4C1294
Thunderboard Sense	$36	1.77"×1.18"	Other	32MHz	32-bit ARM Cortex-M4
TinyLily Mini	$10	0.55" dia.	Arduino	8MHz	8-bit ATmega328P
tinyTILE	$39	1.38"×1.02"	Arduino, Intel Curie ODK	32MHz	32-bit Intel Curie
WiPy	$32	1.7"×1.0"	Arduino	32MHz	32-bit TI CC3200 ARM Cortex-M4

FIELD-PROGRAMMABLE GATE ARRAY BOARD (FPGA)

Board Name	Price	Dimensions	Software	Clock Speed	Processor
Snickerdoodle Black	$195	2.0"×3.5"	Linux	866MHz	Dual-core Xilinx Zynq 7020 with ARM Cortex-A9
Snickerdoodle Prime	$145	2.0"×3.5"	Linux	667MHz	Dual-core Xilinx Zynq 7020 with ARM Cortex-A9

Memory	Digital Pins	Analog Pins	Radio	Video	Ethernet On Board	Input Voltage	Operating Voltage	Website
512KB flash, 128KB RAM	21	8	Wi-Fi	Composite and VGA	–	3.5V–5V	3.3V	espruino.com
32KB flash	5	4	–	–	–	2.7V–5.5V	3.3V	sparkfun.com
16MB flash, microSD	11–20	1–3	Wi-Fi, Bluetooth	–	–	3.7V–5V	3.3V	seeedstudio.com
1024KB flash, microSD	21–50	13+		–	–	3.6V–10V	3.3V	micropython.org
384KB flash	21–50	4–6	–	–	–	7.5V–12V	3.3V	netduino.com
microSD	18	4	–	HDMI	–	6V–9V	5V	parallax.com
1MB flash	21–50	7–12		–	–	3.9V–12V	3.3V	particle.io
1MB flash	11–20	7–12	Wi-Fi	–	–	3.6V–5.5V	3.3V	particle.io
256KB flash	21–50	13+	–	–	–	3.6V–6V	3.3V	pjrc.com
32KB flash	11–20	1–3	Wi-Fi, Bluetooth	–	–	2.6V–3.6V	3V	punchthrough.com
1MB flash, 512KB RAM	11–20	0	Wi-Fi	–	–	5V	3.3V	realtek.com
128KB flash	1–10	1	Wi-Fi, Bluetooth	–	–	2.1V–3.6V	2.1V	rfduino.com
5MB flash	16	0	–	Mini-HDMI	–	3.3V–5V	3.3V	seeedstudio.com
32KB flash	20	12	–	–	–	3.7V–20V	3.3V	seeedstudio.com
4MB flash, ~50KB RAM	1–10	4–6	Wi-Fi	–	–	3.7V–6V	3.3V	sparkfun.com
16MB flash, 520KB RAM	28	18	Wi-Fi, Bluetooth	–	–	5V	3.3V	sparkfun.com
512KB flash	7	1	Wi-Fi	–	–	3.3V–6V	3.3V	sparkfun.com
32KB flash	12 (3 PWM)	6	–	–	–	3.3V–16V	3.3V	sparkfun.com
32KB flash	14 (6 PWM)	6	–	–	–	7V–15V	3.3V	sparkfun.com
32KB flash	14 (6 PWM)	8	–	–	–	2V–6V	5V	sparkfun.com
1MB flash, 256KB RAM, 6KB EEPROM	21–50	13+	–	–	✓	5V	3.3V	ti.com
256KB flash	11–20	13+	Wi-Fi, Bluetooth	–	–	2V–5.5V	3.3V	silabs.com
32KB flash	1–10	4–6	–	–	–	2.7V–5.5V	3V	tiny-circuits.com
384KB flash, 2MB storage	14 (4 PWM)	6	Bluetooth	–	–	3.7V–17V	3.3V	element14.com
2MB flash	21–50	1–3	Wi-Fi	–	–	3.3V–5.5V	3.3V	pycom.io

Memory	Digital Pins	Analog Pins	Radio	Video	Ethernet On Board	Input Voltage	Operating Voltage	Website
1GB RAM, microSD	182	36	Wi-Fi, Bluetooth, BLE	–	–	3.7V–17V	1.8V–3.3V	krtkl.com
512MB RAM, microSD	182	36	Wi-Fi, Bluetooth, BLE	–	–	3.7V–17V	1.8V–3.3V	krtkl.com

SINGLE-BOARD COMPUTERS (SBC)

Board Name	Price	Dimensions	Software	Clock Speed	Processor
Asus Tinker Board	$60	3.37"×2.125"	Debian Linux	1.8GHz	64-bit RK3288
Banana Pi	$65	3.6"×2.4"	Arduino	1GHz	Dual-core 32-bit Allwinner A20 ARM Cortex-A7
BeagleBoard-X15	$239	4.0"×4.2"	Linux	1GHz	32-bit AM5728 ARM Cortex-A15
BeagleBone Black	$55	3.4"×2.1"	Linux	1GHz	32-bit AM335X ARM Cortex-A8
BeagleBone Blue	$82	3.4"×2.1"	Debian Linux with Cloud9 IDE and libroboticscape	1GHz	32-bit ARM Cortex-A8, ARM Cortex-M3, TI PRU
FriendlyARM NanoPi M1	$15 for 512MB / $20 for 1 GB	2.52"×1.97"	Ubuntu	1GHz	Quad-core 64-bit Allwinner H3 Cortex-A7
Intel Edison (with Arduino breakout)	$84	1.4"×1.0"	Linux	100MHz	Dual-core 32-bit Intel Atom
Intel Joule 550x Dev Kit	$289	3.35"×2.75"	Ubuntu Classic, Core; Windows IoT Core; Ref. Linux OS for IoT	1.5GHz	Quad-core 64-bit Intel Atom T5500
Intel Joule 570x Dev Kit	$335	3.35"×2.75"	Ubuntu Classic, Core; Windows IoT Core; Ref. Linux OS for IoT	1.7GHz Boost to 2.4GHz	Quad-core 64-bit Intel Atom T5700
Kinoma Create	$150	5.13"×5.2"	Linux	800MHz	32-bit Marvel Aspen ARM
LattePanda 2G/4G	$129/$159	2.75"×3.42"	Windows 10	1.92GHz	64-bit Intel Cherry Trail
MinnowBoard Max	$145	2.9"×3.9"	Linux	1GHz	Dual-core 64-bit Intel Atom E3825
Next Thing C.H.I.P.	$9	1.5"×2.3"	Linux	1GHz	32-bit Allwinner ARM R8
Next Thing C.H.I.P. Pro	$16	1.77"×1.18"	Linux	1GHz	32-bit ARMv7-A
Nvidia Jetson TK1 Dev Kit	$192	5.0"×5.0"	Linux	1.9GHz	Quad-core 32-bit ARM Cortex-A15
Nvidia Jetson TX1 Dev Kit	$499	6.7"×6.7"	Linux	1.73GHz	Quad-core 64-bit ARM Cortex-A57
Nvidia Jetson TX2 Dev Kit	$599	6.7"×6.7"	Linux	2GHz	Quad-core 64-bit ARM Cortex-A57 + dual-core Denver 2
Onion Omega2	$5	1.1"×1.7"	Linux	580MHz	32-bit MIPS
Parallella	$99	3.5"×2.1"	Linux	1GHz	Dual-core 32-bit ARM Cortex-A9 with NEON at 1GHz
pcDuino Acadia	$120	4.7"×2.6"	Linux	1GHz	32-bit ARM Cortex-A8
Qualcomm DragonBoard 410c	$75	2.12"×3.35"	Android, Linux, Win 10 IoT	1.2GHz	64-bit Snapdragon 410
Raspberry Pi 2	$35	3.4"×2.2"	Linux	100MHz	Quad-core 32-bit Broadcom ARM Cortex-A7
Raspberry Pi 3	$35	3.4"×2.2"	Linux	1.2GHz	64-bit Broadcom BCM2837
Raspberry Pi Zero	$5	1.18"×2.56"	Linux	1GHz	32-bit Broadcom ARMv6
Raspberry Pi Zero W	$10	1.18"×2.56"	Linux	1GHz	32-bit Broadcom ARMv6
RIoTboard	$79	3.0"×4.7"	Linux	1GHz	32-bit Freescale i.MX 5Solo ARM Cortex-A9
Samsung Artik 10	$150	6.3"×4.13"	Linux	1GHz	Quad-core 32-bit Cortex-A15 & Quad-Core Cortex-A7
Seeed Studio BeagleBone Green Wireless	$45	3.4"×2.1"	Linux	1GHz	32-bit ARM AM335x Cortex-A8
UDOO Neo Full	$65	3.5"×2.3"	Linux	1GHz	32-bit Freescale i.MX 6SoloX ARM Cortex-A9
VoCore2	$18	1.0"×1.0"	Linux	100MHz	16-bit MT7628AN, 580 MHz, MIPS 24K

Memory	Digital Pins	Analog Pins	Radio	Video	Ethernet On Board	Input Voltage	Operating Voltage	Website
2GB Dual Channel DDR3	40	0	Wi-Fi, Bluetooth	HDMI	✓	5V	5V	asus.com
SD	21–50	0	Wi-Fi	HDMI	✓	5V	3.3V	bananapi.org
4GB 8-bit eMMC	50+	0	—	HDMI	✓	12V	3.3V	beagleboard.org
4GB eMMC	50+	7–12	Wi-Fi	Micro-HDMI	✓	5V	1.8V and 3.3V	beagleboard.org
512MB RAM, 4GB eMMC flash	8	4	Wi-Fi, Bluetooth	—	—	9V–18V	1.8V–7.4V	beagleboard.org
512MB, or 1GB	1–10	13+	—	—	✓	5V	3.3V	friendlyarm.com
4GB eMMC flash	11–20	4–6	Wi-Fi, Bluetooth	—	—	7V–15V	5V	intel.com
3GB LPDDR4, 8GB eMMC	48	0	Wi-Fi, Bluetooth	Micro-HDMI, MIPI DSI	—	4V–20V	1.8V	intel.com
4GB RAM, 16GB flash	48	4–6	Wi-Fi, Bluetooth	Micro-HDMI, MIPI DSI	—	4V–20V	1.8V	intel.com
microSD	16	3	Wi-Fi, Bluetooth	Built-in touchscreen	—	3.7V–5V	3.3V	kinoma.com
2GB/4GB	12	6	Wi-Fi, Bluetooth	HDMI and MIPI-DSI	✓	5V	5V	lattepanda.com
8MB SPI flash, microSD	1–10	0	—	Micro-HDMI	✓	5V	3.3V	minnowboard.org
4GB eMMC	1–10	1–3	Wi-Fi, Bluetooth	Composite via TRRS jack	—	3.7V–5V	3.3V	getchip.com
256MB/512MB	27	1	Wi-Fi, Bluetooth	—	—	5V	3.3V	getchip.com
16GB eMMC, SD	40+	0	—	HDMI	✓	9.5V–13.2V	12V	developer.nvidia.com
4GB 64-bit LPDDR4 memory	40+	0	Wi-Fi, Bluetooth	HDMI	✓	5.5V–19.6V	19V	developer.nvidia.com
8GB 128-bit LDDR4 memory	40+	0	Wi-Fi, Bluetooth	HDMI	✓	5.5V–19.6V	19V	developer.nvidia.com
128MB	18	0	Wi-Fi	—	—	3.3V	3.3V	onion.io
1GB DDR3	21–50	0	Wi-Fi	Micro-HDMI	✓	3.3V	1.5V	parallella.org
microSD	11–20	4–6	—	HDMI	✓	5V	3.3V	linksprite.com
1GB LPDDR3 533MHz, 8GB flash	12	0	Wi-Fi, Bluetooth	HDMI	—	6.5V–18V	1.8V	qualcomm.com
microSD	21–50	0	—	HDMI	✓	5V	3.3V	raspberrypi.org
1GB LPDDR2-900 SDRAM	29	0	Wi-Fi, Bluetooth	HDMI	✓	5V	3.3V	raspberrypi.org
microSD	21–50	0	—	Micro-HDMI	✓	5V	3.3V	raspberrypi.org
microSD	21–50	0	Wi-Fi, Bluetooth	Micro-HDMI	—	5V	3.3V	raspberrypi.org
4GB eMMC, SD, microSD	21–50	0	—	HDMI	✓	5V	3.3V	riotboard.org
2GB DRAM, 16GB flash	11–20	7–12	Wi-Fi, Bluetooth	Mini-HDMI	✓	3.4V–5V	3.3V	artik.io
512MB RAM (4GB eMMC)	50+	7–12	Wi-Fi, Bluetooth	—	—	5V	1.8V and 3.3V	seeedstudio.com
microSD	21–50	4–6	Wi-Fi, Bluetooth	Micro-HDMI	✓	6V–15V	3.3V	udoo.org
128MB, DDR2, 166MHz	21–50	4–6	Wi-Fi	—	✓	3.6V–6.0V	3.3V	vocore.io

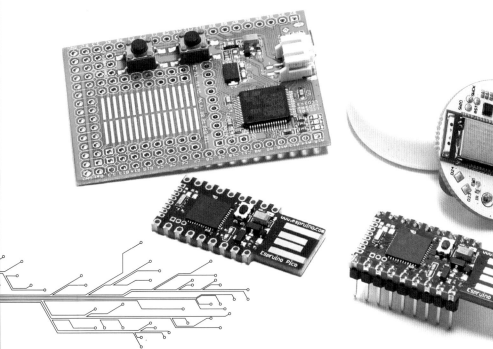

Clockwise from top left: original Espruino; Puck.js; Espruino WiFi; Espruino Pico (with and without pins).

The first time Espruino was running on actual hardware, 2012 (STM32VLDISCOVERY board).

Packing rewards up for Espruino's first Kickstarter campaign.

everything and be able to spend more time on Espruino, and if it didn't, then I'd shelve it and get a proper job. It went better than I ever could have hoped, and I got over £100,000 in funding from a video my wife and I had knocked together with a cheap camera and iMovie. So I started working on it full time.

The whole Kickstarter experience was amazing — but it was hugely stressful and took a massive amount of time. I was pretty new to designing PCBs, so I used something called the OPL (Open Parts Library) from Seeed Studio. This was a part kit you could buy that also included all the part outlines for PCB design tools. Once I'd put a working prototype together, I was able to give the designs to Seeed, who would manufacture the board with all the parts they already had in stock. This meant that even though everything had taken longer than planned, I was able to ship the boards just one month after the expected ship date.

Seeed mailed the individual Espruino boards for me; however, I had also offered some starter kits to customers containing a lot of different electronic components, so we had to assemble them ourselves. That was a bit of an eye-opener. When I make software, 500 downloads doesn't seem like that many at all — but it looks quite different when you have to pack kits, label them, and make sure they are delivered!

Now, almost five years after writing my first lines of code, I've just completed shipping out all of the rewards for a third Kickstarter campaign: Puck.js, a programmable Bluetooth button. There's now a great community of users around Espruino and a forum with over 20,000 posts — fueled mainly by the enthusiasm of my Kickstarter backers. Everything is open source (hardware and software), and yet I'm finally at the stage where monthly sales of Espruino boards are

RUNNING AN OPEN SOURCE HARDWARE AND SOFTWARE COMPANY HAS ITS REWARDS. BUT IT ALSO HAS ITS CHALLENGES.

Written by Gordon Williams

GORDON WILLIAMS is a software and hardware enthusiast who has turned his passion into a business.

I'VE SPENT THE LAST 13 YEARS AS A SOFTWARE ENGINEER, WORKING MAINLY ON 3D GRAPHICS AND COMPILERS. Developing for microcontrollers had always been a hobby, but I found the existing ARM microcontroller development tools to be very difficult to install and use, especially on Linux. Spending hours wrestling with software tools in the evenings after I'd already spent a full day in front of a computer was extremely frustrating, so I set out to create something I'd find enjoyable to use, not painful.

I wanted to move all of the toolchain onto the microcontroller itself, allowing anyone to program it, from any platform, using JavaScript. My goal was that someone with minimal programming knowledge could start blinking a light on a microcontroller in just a few minutes, rather than hours. With that in mind, I started a project I called Espruino — the name is a portmanteau of Espresso (given the coffee associations of Java and JavaScript), and Arduino (whose "uino" ending has now become synonymous with microcontrollers). I'd written an extremely basic JavaScript-like language interpreter called TinyJS for another project of mine, and five years ago, after a mammoth hacking spree in which I rewrote it from scratch to use statically allocated memory, I committed my first code into a Git repository.

A few months later, on a vacation in Wales with friends, I got it to work. I remember the feeling of accomplishment as I saw the little ST Discovery board print out a Mandelbrot fractal

Hep Svadja

line by line. However that was just the start of a long journey, which has now turned into a full-time job for me.

FREEMIUM SOFTWARE
Shortly after, I decided to put my work online — not open source initially, but free to download. I soon found myself spending a lot of time trying to help users through the arduous process of flashing firmware onto the microcontrollers themselves. I realized that if I was ever going to be able to keep working on Espruino properly, I needed to spend a lot more time on it, which meant finding a way to provide myself with a salary.

My first attempt involved making Espruino "freemium." I added the ability to save an image of the currently running code into flash memory and charged $4 for it — unfortunately, over an entire year, I only made $40 despite spending weeks helping users out. I had significant downloads, but very few people were able to install the firmware and get far enough past the "Hello World" of blinking LEDs to even save what they'd done.

I tried to contact all of the STM32 board manufacturers I could find about preinstalling Espruino, but none were willing to take a risk on what was, at the time, a relatively unknown bit of software. So I decided to do something myself.

KICKSTARTING A BOARD
At around this time, Kickstarter had just opened its doors to creators in England, and I thought I'd give it a try by making my own board. If it went well, I would open source